Cases on Economics Education and Tools for Educators

Brad Scott
Rowan-Cabarrus Community College, USA

Melanie E. Fox
Purdue University, USA

A volume in the Advances in Educational Technologies and Instructional Design (AETID) Book Series

IGI Global
PUBLISHER of TIMELY KNOWLEDGE

Published in the United States of America by
IGI Global
Business Science Reference (an imprint of IGI Global)
701 E. Chocolate Avenue
Hershey PA, USA 17033
Tel: 717-533-8845
Fax: 717-533-8661
E-mail: cust@igi-global.com
Web site: http://www.igi-global.com

Library of Congress Cataloging-in-Publication Data

Names: Scott, A. Bradley, 1989- editor. | Fox, Melanie, editor.
Title: Cases on economics education and tools for educators / edited by: A. Bradley Scott, and Melanie Fox.
Description: Hershey PA : Business Science Reference, [2024] | Includes bibliographical references. | Summary: "This book aims to provide relevant cases and examples of effective economics education topics suited for K-12 educators. The cases are written with current and future practitioners in mind who are teaching or planning to teach economics in the K-12 classroom. Topics covered in this book aim to assist current and future economic educators in pedagogy, methodology, practitioner examples, and practices that support a learning environment that engages and includes all learners and especially groups that have been under-represented in economics"-- Provided by publisher.
Identifiers: LCCN 2023019984 (print) | LCCN 2023019985 (ebook) | ISBN 9781668475836 (hardcover) | ISBN 9781668475843 (paperback) | ISBN 9781668475850 (ebook)
Subjects: LCSH: Economics--Study and teaching--Case studies.
Classification: LCC HB74.5 .C385 2024 (print) | LCC HB74.5 (ebook) | DDC 330.071--dc23/eng/20230616
LC record available at https://lccn.loc.gov/2023019984
LC ebook record available at https://lccn.loc.gov/2023019985

This book is published in the IGI Global book series Advances in Educational Technologies and Instructional Design (AETID) (ISSN: 2326-8905; eISSN: 2326-8913)

British Cataloguing in Publication Data
A Cataloguing in Publication record for this book is available from the British Library.

Advances in Educational Technologies and Instructional Design (AETID) Book Series

ISSN:2326-8905
EISSN:2326-8913

Editor-in-Chief: Lawrence A. Tomei, Robert Morris University, USA

MISSION

Education has undergone, and continues to undergo, immense changes in the way it is enacted and distributed to both child and adult learners. In modern education, the traditional classroom learning experience has evolved to include technological resources and to provide online classroom opportunities to students of all ages regardless of their geographical locations. From distance education, Massive-Open-Online-Courses (MOOCs), and electronic tablets in the classroom, technology is now an integral part of learning and is also affecting the way educators communicate information to students.

The **Advances in Educational Technologies & Instructional Design (AETID) Book Series** explores new research and theories for facilitating learning and improving educational performance utilizing technological processes and resources. The series examines technologies that can be integrated into K-12 classrooms to improve skills and learning abilities in all subjects including STEM education and language learning. Additionally, it studies the emergence of fully online classrooms for young and adult learners alike, and the communication and accountability challenges that can arise. Trending topics that are covered include adaptive learning, game-based learning, virtual school environments, and social media effects. School administrators, educators, academicians, researchers, and students will find this series to be an excellent resource for the effective design and implementation of learning technologies in their classes.

COVERAGE

- Game-Based Learning
- Curriculum Development
- Instructional Design Models
- Adaptive Learning
- K-12 Educational Technologies
- Digital Divide in Education
- Educational Telecommunications
- E-Learning
- Bring-Your-Own-Device
- Collaboration Tools

IGI Global is currently accepting manuscripts for publication within this series. To submit a proposal for a volume in this series, please contact our Acquisition Editors at Acquisitions@igi-global.com or visit: http://www.igi-global.com/publish/.

The Advances in Educational Technologies and Instructional Design (AETID) Book Series (ISSN 2326-8905) is published by IGI Global, 701 E. Chocolate Avenue, Hershey, PA 17033-1240, USA, www.igi-global.com. This series is composed of titles available for purchase individually; each title is edited to be contextually exclusive from any other title within the series. For pricing and ordering information please visit http://www.igi-global.com/book-series/advances-educational-technologies-instructional-design/73678. Postmaster: Send all address changes to above address.

Titles in this Series

For a list of additional titles in this series, please visit:
http://www.igi-global.com/book-series/advances-educational-technologies-instructional-design/73678

Contemporary Challenges in Education Digitalization, Methodology, and Management
Anna A. Arinushkina (Lomonosov Moscow State University, Russia) Alexander V. Morozov (Moscow Social Pedagogical Institute, Russia) and Irena V. Robert (Institute for Strategy of Education Development, Russia)
Information Science Reference • © 2023 • 359pp • H/C (ISBN: 9798369318263) • US $285.00

Perspectives on Learning Analytics for Maximizing Student Outcomes
Gürhan Durak (Balıkesir University, Turkey) and Serkan Cankaya (Izmir Democracy University, Turkey)
Information Science Reference • © 2023 • 453pp • H/C (ISBN: 9781668495278) • US $230.00

Reconceptualizing Language Norms in Multilingual Contexts
Sarah Jones (University of Toronto, Canada) Rebecca Schmor (University of Toronto, Canada) and Julie Kerekes (University of Toronto, Canada)
Information Science Reference • © 2023 • 330pp • H/C (ISBN: 9781668487617) • US $215.00

Architecture and Technological Advancements of Education 4.0
Rajiv Pandey (Amity University, Uttar Pradesh, India) Nidhi Srivastava (Amity University, Uttar Pradesh, India) and Parag Chatterjee (National Technological University Buenos Aires, Argentina)
Information Science Reference • © 2024 • 320pp • H/C (ISBN: 9781668492857) • US $225.00

For an entire list of titles in this series, please visit:
http://www.igi-global.com/book-series/advances-educational-technologies-instructional-design/73678

IGI Global
PUBLISHER of TIMELY KNOWLEDGE

701 East Chocolate Avenue, Hershey, PA 17033, USA
Tel: 717-533-8845 x100 • Fax: 717-533-8661
E-Mail: cust@igi-global.com • www.igi-global.com

Table of Contents

Detailed Table of Contents

and development project (RDP). The RDP is the continuation of previous works and findings that are used to prove RTBLP's feasibility and to offer a polymathics' curriculum for the secondary school cycle.

Effective teaching is a delicate balance of deep content knowledge and adept pedagogical skills. Pedagogical content knowledge (PCK), introduced by Shulman in 1987 captures the essence of this synergy, emphasizing the transformative capability of educators in delivering subject content in ways that engage students. This chapter dives into the nuances of PCK, its foundational role in teacher education, and its expansive relevance across academic fields, with special emphasis on economic educators. Rooted in Shulman's groundbreaking research, with insights from various educational researchers, the chapter underscores the importance of melding content mastery with pedagogical techniques. It further explores the historical and contemporary perspectives on the confluence of content and pedagogy, featuring case studies for analysis. The chapter contributes to the broader conversation on the necessity for teachers to become more adaptable within teaching approaches.

The purpose of the study reported on in this chapter is to investigate the impact of learner content and user interface design on improving e-learning quality and to harness the full potential of e-learning in Ghana at the basic school level. Against the background of cases on economics education and tools for educators, the main focus will be on the effective use of technologies, such as social media, movies, and TV shows, as well as, for example, music, team-based learning, think-pair-share, and other forms of active learning and computer-based learning in the classroom.

The incorporation of social media into economics education is a transformative journey characterized by innovation, the resolution of obstacles, and the creation of promising opportunities. It emphasizes social media's power in engaging students, making economics concepts accessible, and promoting critical thinking. Considerations

This chapter consists of an investigation on the motivational factors that entail the use of the Moodle platform as an auxiliary tool within the teaching-learning process. The objective of the research was to recognize the student's perception of the use of virtual educational platforms (Moodle) as a motivational and influential factor in their learning process focused on the results it achieves. According to the results, it is possible to affirm that there is a high motivational level of the students regarding the use of the Moodle platform as well as an elevated level of motivational perception. In the same way, it was observed that there are five main components that summarize the variation between the items, motivational characteristics that were obtained and proposed as a conclusion for the effective obtaining of results when using the Moodle platform within the teaching-learning process.

In this chapter, the authors outline a plan for implementing CBL in economics education and highlight some of the key tools and resources that can be used to enhance the learning experience. They provide access to data analysis tools for the students that can provide access to data analysis tools such as statistical software packages and online databases. This can enable them to analyze economic data more effectively and develop their data analysis skills. There is the platform to study all types of data analysis tools that may be useful to both educators and students for learning the economics. The chapter emphasizes the importance of conducting a needs assessment, developing digital resources, establishing the necessary technology infrastructure, providing faculty training, and implementing the CBL strategy across all economics courses. The chapter also highlights some of the tools and resources that can be used to support CBL in economics education, including Microsoft Excel, statistical software packages, geographic information systems, and business intelligence (BI) software.

Preface

In an ever-evolving world, economics education has become an integral part of preparing young minds for the complexities of the modern age. With the majority of U.S. state high school graduation requirements mandating economics coursework, and an increasing number of states weaving economics into their curriculum starting from Kindergarten, the importance of equipping educators with the right tools and resources cannot be overstated. The responsibility to impart economic literacy upon our students is a shared one, and it is a collective duty that necessitates support and collaboration. While the U.S. importance is stressed for the editors, this work serves as a global force that represents authors from around the world, sharing ideas and concepts that beginning teachers or veteran teachers can use to forge their approaches. Several other countries, like Italy, have began to take notice of the importance of economics – often, tied with personal finance – as a subject worth while in K-12 education.

Cases on Economics Education and Tools for Educators is a testament to the commitment we share in ensuring that economics education reaches its full potential in K-12 classrooms. As editors, we recognized a growing demand for a curated collection of materials to aid educators on this journey. This book was carefully crafted to showcase an international presence and embrace diversity in teaching methods and learning styles.

Economics education is not a one-size-fits-all endeavor, and this book reflects that reality. Our aim is to provide K-12 educators with a diverse array of cases and examples, rooted in effective pedagogy, methodology, and practitioner experiences. These resources are designed to foster a learning environment that engages and includes all students, with particular emphasis on those who have historically been underrepresented in the field of economics.

While the primary audience for this book is college students aspiring to teach economics in K-12 classrooms, we also extend our hand to the broader community of practitioners and curriculum design professionals who are committed to enhancing and supporting student success. The cases presented within these pages are versatile and can be adapted for various educational contexts, ensuring that educators have the flexibility to choose what best suits their students and teaching styles.

This collection covers different pedagogical practices and blends the importance of using popular culture, social media, and instructor-created games to explore financial economics topics. Additionally, these works take the time to showcase a wide range of resources through the writing and references of each chapter. As educators and advocates for robust economics education, we understand the importance of equipping teachers with the right tools and knowledge. We hope that this book serves as a valuable resource, offering insights, inspiration, and practical guidance to those who are passionate about teaching economics to the next generation. Together, we can create a brighter economic future for our students and society as a whole.

Brad Scott
Rowan-Cabarrus Community College, USA

Melanie E. Fox
Purdue University, USA

Acknowledgment

We would like to thank the authors of each chapter for the continued revision of their work. Additionally, we deeply appreciate the feedback from the anonymous reviewers, whose thoughtful critiques and suggestions greatly enriched this work.

Chapter 1
Team-Based Learning: Enhancing Student Engagement and Learning Outcomes

Iris-Panagiota Efthymiou
https://orcid.org/0000-0001-9656-8378
University of East London, UK & University of Greenwich, UK

Symeon Sidiropoulos
University of Piraeus, Greece

EXECUTIVE SUMMARY

This chapter delves into the topic of team-based learning (TBL) and its impact on student engagement and learning outcomes in higher education. The chapter begins by discussing the need for innovative pedagogical approaches that encourage students to become active participants in the learning process. It then goes on to outline the principles and process of TBL, including the various stages of pre-class preparation, in-class activities, and individual and team assessments. The chapter also discusses the benefits of TBL, including its ability to enhance critical thinking, problem-solving, and communication skills, as well as to foster a sense of community and shared responsibility among students. Additionally, the chapter explores practical considerations for implementing TBL in the classroom, such as designing effective team assignments and providing adequate resources and support for students. Overall, the chapter provides a comprehensive overview of TBL and its potential to enhance student engagement and learning outcomes in higher education settings.

DOI: 10.4018/978-1-6684-7583-6.ch001

INTRODUCTION

Team-Based Learning (TBL) is an "active learning and collaborative teaching strategy" that emphasizes student engagement and quality learning by following a structured process. The strategy involves individual and group activities and immediate feedback that increase student accountability and motivation. It transfers the emphasis of classroom time away from the teacher's delivery of course concepts and towards the application of those concepts by student teams. The strategy may be used in a variety of situations, disciplines, and classroom settings (Team-Based Learning Collaborative, n.d.). The TBL process involves dividing students into permanent groups, studying assigned material, taking both the "Group Readiness Assurance Test (gRAT)" and "Individual Readiness Assurance Test (iRAT)," and taking part in in-class activities that encourage students to use what they've learned to solve problems (FeedbackFruits, 2021). This type of learning is effective at improving students' communication, collaboration, and critical thinking, which are important in today's workforce. TBL has been adopted effectively in various educational settings, including medical schools, business schools, and STEM disciplines. Its success in encouraging active learning and student participation has contributed to its rising popularity in education (Currey et al., 2015).

BENEFITS

Studies have shown that students who were taught using interactive engagement methods such as TBL showed over two standard deviations better learning outcomes than students in traditional courses (Center for Teaching, n.d.). The TBL process is organised into a "rhythm" of "out-of-class preparation, readiness assurance testing, and application activities." TBL is based on four pillars: groups, accountability, feedback, and assessment. Instructors must consider factors such as resources, avoiding coalitions, and time when creating groups. Students should be held responsible for their "individual and group" work quality, and feedback is provided immediately to enhance learning (FeedbackFruits, 2021). TBL has several benefits, including improving problem-solving skills, building trust among team members, and outperforming the best member. TBL is now frequently utilised in large classes and is even possible in challenging classroom settings (Team-Based Learning Collaborative, n.d.).

TBL helps foster accountability and a sense of agency in students, allowing them to organize themselves independently, create solutions, and develop a sense of accountability towards each other. The TBL process involves several stages, including preparation, readiness assurance testing, clarification, group discussion, and the submission and showcase of group work. While TBL has numerous advantages for students, there might be difficulties in enabling various stages, such as free-riding, lack of engagement, and workload, due to the flipped classroom model. To overcome these challenges, teachers must be well-organized facilitators who understand how to employ various pedagogical instruments. FeedbackFruits is a tool suite that helps instructors design and structure TBL activities that optimise student engagement, learning, and retention. FeedbackFruits Interactive Study Material, Team-Based Learning, Discussion Assignment, and Group Member Evaluation tools can be used in different stages of TBL to give students meaningful and engaging learning experiences. By combining these tools, instructors can facilitate a smooth and effective TBL process that maximises the power of collaboration (FeedbackFruits, 2021).

OVERVIEW

TBL is a collaborative learning approach that encourages student engagement and active learning (Michaelsen et al., 2004). It is an interactive, small-group, teacher-directed instructional strategy that promotes problem-solving, communication skills, team-building, and critical thinking necessary for students' future practice (Cevik et al., 2019). TBL is a type of small group learning in which students are divided into different teams of 5-7 members who collaborate throughout the class. Students prepare for every unit or module of the course by reading before class. In the module's first class, students take part in a "Readiness Assurance Process (RAP)," which includes a test taken individually (iRAT) and with their group members (gRAT). Both scores are used to determine the student's grade. Following the test, the instructor offers a mini lecture focusing on the concepts with which the pupils had the greatest difficulty. The process prepares teams for in-class application activities that demand them to make a precise decision regarding a serious challenge. Peer evaluation is a crucial component of TBL since it holds students accountable to their peers. TBL contains key constructivist learning aspects and has been proven to yield learning improvements in a range of "healthcare education classrooms" (Center for Teaching, n.d.).

PRINCIPLES

The principles that underpin TBL include constructivist learning, small groups, readiness assurance, team performance, application exercises, real-world contexts, multiple perspectives, provision of feedback, and reflection (Michaelsen et al., 2004). "Constructivist learning theory" emphasizes that learning is an active procedure of constructing knowledge through social interaction and collaboration. In TBL, students work collaboratively in small groups of 5-7 to solve problems and complete tasks. The readiness assurance process, which consists of individual preparation work before class followed by a test of individual performance on teacher-assigned tasks connected to certain goals, assists students in preparing for team activities. Team performance is also assessed on the same instructor-assigned tasks, which encourages collaboration and communication within the group. The application exercises in TBL are designed to encourage the application of team communication, problem-solving skills, knowledge, and reasoning, with tasks situated in real-world contexts to help students apply their skills and knowledge to solve real-world problems. TBL also promotes the development and sharing of alternative viewpoints, discussions, and debates through the examination of diverse perspectives and collaborative learning. Feedback is emphasised both by the teacher and by peers to enhance learning and support student development. TBL also encourages pupils to reflect on their learning and engage in metacognitive processes to enhance their learning and understanding of the subject matter (Michaelsen et al., 2004).

"Kolb's Experiential Learning Theory (ELT)" proposes that learners acquire knowledge and skills by engaging in concrete experiences, reflecting on those experiences, conceptualising them, and then applying the resulting knowledge to new situations (Kolb, 1984). TBL incorporates this principle by presenting students with real-world scenarios to enable them to apply their skills and knowledge to authentic problems. By situating tasks in real-world contexts, TBL encourages learners to explore multiple perspectives, debate, discuss, and share alternative viewpoints, ultimately leading to the qualitative reorganisation and co-construction of their knowledge constructions (Michaelsen et al., 2004). This approach fosters active learning and enables students to develop the competencies necessary for clinical practice (Parmelee & Michaelsen, 2010).

"Self-Determination Theory (SDT)" proposes that three innate psychological needs—"autonomy, competence, and relatedness"—drive human motivation" (Ryan & Deci, 2000). TBL is designed to fulfil these needs by providing learners with a feeling of authority over their learning, opportunities to develop and demonstrate their competencies, and a supportive learning environment that fosters social connections and collaboration (Michaelsen et al., 2004). By satisfying these needs, TBL can promote intrinsic motivation and enhance learning outcomes (Haidet et al., 2008).

Studies have found that TBL is an effective instructional strategy for promoting self-determination in learners (Fatmi et al., 2013; Rajalingam & Rotgans, 2018). For instance, one study highlighted those medical students participating in TBL showed higher levels of autonomy and competence compared to those in traditional lecture-based courses (Fatmi et al., 2013). Similarly, a study of undergraduate nursing students revealed that TBL improved their sense of relatedness and satisfaction with the learning experience (Rajalingam & Rotgans, 2018). These findings suggest that TBL aligns well with the SDT and can contribute to learners' motivation and engagement in the learning process.

"Social Learning Theory (SLT)" posits that individuals acquire knowledge and skills by observing and imitating the behaviours of others in social contexts (Bandura, 1977). TBL provides a structured setting where students can observe and model their peers' behaviours, facilitating social learning and teamwork (Michaelsen, Knight, & Fink, 2002). TBL aligns with SLT, emphasising collaboration and cooperation, and can promote social learning in a supportive and organised learning environment, thereby enhancing the effectiveness of learning experiences. Thus, TBL represents a valuable pedagogical approach to fostering social learning and teamwork among students (Bandura, 1977; Michaelsen, Knight, & Fink, 2002).

COLLABORATIVE LEARNING

TBL is a collaborative learning approach that stands out from other methods due to its combination of individual pre-work, readiness assurance, and team application activities (Michaelsen et al., 2002). This approach emphasises the importance of individual accountability, promoting learners' responsibility for their own learning. The readiness assurance process also helps learners assess their comprehension of key concepts, identify their weaknesses and strengths, and focus on areas that require additional work (Sweet & Michaelsen, 2012).

Unlike other collaborative learning methods, TBL emphasizes team-based learning activities that require learners to work together to complete tasks or solve problems. These activities promote a "sense of community and belonging" among pupils while providing chances to develop necessary skills like communication, leadership, and collaboration, which are critical for success in various settings (Haidet et al., 2014).

TBL's use of immediate feedback is another unique aspect that enables learners to receive prompt feedback on their performance and adjust their learning strategies accordingly. This feedback helps learners identify areas where they need improvement and adjust their approach accordingly (McLaughlin et al., 2014). So, TBL's focus on individual preparation, readiness assurance, team-based learning activities, immediate feedback, and skill development sets it apart from other collaborative learning approaches (Parmelee & Michaelsen, 2010; Hrynchak & Batty, 2012). These unique features make TBL an effective method for promoting a sense of accountability among learners, fostering a sense of community, and developing critical skills.

BENEFITS

TBL has been widely used in numerous fields, including engineering, business, and medical education, and it consistently gives beneficial results. One of the main advantages of TBL is that it encourages students to participate in interactive activities and discussions, which supports active learning (Burgess et al., 2020). Students are encouraged to study and use their critical thinking abilities to solve issues as a result of participating in such activities. In TBL, students examine and discuss case studies in teams so they may learn from one another and consider different viewpoints (Michaelsen et al., 2002).

Students may learn problem-solving and critical thinking techniques using this method, which will be helpful in both their academic and professional lives. TBL also gives students the chance to own their learning, which has been found to increase student motivation and involvement (Espey, 2018). TBL promotes a learning atmosphere where students are motivated to be active learners, take ownership of their education, and show a greater interest in the subject matter. Students may share their knowledge and skills by working in teams, which can increase confidence and engagement (YN & Ladd, 2018).

TBL has also been shown to support cooperative learning, in which students cooperate to achieve a common goal. Students can benefit from one another's knowledge, cooperate on schoolwork, and form bonds with their peers by working in groups. Enhancing social, communication, and teamwork abilities via this kind of engagement may be beneficial in all facets of life (Parmelee & Michaelsen, 2010).

The utilization of TBL in education yields several advantages in fostering problem-solving, critical thinking, and decision-making skills among students. Through collaborative work, students participate in activities that encourage them to discuss ideas, defend positions using evidence-based reasoning, and think critically (Currey et al., 2015). This method challenges students to analyze information, apply knowledge, and evaluate the effectiveness of solutions, developing skills that are valuable in real-life problem-solving scenarios (Burgess et al., 2018). In addition, TBL encourages the exploration of diverse viewpoints and deepens understanding of the complexities of real-world challenges, thereby advancing critical thinking skills (Burgess & Matar, 2020).

Through TBL, students collaborate to recognize problems, evaluate possible solutions, and devise action plans supported by robust evidence (Hmelo-Silver, 2004). This approach cultivates the ability to think creatively, apply knowledge, and generate original solutions. Additionally, TBL motivates students to take their own learning responsibility, resulting in increased motivation and participation in the problem-solving process (Vasan, DeFouw, & Compton, 2011).

Moreover, TBL promotes the development of decision-making skills by providing students with opportunities to make informed decisions based on evidence and sound reasoning. Students evaluate information, compare, and contrast different options, and make informed decisions based on the available evidence (Roberson & Franchini, 2014). Consequently, students develop decision-making skills that are vital in various aspects of life, including personal, academic, and professional settings.

VERSATILE APPLICATION

The effectiveness of TBL has been demonstrated in a variety of educational contexts (Parmelee & Michaelsen, 2010; Hrynchak & Batty, 2012). It is a significant pedagogical approach for educators to take into consideration since it can enhance learning outcomes and increase student engagement in a variety of academic disciplines (Christensen et al., 2019). It has been effectively used in language learning, online learning, undergraduate accounting education, and medical education (Parmelee & Michaelsen, 2010; Hrynchak & Batty, 2012).

In the medical field, TBL is a successful teaching strategy since it enables students to grow their critical thinking abilities and collaborate with their classmates and healthcare experts. Middleton-Green and Ashelford (2013) used TBL to successfully teach medical students about the pathophysiology of numerous disorders like cancer, diabetes, depression, and pain. The findings revealed that students who got TBL-based training outperformed those who received conventional lecture-based education on a post-test measuring their understanding of the subject.

Similarly, Opdecam et al. (2014) found that TBL was a helpful tool for teaching students about the creation and analysis of financial statements in the context of undergraduate accounting education. When compared to students who got traditional lecture-based training, those who received TBL-based instruction performed better academically and expressed greater levels of satisfaction with their educational experience. This demonstrates how TBL can improve student engagement and learning results across a range of academic disciplines. Language learning has also shown success with TBL. Helwa (2015) taught English as a foreign language to Turkish university students using TBL. The findings revealed that students who got TBL-based instruction outperformed those who received traditional instruction in terms of test scores on a grammar section as well as in terms of student engagement.

TBL has also been employed successfully in online education. Jacobson (2012) used TBL to teach undergraduate students in an online course on information literacy. The findings revealed that students who received TBL-based instruction had better grade point averages and expressed greater levels of satisfaction with their educational experiences than those who only got traditional online instruction.

It has been demonstrated that implementing TBL improves students' abilities for critical thinking, collaboration, and self-directed learning. The effective use of TBL in many educational settings demonstrates how adaptable and successful it is as a teaching approach (Christensen et al., 2019).

IMPLEMENTATION

Successful TBL needs effective team structures, application activities, and feedback to support student learning and engagement (Sweet & Michaelsen, 2012). One significant element of TBL is creating effective team structures that encourage student participation and collaboration. Teams should be heterogeneous in terms of skill level, academic background, and diversity to maximize knowledge sharing and peer learning (Michaelsen et al., 2002). To facilitate effective teamwork, team roles and responsibilities must be clearly defined, and team-building activities should be conducted to promote trust and rapport among team members (Yukelson, 1997). Furthermore, regular peer evaluations can be used to monitor individual participation and team performance, which can enhance accountability and motivation (Wilkinson, 1998).

Another key element of TBL is developing effective application activities that promote active learning and critical thinking. Application activities should be relevant, challenging, and aligned with learning objectives (Gleason et al., 2011). For example, case studies, simulations, and problem-solving exercises can provide students with real-world scenarios to apply and integrate their knowledge (Jurdak, 2006). In addition, readiness assurance tests (RATs) can be used to assess students' prior knowledge and provide immediate feedback, which can enhance their self-regulation and motivation (Restall & Clark, 2021).

Finally, providing appropriate feedback is critical to TBL's success. Feedback should be timely, specific, and constructive to promote learning and improvement (Cestone, Levine, & Lane, 2008). For instance, team-based feedback can be utilized to evaluate team procedures and outcomes and identify areas for improvement (Ofstad & Brunner, 2013). In addition, individual feedback can be provided through peer evaluations and RATs, which can assist students in identifying their strengths and shortcomings and developing improvement strategies (Gleason et al., 2011).

ALIGNMENT

Active learning techniques, such as TBL, have garnered increased attention in educational spheres, as noted by Bean & Melzer (2021). TBL's potential to enhance student outcomes is undeniable, but its alignment with course objectives and learning outcomes is pivotal for maximum efficiency (Zhang, Wu, & Li, 2018). This alignment between TBL and course objectives is paramount for several reasons. Primarily, given the extensive time and resources TBL demands, ensuring activities align with specific course objectives and learning outcomes is essential. Without such congruence, there's a risk that TBL exercises may deviate from course content or fail to meet set learning goals, leading to potential inefficiencies (Michaelsen & Sweet, 2012).

Additionally, harmonizing TBL with course outcomes can elevate student motivation and engagement. A direct link between TBL activities and the course's set objectives often results in heightened student involvement. Such profound engagement can, in turn, spark motivation, a key ingredient for fostering learning (Alvarez-Bell et al., 2017). Furthermore, aligning TBL with course objectives can pave the way for refined assessment protocols. With TBL exercises mapped to the course's targets, educators can more adeptly gauge student progress and offer feedback. Consequently, this feedback becomes increasingly insightful, and educators can effectively determine TBL's contribution to the learning objectives (Michaelsen & Sweet, 2008).

To ensure this alignment, instructors are advised to pinpoint course objectives and learning outcomes that resonate with TBL activities. A thorough overview of course materials, the syllabus, and set learning objectives can facilitate this alignment. Collaboration with colleagues and instructional design experts can also be beneficial. Once the course's objectives are discerned, instructors can then devise TBL exercises that foster students' analytical, problem-solving, and decision-making prowess (Whitley et al., 2015).

BEST PRACTICES

TBL, as an instructional strategy, prioritizes active student engagement, honing their communication, teamwork, and cognitive skills. For TBL's successful execution, adhering to certain best practices is imperative. Initially, well-defined learning objectives should be established, as highlighted by Parmelee & Michaelsen (2010). These objectives, which should be clear, quantifiable, and aligned with course content, need to be communicated to students upfront. Taking a biology course as an example, objectives might encompass understanding cellular structures or elucidating DNA replication processes, as noted by Bissell & Lemons (2006). The subsequent best practice emphasizes curating effective learning resources. These resources, catering to the established learning objectives, should be accessible to all students and diversely formatted, encompassing readings, multimedia, and engaging simulations. The content should be challenging without being discouraging and delivered in an appealing manner, as suggested by Michaelsen & Sweet (2008).

Designing TBL sessions to foster active student participation forms the third best practice. Activities, geared towards realizing learning objectives, should be embedded both at individual and group levels within these sessions. Moreover, these sessions should incorporate opportunities for peer assessment and feedback to nurture teamwork and communication, as outlined by Farland et al. (2013). The fourth practice underscores the significance of timely feedback. As Michaelsen & Sweet (2012) indicate, feedback within TBL is crucial for students to discern their strengths and areas of improvement. Feedback sources can span from instructors, peers, or introspective reflections, and it should always align with the learning objectives.

Lastly, the importance of evaluating TBL's effectiveness forms the fifth best practice. Evaluative measures, both formative and summative, should be anchored on the learning objectives. While summative evaluations capture the holistic learning experience, formative assessments pinpoint specific areas of improvement for students, as delineated by Chung et al. (2009).

EVALUATION

Due to its complexity and multifaceted nature, TBL evaluation is not an easy process and presents challenges for educators as well as researchers. The lack of a consistent evaluation framework that can be used in a wide range of circumstances and disciplines is one of the challenges in evaluating TBL. TBL requires that students participate in active learning and critical thinking, which can be challenging to assess and measure using traditional assessment methods (Zhang et al., 2018). TBL also promotes cooperation and collaboration, which might make evaluation more difficult because it could be difficult to distinguish between individual achievement and group performance. These challenges might make it difficult to compare the results of different research and limit the generalizability of assessment findings (Lerner et al., 2009).

TBL has been evaluated using a variety of techniques to address these challenges. Using multiple-choice questions (MCQs) to evaluate student learning outcomes is a common approach. MCQs are frequently employed to assess students' memory and information retention. Yet MCQs might not test problem-solving and critical thinking abilities, which are essential elements of TBL (Tan et al., 2022). Peer evaluation is another approach used to evaluate TBL. Students that participate in peer evaluation provide their team members with comments on their efforts in the group project. In addition to offering insights into individual performance, this approach encourages teamwork and accountability. Peer evaluation, however, could be biased and might not correctly reflect each person's contributions to the group (Burgess et al., 2021).

Another approach for assessing TBL is self-assessment. Students self-assess their learning and performance by reflecting on them. In addition to giving students insights into their learning processes and metacognitive abilities, this approach enables them to accept responsibility for their own learning and development. However, students may overestimate their learning and performance when they self-assess, a phenomenon known as overestimation bias (Rodríguez et al., 2019). The multifaceted nature of TBL, which necessitates active learning, critical thinking, and cooperation, may not be adequately measured by conventional evaluation methods. TBL has been evaluated using a variety of techniques, including MCQs, peer review, and self-assessment, to address these challenges. Each of these methods has advantages and disadvantages, so it's crucial to carefully analyse them depending on the objectives and learning outcomes of the instructional strategy.

FEEDBACK

Providing feedback to students is essential for helping them understand their strengths and weaknesses, identify possibilities for growth, and develop self-regulated learning skills. According to Chan et al. (2014), feedback, which may increase learning outcomes by up to 50%, is one of the most potent influences on student learning and accomplishments. The task, process, and self-regulation levels of learning should emphasise feedback, which should also be fast, precise, and actionable (Ley & Young, 2001).

By highlighting areas for development and informing instructional decisions, assessment data may also be used to enhance the TBL process. TBL depends heavily on assessments to evaluate students' learning growth and assess their learning outcomes. By reviewing assessment results, teachers may identify areas where students' understanding is weak, modify the TBL activities and discussions to fill up these gaps, and provide relevant feedback to help students advance (Cestone et al., 2008). Moreover, evaluation data may be utilised to examine the efficiency of the TBL process and identify areas for enhancement in terms of its design, implementation, and facilitation (Burgess et al., 2022).

The TBL process may dramatically enhance learning results by using feedback and evaluation data. While assessment information can guide instructors' instructional decisions and assist them in evaluating the efficacy of the TBL process, appropriate feedback can assist students in improving their understanding of the content and building self-regulated learning skills (Reimschisel et al., 2017). To make informed decisions and continuously improve the TBL process, teachers should place a high priority on giving students quick, detailed, and actionable feedback.

CASES ON TBL

It is important to use evaluation strategies that accurately measure students' performance and learning outcomes to assess the efficacy of TBL. The use of RATs is one practical strategy. RATs are frequently administered at the start of every TBL session to make sure that students have read the essential material and are prepared to participate in team-based discussions. With RATs, educators may evaluate how well their students comprehend the subject matter and modify their teaching methods accordingly (Fujikura et al., 2013).

Peer evaluations constitute another successful TBL evaluation strategy. Peer evaluations can be used to rate each member's contributions to group discussions and projects. Students can use this technique to evaluate their own performance and get input from their peers. Peer evaluations can motivate students to hold one another accountable and cooperate to accomplish common goals (Cestone et al., 2008).

Finally, using student surveys to measure the TBL's overall efficacy can be effective. At the end of each TBL session or the end of the semester, surveys might be conducted. Students can give feedback on how well TBL has improved their learning outcomes and strengthened their cooperation and communication skills using this evaluation strategy (Chad, 2012).

SCALING UP

TBL improves the learning outcomes and critical thinking abilities of students. TBL scaling, however, might be difficult due to the barriers that can arise. Faculty members' resistance to implementing new teaching methods is one possible barrier (Reid, 2014). This may be avoided by offering instruction and assistance to faculty members so they feel more confident using TBL (Thompson et al., 2007). The need for significant resource expenditure, including time and money, is another possible barrier. Institutions may overcome this barrier by giving faculty members institutional and financial assistance so they can create and use TBL in their classes (Sparrow & McCabe, 2012). Institutions should also promote cooperation and resource sharing among faculty members to lower the total cost of adopting TBL.

The need for significant changes in the curriculum and assessment methods is another possible barrier to scaling up TBL. This may be resolved by conducting regular assessments and evaluations of TBL's effectiveness, which can assist identify areas that require development and adapting the curriculum and assessment strategies accordingly (Wong et al., 2021). Moreover, scaling up TBL may be difficult due to the necessity for strong faculty-student collaboration and communication. By giving faculty members and students the resources and tools they need to communicate and collaborate, such as online discussion boards and collaborative workspaces, institutions may overcome this (Lowry, 2007).

APPROPRIATE SUPPORT

TBL adoption involves several essential elements, including faculty buy-in, institutional support, and efficient training. For TBL to be implemented successfully, faculty support is necessary because it ensures that teachers are dedicated to the strategy and are prepared to put in the time and effort needed to make it succeed (Allen et al., 2013). Institutional support is also essential to offer the infrastructure and resources required for TBL, including technology, facilities, and administrative assistance (Motlagh et al., 2015).

For the TBL implementation to be successful, effective training is also important. Faculty members must get training in the TBL's principles and processes, including how to build efficient team structures, develop relevant evaluations, and lead group discussions (Michaelsen & Sweet, 2012). Lack of training might make it difficult for teachers to use TBL successfully, which would frustrate both teachers and pupils and result in poor outcomes. In addition, instructors who have received the necessary training in TBL are more likely to see its advantages and use it as a teaching method (Elshama, 2021).

EXAMPLES

TBL has been effectively implemented at scale by various institutions, and numerous studies have highlighted its advantages in a wide range of situations and disciplines. The "University of California, San Francisco (UCSF) School of Medicine" is one university that uses TBL in its preclinical curriculum. To integrate TBL modules, classes had to be restructured, and faculty members had to receive TBL training. In comparison to the conventional lecture-based style, the findings revealed considerable improvements in students' performance, including higher exam scores and knowledge retention (McOwen & Farmakidis, 2020).

The "University of Michigan Medical School" employed TBL in a large introductory course for first-year medical students, which was another effective example of TBL being applied on a large scale. The TBL modules on numerous subjects in the course proved to be more effective than in previous years, resulting in increased exam scores, higher student engagement, and higher information retention (University of Michigan, 2014).

Further, the "College of Business at Iowa State University" implemented TBL in a large-enrolment course for engineering students. The use of TBL aligns with the increasing need for active learning by both faculty and students and the importance of developing teamwork skills for future employment. However, managing conflict, creating fair methods of assessment for team-based work, and differing levels of effort by students can be challenging. Strategies used for team selection and development, as well as optimization of the TBL process, have been implemented to overcome these challenges. Student performance on TBL activities and evaluations of the TBL experience has been positive. This example shows the potential of TBL for promoting engaged and transformative learning in large-enrolment courses for engineering and engineering technology students (Mosher, 2021).

Adding to the above thoughts, it should be noted that Adopting AI in education, especially Team-Based Learning (TBL), necessitates a collaborative strategy involving specialists from a variety of professions, including computer science, social science, and law, among others. As artificial intelligence (AI) becomes more widespread in education, particularly TBL, ethical and legal concerns arise. These may include concerns about data privacy, AI algorithm bias, accountability, and transparency (Efthymiou–Egleton, et al., 2020). To ensure responsible and ethical use of AI in education, professionals in domains such as computer science, social science, and law must collaborate to produce ethical principles, rules, and policies (Efthymiou-Egleton et al., 2020).

CONCLUSION

The chapter discusses the concept of TBL, a collaborative teaching strategy that emphasizes student engagement and quality learning through individual and group activities with immediate feedback. TBL is adaptable to various situations and disciplines and involves dividing students into permanent groups, studying assigned material, taking "individual and team readiness assurance tests, and participating in in-class activities that require students to apply the study content for problem-solving." The benefits of TBL for improving student engagement, collaboration, and learning outcomes are highlighted, including improving problem-solving skills, building trust among team members, and outperforming the best member. The TBL process is organized into a "rhythm" of "out-of-class preparation, readiness assurance testing, and application activities" based on four pillars: groups, accountability, feedback, and assessment.

Designing and implementing TBL requires effective team structures, the development of application activities, and appropriate feedback. TBL needs to align with learning objectives and course outcomes, and examples of best practices for designing and implementing TBL are provided. TBL activities challenge students to use "critical thinking and problem-solving skills" and also help them develop transferable skills that are highly valued by employers. Therefore, TBL is a valuable educational strategy for preparing students for the workforce. The challenges of evaluating TBL are discussed, and different methods used to measure student learning and performance, feedback, and assessment data to improve the TBL process are presented.

Scaling up TBL requires overcoming barriers, faculty buy-in, institutional support, and effective training for successful TBL implementation. Examples of successful TBL implementations at scale are also provided. Overall, TBL helps foster accountability and a sense of agency in students, allowing them to organize themselves independently, create solutions, and develop a sense of accountability towards each other. TBL is designed in such a manner that students may collaborate in groups to solve issues, discuss case studies, and engage in simulations. TBL has the potential to enhance student engagement and learning outcomes in higher education. One of the most significant advantages of TBL is that it encourages active and collaborative learning, which can lead to increased student engagement (Ofstad & Brunner, 2013). Students are motivated to engage actively in their learning process by working in groups, which can boost their enthusiasm and interest in the subject matter (Al Kawas & Hamdy, 2017). TBL activities are also meant to be challenging, requiring students to use "critical thinking and problem-solving skills," (Efthymiou, I. P., 2020), which can increase student engagement and learning results (Dearnley et al., 2018).

Moreover, TBL has been demonstrated to increase learning outcomes in higher education. Haidet, Kubitz, and McCormack (2014) demonstrated, for example, that students who engaged in TBL activities outperformed their peers in conventional lecture-based courses in terms of both knowledge acquisition and retention. Similarly, Espey (2018) found in a meta-analysis that TBL was connected with greater academic achievement and enhanced critical thinking abilities when compared to conventional teaching approaches.

TBL can also help with the growth of important transferable skills like collaboration, communication, and leadership (Zhang et al., 2018). Working in groups requires students to communicate effectively, exchange ideas, and distribute tasks, which can help them improve these abilities. Institutions place a high emphasis on transferable skills, making TBL a viable educational strategy for preparing students for the job (Vlachopoulos et al., 2020).

FUTURE RESEARCH

Below are some research gaps that may be addressed in the future on the topic of team-based learning (TBL):

- TBL effectiveness in different disciplines: While TBL has been effectively applied in a variety of disciplines, it is unclear if it is equally beneficial across all disciplines. Future studies might look at the effectiveness of TBL in different disciplines and identify factors that may impact its effectiveness.
- Long-term learning results of TBL: While TBL has been found to increase immediate learning outcomes, it is unclear if it has a long-term influence on students' skills and knowledge. Future studies might look into the influence of TBL on long-term learning outcomes and knowledge retention.
- The impact of TBL on diverse student populations: TBL is successful in improving student engagement and collaboration, but it is unclear if it works equally well for diverse student populations, especially students from underrepresented groups. Future studies might look at the influence of TBL on different student populations and develop measures to make it more inclusive.
- TBL team size and composition: Since TBL includes grouping students, it is unclear what the best team size and composition are for optimising learning outcomes. Future studies might look at the influence of team size and composition on TBL efficacy and identify best practices for team formation.
- Technology's Role in TBL: While TBL may be implemented without the use of technology, it is unclear what role technology can play in improving TBL effectiveness. Future studies might look at how technology affects TBL effectiveness and identify best practices for using technology in TBL.

REFERENCES

Abreu, M., Veiga, F. H., Antunes, J., & Ferreira, A. (2006). Attitudes towards the school and self-interest in students from different family contexts. Activação do desenvolvimento psicológico: Actas do simpósio internacional, 194-200.

Ainsworth, J. (2021). Team-Based Learning in professional writing courses for accounting graduates: Positive impacts on student engagement, accountability and satisfaction. *Accounting Education*, *30*(3), 234–257. doi:10.1080/09639284.2021.1906720

Al Kawas, S., & Hamdy, H. (2017). Peer-assisted learning associated with team-based learning in dental education. *Health Profession Education, 3*(1), 38–43. doi:10.1016/j.hpe.2016.08.003

Allen, R. E., Copeland, J., Franks, A. S., Karimi, R., McCollum, M., Riese, D. J. II, & Lin, A. Y. (2013). Team-based learning in US colleges and schools of pharmacy. *American Journal of Pharmaceutical Education, 77*(6), 115. doi:10.5688/ajpe776115 PMID:23966718

Alvarez-Bell, R. M., Wirtz, D., & Bian, H. (2017). Identifying keys to success in innovative teaching: Student engagement and instructional practices as predictors of student learning in a course using a team-based learning approach. *Teaching & Learning Inquiry, 5*(2), 128–146. doi:10.20343/teachlearninqu.5.2.10

Bandura, A. (1977). *Social learning theory*. Prentice Hall.

Bean, J. C., & Melzer, D. (2021). *Engaging ideas: The professor's guide to integrating writing, critical thinking, and active learning in the classroom*. John Wiley & Sons.

Bissell, A. N., & Lemons, P. P. (2006). A new method for assessing critical thinking in the classroom. *Bioscience, 56*(1), 66–72. doi:10.1641/0006-3568(2006)056[0066:ANMFAC]2.0.CO;2

Burgess, A., & Matar, E. (2020). Team-based learning (TBL): theory, planning, practice, and implementation. *Clinical Education for the Health Professions: Theory and Practice*, 1-29. doi:10.1007/978-981-13-6106-7_128-1

Burgess, A., Roberts, C., Ayton, T., & Mellis, C. (2018). Implementation of modified team-based learning within a problem based learning medical curriculum: A focus group study. *BMC Medical Education, 18*(1), 1–7. doi:10.118612909-018-1172-8 PMID:29631579

Burgess, A., Roberts, C., Lane, A. S., Haq, I., Clark, T., Kalman, E., Pappalardo, N., & Bleasel, J. (2021). Peer review in team-based learning: Influencing feedback literacy. *BMC Medical Education, 21*(1), 426. doi:10.118612909-021-02821-6 PMID:34384418

Burgess, A., van Diggele, C., Roberts, C., & Mellis, C. (2020). Team-based learning: Design, facilitation and participation. *BMC Medical Education, 20*(2), 1–7. doi:10.118612909-020-02287-y PMID:33272267

Center for Teaching. (n.d.). *Team-Based Learning*. Vanderbilt University. Online available at: https://cft.vanderbilt.edu/guides-sub-pages/team-based-learning/

Cestone, C. M., Levine, R. E., & Lane, D. R. (2008). Peer assessment and evaluation in team-based learning. *New Directions for Teaching and Learning, 2008*(116), 69–78. doi:10.1002/tl.334

Cevik, A. A., ElZubeir, M., Abu-Zidan, F. M., & Shaban, S. (2019). Team-based learning improves knowledge and retention in an emergency medicine clerkship. *International Journal of Emergency Medicine, 12*(1), 1–8. doi:10.118612245-019-0222-2 PMID:31179926

Chad, P. (2012). The use of team-based learning as an approach to increased engagement and learning for marketing students: A case study. *Journal of Marketing Education, 34*(2), 128–139. doi:10.1177/0273475312450388

Chan, P. E., Konrad, M., Gonzalez, V., Peters, M. T., & Ressa, V. A. (2014). The critical role of feedback in formative instructional practices. *Intervention in School and Clinic, 50*(2), 96–104. doi:10.1177/1053451214536044

Christensen, J., Harrison, J. L., Hollindale, J., & Wood, K. (2019). Implementing team-based learning (TBL) in accounting courses. *Accounting Education, 28*(2), 195–219. doi:10.1080/09639284.2018.1535986

Chung, E. K., Rhee, J. A., Baik, Y. H., & A, O.-S. (2009). The effect of team-based learning in medical ethics education. *Medical Teacher, 31*(11), 1013–1017. doi:10.3109/01421590802590553 PMID:19909042

Currey, J., Eustace, P., Oldland, E., Glanville, D., & Story, I. (2015). Developing professional attributes in critical care nurses using Team-Based Learning. *Nurse Education in Practice, 15*(3), 232–238. doi:10.1016/j.nepr.2015.01.011 PMID:25704795

Dearnley, C., Rhodes, C., Roberts, P., Williams, P., & Prenton, S. (2018). Team based learning in nursing and midwifery higher education; a systematic review of the evidence for change. *Nurse Education Today, 60*, 75–83. doi:10.1016/j.nedt.2017.09.012 PMID:29045913

Efthymiou, I. P. (2020). Non-Cognitive Skills and AI: A New Era of Learning and Development. *International Case Studies Journal, 9*(10), 42–46.

Efthymiou-Egleton, I. P., Egleton, T. W. E., & Sidiropoulos, S. (2020). Artificial Intelligence (AI) in Politics: Should Political AI be Controlled? *International Journal of Innovative Science and Research Technology, 5*(2).

Efthymiou–Egleton, T. W., Sidiropoulos, S., Spanos, E., & Stougiannou, E. (2020). Big Data and Democracy. *HAPSc Policy Briefs Series*, *1*(2), 18–25. doi:10.12681/hapscpbs.26473

Elshama, S. S. (2021). How to Apply Team-Based Learning in Medical Education? *Quantum Journal of Medical and Health Sciences*, *1*(2), 15–22.

Espey, M. (2018). Enhancing critical thinking using team-based learning. *Higher Education Research & Development*, *37*(1), 15–29. doi:10.1080/07294360.2017.1344196

Farland, M. Z., Sicat, B. L., Franks, A. S., Pater, K. S., Medina, M. S., & Persky, A. M. (2013). Best practices for implementing team-based learning in pharmacy education. *American Journal of Pharmaceutical Education*, *77*(8), 177. doi:10.5688/ajpe778177 PMID:24159218

Fatmi, M., Hartling, L., Hillier, T., Campbell, S., Oswald, A. E., & Brown, M. (2013). The effectiveness of team-based learning on learning outcomes in health professions education: BEME Guide No. 30. *Medical Teacher*, *35*(12), e1608–e1624. doi:10.3109/0142159X.2013.849802 PMID:24245519

FeedbackFruits. (2021, August 5). *What is team-based learning*? FeedbackFruits. Retrieved from https://feedbackfruits.com/blog/what-is-team-based-learning

Fujikura, T., Takeshita, T., Homma, H., Adachi, K., Miyake, K., Kudo, M., Takizawa, T., Nagayama, H., & Hirakawa, K. (2013). Team-based learning using an audience response system: A possible new strategy for interactive medical education. *Journal of Nippon Medical School*, *80*(1), 63–69. doi:10.1272/jnms.80.63 PMID:23470808

Gleason, B. L., Peeters, M. J., Resman-Targoff, B. H., Karr, S., McBane, S., Kelley, K., Thomas, T., & Denetclaw, T. H. (2011). An active-learning strategies primer for achieving ability-based educational outcomes. *American Journal of Pharmaceutical Education*, *75*(9), 186. doi:10.5688/ajpe759186 PMID:22171114

Haidet, P., Kubitz, K., & McCormack, W. T. (2014). Analysis of the Team-Based Learning Literature: TBL Comes of Age. *Journal on Excellence in College Teaching*, *25*(3&4), 303–333. PMID:26568668

Haidet, P., O'Malley, K. J., & Richards, B. (2008). An initial experience with "team learning" in medical education. *Academic Medicine*, *83*(10), 10–16. doi:10.1097/ACM.0b013e318183eafd PMID:11788321

Helwa, H. S. (2015). Using Computer mediated Team based Learning for Developing EFL Prospective Teachers' Presentation Skills and reducing their Foreign Language Anxiety. *Arabic Studies in Education and Psychology, 58*(58), 345-388. doi:10.12816/0022419

Hmelo-Silver, C. E. (2004). Problem-based learning: What and how do students learn? *Educational Psychology Review*, *16*(3), 235–266. doi:10.1023/B:EDPR.0000034022.16470.f3

Hosseini, S. M. H. (2014). Competitive team-based learning versus group investigation with reference to the language proficiency of Iranian EFL intermediate students. *International Journal of Instruction*, *7*(1), 37–47. https://dergipark.org.tr/en/pub/eiji/issue/5136/69994

Hrynchak, P., & Batty, H. (2012). The Educational Theory Basis of Team-Based Learning. *Medical Teacher*, *34*(10), 796–801. doi:10.3109/0142159X.2012.687120 PMID:22646301

Hrynchak, P., & Batty, H. (2012). The educational theory basis of team-based learning. *Medical Teacher*, *34*(10), 796–801. doi:10.3109/0142159X.2012.687120 PMID:22646301

Jacobson, T. E. (2012). Team-based learning in an information literacy course. *Communications in Information Literacy*, *5*(2), 82–101. doi:10.15760/comminfolit.2012.5.2.105

Jarjoura, C., Abou Tayeh, P., & Zgheib, N. K. (2015). Using team-based learning to teach grade 7 biology: Student satisfaction and improved performance. *Journal of Biological Education*, *49*(4), 401–419. doi:10.1080/00219266.2014.967277

Jurdak, M. E. (2006). Contrasting perspectives and performance of high school students on problem solving in real world, situated, and school contexts. *Educational Studies in Mathematics*, *63*(3), 283–301. doi:10.100710649-005-9008-y

Kolb, D. A. (1984). *Experiential learning: Experience as the source of learning and development*. Prentice-Hall.

Lerner, S., Magrane, D., & Friedman, E. (2009). Teaching teamwork in medical education. *Mount Sinai Journal of Medicine: A Journal of Translational and Personalized Medicine: A Journal of Translational and Personalized Medicine, 76*(4), 318-329. doi:10.1002/msj.20129

Ley, K., & Young, D. B. (2001). Instructional principles for self-regulation. *Educational Technology Research and Development*, *49*(2), 93–103. doi:10.1007/BF02504930

Lowry, A. E. (2007). *Effects of online versus face-to-face professional development with a team-based learning community approach on teachers' application of a new instructional practice*. The Johns Hopkins University.

McLaughlin, J. E., Roth, M. T., Glatt, D. M., Gharkholonarehe, N., Davidson, C. A., Griffin, L. M., Esserman, D. A., & Mumper, R. J. (2014). The Flipped Classroom: A Course Redesign to Foster Learning and Engagement in a Health Professions School. *Academic Medicine*, *89*(2), 236–243. doi:10.1097/ACM.0000000000000086 PMID:24270916

McOwen, K. S., & Farmakidis, A. L. (2020). A snapshot of medical student education in the United States and Canada: Reports from 145 schools. *Academic Medicine*, *95*(9, suppl), S1–S606.

Michaelsen, L. K., Knight, A. B., & Fink, L. D. (2002). *Team-based learning: A transformative use of small groups*. Greenwood Publishing Group.

Michaelsen, L. K., Knight, A. B., & Fink, L. D. (2004). *Team-Based Learning: A Transformative Use of Small Groups in College Teaching*. Stylus Publishing, LLC.

Michaelsen, L. K., & Sweet, M. (2008). The essential elements of team-based learning. *New Directions for Teaching and Learning*, *2008*(116), 7–27. doi:10.1002/tl.330

Michaelsen, L. K., & Sweet, M. (2012). Fundamental principles and practices of team-based learning. In L. K. Michaelsen, A. Knight, & L. D. Fink (Eds.), *Team-based learning for health professions education: A guide to using small groups for improving learning* (pp. 9–34). Stylus Publishing, LLC.

Middleton-Green, L., & Ashelford, S. (2013). Using team-based learning in teaching undergraduate pathophysiology for nurses. *Health and Social Care Education*, *2*(2), 53–58. doi:10.11120/hsce.2013.00031

Mosher, G. A. (2021). *Formation and development of effective student teams to facilitate team-based learning. 2013 North Midwest Section Meeting*.

Motlagh, M. K., Najarkolai, A. R., & Keshmiri, F. (2015). Team-Based learning in medical universities: Infrastructure and requirements. *Thrita*, *4*(3), e29549. doi:10.5812/thrita.29549

Ofstad, W., & Brunner, L. J. (2013). Team-based learning in pharmacy education. *American Journal of Pharmaceutical Education, 77*(4), 70. doi:10.5688/ajpe77470 PMID:23716738

Opdecam, E., Everaert, P., Van Keer, H., & Buysschaert, F. (2014). Preferences for team learning and lecture-based learning among first-year undergraduate accounting students. *Research in Higher Education, 55*, 400–432. doi:10.100711162-013-9315-6

Palsolé, S., & Awalt, C. (2008). Team-based learning in asynchronous online settings. *New Directions for Teaching and Learning, 2008*(116), 87–95. doi:10.1002/tl.336

Parmelee, D. X. (2008). Team-based learning in health professions education. In L. K. Michaelsen, A. Knight, & L. D. Fink (Eds.), *Team-based learning for health professions education* (pp. 1–14). Stylus Publishing, LLC.

Parmelee, D. X., & Michaelsen, L. K. (2010). Twelve tips for doing effective team-based learning (TBL). *Medical Teacher, 32*(2), 118–122. doi:10.3109/01421590903548562 PMID:20163226

Rajalingam, P., & Rotgans, J. I. (2018). Team-based learning improves nursing students' knowledge acquisition, retention, and satisfaction: A mixed-methods study. *Journal of Nursing Education and Practice, 8*(3), 29–39. doi:10.5430/jnep.v8n3p29

Reid, P. (2014). Categories for barriers to adoption of instructional technologies. *Education and Information Technologies, 19*(2), 383–407. doi:10.100710639-012-9222-z

Reimschisel, T., Herring, A. L., Huang, J., & Minor, T. J. (2017). A systematic review of the published literature on team-based learning in health professions education. *Medical Teacher, 39*(12), 1227–1237. doi:10.1080/0142159X.2017.1340636 PMID:28664760

Restall, G. C., & Clark, M. C. (2021). Team-based learning and the community of inquiry model. *New Directions for Teaching and Learning, 2021*(165), 65–76. doi:10.1002/tl.20437

Roberson, B., & Franchini, B. (2014). Effective task design for the TBL classroom. *Journal on Excellence in College Teaching, 25*(3&4), 275–302. https://learntbl.ca/wp-content/uploads/2016/01/v25n34-RobersonFranchini.pdf

Rodríguez, M. C., Ramírez, L. J., & Camargo, J. M. (2019). TBL, self-assessment, and use of ICT: A methodological option to benefit the English learning process in a Colombian university. *Journal of Language Teaching and Research, 10*(6), 1162–1172. doi:10.17507/jltr.1006.04

Ryan, R. M., & Deci, E. L. (2000). Self-determination theory and the facilitation of intrinsic motivation, social development, and well-being. *The American Psychologist, 55*(1), 68–78. doi:10.1037/0003-066X.55.1.68 PMID:11392867

Shashidhara, Y. N., & Ladd, E. (2018). Team Based Learning an Active Teaching and learning Pedagogy: A Narrative Literature Review. *Indian Journal of Public Health Research & Development, 9*(10), 242–248. doi:10.5958/0976-5506.2018.01349.9

Sparrow, S. M., & McCabe, M. S. (2012). Team-based learning in law. *Legal Writing. J. Legal Writing Inst., 18*, 153.

Sweet, M., & Michaelsen, L. K. (2012). *Team-Based Learning in the Social Sciences and Humanities: Group Work That Works to Generate Critical Thinking and Engagement*. Stylus Publishing, LLC.

Tan, S. H. S., Thibault, G., Chew, A. C. Y., & Rajalingam, P. (2022). Enabling open-ended questions in team-based learning using automated marking: Impact on student achievement, learning and engagement. *Journal of Computer Assisted Learning, 38*(5), 1347–1359. doi:10.1111/jcal.12680

Team-Based Learning Collaborative. (n.d.). *What is TBL*? Online available at: https://docs.lamsfoundation.org/tbl/

Thompson, B. M., Schneider, V. F., Haidet, P., Levine, R. E., McMahon, K. K., Perkowski, L. C., & Richards, B. F. (2007). Team-based learning at ten medical schools: Two years later. *Medical Education, 41*(3), 250–257. doi:10.1111/j.1365-2929.2006.02684.x PMID:17316209

University of Michigan. (2014). *Medical Education Day*. Program Guide Dow Auditorium and Towsley Center Lobby. Retrieved from https://medicine.umich.edu/sites/default/files/MedEdDayProgram2014.pdf

Vasan, N. S., DeFouw, D. O., & Compton, S. (2011). Team-based learning in anatomy: An efficient, effective, and economical strategy. *Anatomical Sciences Education, 4*(6), 333–339. doi:10.1002/ase.257 PMID:21998012

Vlachopoulos, P., Jan, S. K., & Buckton, R. (2020). A case for team-based learning as an effective collaborative learning methodology in higher education. *College Teaching, 69*(2), 69–77. doi:10.1080/87567555.2020.1816889

Whitley, H. P., Bell, E., Eng, M., Fuentes, D. G., Helms, K. L., Maki, E. D., & Vyas, D. (2015). Practical team-based learning from planning to implementation. *American Journal of Pharmaceutical Education, 79*(10), 149. doi:10.5688/ajpe7910149 PMID:26889061

Wilkinson, A. (1998). Empowerment: Theory and practice. *Personnel Review*, *27*(1), 40–56. doi:10.1108/00483489810368549

Wong, P., Jumat, M. R., Lee, I. C. J., Foo, K. X., Goh, S. P. L., Ganapathy, S., Lai, S. H., & Hwang, N. C. (2020). Redesigning team-based learning facilitation for an online platform to deliver preclinical curriculum: A response to the COVID-19 pandemic. *MedEdPublish*, *9*(135), 135. doi:10.15694/mep.2020.000135.1

Yukelson, D. (1997). Principles of effective team building interventions in sport: A direct services approach at Penn State University. *Journal of Applied Sport Psychology*, *9*(1), 73–96. doi:10.1080/10413209708415385

Zhang, J., Wu, W., & Li, H. (2018). Enhancing building information modeling competency among civil engineering and management students with team-based learning. *Journal of Professional Issues in Engineering Education and Practice*, *144*(2), 05018001. doi:10.1061/(ASCE)EI.1943-5541.0000356

Chapter 2
Developing Skills With Team-Based Learning

Nitish Kumar Minz
https://orcid.org/0009-0000-4770-0336
K.R. Mangalam University, India

Anshul Saluja
K.R. Mangalam University, India

EXECUTIVE SUMMARY

Team-based learning (TBL) is a pedagogical strategy that has gained significant attention in recent years for its effectiveness in promoting active learning, critical thinking, and collaborative skills among students. This research paper explores the principles, benefits, and challenges of team-based learning, examines its application across different educational settings, and discusses its potential impact on student engagement and learning outcomes. By fostering a student-centered environment, TBL encourages a deeper understanding of complex concepts, enhances communication skills, and prepares students for real-world challenges. This chapter also highlights strategies for successful implementation and offers insights into the future directions of team-based learning in education.

INTRODUCTION

The field of education is currently experiencing a dynamic transformation driven by the pursuit of more effective teaching methodologies that actively engage students and cultivate critical thinking and practical knowledge application (Davidson, Major, & Michaelsen, 2014). In recent years, Team-Based Learning (TBL) has emerged as

DOI: 10.4018/978-1-6684-7583-6.ch002

a prominent and innovative educational approach that aligns with these objectives. This introduction sets the stage for our exploration of TBL, offering insights into its background, purpose, and the scope of our study.

TBL, rooted in active learning, collaboration, and practical knowledge application, represents a departure from traditional lecture-based instruction (Michaelsen & Sweet, 2004). It emphasizes dynamic and interactive learning experiences, with students working collaboratively in teams to address complex problems and engage deeply with course material. This approach fosters a sense of shared responsibility among students, promoting both individual and collective learning.

Our study delves into the evolution and effectiveness of TBL as a pedagogical approach, drawing on a range of scholarly works to provide a comprehensive analysis of its impact on educational practices and outcomes. Through this exploration, we aim to contribute valuable insights to the ongoing discourse on innovative teaching methodologies in education.

BACKGROUND

Traditional lecture-based teaching, a longstanding pillar of education, has increasingly faced criticism for its limitations in fully engaging students, promoting critical thinking, and adequately preparing them for the multifaceted challenges of the modern world. In the conventional lecture format, students often assume passive roles, limiting their interaction with the subject matter and their peers (Ruder, Maier, & Simkins, 2021). Moreover, the one-size-fits-all approach fails to account for individual learning styles and diverse needs in today's diverse classrooms (Espey, 2018).

As educational paradigms evolve to meet the demands of the 21st century, there is a growing recognition of the imperative to employ more dynamic and participatory teaching methods (Hettler, 2015). One such innovative pedagogical approach that has gained traction in recent years is Team-Based Learning (TBL). TBL is grounded in the principles of active learning, collaboration, and the practical application of knowledge (Davidson, Major, & Michaelsen, 2014). It marks a profound departure from traditional lectures by offering a dynamic platform for interactive and collaborative learning experiences.

In TBL, students are organized into teams to tackle complex problems, engage in in-depth discussions about course material, and apply key concepts to real-world scenarios (Green & de Bodisco, 2020). This approach fosters a sense of collective responsibility and accountability among students, encouraging them to actively contribute to their own and their team's learning.

The roots of TBL can be traced back to Dr. Larry Michaelsen's pioneering work in the late 1970s (Michaelsen & Sweet, 2004). Over the ensuing years, TBL has evolved into a versatile and widely recognized pedagogical approach that transcends disciplinary boundaries. Its structured methodology and core principles have made it an invaluable tool for educators across diverse educational settings who aim to create impactful and meaningful learning experiences.

TBL's emergence as a prominent pedagogical approach underscores the urgency of adopting modern teaching methods that foster critical thinking, collaboration, and the development of practical skills—essential attributes for success in today's fast-paced and ever-changing world (Simkins, Maier, & Ruder, 2021) (Huang & Lin, 2017).

Purpose and Scope

This research paper seeks to comprehensively explore the principles, benefits, challenges, and applications of TBL, drawing on a rich body of literature. It aims to provide educators, instructional designers, and educational researchers with a deep understanding of this pedagogical approach and its potential to reshape education.

Our exploration will encompass the following key areas:

i. **Fundamental Principles:** We will delve into the foundational principles underpinning TBL, such as the emphasis on collaboration, active learning, and accountability.
ii. **Benefits:** Our analysis will highlight the myriad benefits of TBL, including improved critical thinking skills, enhanced communication abilities, increased student engagement, and better preparation for real-world challenges.
iii. **Challenges:** We will discuss the challenges educators may encounter when implementing TBL, such as managing group dynamics and designing effective assessment strategies, along with strategies to address these challenges.
iv. **Applications:** We will examine the diverse applications of TBL across various educational contexts, from higher education to K-12 settings, health sciences education, and interdisciplinary courses.
v. **Implementation Strategies:** This paper will provide insights into strategies for successfully implementing TBL, including designing effective team activities, facilitating productive student discussions, aligning TBL with learning objectives, and evaluating student performance.
vi. **Future Directions:** Lastly, we will explore the future of TBL, considering potential innovations, the integration of technology, and identifying research opportunities to enhance its effectiveness.

Figure 1. Mind map representation of research paper structure on team-based learning (TBL)
Source: Author's Compilation

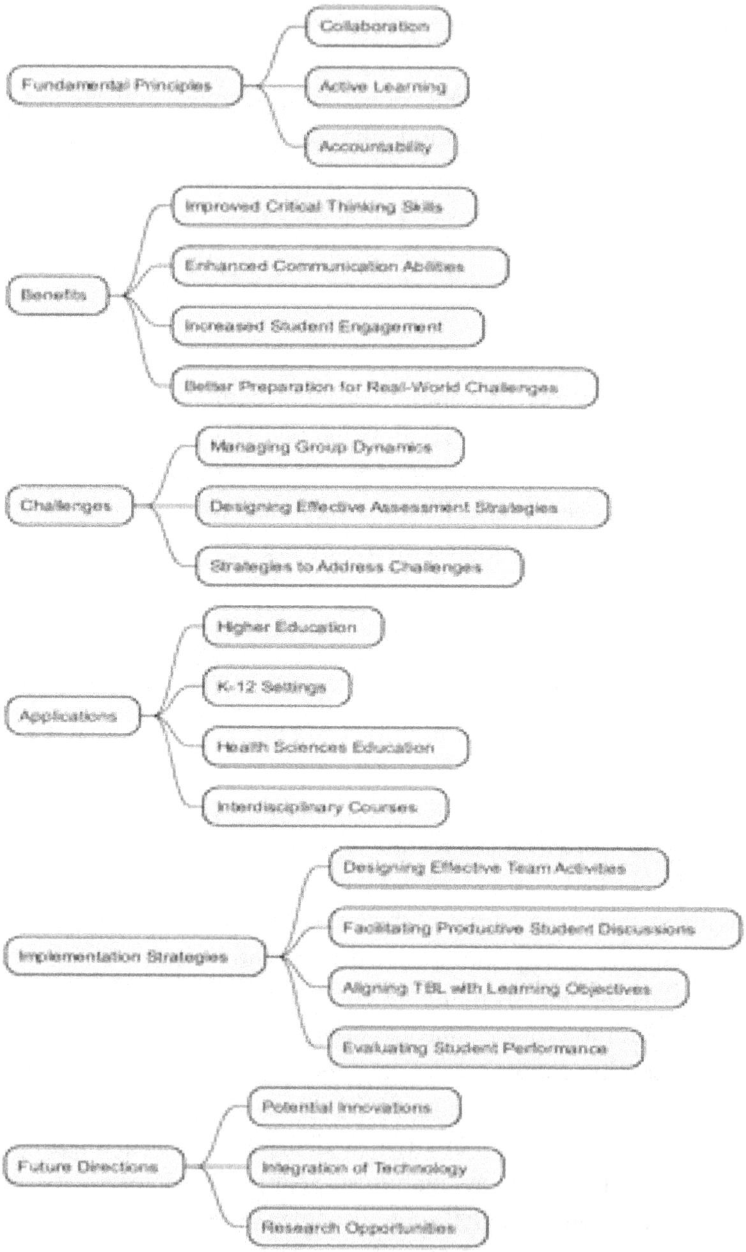

This research endeavour aims to equip educators with a comprehensive resource that illuminates the principles and practical applications of Team-Based Learning. By the conclusion of this paper, readers will have gained valuable insights into how TBL can enrich learning experiences and prepare students for the challenges of the modern educational landscape.

LITERATURE REVIEW

Davidson Higher education landscape is evolving, with a growing emphasis on innovative pedagogical approaches that actively engage students and promote deeper learning. Team-Based Learning (TBL) has emerged as a powerful strategy that aligns with these educational goals.

Ruder, Maier, & Simkins (2021) introduced the concept of Team-Based Learning (TBL) within the realm of economic education. Their work served as a valuable starting point for educators interested in adopting TBL methodologies. The study offered a comprehensive overview of TBL, including its foundational principles and practical implementation. By highlighting the benefits and challenges of TBL, this reference equipped instructors with the necessary tools to initiate TBL in their classrooms. It provided insights into TBL's adaptability and effectiveness in engaging students in active learning.

Espey (2018) focused on the application of Team-Based Learning (TBL) to enhance critical thinking skills in the higher education context. The study emphasized the practical strategies employed to incorporate TBL in courses and evaluated its impact on students' engagement and cognitive development. Espey's work underlined the significance of TBL as a pedagogical approach to stimulate critical thinking, urging educators to consider its potential to augment learning outcomes. This reference served as a valuable resource for those seeking to understand the cognitive benefits of TBL and its practical implementation.

Hettler (2015) delved into the influence of student demographics on the outcomes of Team-Based Learning (TBL). This reference evaluated how factors such as gender, age, and prior educational experiences could affect the effectiveness of TBL strategies in economics education. By analyzing the relationships between student characteristics and TBL performance, Hettler provided insights into the diversity of TBL outcomes among different student groups. The research encouraged educators to consider the individualized impact of TBL based on student demographics and adapt their pedagogical approaches accordingly. This reference was valuable for those interested in tailoring TBL to diverse student populations.

Green & de Bodisco (2020) explored the utilization of Team-Based Learning (TBL) in discussion and writing classes, expanding the scope of TBL beyond traditional lecture-based formats. This reference discussed innovative methods of incorporating TBL into diverse educational contexts. By considering its application in discussion and writing classes, the study emphasized the adaptability of TBL to different subject areas and teaching methodologies. The research highlighted how TBL could promote active engagement and collaborative learning, making it a versatile approach for enhancing student participation in discussion and writing courses.

Simkins, Maier, & Ruder (2021) focused on the integration of learning sciences research into economics education through Team-Based Learning (TBL). This reference offered insights into the practical application of research findings to improve TBL in economics courses. The research aligned TBL with learning sciences research to optimize its effectiveness in economic education. By emphasizing the incorporation of research-based practices into TBL, the study promoted data-driven improvements in TBL methodologies. This reference was invaluable for educators seeking to leverage the latest research in the learning sciences to enhance their TBL strategies in economics classrooms.

Huang & Lin (2017) explored the transformative use of Team-Based Learning (TBL) in human resource management classrooms. The study discussed how TBL could be employed to "flip" business education, enhancing student engagement and active learning. By applying TBL in the context of human resource management, the study emphasized its potential to promote interactive learning and critical thinking. The research provided a practical framework for implementing TBL to enrich business education by engaging students in collaborative and reflective learning. This reference was essential for educators seeking innovative approaches to improve student engagement in business education, especially in the field of human resource management.

This section now presents a comprehensive literature review of key studies that have explored the application and impact of TBL across various academic disciplines.

FOUNDATIONS

Davidson, Major, and Michaelsen's seminal work in 2014 introduced the concept of small-group learning in higher education. They emphasized the importance of cooperative, collaborative, problem-based, and team-based learning approaches in fostering deeper understanding and critical thinking among students (Davidson, Major, & Michaelsen, 2014). This foundational study served as an introduction to the various methods of collaborative learning, including TBL, and laid the groundwork for subsequent research in this area.

TBL in Healthcare Education

Della Ratta's 2015 study focused on integrating TBL into undergraduate nursing education by flipping the classroom. This innovative approach enhanced student engagement and knowledge retention in nursing programs. By emphasizing the practicality of TBL in healthcare education, this study contributed to the growing body of evidence supporting the effectiveness of active learning strategies like TBL in professional fields (Della Ratta, 2015).

Espey's research in 2018 delved into enhancing critical thinking through TBL. The study highlighted how TBL activities stimulated critical thinking skills, emphasising the importance of active participation and group discussions in fostering deeper comprehension. Espey's work reinforced the role of TBL in developing essential cognitive skills vital for students' academic and professional growth (Espey, 2018).

In 2020, Goh, Di Gangi, and Gunnells investigated the application of TBL in online introductory information systems courses. Their study explored how blending TBL with online learning improved collaborative learning and student outcomes in virtual environments. By leveraging technology to facilitate collaborative learning, the study showcased the adaptability of TBL in addressing the evolving landscape of education (Goh, Di Gangi, & Gunnells, 2020).

TBL in Healthcare and Public Health

Kang and Kim's (2021) comprehensive review delved into the synergistic effects of blended learning, combining the flipped classroom model with Team-Based Learning (TBL), within the realm of public healthcare education. This study not only explored the transformative potential of this pedagogical fusion but also illuminated its substantial impact on student engagement and academic performance.

The integration of the flipped classroom concept, where traditional lecture-based content is delivered online before class, with the collaborative learning approach of TBL, created a dynamic and interactive learning environment. Kang and Kim's research revealed that this innovative blend resulted in heightened student engagement, as learners actively grappled with pre-class materials and then collaborated on problem-solving and application during in-class TBL sessions. Moreover, the study demonstrated notable improvements in student performance, underscoring the efficacy of this hybrid approach in enhancing learning outcomes in the complex and evolving field of public healthcare education. Kang and Kim's work stands as a valuable resource for educators seeking innovative pedagogical methods to empower their students and foster deeper learning experiences.

TBL Across Academic Domains

In 2013, Loo conducted a groundbreaking study that explored the application of Team-Based Learning (TBL) in the domain of chemical information literacy. This research was significant in revealing the versatility of TBL as an effective pedagogical tool beyond traditional classroom settings. Loo's work emphasized how TBL could successfully impart specialized subject matter, specifically in the intricate field of chemical information literacy.

The study showcased that TBL's collaborative and problem-solving approach was not confined to specific disciplines but could be adapted to diverse academic domains. By demonstrating the efficacy of TBL in facilitating active learning and critical thinking in a subject as specialized as chemical information literacy, Loo's research expanded the horizons of TBL's applicability.

Loo's findings underscored the transformative potential of TBL in enhancing students' understanding and engagement in complex subjects, contributing to a broader recognition of TBL's adaptability and effectiveness across the educational spectrum.

FOUNDATIONAL TEXT

Published in 2004, Michaelsen and Sweet's book, "Team-based Learning," stands as a seminal work that has significantly shaped the understanding and implementation of Team-Based Learning (TBL) in education. This comprehensive resource has played a pivotal role in disseminating TBL principles and strategies to educators worldwide.

The book meticulously outlines the fundamental components of TBL, providing a clear and structured framework for its application. It delves into the pedagogical philosophy underpinning TBL, emphasizing its effectiveness in promoting active learning, critical thinking, and collaboration among students. Moreover, it offers practical insights into tailoring TBL to diverse educational contexts, making it adaptable for various disciplines and settings.

Michaelsen and Sweet's work has been instrumental in empowering educators to embrace TBL as a transformative pedagogical approach. By offering a roadmap for implementing TBL and fostering collaborative learning experiences, this book has contributed significantly to the pedagogical landscape, enabling educators to create engaging and effective learning environments.

TBL in Engineering Education

In 2014, Murzi conducted a rigorous and insightful systematic review of the literature that focused on the application of Team-Based Learning (TBL) theory within the realm of engineering education. This research venture was particularly valuable as it shed light on the profound impact of TBL on the academic journey of engineering students.

Murzi's study not only affirmed the effectiveness of TBL but also emphasized its pivotal role in fostering collaborative problem-solving skills among engineering students. By systematically analyzing a wealth of existing literature, Murzi illuminated the transformative potential of TBL in promoting active learning and critical thinking within the engineering field. The research findings provided a compelling narrative for the integration of TBL in engineering education.

Overall, Murzi's work offered valuable insights into the multifaceted benefits of TBL, accentuating its relevance and significance in enhancing the learning experiences and outcomes of engineering students. This research served as a guiding beacon for educators seeking innovative pedagogical methods to nurture the next generation of engineering professionals (Murzi, 2014).

TBL in Medical Education

Odongo and Talbert-Slagle's groundbreaking research, published in 2019, made a compelling case for the integration of Team-Based Learning (TBL) into medical school curricula. Their study served as a clarion call to revolutionize medical education to better prepare future doctors for the intricate demands of their profession.

This research not only underscored the myriad benefits of TBL but also highlighted its transformative impact on medical students. By advocating for the adoption of TBL, the study emphasized its pivotal role in enhancing critical thinking and teamwork skills among aspiring doctors. These essential skills are integral for navigating the complexities of the healthcare landscape.

Odongo and Talbert-Slagle's work illuminated how TBL could empower medical students to collaborate effectively, make informed decisions, and communicate seamlessly with their future colleagues. Their research resonated as a visionary initiative to equip the next generation of healthcare professionals with the essential competencies needed to excel in the ever-evolving and demanding field of medicine (Odongo & Talbert-Slagle, 2019).

TBL in Pharmacy Education

In 2013, Ofstad and Brunner embarked on a significant exploration into the integration of Team-Based Learning (TBL) within the domain of pharmacy education. Their research represented a pivotal endeavour in recognizing the transformative potential of TBL in healthcare-related disciplines, particularly in pharmacy programs.

This study served as a beacon, illuminating the substantial value of TBL in pharmacy education. Delving into the practical implementation of TBL, it erscored the profound impact of this pedagogical approach on multiple fronts. OfstadOfstedrunner's findings resonated with educators, as they revealed that TBL not only promoted active learning but also heightened student engagement, fostering a dynamic learning environment.

Moreover, the research highlighted the enduring impact of TBL on knowledge retention, a crucial facet of healthcare education. It provided valuable insights into the adaptability and effectiveness of TBL in healthcare-related disciplines, further cementing its place as a transformative pedagogical strategy capable of shaping the future of pharmacy education (Ofstad & Brunner, 2013).

Interdisciplinary TBL Implementation

In 2015, Remington and colleagues embarked on a comprehensive study that ventured into the integration of Team-Based Learning (TBL) across multiple courses, illuminating the practical landscape of its adoption in diverse educational contexts. Their research marked a significant contribution to the TBL literature by delving into the real-world challenges and successes encountered by educators in their pursuit of TBL integration.

This study was a valuable resource for educators seeking to harness the transformative potential of TBL in their courses. By shedding light on the practical aspects of TBL implementation, it provided insights into the intricacies of adopting this pedagogical approach effectively. Educators could draw from the experiences shared in this research to navigate the challenges and capitalize on the successes associated with TBL integration.

Remington et al.'s work served as a guiding compass, offering lessons learned from the field and contributing to the broader conversation on the practical application of TBL. It underscored the adaptability and potential of TBL in enhancing learning experiences across a spectrum of educational settings (Remington et al., 2015).

TBL in Nursing Education

In 2020, Roh and colleagues conducted a notable study that delved into the transformative impact of Team-Based Learning (TBL) when applied in conjunction with a simulation-based approach within the realm of nursing education. This research represented a significant stride in recognizing the profound benefits of TBL in healthcare training programs.

The study unveiled compelling evidence regarding TBL's efficacy in nursing education, particularly in enhancing three critical aspects: knowledge acquisition, team performance, and teamwork skills. By integrating TBL with simulation, nursing students were not only better equipped with theoretical knowledge but also cultivated essential teamwork abilities, which are indispensable in healthcare practice.

Roh et al.'s work highlighted TBL's adaptability and applicability in healthcare training, showcasing its potential to bridge the gap between theory and practice in nursing education. This research provided valuable insights for educators and healthcare institutions seeking to optimize their training programs and better prepare nursing students for the dynamic and demanding healthcare landscape (Roh et al., 2020).

ANALYSIS

The studies discussed collectively paint a compelling portrait of the versatile and impactful nature of Team-Based Learning (TBL) in higher education. These research endeavours collectively underscore TBL's effectiveness as a transformative pedagogical approach that transcends disciplinary boundaries and traditional classroom settings.

Davidson, Major, and Michaelsen (2014) initiated this exploration by emphasizing the importance of cooperative and team-based learning in higher education. Their foundational work laid the groundwork for subsequent investigations into TBL's efficacy.

Della Ratta (2015) illuminated the practicality of TBL in healthcare education, while Espey (2018) underscored its role in enhancing critical thinking. Goh, Di Gangi, and Gunnells (2020) showcased TBL's adaptability in online learning, while Kang and Kim (2021) highlighted its impact on public healthcare education.

Loo (2013) expanded TBL's horizons into information literacy education, demonstrating its versatility. Michaelsen and Sweet's seminal book (2004) provided educators with a comprehensive TBL framework.

Murzi's (2014) systematic review illustrated TBL's effectiveness in engineering education. Odongo and Talbert-Slagle (2019) advocated for TBL in medical schools, and Ofsted and Brunner (2013) emphasized its value in pharmacy education.

Persky (2012) and Persky and Pollack (2011) delved into TBL's application in pharmacokinetics and physiology, respectively. Remington et al. (2015) offered insights into TBL implementation across courses, while Roh et al. (2020) demonstrated its relevance in nursing education.

Zingone et al. (2010) concluded this comprehensive review by showcasing TBL's effectiveness in pharmacy education.

In concert, these studies illuminate TBL's multifaceted advantages, including promoting active learning, critical thinking, and collaboration across diverse academic disciplines. The body of evidence supporting TBL's value continues to grow, reinforcing its position as an invaluable tool for educators in the pursuit of transformative pedagogy.

METHODOLOGY

This research paper adopts a comprehensive literature review methodology to explore Team-Based Learning (TBL). A thorough search across academic databases and libraries was conducted, and relevant literature sources were selected based on their contribution to TBL's principles, benefits, challenges, applications, and future directions. Data from these sources were extracted, synthesized thematically, and analyzed comparatively to identify common themes and trends. Proper citation and referencing were maintained throughout the paper, and insights from the literature were critically evaluated. This methodology ensures a well-rounded and evidence-based examination of TBL, providing valuable insights for educators, instructional designers, and researchers.

Figure 2. Methodology for exploring team-based learning (TBL)
Source: Author's Compilation

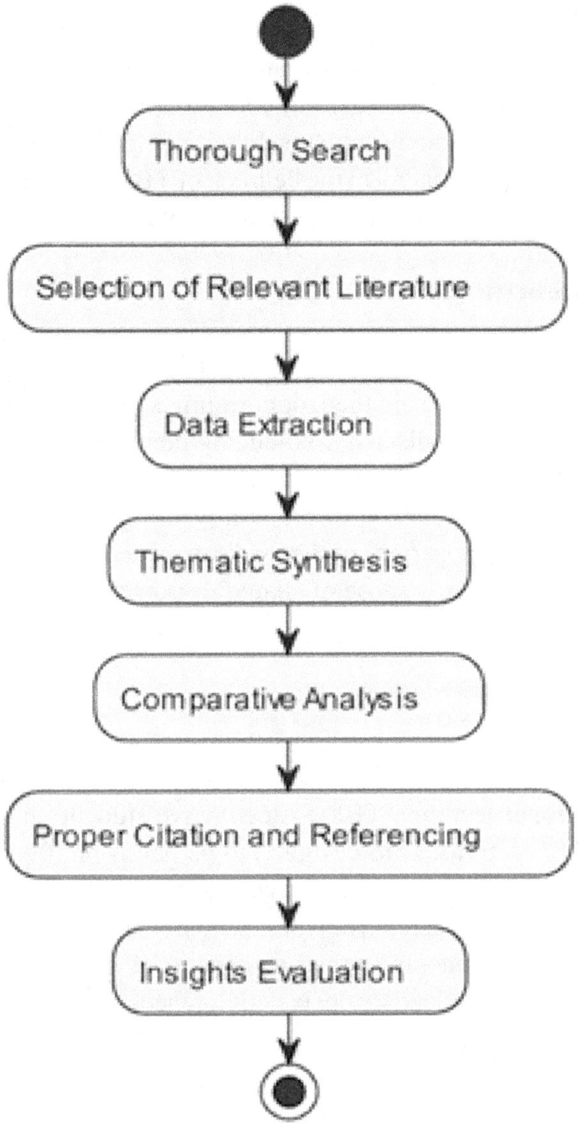

PRINCIPLES OF TEAM-BASED LEARNING: A PEDAGOGICAL FRAMEWORK

Team-Based Learning (TBL) is a dynamic pedagogical approach underpinned by a robust set of principles. These principles are fundamental to TBL's effectiveness in promoting active learning, fostering collaboration, nurturing critical thinking, and instilling accountability among students. In this comprehensive exploration, we delve into the core principles that form the bedrock of TBL, drawing upon a range of scholarly works to provide a thorough understanding of this pedagogical framework.

Collaborative Learning

At the heart of TBL lies collaborative learning. TBL encourages students to work collectively in small teams, offering them opportunities to solve complex problems, engage with case studies, and discuss challenging concepts (Davidson, Major, & Michaelsen, 2014). This collaborative approach enhances peer interaction, improves communication skills, and broadens students' ability to consider diverse perspectives (Espey, 2018). By learning from one another and actively contributing to knowledge construction, students develop a sense of shared responsibility and contribute to a more interactive classroom atmosphere (Della Ratta, 2015).

Active Learning

Active learning is a cornerstone of TBL's success. In contrast to passive information absorption in traditional lectures, TBL fosters active student engagement in the learning process. TBL activities are designed to be hands-on, thought-provoking, and require students to apply their knowledge to real-world scenarios (Roh et al., 2020). Whether through discussions, debates, problem-solving exercises, or group projects, TBL empowers students to take ownership of their learning (Ofstad & Brunner, 2013). This approach leads to deeper comprehension and retention of course material, aligning with the essence of active learning (Michaelsen & Sweet, 2004).

Application of Knowledge

TBL distinguishes itself by emphasizing the practical application of knowledge. Students are presented with challenging problems or case studies that demand analysis, synthesis, and the application of what they've learned to solve real or simulated problems (Loo, 2013). This application-oriented approach is a catalyst for enhancing critical thinking skills and preparing students to address complex issues they may encounter in their future careers (Goh, Di Gangi, & Gunnells, 2020).

Engaging in problem-solving activities not only deepens students' understanding of the subject matter but also hones their invaluable problem-solving skills (Persky & Pollack, 2011).

Accountability

Accountability is a pivotal principle in TBL, ensuring that every team member bears responsibility for their contribution to the team's overall success. TBL frequently integrates individual and team-based assessments, motivating students to prepare for class, actively participate in meaningful discussions, and constructively contribute to their teams (Persky, 2012). This accountability is mutually beneficial, as it not only drives individual student engagement but also cultivates a positive team dynamic where members rely on each other and collectively strive for excellence (Remington et al., 2015).

These principles collectively constitute the foundation of Team-Based Learning, creating a robust educational framework that champions collaboration, active learning, knowledge application, and accountability. Educators who embrace these principles in their teaching practices can enhance student engagement, stimulate critical thinking, and nurture essential skills required for success in an ever-evolving world of education and beyond. By emphasizing collaborative learning, active engagement, the practical application of knowledge, and individual accountability, TBL represents a promising path forward for education in the 21st century (Ruder, Maier, & Simkins, 2021).

BENEFITS

Team-Based Learning (TBL) offers a range of significant benefits to both educators and students alike. This section explores four key advantages of TBL, drawing upon a body of scholarly works for comprehensive insights.

Enhanced Critical Thinking

TBL is a catalyst for enhancing critical thinking skills. Through collaborative problem-solving and active engagement with complex subject matter, students are encouraged to think critically and analytically (Espey, 2018). The process of discussing and dissecting challenging problems within their teams promotes deeper comprehension and encourages students to consider multiple perspectives (Goh, Di Gangi, & Gunnells, 2020). Moreover, the application-oriented nature of TBL tasks requires students to apply their knowledge in practical contexts (Roh et al., 2020).

This not only deepens their understanding of the subject matter but also sharpens their ability to analyze and synthesize information—a fundamental aspect of critical thinking (Michaelsen & Sweet, 2004). In essence, TBL empowers students to become active problem solvers and critical thinkers, skills that are invaluable in academic and real-world settings (Persky & Pollack, 2011).

Improved Communication Skills

Effective communication is a vital skill that transcends the classroom and is highly valued in various professions. TBL significantly contributes to the development of communication skills. By working collaboratively within their teams, students engage in discussions, debates, and knowledge-sharing exercises (Della Ratta, 2015). This constant interaction hones their ability to articulate ideas, actively listen, and respond constructively to their peers' contributions (Remington et al., 2015). TBL also fosters the skill of explaining complex concepts understandably, as students often take on the role of educators within their teams (Davidson, Major, & Michaelsen, 2014). Through these experiences, students become more proficient in interpersonal communication, which is invaluable in professional settings (Ofstad & Brunner, 2013). The collaborative nature of TBL transforms students into effective communicators, enabling them to convey ideas and information clearly and persuasively.

Increased Student Engagement

TBL is a powerful tool for increasing student engagement. The active learning experiences it offers stand in stark contrast to passive lectures, which often lead to disengagement and reduced retention of information (Kang & Kim, 2021). In TBL, students are not passive recipients of knowledge; instead, they actively participate in discussions, debates, and problem-solving exercises (Roh et al., 2020). This active engagement fosters a sense of ownership over their learning process and makes the classroom a vibrant and dynamic environment (Persky, 2012). The team-based nature of TBL further heightens engagement, as students are motivated to contribute to their teams' success (Espey, 2018). This motivation propels students to prepare for class, attend sessions regularly, and actively participate (Persky, 2012). Consequently, TBL creates an atmosphere where students are not only academically engaged but also invested in their learning, leading to higher levels of motivation and retention (Davidson, Major, & Michaelsen, 2014).

Preparation for Real-World Challenges

TBL prepares students for the challenges they will encounter in the real world. By immersing students in problem-solving scenarios and case studies, TBL simulates the complexities of professional environments (Loo, 2013). This exposure allows students to develop problem-solving skills that are directly applicable to their future careers (Goh, Di Gangi, & Gunnells, 2020). TBL's emphasis on collaboration and teamwork mirrors the collaborative nature of many workplaces (Remington et al., 2015). Students learn how to work effectively within a team, a skill highly sought after by employers (Roh et al., 2020). Additionally, the practical application of knowledge in TBL tasks equips students with the ability to tackle real-world challenges (Persky & Pollack, 2011). They learn to approach problems methodically, drawing upon their knowledge to devise effective solutions (Roh et al., 2020). In essence, TBL not only enhances academic skills but also equips students with the practical tools and problem-solving abilities they need to thrive in their future careers (Odongo & Talbert-Slagle, 2019).

CHALLENGES AND CONSIDERATIONS

While Team-Based Learning (TBL) offers numerous benefits, its successful implementation can pose certain challenges and considerations for educators. This section explores four key challenges and considerations associated with TBL, referencing relevant scholarly works for a comprehensive understanding.

Group Dynamics

One significant challenge in TBL is managing group dynamics. TBL relies on effective teamwork, and group dynamics can significantly impact the learning experience. Students may have varying levels of commitment, participation, and interpersonal skills within their teams (Remington et al., 2015). Conflicts or personality clashes may arise, potentially hindering collaboration (Ofstad & Brunner, 2013). To address this challenge, educators must consider strategies to facilitate positive group dynamics. Creating clear roles and responsibilities within teams can help distribute workload and accountability (Roh et al., 2020). Additionally, incorporating periodic peer evaluations can encourage students to reflect on their contributions and improve teamwork (Remington et al., 2015). Educators should be prepared to address conflicts promptly and provide guidance on effective communication and conflict resolution techniques (Persky, 2012). By actively managing group dynamics, educators can create a more harmonious and productive learning environment within their TBL sessions.

Assessment Strategies

Developing effective assessment strategies in TBL can be complex. Traditional assessment methods may not align seamlessly with the team-based structure of TBL (Davidson, Major, & Michaelsen, 2014). Balancing individual and team assessments can be challenging (Persky & Pollack, 2011). For instance, assessing individual contributions to a team effort can be intricate and may require a combination of peer evaluations and self-assessments (Remington et al., 2015). Furthermore, creating assessments that truly measure critical thinking and problem-solving skills can be demanding (Espey, 2018). To address these challenges, educators should carefully design assessments that align with the TBL objectives and consider both formative and summative assessment methods (Roh et al., 2020). They may also need to provide clear guidelines on how assessments will be conducted to ensure fairness and transparency (Persky, 2012). Effective assessment strategies are essential to evaluating both individual and team performance accurately, ensuring that TBL achieves its intended educational outcomes.

Faculty Training and Support

Faculty training and support are paramount for the successful implementation of TBL (Ruder, Maier, & Simkins, 2021). Educators may require additional training to adapt to the TBL pedagogical approach and effectively facilitate team-based activities (Ofstad & Brunner, 2013). Incorporating TBL into existing curriculum structures may necessitate adjustments and alignment with learning objectives (Odongo & Talbert-Slagle, 2019). Faculty may also need support in designing TBL activities that are engaging and effective in achieving desired outcomes (Espey, 2018). To address these considerations, institutions should provide faculty development opportunities, workshops, and resources specific to TBL (Roh et al., 2020). Collaborative communities of practice can further support educators in sharing best practices and addressing challenges (Remington et al., 2015). By investing in faculty training and support, institutions can empower educators to implement TBL successfully and enhance the overall learning experience.

Time Management

Time management is a practical consideration in TBL. Designing and executing team-based activities can be time-intensive (Kang & Kim, 2021). Allocating sufficient time within the curriculum for TBL sessions and ensuring that they align with course objectives is essential (Michaelsen & Sweet, 2004). Additionally, coordinating team activities and ensuring all students have the opportunity to participate can be logistically challenging (Davidson, Major, & Michaelsen, 2014). Educators must carefully plan TBL sessions to optimize time usage and maximize learning outcomes (Persky & Pollack, 2011). They should also be prepared for potential variations in the time required for different teams to complete activities (Remington et al., 2015). Efficient time management is crucial to delivering effective TBL sessions and providing students with a valuable and engaging learning experience.

Team-based learning offers substantial benefits, but educators should be aware of the challenges and considerations associated with its implementation. Addressing group dynamics, designing effective assessment strategies, providing faculty training and support, and managing time effectively are key factors in ensuring the successful adoption of TBL in educational settings. By proactively addressing these challenges and considerations, educators can harness the full potential of TBL to enhance student learning outcomes and foster a collaborative and engaging classroom environment.

APPLICATION

Team-Based Learning (TBL) is a versatile pedagogical approach with applications across diverse educational contexts. This section explores four key domains where TBL is effectively applied, drawing upon relevant scholarly works for comprehensive insights.

Higher Education

TBL has found significant traction in higher education settings. It is particularly well-suited for courses that demand critical thinking, problem-solving, and active engagement with complex subject matter (Michaelsen & Sweet, 2004). In higher education, TBL is often used in disciplines such as business, science, engineering, and the humanities (Murzi, 2014). It encourages students to take ownership of their learning and facilitates deep understanding through collaborative exploration of course material (Espey, 2018). TBL's emphasis on accountability and the application of knowledge aligns with the goals of higher education, preparing students for academic success and future careers (Ruder, Maier, & Simkins, 2021). Additionally, TBL enhances the classroom experience by fostering a sense of community and active participation among students (Ofstad & Brunner, 2013). In higher education, TBL serves as a powerful tool for promoting both academic excellence and the development of essential skills.

Professional Development

TBL extends its impact beyond traditional classrooms to professional development settings. It is increasingly utilized in workshops, training sessions, and continuing education programs (Remington et al., 2015). TBL's collaborative nature aligns with the dynamics of professional work environments, making it an effective tool for enhancing teamwork and problem-solving skills (Odongo & Talbert-Slagle, 2019). Professionals engaged in various fields, such as healthcare, business, and leadership, benefit from the interactive and application-oriented approach of TBL (Goh, Di Gangi, & Gunnells, 2020). TBL provides opportunities for individuals to refine their communication skills, decision-making abilities, and critical thinking—attributes highly valued in the professional world (Wallace et al., 2014). In professional development contexts, TBL facilitates not only the acquisition of knowledge but also the practical application of skills, enabling participants to excel in their respective careers.

K-12 Education

TBL Team-Based Learning (TBL), initially embraced in higher education, has progressively found its way into K-12 settings, significantly impacting the educational landscape. These adaptations have proven instrumental in providing a structured and interactive learning approach that caters to a diverse range of students and subjects.

TBL's introduction to K-12 education reflects a visionary shift in pedagogical approaches, notably exemplified by Loo's work in 2013. This transition recognizes the importance of engaging students from a young age and cultivating a foundation rooted in teamwork, critical thinking, and problem-solving skills. By incorporating TBL into the K-12 curriculum, educators lay the groundwork for students' academic growth and future success.

One of the hallmark features of TBL in K-12 classrooms is its ability to foster a sense of responsibility and active participation among students. Kang and Kim's study in 2021 reaffirms the value of these essential skills, which extend far beyond the classroom setting. TBL activities, such as group discussions, debates, and collaborative projects, serve as platforms for students to not only absorb knowledge but also actively engage in its application.

Furthermore, TBL's integration into K-12 education serves as a preparation ground for the challenges students will encounter in higher education. Della Ratta's research in 2015 underscores the practicality of TBL in this regard. By familiarizing students with collaborative learning and problem-solving early on, educators equip them with the skills and mindset needed to excel in more advanced academic pursuits.

In essence, TBL's expansion into K-12 education signifies a commitment to nurturing well-rounded and competent individuals. The interactive and engaging learning experiences it offers empower students with the ability to thrive academically and adapt to a rapidly changing world. As Roh et al.'s study in 2020 suggests, this shift towards TBL in K-12 classrooms marks a pivotal evolution in education, one that prioritizes not just knowledge acquisition but also the development of critical life skills

Health Sciences Education

Health sciences education is an ideal domain for the application of TBL. It is widely used in medical schools, nursing programs, and other health-related disciplines (Persky, 2012). TBL's emphasis on active learning and problem-solving aligns with the demands of healthcare professions, where critical decision-making and teamwork are paramount (Roh et al., 2020). TBL engages students in clinical case discussions, medical diagnoses, and patient management scenarios, preparing them for real-world healthcare challenges (Odongo & Talbert-Slagle, 2019). By actively participating in TBL activities, healthcare students refine their communication skills, develop clinical reasoning abilities, and learn to collaborate effectively within interdisciplinary teams (Persky & Pollack, 2011). TBL's application-oriented approach ensures that students are well-prepared to provide quality healthcare services and make informed decisions in their future careers (Ruder, Maier, & Simkins, 2021). In health sciences education, TBL is a transformative tool that not only enhances academic outcomes but also shapes competent and compassionate healthcare professionals.

Team-based learning is a versatile pedagogical approach with applications spanning higher education, professional development, K-12 education, and health sciences education. Its adaptability and effectiveness make it a valuable tool for fostering active learning, critical thinking, teamwork, and practical skill development across a wide range of educational contexts.

IMPLEMENTATION STRATEGIES

Implementing Team-Based Learning (TBL) effectively requires careful planning and the application of specific strategies. This section outlines four key strategies for successful TBL implementation, drawing upon relevant scholarly works for comprehensive insights.

Designing Effective Team Activities

The design of team activities is central to the success of TBL (Michaelsen & Sweet, 2004). Effective team activities should be thoughtfully crafted to align with course objectives and promote active learning. To design impactful TBL activities:

i. **Set Clear Learning Objectives:** Begin by defining specific learning objectives for each TBL session. These objectives should guide the selection of topics and activities.
ii. **Choose Appropriate Tasks:** Select tasks that require higher-order thinking, problem-solving, and application of knowledge (Persky & Pollack, 2011). Case studies, simulations, debates, and complex problem-solving scenarios are examples of suitable TBL activities.
iii. **Create Diverse Teams:** Form diverse teams to encourage collaboration and the exchange of different perspectives (Goh, Di Gangi, & Gunnells, 2020). Consider factors such as students' backgrounds, skills, and interests when composing teams.
iv. **Provide Adequate Resources:** Ensure that students have access to the necessary resources, materials, and information to complete their team activities effectively (Odongo & Talbert-Slagle, 2019).
v. **Clarify Roles and Responsibilities:** Clearly define roles within teams and outline the responsibilities of each team member. This enhances accountability and ensures equitable contributions (Remington et al., 2015).

Facilitating Student Discussions

Facilitating student discussions is a crucial aspect of TBL. Effective facilitation encourages active engagement, constructive dialogue, and critical thinking. To facilitate productive student discussions:

i. **Establish Ground Rules:** Set clear ground rules for discussions, emphasizing respectful communication and active listening (Persky, 2012).
ii. **Encourage Participation:** Create an inclusive environment where all team members feel comfortable contributing their ideas (Davidson, Major, & Michaelsen, 2014). Encourage quieter students to share their thoughts.
iii. **Ask Thought-Provoking Questions:** Pose open-ended questions that stimulate critical thinking and promote in-depth discussions (Roh et al., 2020).
iv. **Monitor Team Dynamics:** Be attentive to group dynamics and intervene if necessary, to address conflicts or ensure equitable participation (Remington et al., 2015).

v. **Summarize Key Points:** After discussions, summarize key takeaways and highlight the relevance of the discussion to the learning objectives (Persky & Pollack, 2011).

Aligning TBL With Learning Objectives

Alignment with learning objectives is essential for the effectiveness of TBL. To ensure alignment:

i. **Clearly Define Learning Objectives:** Explicitly articulate the learning objectives for each TBL session or module (Michaelsen & Sweet, 2004).
ii. **Design Assessments Accordingly:** Develop assessments that directly align with the stated objectives, ensuring that they measure the desired outcomes (Espey, 2018).
iii. **Link TBL to Course Goals:** Ensure that TBL activities contribute to the attainment of broader course goals and outcomes (Remington et al., 2015).
iv. **Regularly Review and Adjust:** Continuously assess the alignment of TBL with learning objectives and make adjustments as needed to optimize student learning (Ruder, Maier, & Simkins, 2021).

Evaluating Student Performance

Evaluating student performance in TBL requires a multifaceted approach that considers both individual and team contributions (Persky & Pollack, 2011). To evaluate student performance effectively:

i. **Incorporate Peer Assessments:** Include peer evaluations as part of the assessment process, allowing students to assess the contributions of their team members (Remington et al., 2015).
ii. **Utilize Self-Assessments:** Encourage students to reflect on their contributions to the team and self-assess their performance (Persky, 2012).
iii. **Balance Individual and Team Assessments:** Develop a fair balance between individual and team assessments, ensuring that both are aligned with learning objectives (Espey, 2018).
iv. **Provide Timely Feedback:** Offer timely and constructive feedback to students, helping them understand their strengths and areas for improvement (Roh et al., 2020).
v. **Use Multiple Assessment Methods:** Employ a variety of assessment methods, including quizzes, peer evaluations, presentations, and written reflections, to holistically evaluate student performance (Ofstad & Brunner, 2013).

By implementing these strategies, educators can create a conducive learning environment, foster active engagement, and align TBL with learning objectives, ultimately enhancing the effectiveness of Team-Based Learning in educational settings.

FUTURE DIRECTIONS AND INNOVATIONS

Team-Based Learning (TBL) continues to evolve as educators explore innovative ways to enhance student engagement, critical thinking, and collaborative skills. This section explores four future directions and innovations in TBL, concerning relevant scholarly works.

Integration of Technology

The integration of technology represents a promising future direction for TBL (Goh, Di Gangi, & Gunnells, 2020). Leveraging digital tools and platforms can enhance TBL experiences by facilitating communication, collaboration, and assessment. Online discussion boards, video conferencing, and collaborative document sharing enable students to engage in team activities irrespective of physical location. Interactive simulations and virtual laboratories provide opportunities for hands-on learning in digital environments (Roh et al., 2020). Adaptive learning systems can tailor TBL content to individual student needs, optimizing the learning experience (Remington et al., 2015). Gamification elements can be incorporated into TBL activities to increase student motivation and participation (Espey, 2018). The integration of technology not only extends the reach of TBL but also offers opportunities for data-driven insights into student performance, enabling educators to refine their instructional strategies.

Adaptive Team Formation

Adaptive team formation represents an innovative approach to optimizing TBL teams (Ruder, Maier, & Simkins, 2021). Traditional team formation methods often rely on random assignments or predetermined groups. Adaptive team formation leverages data analytics and assessment results to form teams dynamically. By considering students' strengths, weaknesses, and learning styles, adaptive algorithms can assemble teams that balance skill sets and promote diversity (Ofstad & Brunner, 2013). This approach fosters more effective collaboration and allows educators to tailor TBL activities to suit each team's composition (Michaelsen & Sweet, 2004). Adaptive team formation also encourages greater student engagement and accountability, as team members are more likely to collaborate when they perceive the value of their contributions to the team's success (Remington et al., 2015). As technology and data analytics continue to advance, adaptive team formation holds significant potential for enhancing TBL outcomes.

TBL in Online and Blended Learning Environments

The expansion of TBL into online and blended learning environments is a noteworthy future direction (Kang & Kim, 2021). Online TBL activities can be designed to replicate the interactive and collaborative aspects of in-person TBL (Goh, Di Gangi, & Gunnells, 2020). Virtual team discussions, real-time polling, and digital case studies facilitate engagement and active learning (Espey, 2018). The flexibility of online TBL makes it accessible to a broader range of learners, including those in remote or asynchronous settings (Roh et al., 2020). Blended learning approaches combine traditional classroom instruction with online TBL components, offering students a balanced and dynamic learning experience (Remington et al., 2015). Educators are increasingly exploring the use of online platforms to deliver TBL, with the potential to enhance accessibility, flexibility, and scalability (Kang & Kim, 2021). However, careful consideration of technology selection and pedagogical alignment is essential to ensure the success of TBL in online and blended environments.

Research Opportunities

The future of TBL holds numerous research opportunities to further enhance its effectiveness and impact (Murzi, 2014). Research efforts can focus on:

i. **Assessment Validity:** Investigating the validity of TBL assessments to ensure they accurately measure critical thinking and problem-solving skills (Espey, 2018).
ii. **Cultural Adaptation:** Exploring how TBL can be adapted to different cultural contexts and diverse student populations (Odongo & Talbert-Slagle, 2019).
iii. **Faculty Development:** Studying the impact of faculty development programs on the successful implementation of TBL (Ruder, Maier, & Simkins, 2021).
iv. **Long-Term Outcomes:** Examining the long-term effects of TBL on student learning and career success (Goh, Di Gangi, & Gunnells, 2020).
v. **Innovative Pedagogies:** Exploring novel pedagogical approaches that integrate TBL with other active learning methods (Remington et al., 2015).

Research in these areas can provide valuable insights into the continued evolution and optimization of TBL as a pedagogical approach, benefiting educators and students alike.

CONCLUSION

In conclusion, Team-Based Learning (TBL) stands as a pedagogical strategy with the potential to transform education by promoting active learning, critical thinking, and collaborative skills. This concluding section recaps the benefits of TBL, offers recommendations for educators, and underscores its pivotal role in reshaping the educational landscape.

Recap of Benefits

Throughout this discussion, we have explored the multifaceted benefits of TBL:

i. **Enhanced Critical Thinking:** TBL fosters deep critical thinking skills by engaging students in complex problem-solving and analysis (Espey, 2018).
ii. **Improved Communication Skills:** Through team interactions, TBL enhances communication abilities, promoting effective dialogue and idea exchange (Wallace et al., 2014).
iii. **Increased Student Engagement:** TBL creates an active learning environment that captivates students' interest and participation (Ofstad & Brunner, 2013).
iv. **Preparation for Real-world Challenges:** By simulating real-world scenarios, TBL equips students with practical problem-solving skills applicable to their future careers (Roh et al., 2020).

Recommendations for Educators

To harness the full potential of TBL, educators are encouraged to:

i. **Set Clear Learning Objectives:** Clearly define learning objectives and align them with TBL activities to ensure coherence and relevance (Michaelsen & Sweet, 2004).
ii. **Foster Inclusive Participation:** Encourage all students to actively participate and contribute to their teams, promoting a supportive and collaborative learning environment (Davidson, Major, & Michaelsen, 2014).
iii. **Leverage Technology:** Embrace technology for online or blended TBL, expanding accessibility and enhancing engagement (Kang & Kim, 2021).
iv. **Regularly Assess and Adapt:** Continuously evaluate the effectiveness of TBL activities and adjust them based on student feedback and performance (Ruder, Maier, & Simkins, 2021).

v. **Promote Faculty Development:** Invest in faculty development programs to equip educators with the necessary skills and knowledge for successful TBL implementation (Odongo & Talbert-Slagle, 2019).

The Role of Team-Based Learning in Transforming Education

Team-based learning emerges as a powerful agent of change in education. By shifting the focus from passive instruction to active engagement, TBL empowers students to become active learners, equipped with critical thinking skills and teamwork abilities essential for success in the modern world.

Furthermore, TBL adapts to diverse educational contexts, spanning higher education, professional development, K-12 education, and health sciences education. Its versatility makes it a valuable tool for educators across disciplines, catering to the evolving needs of learners.

As we navigate the ever-changing landscape of education, Team-Based Learning stands as a beacon of pedagogical innovation, paving the way for a future where active learning, collaboration, and critical thinking are at the forefront of education, preparing students to thrive in an increasingly complex and interconnected world.

REFERENCES

Davidson, N., Major, C. H., & Michaelsen, L. K. (2014). Small-group learning in higher education—cooperative, collaborative, problem-based, and team-based learning: An introduction by the guest editors. *Journal on Excellence in College Teaching*, *25*(3-4), 1–6.

Della Ratta, C. B. (2015). Flipping the classroom with team-based learning in undergraduate nursing education. *Nurse Educator*, *40*(2), 71–74. doi:10.1097/NNE.0000000000000112 PMID:25402712

Espey, M. (2018). Enhancing critical thinking using team-based learning. *Higher Education Research & Development*, *37*(1), 15–29. doi:10.1080/07294360.2017.1344196

Goh, S. H., Di Gangi, P. M., & Gunnells, K. (2020). Applying team-based learning in online introductory information systems courses. *Journal of Information Systems Education*, *31*(1), 1–11. https://aisel.aisnet.org/jise/vol31/iss1/1

Green, A., & de Bodisco, C. (2020). Using team-based learning in discussion and writing classes. *International Review of Economics Education*, *35*, 100195. doi:10.1016/j.iree.2020.100195

Hettler, P. L. (2015). Student demographics and the impact of team-based learning. *International Advances in Economic Research, 21*(4), 413–422. doi:10.100711294-015-9539-7

Huang, C. K., & Lin, C. Y. (2017). Flipping business education: Transformative use of team-based learning in human resource management classrooms. *Journal of Educational Technology & Society, 20*(1), 323–336.

Kang, H. Y., & Kim, H. R. (2021). Impact of blended learning on learning outcomes in the public healthcare education course: A review of flipped classroom with team-based learning. *BMC Medical Education, 21*(1), 1–8. doi:10.118612909-021-02508-y PMID:33509176

Loo, J. L. (2013). Guided and team-based learning for chemical information literacy. *Journal of Academic Librarianship, 39*(3), 252–259. doi:10.1016/j.acalib.2013.01.007

Michaelsen, L., & Sweet, M. (2004). *Team-based learning*. Sterling.

Murzi, H. G. (2014, June). Team-based learning theory applied to engineering education: A systematic review of literature. In *2014 ASEE Annual Conference & Exposition* (pp. 24-1175). 10.18260/1-2--23108

Odongo, C. O., & Talbert-Slagle, K. (2019). Training the next generation of Africa's doctors: Why medical schools should embrace the team-based learning pedagogy. *BMC Medical Education, 19*(1), 1–8. doi:10.118612909-019-1845-y PMID:31699081

Ofstad, W., & Brunner, L. J. (2013). Team-based learning in pharmacy education. *American Journal of Pharmaceutical Education, 77*(4), 70. Advance online publication. doi:10.5688/ajpe77470 PMID:23716738

Persky, A. M. (2012). The impact of team-based learning on a foundational pharmacokinetics course. *American Journal of Pharmaceutical Education, 76*(2), 31. Advance online publication. doi:10.5688/ajpe76231 PMID:22438603

Persky, A. M., & Pollack, G. M. (2011). A modified team-based learning physiology course. *American Journal of Pharmaceutical Education, 75*(10), 204. Advance online publication. doi:10.5688/ajpe7510204 PMID:22345723

Remington, T. L., Hershock, C., Klein, K. C., Niemer, R. K., & Bleske, B. E. (2015). Lessons from the trenches: Implementing team-based learning across several courses. *Currents in Pharmacy Teaching & Learning, 7*(1), 121–130. doi:10.1016/j.cptl.2014.09.008

Roh, Y. S., Kim, S. S., Park, S., & Ahn, J. W. (2020). Effects of a simulation with team-based learning on knowledge, team performance, and teamwork for nursing students. *CIN: Computers, Informatics. Computers, Informatics, Nursing*, *38*(7), 367–372. doi:10.1097/CIN.0000000000000628 PMID:32349024

Ruder, P., Maier, M. H., & Simkins, S. P. (2021). Getting started with team-based learning (TBL): An introduction. *The Journal of Economic Education*, *52*(3), 220–230. doi:10.1080/00220485.2021.1925187

Simkins, S. P., Maier, M. H., & Ruder, P. (2021). Team-based learning (TBL): Putting learning sciences research to work in the economics classroom. *The Journal of Economic Education*, *52*(3), 231–240. doi:10.1080/00220485.2021.1925188

Wallace, M. L., Walker, J. D., Braseby, A. M., & Sweet, M. S. (2014). Now, What Happens During Class?" Using Team-Based Learning to Optimize the Role of Expertise Within the Flipped Classroom. *Journal on Excellence in College Teaching*, 25.

Zingone, M. M., Franks, A. S., Guirguis, A. B., George, C. M., Howard-Thompson, A., & Heidel, R. E. (2010). Comparing team-based and mixed active-learning methods in an ambulatory care elective course. *American Journal of Pharmaceutical Education*, *74*(9), 160. Advance online publication. doi:10.5688/aj7409160 PMID:21301594

Chapter 3
Blended Learning:
Maximizing the Benefits of Technology in the Classroom

Iris-Panagiota Efthymiou
https://orcid.org/0000-0001-9656-8378
University of Greenwich, UK & University of East London, UK

EXECUTIVE SUMMARY

The chapter provides an overview of blended learning, an instructional method that integrates traditional classroom instruction with eLearning experiences. Blended learning offers a flexible and dynamic learning experience that allows learners to benefit from the interaction and guidance of in-person instruction while also having access to self-paced, personalized eLearning content outside of the classroom. It discusses the various forms and methods of delivering blended learning, including flipped classrooms, web-enhanced courses, flexible labs, and combined modes. The chapter also discusses challenges associated with blended learning and highlights the benefits it offers for learners, teachers, and organizations. These benefits include improved student performance, enhanced teacher effectiveness, and cost savings for organizations. Finally, it provides practical strategies for implementing blended learning in the classroom and features case studies and examples of blended learning in education, such as Rocketship Education and Khan Academy.

DOI: 10.4018/978-1-6684-7583-6.ch003

INTRODUCTION

Blended learning is a teaching approach that combines traditional face-to-face instruction with online learning. This method allows learners to access a range of online learning materials and interact with their instructors and peers virtually, while still enjoying the benefits of the traditional classroom environment (Ryan et al., 2016; Watson, 2008). Blended learning can take on various forms and can be personalized to meet the particular needs of individual learners (Kumar et al., 2021). This chapter will explore the benefits of blended learning and provide practical strategies for implementing it effectively in the classroom.

Blended Learning

Blended learning refers an educational approach that combines traditional face-to-face learning with online learning experiences (Hrastinski, 2019; Kumar et al., 2021). The blended learning approach is a learning model that has gained momentum due to improvements in digital technology, flexible school curriculum and dynamic learning experiences (Suartama et al., 2019). This approach allows learners to benefit from the interaction and guidance of in-person instruction while also having access to self-paced, personalized eLearning content outside of the classroom (Horn & Staker, 2014; Tucker et al., 2016).

Blended learning leverages the strengths of both methods, providing learners with opportunities for role-playing, immediate feedback, and social interaction during in-class sessions, while offering dynamic and interactive eLearning components such as "games, videos, tutorials, quizzes, and social media features" that can be accessed from a learner's home page in the mobile device or the Learning Management System (LMS) (ELM Learning, n.d). Economics educators have been supportive of using games, videos, and social media within the classroom (Al-Bahrani et al., 2018; Rogmans, 2018; Scott, 2023).

Blended learning can take on various forms, including flipped classrooms, hybrid learning, and remote learning, and can use a range of resources and tools, such as Google Classroom, YouTube, Zoom, and Microsoft Teams (Megahed & Hassan, 2022; Zimmerman, 2019). Blended learning aims to improve the learning experience by utilizing both in-person and online instructional methods in a complementary manner. It is considered effective when technology and teaching methods work together to cater to the diverse learning styles of students (Goffe & Sosin, 2010; Margolis et al., 2017; Swoboda & Feiler, 2016).

Blended learning is different from pure eLearning because it does not replace face-to-face teaching entirely (Tayebinik & Puteh, 2013). Instead, teachers use technology to enhance the learning experience and provide additional resources that can be accessed online, such as videos, quizzes, and interactive modules. Students may watch videos or complete online activities at home and then discuss them in class with their teacher and peers. Blended learning is more than just a merging of traditional classroom instruction and digital resources (Lapitan et al., 2021).

DELIVERY METHODS

Blended learning is a versatile approach to education that can be used in various ways in the classroom. Below are some popular methods of delivering blended learning in the education field:

Flipped Classrooms

The flipped classroom method requires educators to upload lecture materials to an online platform and assign reading materials for students to review at home (Long et al., 2017). In-class activities are then focused on interactive, student-centred exercises such as discussions, simulations, role-playing scenarios, and problem-solving activities. This approach can make in-class time more productive than traditional lecture formats and may also reduce the time spent in class (LTomesko et al. 2022).

The flipped classroom model aims to shift the focus of traditional teaching methods from lectures to active learning activities (Keengwe et al., 2014a). By providing pre-recorded lectures for students to watch on their own time, instructors can spend more class time engaging students in interactive activities that encourage collaboration, critical thinking, and problem-solving. This allows students to concentrate more intently on the subject matter and apply what they have learned in practical situations (Basal, 2015).

One potential advantage of the flipped classroom model is the capability to optimize class time by allowing instructors to incorporate students into practical tasks that can enhance their understanding of the subject matter (Roehl et al., 2013). Furthermore, students can learn at their own pace and could review the material as needed by having access to it before class (Pavanelli, 2018).

Web-Enhanced Courses

One method to incorporate technology into traditional classroom learning is through web-enhanced courses. As described by Driver (2002), these courses offer students the opportunity to participate in online activities outside of class time, such as participating in virtual discussions, viewing instructional videos, completing online assessments, or engaging in interactive simulations and labs. The goal of these activities is to enhance student engagement with the course material (Stine, 2010).

Web-enhanced courses aim to complement traditional classroom instruction by providing additional online activities that students can complete at their own pace (MacEntee & Lewis, 2004). Incorporating technology into the learning process can promote engagement and improve retention of course material among students. Some of the activities that can be integrated into the learning process include online simulations and labs, quizzes, online discussions, and watching educational videos. Web-enhanced courses can also benefit students who prefer independent learning or require additional support outside of class (Buckey, 2003).

However, it is important to recognize that not all subjects or learning styles may be suitable for web-enhanced courses. Students may also struggle with adapting to the online learning environment or experiencing inconsistent internet access. These challenges can be mitigated by providing appropriate resources and assistance, such as technical support and clear instructions for online activities (Shea et al., 2006).

Flexible Labs

Flexible laboratories are a type of learning environment where regular lab times are eliminated and students are free to complete lab tasks at their own pace and convenience (Fernandez et al., 2012). The lab may be supported by online resources, such as video tutorials or virtual simulations that students can access outside of the classroom. This combination of "face-to-face and online learning" can be considered a form of blended learning (Gamage et al., 2021).

This method establishes a learning commons where students may go if they want assistance or direction. Generally, lab assistants and tutors are available in flexible lab environments. To help the students with their lab work, the learning commons space may also be furnished with tools including books, movies, and computer software (Marques et al., 2013).

With the flexible laboratories' method, students have more control over their learning since they can choose how much time to spend on each activity and focus on the tasks that most interest them. Since it enables them to work at their own pace and in a more comfortable setting, this method is especially helpful for students who might not learn well in conventional laboratory settings (Hoic-Bozic et al., 2008).

Combined Modes

Combined modes refer to a type of blended learning that integrates different forms of instructional methods into one course or program. In this approach, students experience a mix of traditional classroom instruction and online learning through various formats such as virtual classes, interactive modules, or pre-recorded lectures (Hrastinski, 2019). For example, the flipped classroom model involves students viewing "pre-recorded lectures" outside of class and then attending in-person sessions to collaborate on hands-on activities and projects with their peers (Johnson, 2013). Meanwhile, flexible labs may also be incorporated, allowing students to conduct experiments or other activities in a self-paced, independent manner (Ng, 2022).

By using combined modes of blended learning, educators can give a more comprehensive and adaptable learning experience that caters to diverse student needs and learning styles. This approach allows for greater flexibility, engagement, and personalization of instruction, as well as increased collaboration among students and instructors. However, it also needs careful planning and implementation to ensure that the different modes of instruction work effectively together and support each other to attain the intended learning outcomes (Azizan, 2010).

Benefits of Blended Learning

Blended learning offers numerous benefits for learners, instructors, and institutions. Below are some of the benefits associated with this approach:

The benefits of blended learning for students (Albiladi & Alshareef, 2019; Azizan, 2010; Tayebinik & Puteh, 2013):

- Safer learning environment: Blended learning can offer a safer learning environment by minimizing the amount of time that learners spend together in person, while still providing opportunities for real-time communication.
- Interactive learning process: Blended learning uses a variety of tools such as game-like courses, simulations, and interactive activities to make the learning process engaging and fun.
- Learner autonomy: A flexible and personalized learning experience can be achieved through blended learning, allowing learners to manage their learning schedule based on their lifestyle and preferences.
- Greater learner engagement: Blended learning increases student engagement by offering multiple opportunities and utilizing digital tools (Harmon & Szarka, 2018).
- Better understanding: A teaching method employed in blended learning, known as the flipped classroom model, allows learners to study theoretical content at their preferred pace and apply new knowledge during face-to-face sessions, resulting in improved comprehension.
- Detailed analytics: Blended learning allows organizations to track learner progress and performance through detailed analytics, helping to identify areas that need improvement.

- Diverse learning styles: Blended learning offers different learning styles and allows students to mix up how they learn. This includes technology-based activities, group projects, and access to learning materials outside of core teaching hours.
- Improved accessibility and flexibility: Blended learning allows students to learn in more flexible ways, with webinars, videos, and other key aspects being done online. This makes learning more accessible to those who struggle with the classroom environment, those who may not be able to attend classes, or those who need to structure their learning around work or care.
- Lower costs: With part or all a lesson delivered online, costs can be kept much lower, making it easier for students to afford to attend and learn.
- Encourages social learning: Blended learning encourages social learning, where students can seek support from each other or from the instructor (Dakhi et al., 2020).

Benefits of blended learning for teachers (Alammary et al., 2014; Jeffrey et al., 2014; Lalima & Dangwal, 2014):

- Personalized lessons: Using technology and other e-learning methods, teachers can personalize lessons to cater to different learning styles, such as videos for visual learners, group tasks for social learners, or gamification for different styles.
- Tracking progression: Teachers can track progress, showing how far along a student is on a piece of work or by creating online quizzes and tests to test a student's knowledge.
- Fluid lesson planning: Blended learning allows for both online and offline teaching, enabling lesson plans to be created that allow for each. This makes it easier for teachers to demonstrate certain subjects in class while other subjects may be more effectively learned from online resources.

Benefits of blended learning for organizations (Biewener, 2023):

- Cost-effective: Blended learning offers a cost-effective approach to learning as it reduces the need for physical classrooms, travel expenses, and other associated costs.
- Flexible learning: Blended learning offers greater flexibility to organizations as learners can access courses 24/7, which can be particularly useful for organizations with remote or distributed teams.
- Improved retention rates: Blended learning has been shown to improve retention rates by providing learners with a variety of learning experiences.

- Customizable learning: Blended learning allows organizations to customize learning experiences for their learners, which can help to improve learning outcomes.

Implementation Strategies

Blended learning is becoming increasingly popular due to its flexibility and ability to engage students (George-Walker & Keeffe, 2010). Here are some strategies that can be used to make the most out of blended learning:

- Game-based and project-based learning methods: Game-based learning can be particularly effective at engaging students who may struggle with traditional classroom instruction or who are more motivated by interactive and hands-on learning experiences, can make the classroom more engaging and interesting. These methods can help students apply their learning in practical and fun ways, promoting better retention and understanding of course material. This approach immerses students in a single project or challenges over a while, either face-to-face or entirely assignment based. By working on a project that is relevant and meaningful to them, students are more likely to be motivated and invested in their learning. In addition, project-based learning can help students develop important skills, such as critical thinking, problem-solving, and communication, combining project-based learning with a blended approach allows students to push themselves even further (Jääskä & Aaltonen, 2022). Overall, employing game-based and project-based learning methods can be a highly effective way to make the classroom more engaging and interesting for students. By creating a dynamic and interactive learning environment, teachers can help students develop a love of learning and a lifelong passion for knowledge.
- Collaborative work in a virtual classroom: Collaborative work in a virtual classroom can help hone problem-solving skills and encourage engagement. By working together in groups, students can learn from one another, share ideas and perspectives, and collectively develop solutions to complex problems. Collaborative work in a virtual classroom can also help to foster a sense of community and belonging, which can be especially important for students who are learning remotely. When students feel connected to their peers and have opportunities to work together towards shared goals, they are more likely to be engaged and motivated to participate in class. In addition, collaborative work in a virtual classroom can help students develop important 21st-century skills, such as communication, collaboration, and critical thinking (Efthymiou, 2021). These skills are highly valued in today's

workforce, and providing students with opportunities to develop them in a safe and supportive learning environment can help prepare them for success in the future. Online materials and reviews can be used to facilitate distance learning (Keengwe et al., 2014b).

- Online tools for motivation and assessments: Online tools can be used to increase student motivation, and assessments can be carried out through automated checking, by providing interactive and personalized learning experiences. For example, digital tools such as educational games, simulations, and virtual reality can make learning more engaging and immersive, while adaptive learning platforms can provide students with personalized feedback and learning pathways that are tailored to their individual needs and abilities (Pereira et al., 2007). Another way online tools can increase student motivation is by providing opportunities for collaboration and communication. For instance, online discussion boards, video conferencing tools, and social media platforms can be used to facilitate peer-to-peer learning, group projects, and online debates, which can help students feel more connected to their classmates and more invested in their learning. In addition, online tools can be used to carry out assessments through automated checking. For example, quizzes and tests can be created using software that automatically grades student responses and provides instant feedback, saving teachers time and enabling them to focus on other aspects of teaching and learning. Automated checking can also help reduce bias and increase the accuracy and consistency of grading.
- Structured learning and flipped classroom: Structured learning methods provide students with clear learning objectives, guidelines, and milestones that help them understand what they need to do to succeed in the course. For instance, using a syllabus, course calendar, or learning management system can help students stay organized and on track with their assignments and assessments. Providing frequent feedback and support can also help students monitor their progress and stay motivated. The flipped classroom model is an effective approach to combining online and offline learning environments. In a flipped classroom, students watch pre-recorded lectures or complete online learning activities at home, and then come to class for interactive discussions, collaborative projects, and hands-on activities. This approach allows students to work at their own pace and frees up class time for more engaging and interactive learning experiences.
- Live online training: Live online training is becoming more popular due to its convenience and ability to accommodate remote learners. Live online training, also known as virtual instructor-led training (VILT), involves delivering training sessions over the internet in real-time, using

video conferencing software or other online tools. VILT allows learners to participate in training sessions from anywhere in the world, as long as they have an internet connection, which makes it a highly convenient and flexible option for busy professionals or remote workers. Blended learning solutions can help facilitate real-time or live training and accommodate learners who cannot attend in person (Holton III et al., 2006).

- Leveraging various elements of online learning: Several components of eLearning can be utilized, such as personalized course material, adjustable pacing, interactive assessments, real-time virtual teaching and teamwork, flipped teaching techniques, and multimedia elements like videos, images, animations, and virtual simulations.
- Rotation blended learning: This approach involves fixed schedules where students move from one type of learning to another. Types of rotation blended learning include station, lab, remote, and flipped learning. In station rotation blended learning, students rotate between different stations within the classroom, where they engage in different learning activities or work on different tasks. For example, one station might involve a teacher-led lesson, while another station might involve an independent learning activity or a group project. In lab rotation blended learning, students rotate between a traditional classroom setting and a computer lab or other digital learning environment, where they engage in online learning activities or complete computer-based assessments. In remote rotation blended learning, students rotate between remote learning and in-person learning, where they attend virtual classes or complete online assignments at home, and then attend in-person classes or small group sessions on campus or at other designated locations. In flipped blended learning, students watch pre-recorded video lectures or complete online learning activities at home, and then come to class for interactive discussions, collaborative projects, and hands-on activities.
- Flexible or self-directed blended learning: This method provides students with access to a centralized curriculum but permits them to learn in their own time at their own pace. Teachers provide mentoring support or answer questions at key points. Flexible blended learning offers several benefits for students and teachers alike. For students, it provides a more personalized and flexible approach to learning, allowing them to learn at their own pace and in their own time. This can help to increase motivation, engagement, and retention, as well as supporting the development of self-directed learning skills. For teachers, flexible blended learning can help to save time and reduce workload, as students take more responsibility for their own learning. It can also provide opportunities for more personalized and differentiated

instruction, as teachers can focus their attention on supporting individual students rather than delivering a one-size-fits-all approach to teaching.

- Gamification: This approach uses technology to help students learn new skills, such as interactive whiteboards or online learning platforms. Gamification can include fun quizzes or interactive activities that require learners to earn points or increase levels. These elements are designed to make learning more fun, interactive, and engaging, and to encourage learners to take an active role in their own learning. One of the key benefits of gamification is that it can help to increase motivation and engagement among learners. By incorporating game-like elements into the learning process, students are more likely to be excited and enthusiastic about learning, which can lead to better learning outcomes and higher levels of achievement.
- Self-blend and supplemental learning: Students use online courses, extra reading, or additional assignments that are supplementary to the work set by their teacher. This additional learning can help them better understand the course content (Reguera & Lopez, 2021). In self-blend and supplemental learning, students are given access to a range of digital resources, such as online courses, e-books, articles, videos, and other learning materials. They can then use these resources to supplement the work set by their teacher, either to deepen their understanding of the topic or to explore related areas of interest. This approach to blended learning is highly flexible and allows students to take greater control over their own learning. It can also help to personalize the learning experience, as students can choose the resources that are most relevant and engaging to them. Supplemental learning can be particularly beneficial for students who may be struggling with certain aspects of the course content, as it provides additional support and resources to help them overcome any challenges or difficulties they may be facing. It can also be useful for high-achieving students who want to explore topics in greater depth or to pursue their own interests and passions (Efthymiou, 2020).
- Outside-in blended learning: This approach relies on remote and virtual learning upfront, followed by bringing everything together in a physical classroom. Students learn via online training, assignments, and coursework in a structured fashion, and then use the classroom as a finishing point to tie together their own learning, encourage collaboration, and provide feedback (Azizan, 2010; Cleveland-Innes & Wilton, 2018). The idea behind outside-in blended learning is to provide students with a strong foundation of knowledge and skills before bringing them together in a physical classroom environment. By using digital resources to learn the basics, students can work at their own pace and build a solid understanding of the course content before coming together with their peers and teacher in person. Once in the

classroom, students can work collaboratively on projects, participate in discussions and debates, and receive personalized feedback and support from their teacher. This approach to blended learning is highly flexible and can be adapted to meet the needs of individual students, allowing them to work at their own pace and to receive personalized support and feedback. Outside-in blended learning is a powerful approach to blended learning that combines the benefits of remote and virtual learning with the social and collaborative aspects of in-person classroom experiences.

To ensure that blended learning is implemented successfully, it is crucial to introduce the new learning model gradually to help students adapt to the changes. As technology continues to evolve, blended learning will become even more effective in improving learning outcomes.

CASE STUDIES AND EXAMPLES OF BLENDED LEARNING

Here are some examples of blended learning in education:

Rocketship Education

Rocketship Education is a public charter school system renowned for its pioneering use of technology to improve learning outcomes. The school system has implemented a blended learning approach that integrates online courses with conventional classroom teaching, catering to a diverse range of academic levels and subjects. The school's experience with blended learning has yielded impressive results, with notable improvements in student performance (Horn & Staker, 2011).

Incorporating blended learning in different subject areas has allowed Rocketship Education to customize learning experiences to suit the interests and unique needs of individual students. For instance, in math, the school uses an adaptive software program that assesses students' mastery of concepts and adjusts learning activities to address gaps in understanding. In literacy, students receive targeted reading instruction and participate in online activities that reinforce skills such as fluency and comprehension (Christensen et al., 2013).

Blended learning has also been successfully implemented across various grade levels at Rocketship Education. For instance, the school has created specialized programs for English Language Learners (ELLs) that incorporate technology to help students improve their language skills (Staker & Horn, 2012).

Despite its many benefits, blended learning also presents challenges and potential pitfalls. One challenge is ensuring that students have access to technology and technical support. Another challenge is ensuring that teachers receive adequate training and support to effectively incorporate technology into their instruction. Finally, there is a risk of over-reliance on technology, which can detract from the human connection between teachers and students.

To overcome these challenges, Rocketship Education has developed a comprehensive support system that includes providing students with access to technology and technical support, offering teachers ongoing training and professional development, and emphasizing the importance of building strong relationships between teachers and students. The school system also regularly evaluates and adjusts its blended learning programs to make sure that they are meeting the requirements of students and teachers (Bailey et al., 2013; Staker & Horn, 2013).

Khan Academy

Khan Academy, a "non-profit educational organization," has incorporated blended learning into its approach to teaching various subjects, such as math, science, and humanities. Their strategy involves creating online videos that students can access at their convenience and pace, followed by in-class activities and exercises to reinforce the concepts learned (Vojtesek & Hutak, 2019).

Blended learning has been implemented across different grade levels and subject areas. Khan Academy's online courses cater to "elementary, middle, and high school students, as well as college and graduate-level learners." The courses cover a broad range of topics, from basic arithmetic to complex calculus, biology, chemistry, and even test preparation for standardized exams such as the SAT (Al-Ansi et al., 2021). Despite the evident benefits of blended learning, there are still potential challenges and pitfalls that educators should be aware of. For example, some students may struggle with the self-discipline required to complete online coursework independently. Others may require additional support and guidance from their teachers to fully comprehend the material covered in online videos.

To overcome these challenges, educators can integrate various strategies, such as personalized learning plans, one-on-one instruction, and group activities that encourage collaboration and peer-to-peer learning. In addition, instructors can leverage technology tools like online discussion boards and interactive whiteboards to assist engagement and participation (Light & Pierson, 2014; Tin-Chun, 2023).

University of Central Florida

Blended learning has been implemented in various subject areas and grade levels, as evidenced by the case study of the "University of Central Florida." The university's blended learning initiative incorporates online modules into traditional classroom activities, resulting in improved student engagement and success rates (Olapiriyakul & Scher, 2006). Despite the benefits of blended learning, there are still potential pitfalls and challenges that must be overcome. One such challenge is ensuring that all students have access to technology and reliable internet connections. In addition, there may be a learning curve for both students and instructors as they adjust to the new mode of instruction. To overcome these challenges, the university can provide access to technology and offer training and support for instructors and students (Moskal et al., 2013).

Michigan Virtual University

Blended learning has been implemented in various subject areas and grade levels, as exemplified by Michigan Virtual University. This online school combines "online learning with face-to-face interactions" to deliver courses to students. The blended learning approach allows students to participate in online activities and also meet with teachers and peers in traditional classrooms (Horn & Staker, 2011). While blended learning can have numerous benefits, it also poses some challenges and potential pitfalls. For instance, teachers may make an effort with the technical aspects of using online tools and resources, and students may lack the necessary digital literacy skills to fully engage with the materials. Additionally, ensuring equitable access to technology and online resources for all students can be a challenge.

To overcome these challenges, educators can provide support and training for both students and teachers in using online tools and resources effectively. They can also explore alternative methods of delivering content, such as video or audio recordings, to accommodate students with varying learning styles and needs. Furthermore, providing access to technology and online resources both in and outside of the classroom can help ensure that all students have an equal chance to engage with the materials (Ferdig & Kennedy, 2014).

Chicago Public Schools

Chicago Public Schools has implemented a personalized learning initiative that employs blended learning to provide a unique education to each student. This involves teachers using online tools to monitor students' progress and offer tailored instruction while allowing students to work at their own pace. Blended learning has been utilized in various subject areas and grade levels throughout the district (Walne, 2012). English Language Arts incorporates online reading and writing programmes that provide customized feedback to students working at their own pace. Math uses online software that adapts to individual student needs and provides instant feedback on performance. In Science, virtual labs and simulations are employed to build a safe environment for students to conduct experiments and explore scientific concepts.

Although blended learning has demonstrated its effectiveness in facilitating personalized learning, it also poses certain difficulties and risks. One of the most significant challenges is ensuring that all students have access to technology and dependable internet connectivity. Additionally, ensuring that teachers are adequately trained to effectively incorporate blended learning technologies into their curriculum is another difficulty.

To address these challenges, Chicago Public Schools has implemented various strategies such as providing students with devices and internet connectivity, offering professional development opportunities for teachers, and partnering with community organizations to provide additional support and resources. The district has also developed a robust system for tracking and evaluating the success of blended learning programs to ensure they meet the requirements of all students (Watson et al., 2013).

These are just a few examples of how blended learning is being used in education. With technology becoming more ubiquitous, blended learning is likely to become even more prevalent in the future.

CHALLENGES

Boelens et al. (2017) identified key challenges to designing and implementing blended learning: "flexibility in integration, interaction, support of student learning, and creating an effective learning environment." These challenges often result in an increased workload for teachers and a lack of professional development for teaching strategies, information technology and communication skills.Blended learning can present challenges for students, including the need to submit assignments electronically and a sense of isolation. Additionally, students who struggle academically may have difficulty adapting to new learning strategies, particularly if they lack internal motivation. Educational institutions may also struggle to address the varied requirements of blended learning, such as a lack of technical infrastructure and insufficient training for teachers to use various ICTs effectively.

To overcome these challenges, educational institutions should provide instructional guidelines for using ICT in learning, pedagogical training for teachers, and course structures that equip students with the abilities and knowledge to work effectively with online learning tools and computers. Schools must also provide necessary tools, such as devices, for online learning and encourage communication between students and teachers. Additionally, teachers must be confident and equipped with the skills to create an effective learning environment and integrate blended learning with teaching (Müller & Wulf, 2022). According to a survey conducted by ProLiteracy

(2020), close to 50% of the respondents who utilized blended learning encountered notable obstacles. The primary difficulty cited was the learners' struggle with self-direction and disinterest in utilizing technology. Other challenges included a lack of knowledge about technology, insufficient planning time, budget constraints, and access issues to Wi-Fi, hardware, or software.

Additionally, there are various challenges that learners may encounter when it comes to blended learning, including insufficient computer or digital skills, distractions, low levels of independence or self-directedness, lack of motivation, discomfort with technology, language barriers, and limited access to the internet or outdated hardware. The obstacles to implementing blended learning can be categorized into four main areas: insufficient resources for adult learners, inadequate knowledge among educators, logistical barriers associated with Wi-Fi and tool accessibility, and resistance. Here are some ways to overcome these challenges of implementing blended learning:

- Provide support and training for learners: Offer training and support to assist learners to develop the necessary digital skills and confidence to use technology effectively.
- Create engaging and interactive content: Use a variety of instructional strategies and media to keep learners engaged and motivated. Provide opportunities for collaboration and interaction with peers and instructors.
- Plan carefully: Allocate sufficient planning time to ensure that the blended learning program is well-designed and meets the needs of learners. Consider the learning objectives, available resources, and technology tools to be used.
- Use appropriate technology: Select appropriate technology tools that are user-friendly, reliable, and accessible to learners. Ensure that learners have access to the necessary hardware and software, and provide technical support as needed.
- Address connectivity issues: Identify and address issues related to Wi-Fi access and connectivity, especially for learners who may not have access to reliable Internet service.
- Foster a culture of learning: Encourage a culture of learning by promoting the advantages of blended learning, creating a supportive learning environment, and providing ongoing feedback and evaluation.
- Address resistance: Address any resistance to blended learning by communicating the benefits of the approach, providing support and training, and addressing any challenges or barriers that learners or instructors may have (Namyssova et al., 2019; ProLiteracy, 2020).

EVALUATING EFFECTIVENESS

Previous research found that blended learning can lead to positive outcomes for both students and teachers (Poon, 2013). Blended learning combines the benefits of "traditional face-to-face" instruction with online teaching using Learning Management System (LMS) functions, which facilitate learning and assessment tasks, as well as goal setting, document organization, and participation. This approach also provides more flexibility for personalized learning and assessment, without being limited by physical space or time constraints (Lin & Wang, 2012).

The research found that blended learning has a positive effect on students' attitudes towards learning. It can increase motivation, improve flexibility, boost self-confidence, enhance group work skills, and promote engagement. Furthermore, blended learning has been found to improve academic achievement and enhance the learning experience. Studies have also demonstrated that personality, learning style, and satisfaction are significant factors that contribute to student progress and achievement. Blended learning can also help students enhance their communication skills, problem-solving abilities, and proficiency in using technology (Sabah, 2020).

Blended learning is advantageous for teachers, as it facilitates one-on-one interaction with students and provides opportunities to tailor or create lesson plans based on individual student's learning progress. Learning Management Systems (LMS) enable teachers to access various representations of subjects and implement alternative methods of teaching by using innovative learning environments and teaching scenarios. Moreover, blended learning enhances teachers' proficiency in incorporating information and digital technology into their teaching practices (Wang et al., 2009).

Blended learning was found to be highly beneficial during the COVID-19 lockdown, as it has led to a notable rise in learner engagement. By leveraging the strengths of every teaching method and integrating the benefits of both "face-to-face and online instruction," the advantages of blended learning can be maximized (Sreehari, 2020).

According to a study conducted by Tong et al. (2022) involving 10th students, blended learning was discovered to be an effective approach to improving students' academic performance and self-study skills. The experimental group showed significantly higher academic achievement than the control group, suggesting that blended learning had a positive effect on student learning attitudes and performance. The study found that students' self-study abilities also improved, which was evident from their feedback and survey responses. Moreover, blended learning increased student-teacher interactions.

CONCLUSION

In conclusion, blended learning is an educational approach that integrates traditional face-to-face teaching with online learning to create a more dynamic and flexible learning experience for students. Blended learning can take on various forms, including flipped classrooms, web-enhanced courses, flexible labs, and combined modes, and can be delivered using a range of resources and tools such as Google Classroom, YouTube, Zoom, and Microsoft Teams. Blended learning is advantageous to students in several ways, such as heightened engagement, better academic achievement, and improved problem-solving and critical thinking abilities. Nevertheless, successful integration of blended learning in classrooms necessitates deliberate preparation, effective communication, and continuous support from educators and management. Some challenges to implementing blended learning include access to technology and internet connectivity, lack of teacher training, and the need for continuous assessment and evaluation.

Despite these challenges, however, the potential benefits of blended learning are significant, and with careful planning and implementation, many schools and education systems have successfully integrated blended learning into their teaching and learning practices. By addressing these challenges head-on and working collaboratively with students, teachers, and other stakeholders, we can create a more effective and engaging learning experience for everyone involved. Blended learning can transform the field of education by utilizing the benefits of both traditional classroom instruction and online learning to establish an enhanced and streamlined learning experience for students. By leveraging the advantages of digital technologies and online learning resources, blended learning allows teachers to personalize instruction and cater to the unique learning needs and preferences of individual students. It also enables students to learn at their own pace, receive immediate feedback, and engage with course materials in a variety of formats, including multimedia, interactive activities, and gamification.

At the same time, blended learning maintains the social and collaborative aspects of traditional classroom instruction, allowing students to interact with their peers, participate in discussions, and receive feedback and guidance from their teacher. This can help to foster a sense of community and belonging, which is crucial for student engagement and motivation.

Overall, blended learning represents a powerful approach to education that can transform the way we teach and learn. By combining the best of both worlds, it has the potential to enhance student outcomes, improve teacher effectiveness, and create a more engaging and enjoyable learning experience for everyone involved.

REFERENCES

Al-Ansi, A. M., Garad, A., & Al-Ansi, A. (2021). ICT-based learning during Covid-19 outbreak: Advantages, opportunities and challenges. *Gagasan Pendidikan Indonesia, 2*(1), 10–26. doi:10.30870/gpi.v2i1.10176

Al-Bahrani, A., Mahon, D., Mateer, G. D., & Murphy, P. R. (2018). Pokémon GO: Applications for the Economics Classroom. *Journal of Economics Teaching, 3*(2), 218–231. doi:10.58311/jeconteach/d8a48467f1a836406126d54c8e97507f474a6525

Alammary, A., Sheard, J., & Carbone, A. (2014). Blended learning in higher education: Three different design approaches. *Australasian Journal of Educational Technology, 30*(4), 387–400. doi:10.14742/ajet.693

Albiladi, W. S., & Alshareef, K. K. (2019). Blended learning in English teaching and learning: A review of the current literature. *Journal of Language Teaching and Research, 10*(2), 232–238. doi:10.17507/jltr.1002.03

Azizan, F. Z. (2010). Blended learning in higher education institution in Malaysia. *Proceedings of regional conference on knowledge integration in ICT, 10*(1), 454-466.

Bailey, J., Martin, N., Schneider, C., Vander Ark, T., Duty, L., Ellis, S., & Terman, A. (2013). Blended learning implementation guide 2.0. In J. Bailey, C. Schneider, & T. Vander Ark (Eds.), Navigating the Digital Shift (pp. 32–39). Academic Press.

Basal, A. (2015). The implementation of a flipped classroom in foreign language teaching. *Turkish Online Journal of Distance Education, 16*(4), 28–37. doi:10.17718/tojde.72185

Biewener, D. (2023, February 21). *5 Big Benefits of Blended Learning*. Simplilearn. https://www.simplilearn.com/benefits-of-blended-learning-article

Boelens, R., De Wever, B., & Voet, M. (2017). Four key challenges to the design of blended learning: A systematic literature review. *Educational Research Review, 22*(1), 1–18. doi:10.1016/j.edurev.2017.06.001

Buckey, K. M. (2003). Evaluation of classroom-based, web-enhanced, and web-based distance learning nutrition courses for undergraduate nursing. *The Journal of Nursing Education, 42*(8), 367–370. doi:10.3928/0148-4834-20030801-09 PMID:12938900

Christensen, C. M., Horn, M. B., & Staker, H. (2013). Is K-12 blended learning disruptive? An introduction to the theory of hybrids. Clayton Christensen Institute for Disruptive Innovation. ERIC No. ED565838.

Cleveland-Innes, M., & Wilton, D. (2018). *Guide to blended learning*. Commonwealth of Learning. https://oasis.col.org/handle/11599/3095

Dakhi, O., Jama, J., & Irfan, D. (2020). Blended learning: A 21st century learning model at college. *International Journal of Multi Science, 1*(7), 50-65. https://multisciencejournal.com/index.php/ijm/article/view/92/72

Driver, M. (2002). Exploring student perceptions of group interaction and class satisfaction in the web-enhanced classroom. *The Internet and Higher Education, 5*(1), 35–45. doi:10.1016/S1096-7516(01)00076-8

Efthymiou, I. P. (2020). Non-Cognitive skills and AI: A new era of learning and development. *International Case Studies Journal, 9*(10), 42–46.

Efthymiou, I. P., (2021). *Soft Skills for Children. A Guide to success for 21st century kids*. Academic Press.

Ferdig, R. E., & Kennedy, K. (2014). *Handbook of research on K-12 online and blended learning*. ETC Press. http://repository.cmu.edu/etcpress/82/

Fernandez, G. C., Ruiz, E. S., Gutierrez, S. M., Gil, M. C., & Perez, F. M. (2012). Flexibility of wireless technologies in learning in robotic laboratories. In *Proceedings of the 2012 IEEE Global Engineering Education Conference (EDUCON)* (pp. 1-5). IEEE. https://doi.org/10.1109/EDUCON.2012.6201060

Gamage, K. A., Wijesuriya, D. I., Ekanayake, S. Y., Rennie, A. E., Lambert, C. G., & Gunawardhana, N. (2020). Online delivery of teaching and laboratory practices: Continuity of university programmes during COVID-19 pandemic. *Education Sciences, 10*(10), 291. doi:10.3390/educsci10100291

George-Walker, L. D., & Keeffe, M. (2010). Self-determined blended learning: A case study of blended learning design. *Higher Education Research & Development, 29*(1), 1–13. doi:10.1080/07294360903277380

Goffe, W. L., & Sosin, K. (2010). Teaching with technology: May you live in interesting times. *The Journal of Economic Education, 36*(3), 278–291. doi:10.3200/JECE.36.3.278-291

Harmon, O., & Szarka, R. (2018). Using Google drawings to create homework exercises. *Journal of Economics Teaching, 2*(2), 68–78. doi:10.58311/jeconteach/cb6e720d514867854cefdc6b43a098f676b69bd6

Hoic-Bozic, N., Mornar, V., & Boticki, I. (2008). A blended learning approach to course design and implementation. *IEEE Transactions on Education, 52*(1), 19–30. doi:10.1109/TE.2007.914945

Holton, E. F. III, Coco, M. L., Lowe, J. L., & Dutsch, J. V. (2006). Blended delivery strategies for competency-based training. *Advances in Developing Human Resources*, *8*(2), 210–228. doi:10.1177/1523422305286153

Horn, M. B., & Staker, H. (2011). *The rise of K-12 blended learning*. Innosight Institute. https://www.christenseninstitute.org/wp-content/uploads/2013/04/The-rise-of-K-12-blended-learning.pdf

Horn, M. B., & Staker, H. (2014). *Blended: Using disruptive innovation to improve schools*. Jossey-Bass.

Hrastinski, S. (2019). What do we mean by blended learning? *TechTrends*, *63*(5), 564–569. doi:10.100711528-019-00375-5

Jääskä, E., & Aaltonen, K. (2022). Teachers' experiences of using game-based learning methods in project management higher education. *Project Leadership and Society*, *3*(1), 100041. doi:10.1016/j.plas.2022.100041

Jeffrey, L. M., Milne, J., Suddaby, G., & Higgins, A. (2014). Blended learning: How teachers balance the blend of online and classroom components. *Journal of Information Technology Education*, *13*(1), 121–140. doi:10.28945/1968

Johnson, G. B. (2013). *Student perceptions of the flipped classroom* [Master's thesis]. The University of British Columbia.

Keengwe, J., Onchwari, G., & Agamba, J. (2014b). Promoting effective e-learning practices through the constructivist pedagogy. *Education and Information Technologies*, *19*(4), 887–898. doi:10.100710639-013-9260-1

Keengwe, J., Onchwari, G., & Oigara, J. N. (Eds.). (2014a). *Promoting Active Learning through the Flipped Classroom Model*. IGI Global. doi:10.4018/978-1-4666-4987-3

Kumar, A., Krishnamurthi, R., Bhatia, S., Kaushik, K., Ahuja, N. J., Nayyar, A., & Masud, M. (2021). Blended learning tools and practices: A comprehensive analysis. *IEEE Access : Practical Innovations, Open Solutions*, *9*, 85151–85197. doi:10.1109/ACCESS.2021.3085844

Lalima, & Dangwal, K. L. (2017). Blended learning: An innovative approach. *Universal Journal of Educational Research, 5*(1), 129-136. doi:10.13189/ujer.2017.050116

Lapitan, L. D. Jr, Tiangco, C. E., Sumalinog, D. A. G., Sabarillo, N. S., & Diaz, J. M. (2021). An effective blended online teaching and learning strategy during the COVID-19 pandemic. *Education for Chemical Engineers*, *35*(1), 116–131. doi:10.1016/j.ece.2021.01.012

Learning, E. L. M. (n.d.). *What is Blended Learning? A Guide to Everything You Need to Know*. Retrieved from https://elmlearning.com/hub/elearning/blended-learning/

Light, D., & Pierson, E. (2014). Increasing student engagement in math: The use of Khan Academy in Chilean classrooms. *International Journal of Education and Development using ICT, 10*(2), 103-119. https://www.learntechlib.org/p/147457/

Lin, W. S., & Wang, C. H. (2012). Antecedences to continued intentions of adopting e-learning system in blended learning instruction: A contingency framework based on models of information system success and task-technology fit. *Computers & Education, 58*(1), 88–99. doi:10.1016/j.compedu.2011.07.008

Long, T., Cummins, J., & Waugh, M. (2017). Use of the flipped classroom instructional model in higher education: Instructors' perspectives. *Journal of Computing in Higher Education, 29*(1), 179–200. doi:10.100712528-016-9119-8

MacEntee, V., & Lewis, B. (2004). Web-enhanced course. *Issues in Informing Science & Information Technology, 1*, 951–964. doi:10.28945/790

Margolis, A. R., Porter, A. L., & Pitterle, M. E. (2017). Best practices for use of blended learning. *American Journal of Pharmaceutical Education, 81*(3), 1–8. doi:10.5688/ajpe81349 PMID:28496269

Marques, M. A., Viegas, M. C., Costa-Lobo, M. C., Fidalgo, A. V., Alves, G. R., Rocha, J. S., & Gustavsson, I. (2013). How remote labs impact on course outcomes: Various practices using VISIR. *IEEE Transactions on Education, 57*(3), 151–159. doi:10.1109/TE.2013.2284156

Megahed, N., & Hassan, A. (2022). A blended learning strategy: Reimagining the post-Covid-19 architectural education. *Archnet-IJAR: International Journal of Architectural Research, 16*(1), 184–202. doi:10.1108/ARCH-04-2021-0081

Moskal, P., Dziuban, C., & Hartman, J. (2013). Blended learning: A dangerous idea? *The Internet and Higher Education, 18*, 15–23. doi:10.1016/j.iheduc.2012.12.001

Müller, F. B., & Wulf, T. (2022). Blended learning environments and learning outcomes: The mediating role of flow experience. *International Journal of Management Education, 20*(3), 100694. Advance online publication. doi:10.1016/j.ijme.2022.100694

Namyssova, G., Tussupbekova, G., Helmer, J., Malone, K., Mir, A., & Jonbekova, D. (2019). Challenges and benefits of blended learning in higher education. *International Journal of Technology in Education, 2*(1), 22–31.

Ng, D. T. K. (2022). Online lab design for aviation engineering students in higher education: A pilot study. *Interactive Learning Environments*, *30*(3), 1–18. doi:10.1080/10494820.2022.2034888

Olapiriyakul, K., & Scher, J. M. (2006). A guide to establishing hybrid learning courses: Employing information technology to create a new learning experience, and a case study. *The Internet and Higher Education*, *9*(4), 287–301. doi:10.1016/j.iheduc.2006.08.001

Pavanelli, R. (2018). The flipped classroom: A mixed methods study of academic performance and student perception in EAP writing context. *International Journal of Language and Linguistics*, *5*(2), 16–26.

Pereira, J. A., Pleguezuelos, E., Merí, A., Molina-Ros, A., Molina-Tomás, M. C., & Masdeu, C. (2007). Effectiveness of using blended learning strategies for teaching and learning human anatomy. *Medical Education*, *41*(2), 189–195. doi:10.1111/j.1365-2929.2006.02672.x PMID:17269953

Poon, J. (2013). Blended learning: An institutional approach for enhancing students' learning experiences. *Journal of Online Learning and Teaching*, *9*(2), 271–289.

ProLiteracy. (2020, February 3). *What are the challenges of implementing blended learning in adult education?* [Blog post]. Retrieved from https://www.proliteracy.org/Blogs/Article/505/What-are-the-Challenges-of-Implementing-Blended-Learning-in-Adult-Education

Reguera, E. A. M., & Lopez, M. (2021). Using a digital whiteboard for student engagement in distance education. *Computers & Electrical Engineering*, *93*, 107268. doi:10.1016/j.compeleceng.2021.107268 PMID:34642507

Roehl, A., Reddy, S. L., & Shannon, G. J. (2013). The flipped classroom: An opportunity to engage millennial students through active learning strategies. *Journal of Family and Consumer Sciences*, *105*(2), 44–49. doi:10.14307/JFCS105.2.12

Rogmans, T. (2018). Teaching macroeconomics with the Econoland simulation game and learning platform. *Journal of Economics Teaching*, *2*(2), 91–103. doi:10.58311/jeconteach/892413d590665dfe858e06a93abd1697c16b00f7

Ryan, S., Kaufman, J., Greenhouse, J., She, R., & Shi, J. (2016). The effectiveness of blended online learning courses at the community college level. *Community College Journal of Research and Practice*, *40*(4), 285–298. doi:10.1080/10668926.2015.1044584

Sabah, N. M. (2020). Motivation factors and barriers to the continuous use of blended learning approach using Moodle: Students' perceptions and individual differences. *Behaviour & Information Technology, 39*(8), 875–898. doi:10.1080/0144929X.2019.1623323

Scott, A. B. (2023). *Using music to enhance pedagogy in the classroom.* Paper presented at the Journal of Economics Teaching Symposium on Economics Teaching (JETSET), Newport, KY. https://doi.org/10.13140/RG.2.2.34710.11847

Shea, P., Li, C. S., & Pickett, A. (2006). A study of teaching presence and student sense of learning community in fully online and web-enhanced college courses. *The Internet and Higher Education, 9*(3), 175–190. doi:10.1016/j.iheduc.2006.06.005

Sreehari, P. (2020). Online learning during the COVID-19 lockdown: Learners' perceptions. *Journal of Critical Reviews, 7*(10), 300–307.

Staker, H., & Horn, M. B. (2012). *Classifying K–12 blended learning.* INNOSIGHT Institute. ERIC. https://files.eric.ed.gov/fulltext/ED535180.pdf

Staker, H., & Horn, M. B. (2013). Blended learning in the K–12 education sector. In A. G. Picciano, C. D. Dziuban, & C. R. Graham (Eds.), *Blended learning: Research perspectives* (Vol. 2, pp. 287–303). Routledge. doi:10.4324/9781315880310

Stine, L. J. (2010). Teaching basic writing in a web-enhanced environment. *Journal of Basic Writing, 29*(1), 33–55. doi:10.37514/JBW-J.2010.29.1.03

Suartama, I. K., Setyosari, P., Sulthoni, S., & Ulfa, S. (2019). Development of an instructional design model for mobile blended learning in higher education. *International Journal of Emerging Technologies in Learning, 14*(16), 4–22. doi:10.3991/ijet.v14i16.10633

Swoboda, A., & Feirler, L. (2016). Measuring the effect of blended learning: Evidence from a selective liberal arts college. *The American Economic Review, 106*(5), 368–372. doi:10.1257/aer.p20161055

Tayebinik, M., & Puteh, M. (2013). *Blended Learning or E-learning?* arXiv preprint arXiv:1306.4085. https://doi.org//arXiv.1306.4085 doi:10.48550

Tayebinik, M., & Puteh, M. (2013). Blended learning or e-learning? *International Magazine on Advances in Computer Science and Telecommunications, 3*(1), 103-110. https://doi.org//arXiv.1306.4085 doi:10.48550

Tin-Chun, L. (2023). Can online discussions benefit students' learning in online courses? Evidence from teaching introduction to microeconomics. *E-Learning and Digital Media.* Advance online publication. doi:10.1177/20427530231170765

Tomesko, J., Cohen, D., & Bridenbaugh, J. (2022). Using a virtual flipped classroom model to promote critical thinking in online graduate courses in the United States: A case presentation. *Journal of Educational Evaluation for Health Professions*, *19*(1), 1–8. doi:10.3352/jeehp.2022.19.5 PMID:35219288

Tong, D. H., Uyen, B. P., & Ngan, L. K. (2022). The effectiveness of blended learning on students' academic achievement, self-study skills and learning attitudes: A quasi-experiment study in teaching the conventions for coordinates in the plane. *Heliyon*, *12657*(12), e12657. Advance online publication. doi:10.1016/j.heliyon.2022.e12657 PMID:36643330

Tucker, C. R., Wycoff, T., & Green, J. T. (2016). *Blended learning in action: A practical guide toward sustainable change*. Corwin Press.

Vojtesek, J., & Hutak, J. (2019). Using multimedia in blended learning. *Software Engineering Methods in Intelligent Algorithms: Proceedings of 8th Computer Science On-line Conference 2019, 18*(1), 249-258.

Walne, M. B. (2012). *Emerging blended-learning models and school profiles*. Community Foundation. Retrieved from http://www.edustart.org/volume2/issue2/Walne.pdf

Wang, M., Shen, R., Novak, D., & Pan, X. (2009). The impact of mobile learning on students' learning behaviours and performance: Report from a large blended classroom. *British Journal of Educational Technology*, *40*(4), 673–695. doi:10.1111/j.1467-8535.2008.00846.x

Watson, J. (2008). Blended learning: The convergence of online and face-to-face education. *Promising Practices in Online Learning,* 2(1), 33-44. https://files.eric.ed.gov/fulltext/ED509636.pdf

Watson, J., Murin, A., Vashaw, L., Gemin, B., & Rapp, C. (2013). *Keeping Pace with K-12 Online & Blended Learning: An Annual Review of Policy and Practice. 10 Year Anniversary Issue*. Evergreen Education Group. https://files.eric.ed.gov/fulltext/ED566139.pdf

Zimmerman, E. (2019). *Microsoft Teams VS Google Classrooms: Tools for Blended Learning. EdTech Magazine*. Retrieved from https://edtechmagazine.com/k12/article/2019/02/google-classroom-and-microsoft-teams-education-find-blended-learning-tool-works-best-perfcon

Chapter 4
Academic and Educational Transformation Projects:
The Role Team-Based Learning in Polymathics (RTBLP)

Antoine Toni Trad
https://orcid.org/0000-0002-4199-6970
IBISTM, France

EXECUTIVE SUMMARY

Iterative academic (and educational) transformation projects (ATP) are fundamental for the enhancements of academic institutions. But ATPs are very complex, because of the reality of the adoption of a holistic concept, which can be considered as a polymathic concept. A polymathic concept promotes the development of an interdisciplinary core and project-based learning for future transformation project's managers and architects. This chapter proposes the applied holistic and poly-mathematical model (AHMM) for ATPs (AHMM4ATP), which is a variant of the author's AHMM and research works. The AHMM4ATP-based RTBLP combines various educational fields that can include business engineering/transformation, enterprise (re)organization, societal changes, business/finance, AI, mathematics, and geopolitical contexts. This research chapter is another topic in the author's research and development project (RDP). The RDP is the continuation of previous works and findings that are used to prove RTBLP's feasibility and to offer a polymathics' curriculum for the secondary school cycle.

DOI: 10.4018/978-1-6684-7583-6.ch004

INTRODUCTION

In the context of secondary cycle teaching and learning. This chapter is based on the author's transformation framework and its related works, like: The Business Transformation Project's Holistic Agile Management (Trad, & Kalpić, 2022c); 2) The selection and training framework for transformation projects; an educational view (Trad, & Kalpić, 2014b); 3) Educational Transformation Project's Remote Group Work (ETPRGW) (Trad, & Kalpić, 2023a); 4) The transformation framework-The role security in the global education system (Trad, 2021a); 5) The business transformation enterprise architecture framework for innovation: The role of artificial intelligence in the global business education (RAIGBE) (Trad, 2021b); 6) Business Transformation Projects: The Role of Psychology-Based Resistance (RPbR) (Trad, 2023b); 7) The Societal and Educational Transformation Projects: The Evolution of the Lebanese Diverse Education (ELDES) (Trad, 2023c); 8) The selection and training framework for managers in business innovation and transformation projects: The Profile and Education of a Business Transformation Manager - An enterprise architecture approach (Trad, & Kalpić, 2014c) and others.

This work has a multi-dimensional approach to RDPs and transformation projects, because it has: 1) An adapted research concept; 2) Shows how to build an in-house transformation framework; 3) Uses an organizational methodological approach that is based Enterprise Architecture (EA); and 4) Polymathic and Interdisciplinary Group Work (PIGW) (Trad, & Kalpić, 2023a). The PIGW uses the Team-Based Learning's (TBL) as its fundament; and the TBL can be used to support a corresponding Polymathic curriculum that can transform educational outcomes. The TBL and RTBLP use integrated: Critical Success Areas (CSA), Critical Success Factors (CSF), Key Performance Indicators (KPI), An authentic research and transformation framework, and An integrated heuristics based Decision Making System (DMS). TBL supports all ATP4SC's activities, and uses existing teaching standards, methodologies, local technics, and also LCSAS practices. The RTBLP focuses on the complex linking of academic and educational fields, like economics, financial engineering, business engineering (BE), information and communication systems (ICS), project management (PM), and other relevant fields, to deliver an adequate PICC.

This chapter is intended for educators, students, researchers, and can also be used by enterprises' human resources to select their future managers or specialists to work in the context of complex transformations and innovations projects; especially when educators want to develop a PICC. The proposed educational concept and PICC are independent of the educational cycle; but where the secondary cycle can be determinant in the sense of: 1) Proactively finding students with Holistic/Polymathic and diversity capabilities and characteristics; 2) Enforcements in PICC related studies and projects, which can be continued in higher education; 3) Support, subsidise, and encourage such rare characteristics; 4) Blends PICC that interconnects existing topics; 5) Define the educators' profile and background; 6) Define core topics and project; 7) Promote ethical values; 8) Working in coordinated PIGWs; and 9) Identify which (multi)cultural communities have such predispositions, which can be promoted (Trad, 2022a). Educational institutions can embrace RTBLP by supporting collaborative environments, accepted classroom management techniques, and supporting interactive technologies.

Educators who use RTBLP can use this approach with a variety curriculum topics. Economics educators (remember, this is an economics education book) could find PICC methods useful in approaching course topics in both quantitative and qualitative lesson designs. An Institution needs to use agile collaboration environments services, educational patterns, educational best practices, and highly interactive multimedia products like the Over-the-Top (OTT). A TBL approach forces the used transformation framework and the related set of existing modules, to synchronize all possible types of educational transformational activities, like the integration of the PIGW which uses automated TBL activities for the secondary cycle. Automated and synchronized agile based TBL coordination environments can produce different types of problems, that can be proactively managed. The author's transformation framework is a pioneering one and its originality lies in that it can be used in any type of transformation project and in any ATP4SC phase. This framework delivers a Action Research (AR) based Learning Process (ARbLP) that can support and enhance learning outcomes.

ATP4SC's crucial problems result from intensive TBL activities and RTBLP's main constraint is the *Entity's* capacity to coherently change and integrate new procedures in all of its departments (keeping local specificities active); this chapter might seem complex to readers and especially the younger ones, but it shows the complexity of Polymath methodologies and concepts. The RTBLP requires a well-defined type of educators and academic educator, which have needed the qualifications to combine complex PICC domains like ICS, mathematics, and other. The RTBLP based PICC links the mentioned topics and defines the relationships. The *Entity's* educator must have the needed set of skills and experience (academic, pedagogic, didactical, and professional project industrial). The educator to manages different types of strongly related TBL based courses and activities.

The RTBLP and the resultant PICC are based on:

1. An integrated version of EA and DMS to support high quality TBL based teaching and learning (Pushpakumara, Jayaweera, & Manjulan, 2021)
2. An internal model like the AHMM4TBL (Trad, & Kalpić, 2020)

3. Classified granular educational services and EA blueprints for ATP4SC (and ATPs in general) platforms (Trad, 2015a, 2015b)
4. Various types of educational/academic templates, patterns and common types of training (Trad, & Kalpić, 2022a, 2022b)
5. Distributed ICS (or the cloud) to support and PIGW (Trad, 2023a)
6. Agile PM coordinates TBL and PIGW activities and PICC's evolution (Spencer, 2016)
7. Implementing latest adapted ICS arteficts like OTT (where OTT does not need any in-depth ICS knowledge) to support TBL based PIGW.
8. To define a dynamic PICC's for future optimal profile (or the Business Transformation Project's Architect's Profile-BTPAP) to be the end-focus (Trad, & Kalpić, 2021a).

This chapter's aim is to prove that the proposed RTBLP can support *Entity's* ATP/ATP4SC and offer an optimal PICC and PIGW. The RTBLP can be designed and evaluated by using the AHMM4TBL, which in turn uses Factors, and on an adapted mixed heuristics-based RDP. The proposed RDP uses the ARbLP that is indented and is optimal for evolutive education, where AR can be used to improve TBL/PIGW based learning and teaching (Trad & Kalpić, 2017; Aksoy, & Ceylan, 2021). The RTBLP problem solving is supported by an ARbLP based DMS for TBL (DMS4TBL), Knowledge Management System for TBL (KMS4TBL) and an agile EA methodology (Blackburn, & Rosen, 1993). The presented Proof of Concept (PoC) uses the following Applied Case Studies (ACS): 1) The insurance domain (Jonkers, Band, & Quartel, 2012a), which is used for ICS, modelling, and EA topics. These topics are good for Polymathic and they support the author's transformation framework which manages the ATP and estimates possible risks of failure; 2) A high school's case of development of teacher collaboration by using a Polymathic curriculum (Fitzgerald, 2005); and 3) A set of online education and TBL/PIGW based ACSs. ATP/ATP4SC's first phase defines: 1) Needed TBL/PIGW and PICC interfaces; 2) Major change steps; 3) Permitted and mandatory activities; and 4) The educator*'s* (that includes educators) ideal profiles and sets of skills.

Figure 1. EURSC's organisation of studies

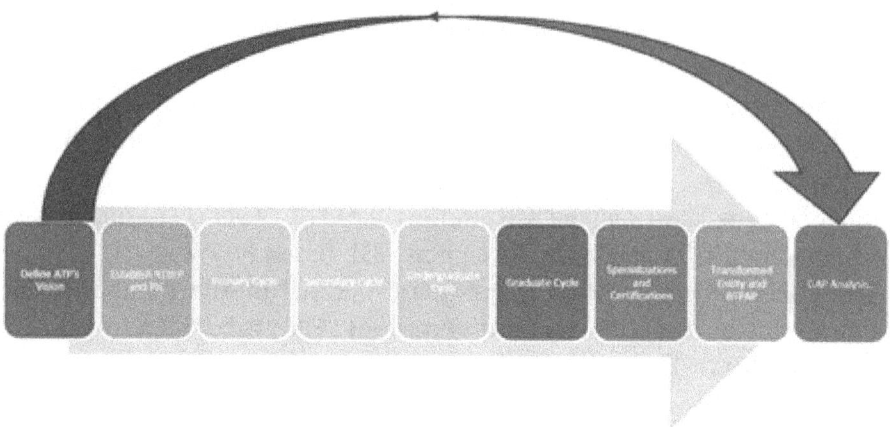

ATP's complexity lies in the transformation of the Legacy Siloed Common Academic/Educational System (LCSAS) into an agile and TBL/PIGW based educational system. RTBLP capable educator

must support ATP's (and ATP4SC's) integration in secondary schools, and such an integration is supported by agile EA methodologies, DMS4TBL, KMS4TBL, and educator*'s* implementation concrete experiences and skills. In the author's previous RDP related works, he has identified an important research gap in the management and coordination of various types of transformation projects, which have very high failure rates that are due to the role and profile of the BTPAP; knowing that failure rates can reach up to 95% (Block, 2022; Dello Ioio, 2023). Such critical Polymath characteristics or profiles must be proactively discovered in early educational phases like secondary cycle (and even primary schools); and such identified profiles must be traced through all other educational phases as shown in Figure 1. Where a Polymath profile can be defined as a Student that can easily apprehend Economics, Math, ICS, Geography (and other) topics and interrelate them in a concrete student project.

Figure 2. EURSC's organisation of studies (EURSC, 2022)

Cycle	Classes	Age
'Early education' (Nursery)	1-2	4 and 5
Primary	1-5	6-10
Secondary Observation cycle Pre-orientation cycle Orientation cycle	 1-3 4-5 6-7	 11-13 14-15 16-18

Because unfortunately today, such complex transformation projects are managed by business managers profiles (who basically specialized accountants), which is the main reason for failures. Transformation projects and ATPs profiles, require educator with cross-functional and/or Polymathic capacities (and set of skills), which can support interconnected PICC topics for the secondary cycle as shown in Figure 2. The PICC for secondary schools' main aim is to provide a multilingual, technical, and cross-functional education for students (EURSC, 2022).

RTBLP CROSS-FUNCTIONAL SET OF CHARACTERISTICS AND SKILLS

Cross-functional/Polymathic skills building is mainly based on common or generic skills with the capability to quickly built specialized skills for a given task and the capacity to improvise in complex environments. This characteristic can be found in limited number of students who are basically a variant of *Technocrats*. The RTBLP needs to be supported by the ARbLP based DMS4TBL and KMS4TBL in order to solve various types of ATP and encountered PICCs' problems.

Figure 3. The interaction between the ATP (hence STP4SC) and the RDP

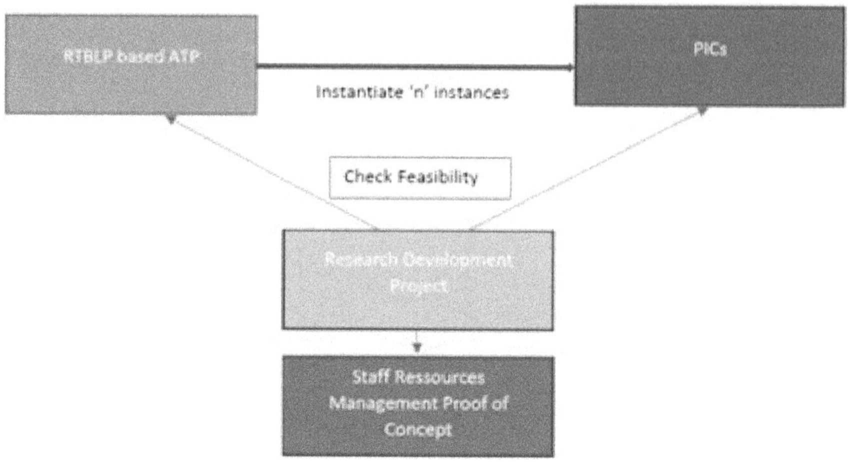

The author uses his established Transformation Research Architecture Development framework (*TRADf*) to show how and can build an inhouse framework to integrate the following components: 1) ICS, TBL/PIGW, OTT technologies; 2) DMS4TBL; 3) KMS4TBL; 4) RTBLP and PICC generators; and 5) RDP as shown in Figure 3, which is the first CSA and its heading are in fact the initial CSFs.

THE RESEARCH DEVELOPMENT PROJECT

ICS and related are exponentially evolving and that implies that businesses and they economical statuses are constantly being transformed; but serious sources state that most of them fail. Therefore, transformation projects are a major challenge and concern. So such projects are doomed from their start (sources: Forbes, McKinsey, BCG, KPMG and Bain & Company…) and failure rates reach 95% (Block, 2022; Dello Ioio, 2023). Mainly because of the lack of Polymathic profiles…

In this chapter the author uses many acronyms, terms and abbreviations, which corresponds to all actual methodologies that are related to Polymathic domains and concepts. *TRADf's* and RDP's iterative concept are recurrent and the author's main concern is that this important subject and this chapter can be considered as unconventional and not to be aligned with standardized academic or educational visions. And the reuse of TRADf, RDP, and other research concepts, which use the same approach, resources, and keywords, can be considered by some simplistic automated/robotized tools as some kind of duplication or cases of similarities… Which is not this approach's case and the extremely high rate of failures justifying the search for some other complex methods and approaches… Knowing that such transformations have very high failure rates (that practically 95%) and that the role of the Polymath profile is essential (Block, 2022; Dello Ioio, 2023). Why shouldn't researchers build their own educational innovation, vision, research/methods, transformation framework, and reuse some parts to deliver a coherent overall RTBLP concept… By just using directed standards, there isn't any creative innovation, especially in complex domains which desperately need new approaches and renewed approach to Polymathic education… To identify the Researched Literature Review (RLR) and Gap.

Research Gap

The RLR and Gap analysis are parts the author's *TRADf*. ATP's complexities and the resulting high rates of failure are due to the integration of cross-functional domains, which needs very advanced Polymathic skills. The ATP4SC recommends the usage of AHMM4TBL and ARbLP based Heuristics Decision Tree (HDT) (where the ARLP and HDT were inspired from AR, which is heavily used in education), to support DMS4TBL's operations (Trad, & Kalpić, 2014a). This work acknowledges an important knowledge gap for a critical topic, which is due to the fact that there isn't any similar: 1) Research approach; 2) High failure rates that justify the search and development of new Polymathic and innovative approaches; 2) No adequate PICC or curriculum; 3) The use of accountant's profiles as managers; and 4) There isn't any concrete profile description of the needed future transformation managers. This RDP's gap was identified because the existing educational methods/curriculums, literature on ATPs (and other transformation projects) very high failure rates, TBL/PIGW, and RTBLP similar concepts do not exist. This RDP checks RTBLP's feasibility and the role that it can play in ATP4SC. Secondary cycle curriculums; Organizational, educational, and technology standards; and is enforced with PIGW related findings. This RDP promotes a Polymathic research process, the usage of the TBL/PIGW, and cross-functional education strategies in various domains, like Economics education, Mathematics, ICS, Business Analysis/Engineering, Management, Sciences, Humanities... Where the RTBLP has an objective, to use critical-thinking based concept that combines: 1) TBL/PIGW, OTT and other online learning topics; 2) The AHMM has been defined and researched previously and the AHMM4TBL, ARbLP and HDT based decision making are adapted versions (Trad, & Kalpić, 2014a, 2020); 3) Educational patterns; 4) Educational engineering for improving used ARbLPs (Smith, 1987); 5) Provides a cross-functional concept and PICC; 7) To use EA blueprints for educational activities and to support the ATP4SC; 8) To integrate TBL/PIGW standards and online technology standards;

and 7) RTBLP's integration and success metrics, based on CSAs, CSFs, and KPIs (simply Factor).

Factors' Management

TRADf is agnostic and supports any type of transformation project and its modules, like the RTBLP based ATP4SC's concepts and modules, which selects the needed CSAs that contain sets of CSFs. A selected CSF is in turn a set of KPIs and each KPI maps to a single ATP/ATP4SC requirement that is a secondary cycle educational requirement. Each KPI maps to a concrete ICS implemented variable, so ATP4SC's evaluation gets real values. Requirement maps to a column of the ARbLP based HDT evaluation Tables (Putri, & Yusof, 2009). The ATP4SC starts with the first phase (or the feasibility phase), which checks the selected Factors (that are stored in DMS4TBL tables), to verify if ATP4SC's and hence RTBLR's objectives were reached, delivers a status value, and possible a set of next actions. Based on the RLR and the selected Factors (especially) CSFs are evaluated by applying the following rules: 1) RTBLP-related references have to be credible and are estimated by the author, DMS4TBL and have to be conform to *TRADf's* classification concept; 2) ATP's iterations are the result of evaluated Factors; 3) EA's modelling language capacities and their mappings to KPIs; 4) To estimate if the Architecture Development Method (ADM) can be used to manage the RTBLP and ATP4SC, by the use of KPIs; 5) The ADM manages *TRADf's* iterations and Factors' tuning; and 6) If the aggregations of all ATP's Factors based Tables are positive (the result is stored in Table 1) and exceed the initially defined minimum, then the ATP4SC continues to PoC's execution, which uses the selected ACSs.

The Selected ACS

Each section (like this RDP) is an ATP CSA, and the PoC is based on RTBLP focused ACSs, which are combined with a common EA based ACS that originates from the Open Group. The EA based ACS covers ATP ICS, EA, modelling, linking KPIs, and basic transformation scenarios. These ACSs were selected because they show cross-functional capabilities and TBL usages. RTBLP's CSFs are automated, tuneable and measurable by the ARbLP based HDT's Rating & Weighting Concept (RWC) that is superficially used the 1st ATP4SC's iteration and then (re)tuned by using ADM's coordination. In each of ADM's iterations, the RTBLP status and progress (or regression) is estimated by using the DMS4TBL. After each ADM's iteration, ARbLPs are enriched by the gained experiences and improved actions, which is typical for AR based education. Therefore, the selected Factors (and especially CSFs) are essential for the ATP4SC and the. selected ACSs are (Felfel et al, 2017):

- The previously mentioned basic ACSs.
- A secondary school case study that presents how to make a difference through collaboration like the TBL/PIGW, which explores cross-functional collaboration in high schools. This ACS explored how students are organized in cross-functional team in a high school project. One of the main aims was to build Polymathic knowledge concept by applying LPs. Another goal was to handle professional risk-making that is frequent in TBL/PIGW based collaborations. Thus, to privilege building a culture of values and risk-taking learning. This ACS examines also the cross-functional professional educator*'s* collaboration in high schools in order to improve Polymathic educators *working together and engaging in reflective dialogue,* with the common goal of improve ARbLP practices and offer Factors that influence cross-functional/Polymathic students' capacities. An important Factor is the impact of collaboration on topics like LP creation in Polymathic fields like ICS, which can be represented by a model of cross-functional collaboration that is shown in Figure 4 (Morse, 2020).
- *Entities* organize *flexible delivery* as a panacea for encountered project problems in education. There are various justifications for the rise to prominence in TBL/PIGW and related teaching/training environments. Which estimated that the main response to mass education and the need to integrate cross-functional student groups. The proposed RTBLP offers the possibility for an emerging educational concept for Polymathic teaching and learning. This ACS is related to *Entity*'s approach by offering TBL/PIGW based courses. The educators of TBL based courses were reskilled with communication capabilities to be able to manage such TBL/PIGW activities. The usage of TBL/PIGW was adopted and no point in this ACS have students and educators suggested that is complex (Postle, 2003).
- Polymathic (like the PICC) curriculums pose major challenges for LCSAS in *Entities*, which want to apply ATP to become capable of delivering TBL/PIGW courses for cross-functional topics. TBL/PIGW was accepted in professional organizations, like governments, high-tech segments… This ACS presents a case that explored the advantages and disadvantages of TBL/PIGW based learning; and it recommends the implementation and use of an ADM based conceptual model for TBL/PIGW (Sagheb-Tehrani, 2009).

Figure 4. Four dimensions of cross-functional/Polymathic collaboration (Morse, 2020)

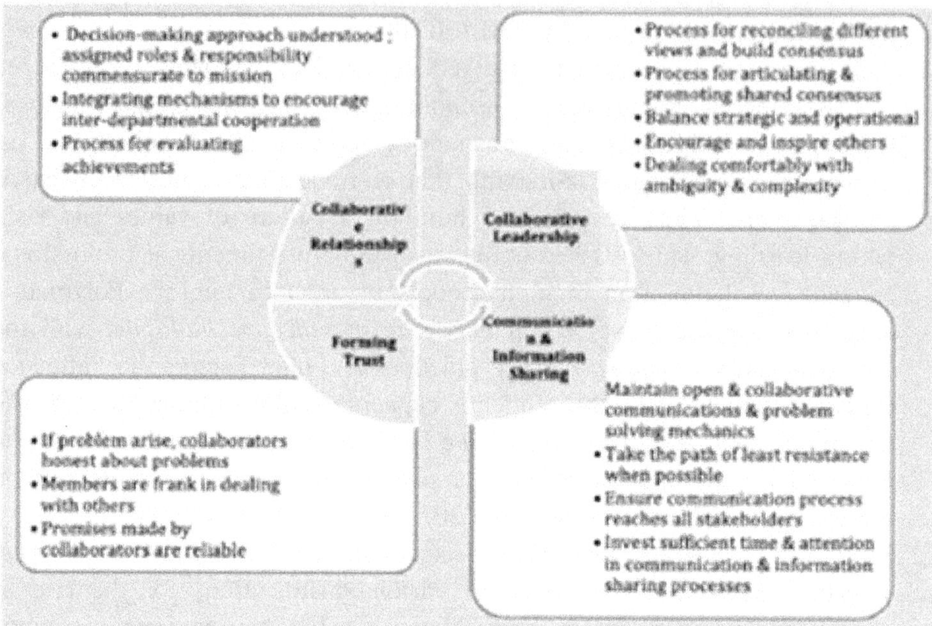

The Use of the ADM for the ATP4SC

This RDP focuses on RQ's feasibility and delivers RTBLP integration possibilities, and it shows also the influence of interactive RTBLP activities, which need the capacity to improvise. In the actual age of distributed ICS, AI hyper-evolution, ARbLP based knowledge collection, TBL/PIGW based education, and efficient infrastructure, there is a need for the ADM to coordinate the ATP4SC. ATP4SC uses can also use internal framework like the TRADf, and the HDT to solve process of RTBLP problems (Markides, 2011). The DMS4TBL offers a set of RTBLP solution types in the form of ATP4SC recommendations, sets of possible actions, and optimal PICCs.

Figure 5. ADM's phases (The Open Group, 2011a, 2011b; Holilah, Girsang, & Saragih, 2019)

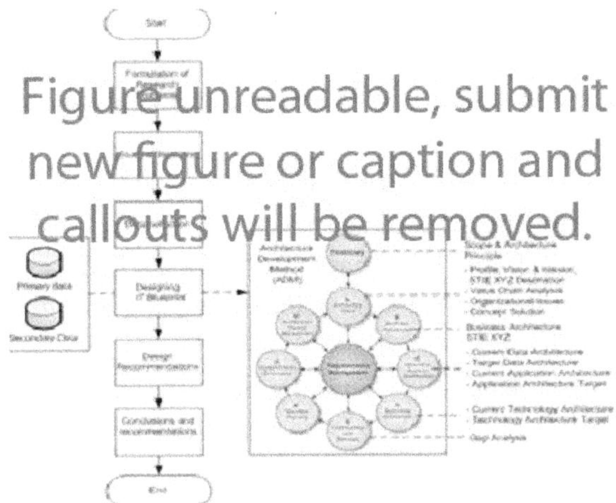

TRADf synchronizes ATP4SC with ADM activities, especially in the concept phase, as shown in Figure 5. Resultant PICCs target a Polymathic profile, who had learned and experienced much (or a universal human) individual whose cross-functional knowledge and expertise includes various domains, that are needed to support complex transformation projects and who is capable to solve their problems (Wikipedia, 2021). RTBLP activities and related profiles can be modelled by using the AHMM4TBL.

The AHMM4TBL

The adoption of a holistic, cross-functional, and Polymathic modelling approach, is supported by the AHMM4TBL, which uses a multi-level unbundling process for ATP. The RTBLP identifies and assesses strategic and critical risks in order to guaranty *Entity's* operations' coherency, by using the AHMM4TBL. For a given ATP4SC and RTBLP requirement (or problem type), the AHMM4TBL based DMS4TBL identifies the initial sets of Factors and sets of actions, to be used by the ARbLP based HDT. There is an immense lack of a Polymathic-holistic approach to ATPs and the RLR used the following resources: 1) Articles and resources related to ATPs, Education, ICS reengineering, AI, …; 2) The author's RDP/RLR works, and TRADf'; 3) ATP's feasibility concept; 4) Initial sets of Factors; and 5) RDP's use of the Empirical Engineering Research Model (EERM). Polderman and Willems (1998) argue that a Polymathic-Mathematical Model (PMM) is a subset of real world's behaviours and possibilities; and that a PMM is a description of a limited reality, which can translated to a PICC and RTBLP usage. Once a PMM is implemented, it offers a set of AHMM analysis arteficts, solutions or explanations. The PMM basics, are:

- A PMM provides abstractions of a real world of a physical system or module (Hinkelmann, 2016).
- Modelling technics are a descriptive design process, which validates PMM principles (Sankaralingam et al, 2013).
- The usage of EA, AI, and HDT can be used by an PMM.
- The gap between the PMM based ATP's adoption and its usage is still very important today (Syynimaa, 2015).
- An PMM that optimizes ATPs by using Factors (Dogan et al, 2015).
- A generic PMM, like the proposed AHMM4TBL (Giachetti, 2012; Kim & Kim, 1999).
- An applied PMM is the description of an *Entity,* ATP, and RTBLP, using mathematical concepts and languages (Sankaralingam et al, 2013).
- Multi-criteria or a multi-Factors model for DMS4TBL needs a mixed method based on qualitative and quantitative criteria, like the ARbLP (Zandia & Tavana, 2011; Kim & Kim, 1999).
- An PMM is optimal for an EERM based RDPs (Easterbrook et al, 2008).

BASIC ELEMENTS

Factors define ATP's initial nodes that are defined as vital for its success and targets to be reached. AHMM4TBL's basic element are used in DMS4TBL processing and the RTBLP uses Factors based DMS4TBL, which is TRADf's specific model. The AHMM4TBL nomenclature is presented in Figure 6:

- The symbol $\sum$ indicates summation of RWC's actions, denoting the relative importance of the set members selected as relevant. Ratings and weightings as integers ranging in ascending importance from 1 to 10.
- The symbol U̲ indicates sets union.

The AHMM4TBL defines the ATP and RTBLP as models, using Factors and RWC.

Figure 6. The applied mathematical model's nomenclature (Trad, & Kalpić, 2020)

Basic Mathematical Model's (BMM) Nomenclature

Iteration	= An integer variable "*i*" that denotes a *Project/ADM iteration*	
microRequirement	= (maps to) KPI	(B1)
CSF	= Σ KPI	(B2)
Requirement	= (maps to) CSF = ⋃ microRequirement	(B3)
CSA	= Σ CSF	(B4)
microMapping microArtifact/Req	= microArtifact + (maps to) microRequirement	(B5)
microKnowledgeArtifact	= ⋃ knowledgeItem(s)	(B6)
neuron	= action->data + microKnowledgeArtifact	(B7)
microArtifact / neural network	= ⋃ neurons	(B8)
microArtifactScenario	= ⋃ microartifact	(B9)
AI/Decision Making	= ⋃ microArtifactScenario	(B10)
microEntity	= ⋃ microArtifact	(B11)
Entity or Enterprise	= ⋃ microEntity	(B12)
EnityIntelligence	= ⋃ AI/Decision Making	(B13)
BMM(*Iteration*) as an instance	= EnityIntelligence(*Iteration*)	(B14)

The Generic AHMM's Formulation

AHMM	= ⋃ ADMs + BMMs	(B15)

AHMM's Application and Instantiation for GA (Implementation Case: LDWPIII)

Domain	= ATP4SC	(B16)
AHMM4(*Domain*)	= ⋃ ADMs + BMMs(*Domain*)	(B17)

The RWC

There various ways on how an ATP generic RWC can be built. An *Entity* can use a standard RWC or like in the case of TRADf, it can build its own one. TRADf's RWC proposes the following rules:

- The selected corresponding weightings to CSF ϵ { 1 … 10 } are integer values.
- The selected corresponding ratings to CSF ϵ { 0.00% … 100.00% } are floating point percentage values.

- A weighting is defined for each RTBLP CSF, and a rating for each KPI.
- The AHMM4TBL applied a research mixed model, which uses a RWC.

The RWC can use standard solutions like:

- The Object Management Group's (OMG) Decision Model and Notation (DMN), where the DMN can be applied the specification of business decisions and business rules. DMN is optimal for ATP's initial checking based on decision making (OMG, 2022). The DMN can be also used for Tables' processing and HDT operations.
- The weighted criteria matrix is a decision-making module that evaluates projects based on defined evaluation criteria weighted by ratings. By evaluating alternatives based on KPIs with respect to individual criteria (Ouye).

The AHMM4TBL applies the HDT which is mainly a qualitative concept which uses specific quantitative method.

A QUANTITATIVE-QUALITATIVE, MIXED METHODS APPROACH

For a selected RTBLP problem, RQ, or Factor the HDT solves by relating breadth and depth tree operations an enriches ARbLPs. The initial set of ATP and PICC problems and their selected Factors are initialized in ATP's preliminary phase or initial iteration. Then, *TRADf's* HDT inputs data sets, which consist(s) of sets of raw data, constraints, and rules, that are stored in ATP' central database. Using only quantitative analysis, is limited and there is the need for a qualitative method. There is also a need to evaluate the activities and behaviour of students, to proactively detect violations to the defined constraints. ARbLP is suitable for academic educator… Because AR is helpful in education and can be defined as the process of TBL/PIGW based learning and improves the quality of educational processes. AR provides the educator with valuable knowledge and tutoring technics on how to improve educational practices and resolve ATP/RTBLP problems. AR uses a systematic process and offers solutions for the educator. Solutions can include: 1) Facilitating *Educator's* professional development; 2) Increasing educator's empowerment; and 3) Bridging the gap between theory, recommendations, and practice (Hine, 2013). ARbLP collected knowledge are used to support ATP's applied transformation model.

THE APPLIED APPLICATION AND TRANSFORMATION MODEL

The AHMM4TBL is composed of: 1) A static view; 2) A dynamic (or behavioural) view; and 3) A pool of reusable ARbLP based scenarios. The AHMM4TBL can be modelled using following formula for Educational Transformation Mathematical Model (*ETMM*) that abstracts the ATP:

AHMM4TBL=Weigthing_1*AHMM4TBL_Qualitative+Weigthing_2*AHMM4TBL_Quantitative (B18).

AHMM4TBL = $\sum$ AHMM4TBL for an ATP iteration (B19).

ETMM = $\sum$ AHMM4TBL instances (B20).

Weigthing_1 and Weigthing_2 are delivered by the RWC. *ETMM's* objective function optimization is done by using constraints and extra variables that need to be tuned. These variable (for maximization or minimization) can be, for example: Students Polymathic capacities, STEM grades, age, costs, or another Factor. For RTBLP's PoC the success will be the main and only constraint and success is quantified as a binary 0 or 1, where the objective function minimizes *ETMM's* risks and identifies RTBLP's efficiency. The *ETMM* is a combination of used methodologies and AHMM4TBL. The AHMM4TBL is a part and the skeleton of *TRADf* that used scenarios to support RTBLP requests (Kim & Lennon, 2017). The initialization phase generates RTBLP problem types and cross-functional aspects to be analysed, which is the second CSA (Agievich, 2014).

CROSS-FUNCTIONAL AND POLYMATHIC ASPECTS

For today's professions it is clear that all educational cycles need to adopt cross-functionally oriented educational practices, especially for secondary education. There are various manners how to structure, design, develop and implement effective cross-functional educational/academic programs, and PICCs. Various concrete cases' analysis show the lack and importance of the development of cross-functional and Polymathic concepts (like the RTBLP) that are needed for the development and implementation of cross-functional PICCs and adequate students projects that need continuous ARbLP based improvements (Crittenden, 2005).

Continuous Improvements

The ATP presents the implications of continuous RTBLP based improvements and quality enhancements. Which have impact on PICC's topics and their applications in secondary schools. Various PICC's topics are analysed, like: 1) The concept of evolutive quality; 2) Enhancements' philosophy; 3) Cross-functional project teams; 4) Reference projects (like the Baldrige educational pilot project, the Muhlenburg College project…; 5) Elementary and secondary school bridging and transformations; 5) School's governance, reorientation, and renewal; 6) Vocational school transformation and renewal; 6) College and university PICCs' transformation; 7) Linking ATP4SC to improve quality in *Entities*. RTBLP's implications in education are derived from various sources related to ATP experiences, technological evolutions, societal changes, literature, professional experiences, and existing recommendations which certify the importance of cross-functional and polymathic teams (Satterlee, 1996).

Cross-Functional and Polymathics Teams

Various research initiatives on the evolution of education, indicate that cross-functional and Polymathic teams are crucial in actual professional environments and students' have to be prepared for that. Parker (1994) has developed recommendations and guidelines for future complex projects' managers to coordinate professional teams, and who are will be responsible for their development and for the integration of cross-functional/Polymathic teams, by (Satterlee, 1996):

- Insisting on defining clear project team goals and implementing plans for achieving these goals.
- Working efficiently to gain the commitment of team members and *Educator* to achieve team goals.
- Emphasize collaborative work-efforts and shared team results.
- Provide just-in-time training that promotes working with diverse student groups.
- Create ARbLP scenarios, policies and procedures that support a team-based environment.
- Noticing that cross-functional teams have the tendency to quickly finish tasks because they apply parallel development rather than serial development.
- Manage complexity, so cross-functional teams improve project's capacity to solve complex problems because such problems transcend traditional siloed disciplines and functions.
- Prepare project teams to focus on the defined requirements.

- Prepare project teams to increase creative capacities by integrating students with different profiles, backgrounds, orientations, cultural values, and styles.
- Apply ARbLP based learning so students learn about other disciplines and develop new skills.
- Applying single point of contact to promote effective teamwork (Parker 1994).
- Promoting leadership that needs a technical background to understand various subjects and to recognize contributions of students from various backgrounds.
- Applying empowerment and authority to promote decision-making skills.
- Concentrate on shared goals that are clearly described are based on defined problem.
- Managing boundaries team's *borders*.
- Using performance appraisal systems verify and encourage students.
- Rewarding by recognition to recognize outstanding students.
- Selects the right sets of Factors.

Factors and TBL Integration

The RTBLP uses Factors like in TBL/PIGW based collaborations, PICC's development and other. These Factors are identified ATP4SC's initial phases and then tuned later (Thune, 2011). The Factors relate to: 1) Used resources, TBL/PIGW fields, ATP features, and used interactive products. To support the TBL/PIGW, agile aspects, practices, and internal resources are needed to support students' activities related to frequent requests and changes. Implementing various types of RTBLP functionalities, like educational patterns and PICC's building, which support educational scenarios, and problems solving. The implementation of RTBLP needs a distributed ICS and a Scaled Agile Framework (SAFe), which can support the TBL/PIGW based intensive Communication (TBLC) (Scaled Agile, 2022).

Using the TBLC

The RTBLP recommends to transform the LCSAS' knowledge and actual LP database, and to integrate a transformed ICS that supports concurrent ARbLP knowledge management. The RTBLP is managed by SAFe, which includes the needed competencies to incorporate the TBL/PIGW based Educational Agility (TEA) that (Kersten, 2021):

- Enables the *Entity* to deliver innovative TBL/PIGW based educational resources.
- Offers agility and enables educators to support quality educational sites.

- The *Educator* uses agile TBL/PIGW practices, as shown in Figure 7.
- The *Educator* show TEA leadership skills.
- The *Educator* has the needed qualities and educational experiences in various fields.
- The ARbLPs is used to store Return on Experience (ROE).

Figure 7. The relation between the educator, students, and program (Kersten, 2021)

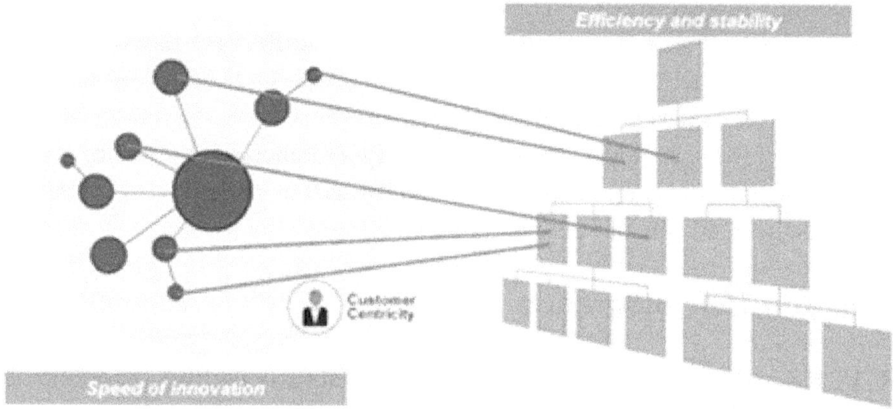

Needed Roe

An *Entity* must build its internal ARbLP, ATP4SC, and ROE concepts, to manage RTBLP's complex problems and the main difficulty lies in the duration of the ATP/ ATP4SC which can take long period to be finalized. ROEs are used to enhance ARbLPs and PICCs. A PICC shows how TBL/PIGW based educational services are related, and these PICCs are modelled using templates which can be enhanced. To apply PICCs efficiently, the following ATP/ATP4SC activities are needed: 1) A system to manage ROEs; 2) EA to support for TBL/PIGW based learning: 3) Virtual environment integration and asynchronous agile interaction; 4) Enabling implementation support: 3) Discovering new capacities from ROEs; 4) Sharing experiences and feedbacks (like Students' reactions); 5) Ethical principles, ... (Hayashi et al, 2022). The developed PICCs support the RTBLP profiles building. ROEs tracing, and defines the Polymathic Students' Collaboration Concept (PSCC).

The PSCC

In educational fields like Science, Technology/ICS, Engineering and Mathematics (STEM), or other topics, educators need to integrate challenge/team-based interaction projects to enforce learning and to prepare students for future transformational and innovation-oriented professions. That all depends on the students' ability to work in PSCCs and that is probably intrinsic to their original capacities. Actions of student groups are classified/categorized as PSCC types, like: Managing, Modelling, Planning, Coordination, Input/Deletion/Updates actions, ... Sequences of PSCC actions are persisted to be used by various groups using the PSCC and are stored in ARbLPs. Such ARbLPs support educators to constitute teams and offer needed support to teamwork; and enhances the used ARbLPs. For Polymathic capable students, PSCC is more adapted than LCSASs, because their Polymathic capacities can progress. But there are different perceptions of PSCC based work and the needed skills between STEM and business students; therefore, there is the need for specialized support and PICC. STEM, and ICS education face challenges because students might not see the importance of such skills for their future professions that is why there is a need to use PSCC. The benefits of PSCC based projects, is that they shows the difficulties in complex inter-related topics, like design and implementation tasks. The PSCC can slow down the diffusion of team-based educational activities, but the adoption of RTBLP can improve this fact. PSCC based teams are structured to complete concrete project goals, in the context of collaborative assignments. Such projects use PSCC in which highly frequent communication between all students is needed and where they can modify their problem-solving method. Interactive PSCC contains: ARbLPs, Context data, Working data, and Support data. Challenge-based education enables problem-solving and is self-regulated by the PSCC, where educators participate as project managers. Educators can use ARbLPs to improve teaching concepts (Pisonia, Gijlersc, Nguyend, & Chene, 2021). The ATP4SC and PSCC needs interconnect TBL/PIGW and LCSAS complex cohabitation, and that can cause resistances from the *Educator* and students. One possible reason for such resistances can be the newly used technology block.

ENTITY'S TECHNOLOGY BLOCKS

Usage of Enterprise Modeling Environments: The ADM

Modelling environments like TOGAF/ADM, Unified Modelling Language (UML), or other, are generic modelling methods/languages that have defined phases, artefICTs, and give the possibility to use iterative project cycles which can be included in the

PICC. Modelling can show the possibilities of designing the future system and its interfaces, and the RTBLP must be capable of defining the set of PICC's modelling requirements and students' usage of the TBL/PIGW with ADM. The ADM manages project's transformation, development, and maintenance processes, which includes also the following phases: The preliminary phase introduces the RTBLP; The architecture vision and domain/educational architecture; ICS' and TBL/PIGW's architectures; Innovative technologies' integration; and ATP4SC's and PICC's requirements management. For the RTBLP, modelling topics like ADM's integration in the PICC is important.

ARCHITECTURE AND MODELING

In general, Economics depend on the roles of EA and ICS, even is some APD specialists consider that EA and ICS are not crucial domains. The EA framework delivers dynamic Economical models and ICS serves as the glue between the institution's components (Zachman, 2015). The ATP4SC uses various types of market frameworks (like TOAGF and SAFe), which show how to apply frameworks and academic standards in PICCs, in order to deliver added educational values to the transformed *Entity*. In order to deliver a meaningful PICC, there is need of add STEM, ICS and other complex topics, and the way they are applied and synchronized. The RTBLP based PICC must be capable of aligning: 1) Building and modelling visions; 2) Applying modelling principles; 3) Iterative transformational activities; 4) Standards' management; 5) PICCs' usage in TBL/PIGW based education and to synchronize PSCC activities; 6) It also enables students to communicate with external teams and partners; and 7) To build and use complex DMSs like the DMS4TBL/KMS4TBL.

The DMS4TBL/KMS4TBL

RTBLP is supported by internal an DMS4TBL/KMS4TBL (simply *Intelligence*) that is based on the ARbLPs and ROEs. *Intelligence* delivers just-in-time possible solutions for pre-defined types of ATP/ATP4SC (or any other type) problems. Possible solution(s) propose recommendations on transformational changes' implications, which minimize related risks. *Intelligence* uses the HDT to solve problems and enhances persisted ARbLPs. RTBLP's integration risks' management is an important pre-requisite to finalize the ATP4SC (Hussain, Dillon, Chang & Hussain, 2010). Therefore, the first step is to transform the LCSAS' KMS and adopt ARbLP concepts. ARbLPs manage Knowledge Items (TbKI), where TbKIs and linked resources are linked to ROEs, gained intelligence, … The KMS4TBL supports the

Entity's underlying mechanics to manage ARbLPs and linked TbKIs. The ATP4SC interfaces the KMS4TBL and its stored TbKIs, which are also linked to Factors. The DMS4TBL/KMS4TBL supports ATP4SC's enhancements. The RTBLP interfaces the DMS4TBL/KMS4TBL to offer TBL/PIGWs based PICCs templates.

TBL/PIGW-Based PICCs

Students need TBL/PIGW skills which are included in PICCs and curricula, in order to support them in complex projects. TBL/PIGW activities can cause problems, due to intensive interactions, like unstable ICS environments or the lack of support. PICCs are applied in interdisciplinary student projects. Therefore, students must find solutions and strategies for solving encountered problems. TBL/PIGW based PICCs contain indications on how students develop problem-solving strategies, actions/ topics to be managed, group interaction/management… PICCs is an important part in Polymathic education which includes TBLC/teamwork, communication, time management, and problem-solving skills. Polymathic skills are included in curricula of students, like TBLC based projects, for various ranges of student groups. Reports on what makes student projects manageable and successful include Factors like, essential educator's guidance and students' Polymathic capabilities. Educators guidance needs skills, so they can support Polymathic student groups; and their role is to support students to become autonomous. That is mainly achieved by using PICCs and PSCC for collaboration scenarios, and the acceptance of TBL/ PIGW. PICCs promote empiric experience acquired from other student groups or the ARbLP based KMS4TBL; which delivers tacit and relevant project knowledge and elaborated practices. The KMS4TBL offers patterns to support TBL/PIGW encountered problems, like: Insufficient Polymathic capacities; Bad communication/ coordination, and Lack of motivation. PICCs include also topics related to design of ARbLP patterns that originated from ROEs. There are various types of patterns in education, like the important *Pedagogical Patterns Project,* a substantial collection of patterns related to Polymathic education. PICCs focus on students' perspective in learning and the use of patterns, and problems' solving. PICCs are based on ROEs from other projects. A PICC can include a set of Polymathic topics, possible professional practices, and generic fields. It can also include actions like: 1) Modelling concepts; 2) Clearing questions; 2) Sharing experiences and explications; 3) Defining clear list of project-tasks; 4) The of ARbLP based KMS4TBLC to support knowledge management; 5) Centralize PM statuses and to follow project's evolution; 6) Mediate and solve conflicts; 7) To keep a high level of motivation; 8) To be efficient and fulfil requirements; and 9) To implement tasks. The used ACSs refer to an external interdisciplinary/Polymathic student project, done at Radboud University Nijmegen. This project used ICS and AI curricula; there were nine groups of students. And each group had different ICS and AI project. Project's EA models and requirements were developed by other student groups from other courses; and the resulting solutions were offered to external real-companies. TBL/PIGW collaboration and achieving project's goals was the main strategic educational goal. At the start PICCs were presented to the students and templates were provided to finalize project tasks. The students were continuously informed that TBL/PIGW was a strategic educational goal and the educator referred to PICCs to drive the supervise and monitor.

Supervision and Monitoring

EA based ATP4SC supports the integration of the hyper-evolution of ICS/ technologies, and tries to detect ICS based Crimes, Cheating, and Irregularities (ICSbCI). ICSbCI affect all educational cycles; but parents' busyness complicates detection processes. Therefore, students must be monitored by a dedicated system. A Students Supervision and Monitoring System (SSMS), as shown in Figure 8, supports supervising students in schools. In Figure 8, some foreign use cases names are used and cannot be translate. The SSMS traces activities and transactions that students that includes activities like teaching and learning… EA improves ICSbCI detections supports a strategy for improving the SMMS, which can be also accessed by parents or educators (Prastiwi et al, 2018). SMSS and other ATP4SC modules need *empirical milestones* to support RTBLP's main blocks.

Figure 8. An EA based SMSS blueprint (Prastiwi, Widagdo, & Kamisutara, 2018)

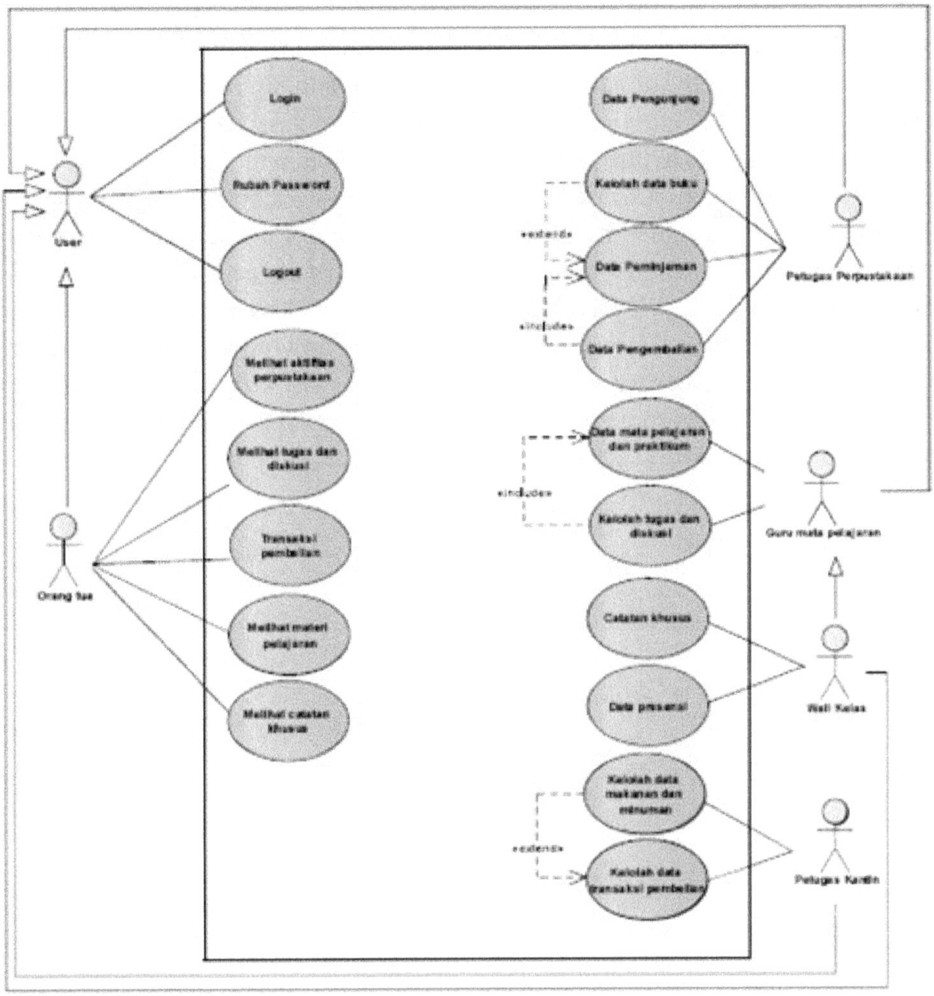

THE RTBLP'S MAIN BLOCKS

TBLC'S Granularity

For LCSAS and TBL/PIGW based classes, a small students-group concept is optimal, which can also generate major issues resulting from groups' granularity; therefore, there is need to find the optimal size. Granularity depends on the original size of the class, the available period, the physical features of the classroom/infrastructure, and the type of TBL/PIGW based team's task. Possible granularity schemes for small teams are (Burke, 2022): 1) Buzz groups, which can have any class size and its main purpose is to generate ideas … 2) *Think-pair-share* which can have any class size, and its main purpose is to generate ideas, increase students' confidence… 3) *Circle of Voices* which can have any class size and its main purpose is to generate structure ideas… 4) *Rotating trios* which can have a class size of 15-30 students and its main purpose is to introduce students to other team members… 5) *Snowball groups/pyramids* which can have a class size of 12-50 students and its main purpose is to generate well-designed models/concepts… 6) *Jigsaw* which can have a class size of 10-50 students and its main purpose is to learn concepts in-depth, develop TBL/PIGW teamwork… 7) *Fishbowl* which ca have a class size of 10-50 students and its main purpose is to observe group interactions, provide real world concepts… 8) *Virtual learning teams* which can have a class has any size, any time frame and its main purpose is to enforce relationships between students, and to increase their confidence. Student TBLC activities need multimedia support.

Multimedia Support for TBLC AND Creativity

Figure 9. OTT-based education (FastEdge, 2023)

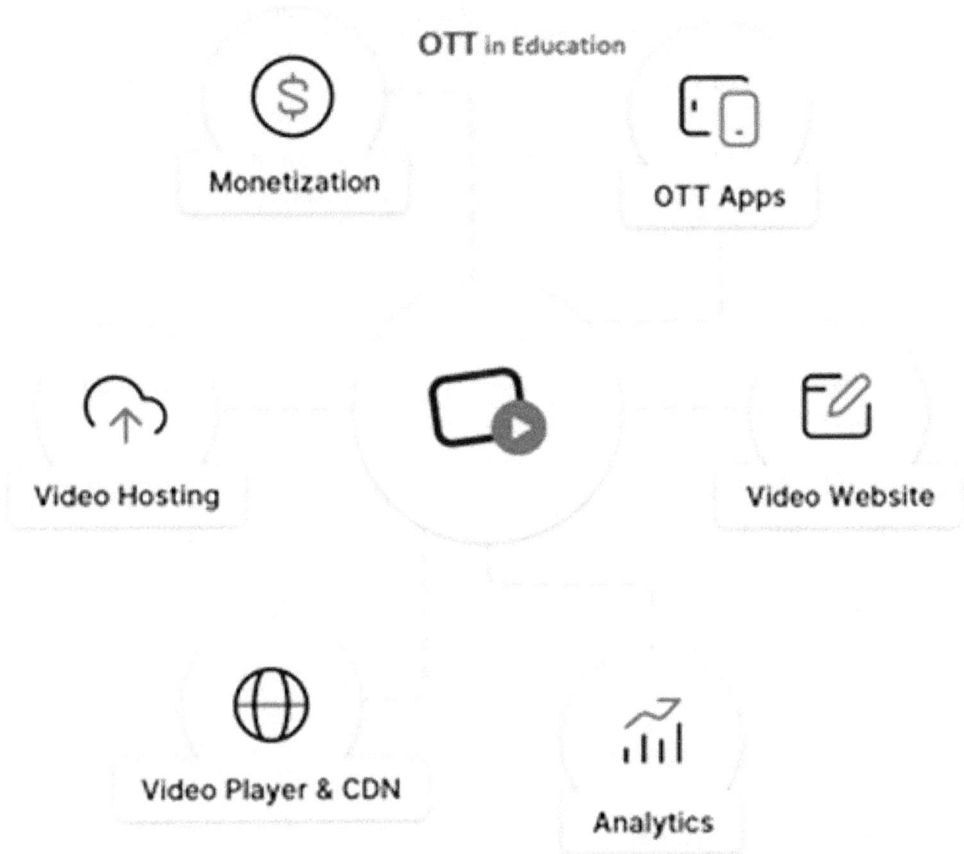

Educational OTT supports classroom experiences, as shown in Figure 9, in which students use video lectures and interact with other students-groups by using TBLC's interaction environments. Digital Transformations (DT) has transformed education and OTT demands have spread beyond entertainment. Educational OTT is very spread today and is used in education, where it provides (FastEdge, 2023; Pappas, 2022):

- Live video instruction from educators and it can be replayed by students to learn independently.
- Is crucial for DT in the education sector and gives students to remotely be in a classroom, and to interactively use quizzes, webinars, exams, and more.

- Students receive just-in-time feedbacks and are supported by the educators and other students
- Support for coursework that includes video lectures, readings, quizzes, and assignments.
- Quality education for students worldwide, much cheaper than LCSAS. It can be tailored to student's requirements, especially in Polymathic fields.
- Students can learn at their capacities and enables them to complete a course ahead of schedule.
- Interactive modules, discussion boards, offer just-in-time support.
- ROEs enhancements of ARbLP and quick evaluations.
- Cloud or distributed e-Learning platforms.

OTT has offers DT capacities for video-enhanced TBL/PIGW based education and for research activities. The ATP can use an OTT platform and OTT based TBL/PIGW Patterns (OTPs) to establish video-based practices. OTPs support interaction using collaboration technologies (Botturi, & Belfer, 2014). OTP practices are influenced by contributions involving close analyses of video and audio-recordings from (Pea, & Lindgren, 2008): 1) Interaction analysis; 2) Sociolinguistic studies of classroom discourse; 3) Anthropological and ethnographic inquiries of learning in formal and informal settings; 4) Studies of socially significant nonverbal behaviors such as *body language*; and other. Modelling and design creativity are crucial Factors and competencies for the RTBLP. Creativity is the basis of Polymathic human intelligence and is a significant Factor in design of ARbLP based problem-solving, innovation initiatives and it is related to educational performances. OTPs support creativity that is associated with designing concepts and is considered a valuable characteristic in STEM education. There is a need for creative business analysts, engineers and scientists, therefore creativity has to be inserted in the PICC and curriculum. Cognitive supports students in creative undertakings, especially in design activities, which is one of the top five competencies needed for professional industrial design. OTP promotes virtual student groups and provides: 1) Access to more information; 2) Stimulate creativity; 3) Project's interactive communication; 4) Better performance; 5) Enforcement of generic and specialized skills. Companies are seeking engineers with advanced Polymathic designing creativity skills (Han et al, 2021).

Design Creativity in Secondary Education

Creativity in design, or design creativity, is a significant PICC topic and is essential part of the conceptual design students' activities. TBLC is a common virtual teaching strategy in education, and it is asserted that students need TBL experience prior to their future undergraduate or professional activities. The main benefits include that it fosters students' abilities and skills in modelling, DMS4TBL, interactive management, interpersonal dynamics, critical reflection, self-study, and social interactions. Students perform better in TBL and use resources effectively. TBL based design education, supports students in experiencing and understanding collaborative analysis design processes, which needs virtual design practice. Virtual design activities need TBL to solve complex design topics and problems. Design creativity has a significant role in practical design and can applicable in all phases of the TBL based design process, including the central detailed design phase. Individual students in economics can be more creative and perform better in TBL especially in interactive brainstorming activities, because of the following facts (Chapman, 2015; Khatkhate, 2009; Inayati et al, 2010):

- TBL based learning gives advantages in modern economics studies and is extremely efficient.
- TBL based techniques of learning or digesting new concepts and ideas, to integrate them with traditional methods.
- Enables an enthusiastic approach that is socially useful.
- TBL based economics studies enhance students' potentials, self-management, personality, intelligence…
- The characteristics of economics topics can cause learning difficulties for students, like in the case of the High School in the City of Malang. Malang that was the subject of research and resulted in: 1) There various categories of difficulties in studying economic subjects; and 2) The manners how solutions were handled.
- Educators have an important role to resolve problems related to learning difficulties; and results from related research (from state senior high schools in the City of Malang) proved the lack of problem-solving capacities.
- Complex problems' solving need: 1) Collecting resources from compulsory economics textbook(s) and electronic books; 2) Interacting with educator(s) regarding the ongoing course and/or project; like in the case of School's Exercise Book, that enhances the comprehension of economics materials' basic concepts.

Virtual creativity development environments can used in modelling and design classes that can involve the following activities like: Brainstorming, Mind mapping, Strength, Weakness, Opportunity and Threat (SWOT), UML, … UML is especially interesting because of its maturity and creativity development environments can used for mass collaboration and education, but they need a special curriculum (Ahmad, 2020; Cress et al, 2016).

CROSS-FUNCTIONAL/POLYMATHIC CURRICULUM

Generic Skills (GS) in education can be done by using Factors, because the importance of GSs has been highlighted both in educational policies and the professional domains, as shown in Figure 10. GSs, like critical thinking, collaboration, communication, modelling, argumentation, and problem-solving skills, are known as cognitive skills is twenty-first century competence and future citizens' literacy. Education for GSs is important for its cycles. But GS courses design demand more resources and its evolution must be monitored (Tuononen, Hyytinen, Kleemola, Hailikari, Männikkö, & Toom, 2022). The complex issue is PICC's implementation for GS, because of problems like: 1) Curriculum overload; 2) Lack of time and resources; and 3) Complicated implementation of cross-functional topics. Various studies have confirmed such problems and show various types of implementation problems. These problems occur in schools' specific context and it looks like that vertical and horizontal continuity in the different stages can create problem. The role of one or more educators can be also a source of problems in Project Oriented Learning (Page, Schagen, Fallus, Bron, De Coninck, Maes, Sleurs, & Van Woensel, 2005).

Figure 10. GS's needed skills (Tuononen et al, 2022)

Main category of generic skills (f)	Subcategories (f)
Professional skills (93)	Professionalism (32), leadership (24), managerial (16), entrepreneurial skills (11), information management (6), project skills (4)
Analytical skills (66)	Critical thinking (23), analytical thinking (20), creative thinking/innovation (18), systems thinking (5)
Applying knowledge (59)	Problem-solving (34), decision making (16), applying theory to practice (9)
Communication skills (59)	Communication (43), writing skills (16)
Collaboration skills (51)	Collaboration skills, teamwork (51)
Time-management skills (29)	Time-management, planning (29)
Study skills (29)	Lifelong learning (10), information searching (8), study skills (5), ability to understand theories (4), knowledge building (2)
Self-knowledge (25)	Self-knowledge including confidence, self-regulation skills, ability to manage emotions and stress, reflection; knowing what study methods are suitable for me; sense of worth and world view; self-criticism (25)
Information technology skills (23)	ICT, computer skills and social media skills (23)
Ethics and responsibility (18)	Research ethics including work ethics, professional moral quality, social responsibility, treat customers data confidentially (18)
Globalization (17)	Globalization, community and citizenship (13), multidisciplinary (4)
Research skills (15)	Research skills, analyze and use numbers and data accurately (15)
Adaptability (10)	Adaptability including adapting to new situations; ability to understand and adapt environment, ability to make changes, flexibility (10)
Personal attributes (10)	Dedication, right personality, perseverance, frankness, open-mindedness, curiosity, resilience, persistence (10)
Foreign language skills (10)	Foreign language (10)
Career skills (5)	Career skills including career planning CV; job applications, interviews, grant applications (5)
Feedback (2)	Utilizing and providing feedback (2)

Integrating POLs

A high-schools educators' collaboration's PICCs include POLs, an they use joint work that is defined as *experiences among educators which are based on shared responsibility for the work of teaching*. POLs promote the concept of the norm of non-interference around RTBLP practices. In TBL/PIGW educators use difficult tasks and questions about Polymathic practices, suggest optimal practices, and challenge POL's termination (Fitzgerald, 2005). POLs emphasise student-centred learning and use real-world problems with needed methods to solve them. Educators are facilitators and students are required to manage their work, POL plans, and collaborate with others. POLs allow students to turn their critical faculties on modelling and implementing tasks. They need skills to: Split a project into *big tasks* and *small tasks*; and to write a report on project's status. POLs enable students to: 1) Integrate skills, by applying knowledge, speculative thinking, and communication; 2) Become autonomous; 3) Express their capabilities; 4) Identify progress; and 5) Apply ARbLPs. POL is a structured development process where educators manage tasks that provide experiences on problem-solving and promoting cognitive shift with regard to students' understanding. POL needs a strategy to reduce unpredictability, by designating specific problems and assignments to students. POL contains the following activities: Researching; Investigating; Specifying; Developing; Optimizations; Planning; Making; and Evaluating (Banks, & Barlex, 2021). RTBLP backed POLs require a specific PICCs, where the *Educator* needs to have the TBL/PIGW and TEA skills, and to establish dynamic PICC based plans. Redesigning secondary education PICCs to include necessary skillsets. It take a generic approach for POLs and students submit their projects before course's end. A critical topic of POLs is thoughtful evaluation, synthesizing, integrating ROEs, and capabilities. There is a gap between the needed skills in business and technical management in modern enterprises. Students choose a real-world project strongly related to Dynamic PICC (Chhatwal, 2023).

The Dynamic PICC

Figure 11. A case of polymathic knowledge and competency curriculum/project (Banks & Barlex, 2021)

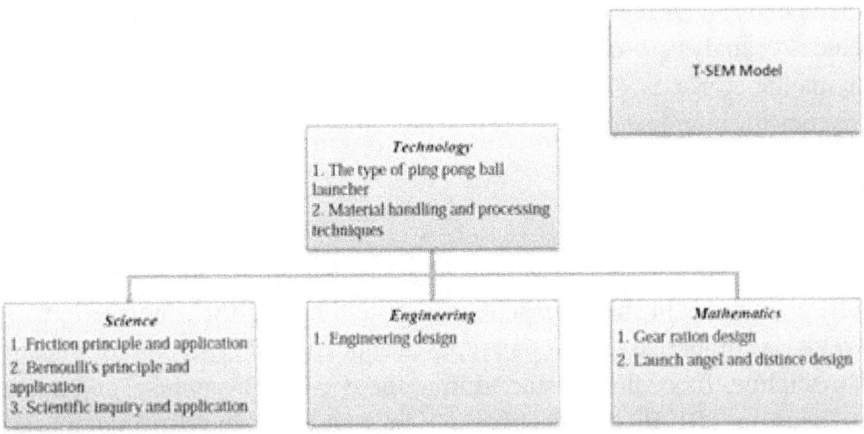

A dynamic PICC can be personalized in cases of exceptional Polymathic cases and it should (UdG, 2023; Banks, & Barlex, 2021; Koppe, van Eekeleny, & Hoppenbrouwersz, 2015):

- Facilitate interrelation between secondary and undergraduate (like polytechnic) educational cycles.
- Strengthen, widen, and improve *Entity's* links with higher education systems, particularly disseminating the research and technological/ICS development to promote vocations in cross-functional fields as well as disseminating advances made in these areas.
- To include STEM and helping educators meet the challenges and use adapted pedagogy.
- Define ways in which Polymathics can interact with the PICC to enhance understanding, and motivation.
- Include real-world projects and provide students with the right support.
- POLs need lets students create portfolios of interests; and include: Language and literature; Maths; Sciences/physics; Geography and/or history; Math; ICS, EA/Modelling; Business analysis; and PM.
- Include 'critical thinking and problem-solving cases.

- POLs permit students to: 1) Choose an authentic 'real-life' project; 2) To take responsibility for conducting their work; 3) Estimate outcomes; and 4) Be aware of skills, and concepts.
- Educators must have the skills to manage POLs.
- Include under 'specified curriculum' the content as found in official documents; and students' acceptance of authority
- Include under 'enacted curriculum' contains what educators teach.
- Includes analysis of natural and technological systems using Polymathic-concepts;
- Didactics for interdisciplinary critical deductive thinking.

Directed Didactics

TBL/PIGW based education as a subdiscipline of pedagogy, addresses the large impact of Polymathics in the enterprise eco-system through its intersection with various fields. In comparison with other types of education, RTBLP based education is a new discipline. Its evolution started in at the end of 20th century, and needed didactics focus on TBL/PIGW teaching and on POL; and such an integration is presented PoC (Koppe, van Eekeleny, & Hoppenbrouwersz, 2015).

THE PROOF OF CONCEPT

This PoC assumes that the selected ACSs have LCSASs, based on traditional educational systems, various types of archaic education services, end students' service department. PoC's objective is to show that the RTBLP and TBL/PIGW can support PICCs and that an *Entity* can implement its framework.

TBL/PIGW-Based Scenarios

Figure 12. Transformation goals (Jonkers, Band, & Quartel, 2012)

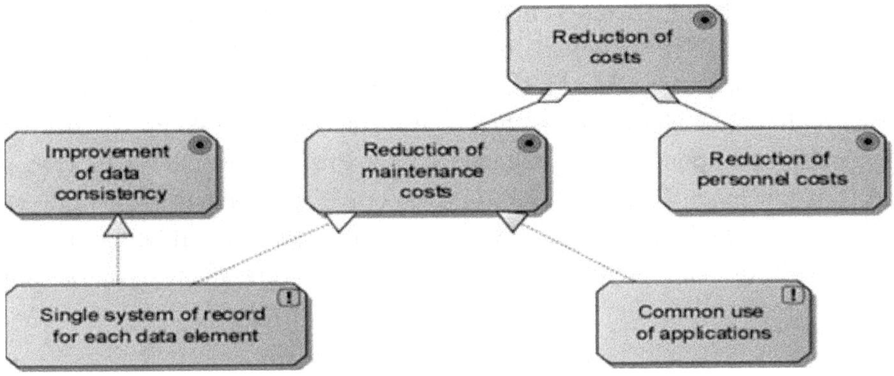

The ATP4SC manages the selected Factors and the used ACSs use a common EA based concept as shown in Figure 13, which tunes the Factors. RTBLP's actions in ADM phases, are: 1) Phase A: To setup TBL/PIGW services' roadmap; 2) Phase B: To setup RTBLP's target architecture; 3) Phase C: To model TBL/PIGW's application landscape; 4) Phase D: Manage the gap analysis and design the infrastructure; and 5) Phases E/F: Verifies RTBLP's implementation and evaluate ATP4SC's status.

PoC's Execution

The RTBLP interfaces the DMS4TBL and its Factors which are presented and evaluated in Figure 13.

Figure 13. The RTBLP RDP's outcome is 8.25

CSA Category of CSFs/KPIs	Transformation Capability	Average Result	Table
The RDP's Integration	Usable-Mature	From 1 to 10: 9.25	1
RTBLP's Feature and Skills	Transformable-Possible-Complex	From 1 to 10: 8.20	2
Cross-functional and Polymathic Aspect	Rare-VeryComplex	From 1 to 10: 7.20	5
Technology Blocks' Integration	Transformable-Possible-Mature	From 1 to 10: 9.40	4
RTBLP'S Main Blocks	Heterogenous-VeryComplex	From 1 to 10: 7.20	5

Evaluate First Phase

The RTBLP-required skills have mappings to ATP4SC's resources and the RTBLP defines relationships between the TBL/PIGW and PICCs. The PoC was implemented using *TRADf* and the initial activity was to setup Factors, then the HDT's automated interface was launched to implement the needed programs to process the Factors/CSAs. After initializing *TRADf's* client, Factors/CSFs were linked to a specific node of the ARbLP/HDT. The programs linked the AHMM4TBL instance to the set of HDT actions which uses DMS4TBL actions. Table 1 presented results concludes PoC's first phase, which shows that the RTBLP can be used in ATPs. RTBLP is not an independent component and is bonded to all the *Project's* overall PICC, TEA, and TBL/PIGW concepts. *TRADf* and its AHMM4TBL's main constraint to implement the RTBLP is that CSAs having an average result below 8.0 will be ignored. This work's conclusion with the result of 8.25 implies that RTBLP's integration is very complex and due to the interpretation of Polymathic profiles.

CONCLUSION AND RECOMMENDATIONS

The complexity is due to siloed concepts and *Educator*'s lack of RTBLP related knowledge. This RDP proposes a set of recommendations on how to used ATP4SCs where the TBL/PIGW supports a teamwork. The usage of the RTBLP uses the ICS/OTT to offer TBL/PIGW services. The most important recommendation that was generated by the previous research phases was that the business transformation manager must be a Polymathic BTPAP, which can describe an educator. The recommendations for the RTBLP are based on the processing of Factors to assert its capabilities, coordination, and effectiveness. RTBLP characteristics are needed to manage students who can be future transformation managers. Because of the low score, 8.25, Table 1 shows that RTBLP's integration is very complex but possible; and the resultant recommendations are:

- Zzzz knowing that failure rates can reach up to 95% (Block, 2022; Dello Ioio, 2023)
- The LCSAS cannot cope with complexity of modern heterogeneous educational systems.
- The author uses his *TRADf* to show how and *Entity* can build an inhouse framework for ATP/ATP4SC.
- This RDP uses a multi-dimensional concept, because it has: 1) An adapted research concept; 2) Shows how to build an internal framework; and 3) A methodological approach based on EA.
- The RLR proved the existence of an important knowledge gap.

- To use a mathematical model (like the AHMM4TBL) and ARbLP based HDT, to support DMS4TBL's operations.
- The HDT supports the RDP is used to create the initial RTBLP concept.
- The RDP proposes a concrete *Framework* on how to support ATP.
- Cross-functional/Polymathic skills building is mainly based on common and GS.
- There is a need for a cross-functional PICC.
- A PICC's content and sequence of Polymathic subjects taught and assessed.
- The RTBLP coordinates PICCs integration to deliver educational blueprints, patterns, …
- Students learning concepts that are recurrent in all cycles (primary, secondary, university…).
- Implementing latest ICS artefícts like OTT to support TBL/PIGW.
- To implement a TBL/PIGW based students' teamwork.
- The *Educator* has to have the needed set of skills and experience (academic, pedagogic, and professional).
- As RTBLP was modelled and the PoC checked its feasibility, and it can replace the LCSAS.
- RTBLP, uses existing frameworks like SAFe, TOGAF to coordinate ATP4SC's activities.
- RTBLP is optimal because it promotes Polymathism, critical-thinking, and opinion-based concepts.
- The RTBLP integration is complex.
- The *Educator* must be an PICC, TEA and TBL experts, who can implement tested blueprints.
- The PoC proved the research feasibility and delivered the recommendations on how to integrate the RTBLP.

REFERENCES

Agievich, V. (2014). *Mathematical model and multi-criteria analysis of designing large-scale enterprise roadmap* [PhD thesis].

Ahmad, G. (2010). *Domain-Oriented Modeling of Indian Education System Through UML*. IUP.

Aksoy, M., & Ceylan, T. (2021). *An Action Research on Improving Classroom Communication and Interaction in Social Studies Teaching*..doi:10.1155/2021/9943194

Ball Hinkelmann, K. (2016). *Modelling in Enterprise Architecture. University of applied sciences northwest Switzerland.* Business School.

Banks, F., & Barlex, D. (2021). *Teaching STEM in the Secondary School-Helping Teachers Meet the Challenge* (2nd ed.). Routledge.

Blackburn, R., & Rosen, B. (1993). Total quality and human resources management: lessons learned from Baldrige Award-winning companies. *Academy of Management Perspectives, 7*(3).

Block, C. (2022). 12 Reasons Your Digital Transformation Will Fail. Forbes Coaches Council. *Forbes*. https://www.forbes.com/sites/forbescoachescouncil/2022/03/16/12-reasons-your-digital-transformation-will-fail/?sh=4e5a5f751f1e

Botturi, L., & Belfer, K. (2014). *Pedagogical patterns for online learning.* ResearchGate.

Burke, J. (2022). *Group Work in the Classroom: Types of Small Groups.* Centre for Teaching Excellence. University of Waterloo. https://uwaterloo.ca/centre-for-teaching-excellence/

Chapman, J. (2015). *Specialization, Polymaths And The Pareto Principle In A Convergence Economy*. TechCrunch. https://techcrunch.com/2015/10/17/specialization-polymaths-and-the-pareto-principle-in-a-convergence-economy/?guccounter=1

Chhatwal, H. (2023). *Redesigning the Business Studies Curriculum of senior secondary education of Central Board of Secondary Education (CBSE), India, in the context of tuition centre in Singapore*. ResearchGate.

Cress, U., Moskaliuk, J., & Jeong, H. (2016). *Mass Collaboration and Education. Computer-Supported Collaborative Learning Series* (Vol. 16). CULS.

Crittenden, V. (2005). Cross-functional education: The need for case development. February 2005. *Journal of Business Research, 58*(7), 955–959. doi:10.1016/j.jbusres.2003.12.004

Dello Ioio, Z. (2023). *5 reasons why digital transformation projects fail (2023).* Enate. https://www.enate.io/blog/why-digital-transformation-projects-fail#:~:text=Technology%20is%20always%20evolving%20and,considering%20making%20their%20own%20changes

Dogan, S., Çalgici, P., Arditi, D., & Gunaydin, H. (2015). *Critical success factors of partnering in the building design process. METU JFA 2015/2*. Department of Architecture, İzmir Institute of Technology.

EURSC. (2022). *Organisation of studies*. Office of the Secretary-General of the European Schools. https://www.eursc.eu/en/European-Schools/studies/studies-organisation#:~:text=The%20European%20School%20system%20consists,seven%20years%20of%20secondary%20education

FastEdge. (2023). *How does educational OTT work*. FastEdge. https://www.fastedge.ai/how-does-educational-ott-work/#:~:text=Educational%20OTT%20can%20be%20thought,through%20web%2Dbased%20discussion%20boards

Felfel, H., Ayadi, O., & Masmoudi, F. (2017). Pareto Optimal Solution Selection for a Multi-Site Supply Chain Planning Problem Using the VIKOR and TOPSIS Methods. *International Journal of Service Science, Management, Engineering, and Technology*. . doi:10.4018/IJSSMET.2017070102

Fitzgerald, J. M. (2005). *A case study of a high school's development of teacher collaboration through interdisciplinary curriculum planning* (Publication No. 3173664) [Doctoral dissertation, Boston College]. ProQuest Dissertations and Theses Global.

Giachetti, R. (2012). *A Flexible Approach to Realize an Enterprise Architecture* [Paper Presentation]. New Challenges in Systems Engineering and Architecting. Conference on Systems Engineering Research (CSER), St. Louis, MO. 10.1016/j.procs.2012.01.031

Han, J., Park, D., Hua, M., & Childs, P. (2021). Is group work beneficial for producing creative designs in STEM design education? *International Journal of Technology and Design Education*. Advance online publication. doi:10.100710798-021-09709-y

Hayashi, K., Shibata, S., Inoue, E., Adachi, S., & Iba, T. (2022). Online Education Patterns, Part 1: Patterns for Linking Separate Worlds. *EuroPLoP'21: 26th European Conference on Pattern Languages of Programs*, 1–16. 10.1145/3489449.3490003

Hine, G. S. C. (2013). The importance of action research in teacher education programs. In *Design, develop, evaluate: The core of the learning. environment. Proceedings of the 22nd Annual Teaching Learning Forum, 7-8 February 2013*. Murdoch University. http://ctl.curtin.edu.au/professional_development/conferences/tlf/tlf2013/refereed/hine.html

Holilah, H., Girsang, A., & Saragih, M. (2019). *Designing IT Blue Print Academic System on Higher Education with Togaf. Journal: Advances in Science*. Technology and Engineering Systems Journal. doi:10.25046/aj040232

Hussain, O., Dillon, Th., Chang, E., & Hussain, F. (2010). Transactional risk-based decision making system in e-business interactions. *International Journal of ComputSystSci & Eng*, *2010*(1), 15–28.

Inayati, R., Sri Handayani, S., Kustiandi, J., Haryono, A., & Wahyono, H. (2010). *The Analysis of the Difficulty in Learning Economics Subject Experienced By Students of Favored State Senior High Schools in City of Malang*. Knowledge E Publishing. https://knepublishing.com/index.php/Kne-Social/article/view/1884/4497 doi:10.18502/kss.v3i3.1884

Jonkers, H., Band, I., & Quartel, D. (2012a). *ArchiSurance Case Study*. The Open Group.

Kersten, M. (2021). *Introducing SAFe® 5*. Your Operating System for Business Agility. Scaled Agile Inc.

Khatkhate, D. (2009). *Harry Johnson: Portrait of a Polymath-A Life in Economics by Donald Moggridge*. EPW. https://www.epw.in/journal/2009/51/review-article-book-reviews/harry-johnson-portrait-polymath.html

Kim, J., & Lennon, Sh. (2017). *Descriptive Content Analysis on E-Service Research. International Journal of Service Science, Management, Engineering, and Technology*. doi:10.4018/IJSSMET.2017010102

Koppe, Ch., van Eekeleny, M., & Hoppenbrouwersz, S. (2015). Improving Student Group Work with Collaboration. Patterns: A Case Study. In *2015 IEEE/ACM 37th IEEE International Conference on Software Engineering*. IEEE. https://ieeexplore.ieee.org/document/7202977

Markides, C. (2011, March). Crossing the Chasm: How to Convert Relevant Research Into Managerially Useful Research. *The Journal of Applied Behavioral Science*, *47*(1), 121–134. doi:10.1177/0021886310388162

Morse, M. (2020). *Making a Difference Through Collaboration: A Case Study Exploring Cross-Functional Collaboration Within an Urban High School in the Northeastern United States* [PhD thesis]. The College of Professional Studies of Northeastern University.

OMG. (2022). *Decision model and notation* (DMN). OMG. https://www.omg.org/dmn/

Page, M., Schagen, S., Fallus, K., Bron, J., De Coninck, Ch., Maes, B., Sleurs, W., & Van Woensel, Ch. (2005). *Cross-curricular themes in secondary education-Report of a CIDREE collaborative project*. Consortium of Institutions for Development and Research in Education in Europe.

Pappas, Ch. (2022). *Cloud Based e-Learning Platforms: 10 Advantages eLearning Professionals Need To Know*. Docebo. https://www.docebo.com/learning-network/blog/cloud-based-elearning-platforms/

Pea, R., & Lindgren, R. (2008). Video Collaboratories for Research and Education: An Analysis of Collaboration Design Patterns. IEEE Transactions on Learning Technologies, 1(4).

Pisonia, G., Gijlersc, H., Ha Nguyend, T., & Chene, H. (2021). Collaboration patterns in students' teams working on business cases. *CEUR Workshop Proceedings*.

Polderman, J., & Willems, J. (1998). *Introduction to Mathematical Systems Theory: A Behavioral Approach (Texts in Applied Mathematics)* (2nd ed.). Springer Verlag. doi:10.1007/978-1-4757-2953-5

Postle, G. (2003). Online Teaching and Learning in Higher Education: A Case Study. Department of Education, Science and Training. University of Southern Queensland.

Prastiwi, S., Widagdo, V., & Kamisutara, M. (2018). Enterprise architecture of education with the TOGAF framework. *The Fourth International Conference on Entrepreneurships*. https://icoen.org/icoen2018/

PushpakumaraH.JayaweeraP.ManjulanW. (2021). *Using the Open Group Architecture Framework (TOGAF) for Quality Assurance in Higher Education Teaching and Learning*. doi:10.2139/ssrn.3808691

Putri, N., & Yusof, S. M. (2009). Critical success factors for implementing quality engineering tools and techniques in malaysian's and indonesian's automotive industries: An Exploratory Study. *Journal Proceedings of the International MultiConference of Engineers and Computer Scientists.*, *2*, 18–20.

Sagheb-Tehrani, M. (2009). The Results of Online Teaching: A Case Study. *ISEDJ, 7*(42). http://isedj.org/7/42/

Sankaralingam, K., Ferris, M., Nowatzki, T., Estan, C., Wood, D., & Vaish, N. (2013). *Optimization and Mathematical Modeling in Computer Architecture*. Morgan & Claypool Publishers.

Satterlee, B. (1996). Continuous Improvement and Quality: Implications for Higher Education. Warner Southern College.

Scaled Agile. (2022). *Succeeding with AI in SAFe.* Scaled Agile, Inc. https://www.scaledagileframework.com/succeeding-with-ai-in-safe/

Smith, A. (1987). Educational Engineering: Heuristics for Improving Learning Effectiveness and Efficiency. *Engineering Education, 77*(5), 274-79.

Spencer, M. (2016). *Agile EA – the MVP – enterprise architect-Building the Business Value Chain…* https://enterprisearchitect.wordpress.com/2016/04/11/agile-ea-the-mvp/1/2

Syynimaa, N. (2015). *Enterprise Architecture Adoption Method for Higher Education Institutions* [Doctoral Thesis]. Informatics Research Centre Henley Business School University of Reading.

The Open Group. (2011a). *Architecture Development Method.* The Open Group. https://pubs.opengroup.org/architecture/togaf9-doc/arch/chap05.html

The Open Group. (2011b). *TOGAF 9.1. The Open Group.* The Open Group.

Thune, T. (2011). Success Factors in Higher Education–Industry Collaboration: A case study of collaboration in the engineering field. *Tertiary Education and Management, 17*(1), 31–50. doi:10.1080/13583883.2011.552627

Trad, A. (2015a). *A Transformation Framework Proposal for Managers in Business Innovation and Business Transformation Projects-Intelligent aBB architecture.* Centeris.

Trad, A. (2015b). *A Transformation Framework Proposal for Managers in Business Innovation and Business Transformation Projects-An ICS's atomic architecture vision.* Centeris.

Trad, A. (2021a). The transformation framework The role security in the global education system. *International Journal of Higher Education Management, 8*(1).

Trad, A. (2021b). The business transformation enterprise architecture framework for innovation: The role of artificial intelligence in the global business education (RAIGBE). The Business & Management Review, 12(1), 82-97.

Trad, A. (2022a). The Societal and Educational Transformation Projects-The Middle East's Educational Construct-The Case of the Lebanese Specific Diverse Educational System (LSDES). *The Business and Management Review, 13*(3).

Trad, A. (2023a). *Business Transformation Project's-The Impact of Rise of Over-the-Top (OTT).* IGI-Global.

Trad, A. (2023b). *Business Transformation Projects: The Role of Psychology-Based Resistance (RPbR). In Considerations on Education for Economic, Social, and Environmental Sustainability*. IGI Global.

Trad, A. (2023c). *The Societal and Educational Transformation Projects: The Evolution of the Lebanese Diverse Education (ELDES). In Global Perspectives on the Internationalization of Higher Education*. IGI Global.

Trad, A., & Kalpić, D. (2014a). The Selection and Training Framework for Managers in Business Innovation and Transformation Projects-An applied mathematics hyper-heuristics model. *Proceedings of the 2014 International Conference on Mathematical Methods, Mathematical Models and Simulation in Science and Engineering (MMSSE 2014)*.

Trad, A., & Kalpić, D. (2014b). *The Selection, and Training Framework selection and training framework (STF) for Manager's in Business Innovation Transformation Projects–Educational Recommendations*. Journal EDEN.

Trad, A., & Kalpić, D. (2014c, June). The selection and training framework for managers in business innovation and transformation projects: The Profile and Education of a Business Transformation Manager - An enterprise architecture approach. *The Business & Management Review, 5*(1), 424–433.

Trad, A., & Kalpić, D. (2017). *An Intelligent Neural Networks Micro Artifact Patterns' Based Enterprise Architecture Model*. IGI-Global.

Trad, A., & Kalpić, D. (2020). *Using Applied Mathematical Models for Business Transformation. IGI Complete Author Book*. IGI Global. doi:10.4018/978-1-7998-1009-4

Trad, A., & Kalpić, D. (2021a). Business transformation project's architect's profile (BTPAP). *The Business & Management Review., 12*(2), 137–153. doi:10.24052/BMR/V12NU02/ART-11

Trad, A., & Kalpić, D. (2022a). Business Transformation Projects based on a Holistic Enterprise Architecture Pattern (HEAP)-The Basics. IGI.

Trad, A., & Kalpić, D. (2022b). Business Transformation Projects based on a Holistic Enterprise Architecture Pattern (HEAP)-The Implementation. IGI.

Trad, A. & Kalpić, D. (2022c). Business Transformation Project's Holistic Agile Management (BTPHAM). *CBER 2022*.

Trad, A., & Kalpić, D. (2023a). *Educational Transformation Project's Remote Group Work (ETPRGW). In Shaping Online Spaces Through Online Humanities Curricula*. IGI Global.

Tuononen, T., Hyytinen, H., Kleemola, K., Hailikari, T., Männikkö, I., & Toom, A. (2022). Systematic Review of Learning Generic Skills in Higher Education—Enhancing and Impeding Factors. Frontiers in Education. *Systematic Review*. doi:10.3389/feduc.2022.885917

UdG. (2023). *Relationships with Secondary Schools-Polytechnic School*. UdG. https://www.udg.edu/en/eps/relacions-amb-secundaria

Wikipedia. (2021). Polymath. In *Wikipedia*. https://en.wikipedia.org/wiki/Polymath

Zachman, J. (2015). *Defining Enterprise Architecture: Economics and the Role of I.T. Business Rules Community*. https://www.brcommunity.com/articles.php?id=b841

Zandia, F., & Tavana, M. (2011). *A fuzzy group multi-criteria enterprise architecture framework selection model*. Elsevier.

Chapter 5
Professional Content Knowledge:
Increasing Instructional Quality

Martha Ann Davis McGaw
Davis McGaw Family Foundation, USA

EXECUTIVE SUMMARY

Effective teaching is a delicate balance of deep content knowledge and adept pedagogical skills. Pedagogical content knowledge (PCK), introduced by Shulman in 1987 captures the essence of this synergy, emphasizing the transformative capability of educators in delivering subject content in ways that engage students. This chapter dives into the nuances of PCK, its foundational role in teacher education, and its expansive relevance across academic fields, with special emphasis on economic educators. Rooted in Shulman's groundbreaking research, with insights from various educational researchers, the chapter underscores the importance of melding content mastery with pedagogical techniques. It further explores the historical and contemporary perspectives on the confluence of content and pedagogy, featuring case studies for analysis. The chapter contributes to the broader conversation on the necessity for teachers to become more adaptable within teaching approaches.

PREFACE

We find few descriptions or analyses of teachers that give careful attention, not only to the management of students in classrooms, but also to the management of ideas within classroom discourse. Both kinds of emphasis will be needed if our portrayals

DOI: 10.4018/978-1-6684-7583-6.ch005

of good practice are to serve as sufficient guides to the design of better education. (Shulman., 1987)

To establish schools that simultaneously nurture and educate, all while fostering individual value, a profound urgency is required (Davis McGaw, 2016; Davis McGraw 2019; Davis McGraw 2020).

INTRODUCTION

Effective teaching resides at the crossroads of profound content knowledge and expert pedagogical skills. Historically, the integration of subject expertise with teaching methodologies has defined the core of impactful education (Shing et al., 2018). Shulman's seminal contribution in 1987 introduced the concept of Pedagogical Content Knowledge (PCK), spotlighting the unique space where educators convert deep subject content into accessible and engaging lessons for students. Rooted in content mastery, adaptability, and reflective thinking, this perspective remains a guiding light in current educational dialogues. The modern educational landscape, with its evolving paradigms, necessitates a fine balance between subject mastery and effective delivery. Achieving this balance is crucial for optimal teaching outcomes (Davis McGaw, 2022). Lee et al. (2018) and Guerriero (2017) further enhance this narrative, detailing the interwoven nature of Subject Matter Knowledge (SMK) and PCK, emphasizing the significant impact of a teacher's sophisticated pedagogical insight on learner outcomes.

Incorporating insights from Shulman's vast research, which is grounded in philosophy, psychology, and a myriad of case studies involving both novice and veteran teachers, the pivotal blending of content knowledge with teaching strategies is underscored. His pioneering work continues to shape teaching standards across all curriculum subjects today (Baptiste & Leck, 2023; Leijen et al., 2022; Ayers, 2016). An important facet of teaching success, as highlighted by Shulman & Sherin (2004), is the educators' deep understanding of both the subject content and its pedagogical representation. While the broader educational community acknowledges the synergy between disciplinary knowledge and teacher evolution, in-depth explorations of their interaction within specific classroom scenarios are comparatively scarce (Grossman, 2008; Shulman, 2011; Davis McGaw, 2016; Heafner, Van Fossen, & Fitchett, 2016).

In the 21st century, the educator's role is not limited to merely delivering knowledge. It extends to weaving contemporary educational insights into refined classroom decisions, offering a more holistic and effective learning experience (Guerriero, 2017). As part of this broader discussion, we delve into the Fostering Communities of Teachers as Learners (FCL) initiative, spearheaded by Shulman in 2004. This initiative, detailed further in Table 1, emerged from a sequence of insightful classroom observations. As articulated by Shulman & Sherin (2004), educational research has historically swayed between phases: sometimes prioritizing subject disciplines and at other times emphasizing overarching instructional principles. Within the FCL framework, four main domain-specific teaching challenges are delineated:

1. Recognition of pivotal concepts or 'big ideas'.
2. Analyzing the divisibility of topics within a subject.
3. The role of existing curriculum patterns in influencing pedagogical shifts.
4. The complexities of applying these insights within a cohesive learning community.

This chapter seeks to unpack the nuances of PCK, highlighting its foundational role in teacher education and its continued relevance across various academic fields (Star, 2023). We also traverse evolving teaching paradigms, enriched with experiences from diverse educational contexts spanning Asia, Europe, and the USA.

Figure 1. Teacher professional knowledge according to Shulman (1987) as seen in Neumann, Kind, and Harms (2018)

PEDAGOGICAL CONTENT KNOWLEDGE

Pedagogical Content Knowledge (PCK) is the scaffolding that connects content expertise with effective teaching practices, equipping educators for diverse classroom environments, be they traditional or digital. Lee et al. (2015) argue that effective teaching extends beyond formal training, melding content knowledge with lived experiences. This sentiment is mirrored by Guerriero (2017), who underscores that PCK's strength lies in its integrative approach, melding content with pedagogical strategies tailored for each subject.

TEACHER KNOWLEDGE FRAMEWORK

Shulman's (1987) exploration into the dimensions of teacher knowledge remains a touchstone in educational research. He delineated this intricate knowledge into several domains, emphasizing the comprehensive skill set educators must cultivate. Among these, two stand out:

- General Pedagogical Knowledge (GPK): Representing foundational teaching principles, methodologies, and strategies that are universal, GPK equips teachers to tackle diverse classroom scenarios, from managing student dynamics to facilitating engagement.
- Pedagogical Content Knowledge (PCK): A more nuanced category, PCK focuses on the synergy between subject content and effective teaching methodologies. As Guerriero (2014) describes, it's the confluence of content mastery with pedagogical finesse, ensuring subjects resonate with students.

Diving deeper, Leijen et al. (2022) provided a meticulous review of the GPK landscape, revealing its evolving definitions and applications. Their study underscored Shulman's enduring influence while also highlighting variations in interpretations across different research traditions. Fascinatingly, while Shulman's ideas were initially aligned with German-speaking educational traditions, recent detailed explorations now draw inspiration from his work, particularly from the König research group.

Gleaning insights from their extensive review, Leijen et al. (2022) synthesized a definition for GPK, encapsulating it as knowledge transcending subjects, centered around learning, teaching, classroom management, and the broader educational context. They also presented a fresh framework that delineates GPK alongside PCK and content knowledge, illustrating their intersections. Despite their study's comprehensiveness, the authors acknowledged potential limitations, emphasizing the importance of ongoing exploration in this domain.

As the field of education continues to evolve, understanding and distinguishing these knowledge dimensions becomes increasingly pivotal for the holistic development of educators.

IMPORTANCE TO ECONOMICS EDUCATORS

For economic educators, the significance of the concepts discussed, especially Pedagogical Content Knowledge (PCK) and the intricate balance between profound content knowledge and refined pedagogical skills, is paramount. The field of economics is often laden with complex theories, intricate models, and data-driven analyses. To make these concepts accessible and engaging for students requires not only an in-depth understanding of the material but also the ability to deliver it in a way that resonates with diverse learner profiles.

Shulman's (1987) introduction of PCK sheds light on the unique nexus where educators can transform intricate economic content into digestible and relevant lessons. By grasping the essence of PCK, economic educators can better navigate the multifaceted demands of contemporary teaching, ensuring that their instruction is both grounded in sound economic principles and attuned to the varied learning needs of their students. The emphasis on both General Pedagogical Knowledge (GPK) and PCK underscores the importance of a dual approach, where foundational teaching principles are married with content-specific strategies tailored to the nuances of economics. As economic paradigms evolve and the world becomes more interconnected, educators in this field are also tasked with integrating global perspectives, emphasizing the real-world implications of economic theories. Thus, understanding and harnessing the concepts of PCK and GPK becomes not just beneficial but essential for economic educators striving for excellence in their classrooms. By doing so, they can ensure that their students not only grasp core economic concepts but also appreciate their broader implications in a dynamic global landscape.

DIFFERENCES AND EVOLVING PERSPECTIVES

In his pivotal work, Knowledge and Teaching: Foundations of the New Reform, Lee Shulman drew attention to the idea that Pedagogical Content Knowledge (PCK) wasn't a newfound concept. Tracing back to the 1950s, educators perceived content and pedagogy as a singular, unified body of knowledge. Content represented 'what is known', and pedagogy outlined 'how to teach it' (Shulman, 1987). Echoing this sentiment, Chien Lee, Rohaida Mohd, and Siow Heng further argued that this unity originally positioned content knowledge and pedagogical techniques as a seamless amalgamation, intertwining what one knows with methods to impart it.

The intricate dance between content and pedagogy finds resonance in Shulman's exploration of 'subject-specific' teacher instruction. Here, Shulman's concept of PCK emerges as a bridge, spanning the chasm between content knowledge and teaching methods (Shulman, 1987). While he staunchly believed in the inherent value of both content and pedagogical knowledge, Shulman contended that these, when viewed in isolation, couldn't capture the sophisticated techniques that standout teachers employed, techniques that markedly enhanced student learning.

A clarion call by Shulman in 2004 underscored the need for more "wisdom of practice" case studies. These studies aimed to delve deep into the interplay between teacher knowledge and the tangible instructional practices showcased by exceptional teachers. Shulman advocated for a cooperative venture, where researchers and educators could collaboratively sculpt codified representations of practical pedagogical insights inherent to proficient teachers. Central to this was understanding the unique PCK—a harmonious integration of content and pedagogy specific to individual subjects (Shulman, p. 8, 2004). A visual representation of Shulman's conceptual grasp of intertwining professional knowledge with Subject Matter Expertise (SME) can be gleaned from Figure 1, as elucidated by Neumann, Kind, and Harms in 2018.

A PARADIGM SHIFT

Recent educational imperatives underscore not just the elevation of student outcomes but also the enhancement of the teaching vanguard's quality. A pivotal work by Lee Shulman and Judith Schulman titled How and what teachers learn: a shifting perspective (2004) presents a pioneering theoretical framework. This blueprint seeks to illuminate the intricacies of preparing teachers to craft, nurture, and impart knowledge within a 'community of learners'. By proposing a fresh perspective on teacher development within varied communities and contexts, the Schulmans present an in-depth exploration of the dynamic interplay between individual student and teacher learning, program-based learning, and the crucial policy environment nuances that bolster ambitious reforms like the 'Fostering a Community of Learners' (FCL) initiative.

Validating his content and pedagogy amalgamation theory, Shulman, in collaboration with Judith Schulman, poses a quartet of pivotal questions in their works from 2004 and 2011:

1. What constitutes the knowledge base for teaching?
2. How can we conceptualize these knowledge sources?
3. What mechanisms drive pedagogical reasoning and action?
4. What ramifications do these insights hold for teaching policies and educational transformation?

By breathing life into the PCK concept, Shulman (1987) revived an age-old premise, suggesting that the act of teaching and the journey of learning to teach ought to be perceived through discipline-specific lenses.

EXAMINING CASE STUDIES FOR INSIGHTS

Case Study 1

In the Netherlands, a study was carried out exploring the "subject matter pedagogy" within Child and Education Studies, specifically in the areas of learning disabilities, student learning, behavioral issues, and clinical work (Vereijken et al., 2023). The research aimed to comprehend the synergy between subject matter, theoretical concepts, and actual teaching methodologies. Some teaching strategies highlighted were:

- Case studies: Assignments that prompt students to apply research or theoretical models to real or hypothetical professional situations unfamiliar to them.
- Group discussions: Encouraging students to reflect on the practical applications of research outcomes.
- Problem-based learning: Engaging students in resolving practical issues through research methods (p. 882).

To garner a deeper understanding, teachers were guided with questions like:

- How is the interplay between theory and practice manifested in this teacher's approach?
- How does the educator perceive the amalgamation of theory and practice?
- What instances or events hold significance for the educator during teaching? (p. 885)

From the narratives gathered, it was deduced that the subject matter serves as the linchpin in intertwining theory and practice in teaching methodologies (p. 880). The study underscored the potential of integrating research into university teaching to foster a more profound grasp of disciplinary knowledge (p.883). However, Vereijken & van der Rijst (2023) concluded that while every lecturer acknowledged the connection between subject matter, theory, and PCK in teaching, each had their unique interpretation, either stemming from a research or practice standpoint. They all faced challenges in clarifying the nexus among these elements to students (p.890).

Case Study 2

A study with 152 prospective secondary mathematics teachers assessed their subject-matter knowledge and its connection with PCK in the context of classroom instruction. Initial data were gathered through an open-ended questionnaire, followed by interviews with 10 participants. Findings revealed that a considerable number of participants had an outdated understanding of PCK. Many could not articulate the significance of professional content knowledge nor how PCK shaped their teaching methods. Alarmingly, a significant portion opted to provide students with rules to follow without emphasizing understanding (Even, 1993).

Case Study 3

Smit et al. (2023) indicated that despite PCK's influence in the education sector, it's not prevalently used in geography education research. A 2023 review by Evens, Elen, and Depaepe unearthed just a single study on this subject. The primary question guiding their research was: 'How is the PCK of individual geography teachers examined in empirical educational studies?' (p.21).

The systematic review process involved:

a) Defining the research scope.
b) Searching and filtering studies based on specific criteria.
c) Evaluating the quality of selected studies.
d) Extracting, analyzing data, and presenting findings.

From the initial 495 articles, only 43 met the study's criteria, representing over 17 countries, including Portugal, Australia, and the USA. The review deduced that the PCK of geography teachers remains an underexplored area. Out of the 43 studies, only nine employed PCK as a guiding framework. Most relied on self-reported data. No decisive conclusions were drawn regarding the quality of geography teachers' PCK. Still, portraits of 16 geography teachers accentuated the crucial role of subject matter knowledge and teaching experience in PCK development (p. 27).

FUTURE RESEARCH

The rapidly changing dynamics of the educational landscape bring forth pivotal questions about the adaptability and relevance of the existing teaching knowledge base, especially in the face of 21st-century educational demands. It's imperative to critically evaluate whether current pedagogical frameworks can effectively support the multidimensional skills required in this age. Specifically, the Technological Pedagogical Content Knowledge (TPACK) concept, which emerges as a defining paradigm of modern-day education, beckons in-depth scrutiny and exploration.

One significant avenue worth probing is culturally responsive pedagogy. The educational success of students, as highlighted by researchers, is often intricately linked to the sensitivity of classroom instruction towards their home cultures (Tyagi & Verma, 2022). This student-centric teaching approach, which seamlessly integrates cultural references in learning, stands as a testament to the profound impacts of recognizing and valuing students' diverse cultural backgrounds (Samuels, 2018). In essence, bridging classroom content with students' cultural contexts can act as a pivotal strategy for enriching both their school and classroom experiences.

Moreover, the intertwined relationship between education and mental health is increasingly coming under the spotlight. With a considerable number of U.S. youth grappling with mental health challenges, often manifesting early in their lives, there's an urgent call for holistic integration of mental health awareness within educational frameworks (Atkins et al., 2010). Pioneering research can pave the way for initiatives that emphasize self-care, personal responsibility for health, and directing students towards essential resources.

Lastly, the proliferation of Artificial Intelligence (AI) in the realm of K-12 education introduces a new dimension of opportunities and challenges. Beyond its transformative potential to reshape pedagogical methods, AI also opens avenues for discussions centered on its ethical dimensions (Krueger, 2023). The integration of AI tools, like ChatGPT, into academic environments necessitates a deeper understanding and adaptation by educators to leverage its full potential responsibly.

APPLICATION OF FRAMEWORK

Technological Pedagogical Content Knowledge (TPACK) outlines the essential knowledge teachers require for efficient technology incorporation. The TPACK framework accentuates the synergy between teachers' grasp of content, pedagogy, and technology, culminating in effective teaching methods (Koehler, Mishra, Kereluik, Shin, Graham, 2014). Koehler and colleagues contend that, despite its novelty, TPACK has made substantial contributions to the spheres of theory, research, and practice in both teacher education and professional development.

Vereijken & van der Rijst (2023) underscore the ambiguity in pinpointing a precise method for imparting the interrelation between theory, practice, and subject matter. They advocate for continuous introspection by educators on aligning these elements. Moreover, they emphasize the role of academic developers in facilitating this reflective process, initiating discussions rooted in the subject matter, and aiding teachers in transposing educational principles into the content being taught (2023, p. 891).

Highlighting the global survey on geography teachers' PCK knowledge, Smit and colleagues stress the potential of PCK. They urge future scholars to delve into broader target groups, encompassing an extensive array of subject matter topics. Ideal research should amalgamate evidence from both teacher knowledge and practice, shedding light on the symbiotic relationship between at least two PCK facets. Consensus from various studies underscores the pivotal role of both pedagogical knowledge and subject matter expertise in enhancing teaching quality and fostering student comprehension. Cochran, a notable figure from Northern Colorado University, advocates for bolstering pedagogical content knowledge in both preliminary and ongoing teacher training. He also emphasizes the significance of teacher participation in research, asserting its critical role in developing subject matter proficiency within the PCK framework, subsequently elevating the standards of science instruction.

CONCLUSION

Gaining insight into the ways in which teachers develop their PCK can be acquired from asking questions such as:

- How does this development take place and
- What prompts these teachers to gain coherence between PCK-elements?
- Where and how does Subject Matter Expertise intersect with PCK to create a more balanced version of classroom instruction?
- What are the implications for teaching policy and educational reform?

Knowing the answer to questions like this could enhance future teacher education and professional development. Understanding how teachers organize subject matter within the context of pedagogical content knowledge will allow teacher colleges and teacher educators to offer relevant, appropriate training. This will improve teacher classroom practice and student learner outcomes will be more successful.

The OECD's Centre for Educational Research and Innovation report, Pedagogical Knowledge and the Changing Nature of the Teaching Profession, concludes:

Highly qualified and competent teachers are fundamental for equitable and effective education systems. Teachers today are facing higher and more complex expectations to help students reach their full potential and become valuable members of 21st century society. The nature and variety of these demands imply that teachers, more than ever before, must be professionals who make decisions based on a robust and updated knowledge base. (Guerriero, 2017)

Educating teachers in PCK must have these goals at the heart of the curriculum:

1. Supporting students' development
2. Support the development of students' learning and collaboration skills and
3. Strengthen the growth of intrinsic motivation (Davis McGaw, 2022).

REFERENCES

Atkins, M. S., Hoagwood, K. E., Kutash, K., & Seidman, E. (2010). Toward the integration of education and mental health in schools. *Administration and Policy in Mental Health, 37*(1-2), 40–47. doi:10.100710488-010-0299-7 PMID:20309623

Ayers, C. A. (2016). Developing preservice and in-service teachers' pedagogical content knowledge in economics. *Social Studies Research & Practice, 11*(1), 73–92. doi:10.1108/SSRP-01-2016-B0005

Baptiste, H. P., & Leck, M. C. (2023). Lee S. Shulman: An icon of teaching. In B. A. Geier (Ed.), *The Palgrave Handbook of Educational Thinkers*. Palgrave Macmillan. doi:10.1007/978-3-030-81037-5_187-1

Davis McGaw, M. A. (2016). The growth of learning colleges including a case study from 2008 revisited in 2015. In E. A. Railean, G. Walker, A. Elçi, & L. Jackson (Eds.), Handbook of research on applied learning theory and design in modern education (pp. 520-544). IGI Global. doi:10.4018/978-1-4666-9634-1.ch025

Davis McGaw, M. A. (2018, November). *A global perspective on the future of education*. Keynote address presented at the National Association of State Directors of Teacher Education and Certification (NASDTEC) Conference, Minneapolis, MN.

Davis McGaw, M. A. (2019). Communities of practice: An ecosystem-based philosophy of harmony in education. In E. A. Railean (Ed.), *Handbook of Research on Ecosystem-Based Theoretical Models of Learning and Communication* (pp. 20–39). IGI Global. doi:10.4018/978-1-5225-7853-6.ch002

Davis McGaw, M. A. (2021). Designing schools as learning centers. In M. Khosrow-Pour (Ed.), *Handbook of Research on Modern Educational Technologies, Applications, and Management* (Vol. 1, pp. 359–376). IGI Global. doi:10.4018/978-1-7998-3476-2.ch022

Davis McGaw, M. A., & Evans, S. M. (2021). *Participatory pedagogy: Emerging research and opportunities*. IGI Global. doi:10.4018/978-1-5225-8964-8

Even, R. (1993). Subject-matter knowledge and pedagogical content knowledge: Prospective secondary teachers and the function concept. *Journal for Research in Mathematics Education, 24*(2), 94–116. doi:10.2307/749215

Grossman, P. L. (1990). *The making of a teacher: Teacher knowledge and teacher education*. Academic Press.

Grossman, P. L., & McDonald, M. (2008). Back to the future: Directions for research in teaching and teacher education. *American Educational Research Journal, 45*(1), 184–205. doi:10.3102/0002831207312906

Guerriero, S. (2014). *Teachers' pedagogical knowledge and the teaching profession: Background report and project objectives*. OECD. https://www.oecd.org/education/ceri/Background_document_to_Symposium_ITEL-FINAL.pdf

Guerriero, S. (2017). Teachers' pedagogical knowledge: What it is and how it functions. In S. Guerriero (Ed.), *Pedagogical Knowledge and the Changing Nature of the Teaching Profession*. OECD., doi:10.1787/9789264270695-6-en

Guerriero, S. (Ed.). (2017). *Teachers' pedagogical knowledge: What it is and how it functions in Pedagogical Knowledge and the Changing Nature of the Teaching Profession. Educational Research and Innovation*. OECD Publishing. doi:10.1787/9789264270695-en

Heafner, T. L., VanFossen, P., & Fitchett, P. G. (2016). *A multilevel model to identify predictors of students' achievement on NAEP-Economics*. Paper presented at the annual meeting of the American Education Research Association, Washington, DC.

Hiebert, J., & Morris, A. K. (2012). Teaching, rather than teachers, as a path toward improving classroom instruction. *Journal of Teacher Education, 63*(2), 92–102. doi:10.1177/0022487111428328

Koehler, M. J., Mishra, P., Kereluik, K., Shin, T. S., & Graham, C. R. (2014). The technological pedagogical content knowledge framework. In J. Spector, M. Merrill, J. Elen, & M. Bishop (Eds.), *Handbook of Research on Educational Communications and Technology*. Springer. doi:10.1007/978-1-4614-3185-5_9

König, J., Blömeke, S., Klein, P., Suhl, U., Busse, A., & Kaiser, G. (2014). Is teachers' general pedagogical knowledge a premise for noticing and interpreting classroom situations? A video-based assessment approach. *Teaching and Teacher Education, 38*, 76–88. doi:10.1016/j.tate.2013.11.004

König, J., Blömeke, S., Paine, L., Schmidt, W. H., & Hsieh, F. J. (2011). General pedagogical knowledge of future middle school teachers: On the complex ecology of teacher education in the United States, Germany, and Taiwan. *Journal of Teacher Education*, *62*(2), 188–201. doi:10.1177/0022487110388664

König, J., Jäger-Biela, D. J., & Glutsch, N. (2020). Adapting to online teaching during COVID-19 school closure: Teacher education and teacher competence effects among early career teachers in Germany. *European Journal of Teacher Education*, *43*(4), 608–622. doi:10.1080/02619768.2020.1809650

Lederman, N. G., & Gess-Newsome, J. (1992). Do subject matter knowledge, pedagogical knowledge, and pedagogical content knowledge constitute the ideal gas law of science teaching? *Journal of Science Teacher Education*, *3*(1), 16–20. https://www.jstor.org/stable/43155929. doi:10.1007/BF02614732

Lee, Y., Capraro, R. M., & Capraro, M. M. (2018). Mathematics teachers' subject matter knowledge and pedagogical content knowledge in problem posing. *International Electronic Journal of Mathematics Education*, *13*(2), 75–90. doi:10.12973/iejme/2698 PMID:31824466

Lee Shing, C., Mohd. Saat, R., & Loke, S. H. (2015). The knowledge of teaching – Pedagogical Content Knowledge (PCK). *The Malaysian Online Journal of Educational Science, 3*(3). Retrieved from https://files.eric.ed.gov/fulltext/EJ1085915.pdf

Leijen, A., Malva, L., Pedaste, M., & Mikser, R. (2022). What constitutes teachers' general pedagogical knowledge and how it can be assessed: A literature review. *Teachers and Teaching*, *28*(2), 206–225. doi:10.1080/13540602.2022.2062710

Neuman, K., Kind, V., & Harms, U. (2018). Probing the amalgam: The relationship between science teachers' content, pedagogical and pedagogical content knowledge. *International Journal of Science Education*, *41*(7), 1–15. doi:10.1080/09500693.2018.1497217

OECD. (2005). *Teachers Matter: Attracting, Developing, and Retaining Effective Teachers*. OECD Publishing.

Rønningsbakk, L., Gudmundsdottir, G. B., & Blikstad-Balas, M. (2020). Sameness and individuality: Teacher adaptation and enactment of an innovative technology-based mathematics curriculum. *Teaching and Teacher Education*, *96*, 103196. doi:10.1016/j.tate.2020.103196

Samuels, A. J. (2018). Exploring culturally responsive pedagogy: Teachers' perspectives on fostering equitable and inclusive classrooms. *SRATE Journal*, *27*(1), 22–30.

Schempp, P. G., Manross, D., Tan, S. K. S., & Fincher, M. D. (1998). Subject expertise and teachers' knowledge. *Journal of Teaching in Physical Education, 17*(3), 342–356. doi:10.1123/jtpe.17.3.342

Schmidt, W. H., Cogan, L., & Houang, R. (2011). The role of opportunity to learn in teacher preparation: An international context. *Journal of Teacher Education, 62*(2), 138–153. doi:10.1177/0022487110391987

Schmidt, W. H., Houang, R. T., Coga, L., Blomeke, S., Tatto, M. T., Hsieh, F. J., Santillan, M., Bankov, K., Han, S., Cedillo, T., Schwille, J., & Paine, L. (2008). Opportunity to learn in the preparation of mathematics teachers: Its structure and how it varies across six countries. *ZDM Mathematics Education, 40*(5), 735–747. doi:10.100711858-008-0115-y

Shulman, J. S. (1993). Teaching as community property: Putting an end to pedagogical solitude. *Change, 25*(6), 6–7. doi:10.1080/00091383.1993.9938465

Shulman, L. (1987). Knowledge and teaching: Foundations of the new reform. *Harvard Educational Review, 57*(1), 1–23. doi:10.17763/haer.57.1.j463w79r56455411

Shulman, L. (2010). Forum: Teaching as community property. Change. *Change, 25*(6), 6–7. doi:10.1080/00091383.1993.9938465

Shulman, L., & Gamoran Sherin, M. (2004). Fostering communities of teachers as learners: Disciplinary perspectives. *Journal of Curriculum Studies, 36*(2), 135–140. doi:10.1080/0022027032000135049

Shulman, L. S. (1986). Those who understand: Knowledge growth in teaching. *Educational Researcher, 15*(2), 4–14. doi:10.2307/1175860

Shulman, L. S. (1998). Theory, practice, & the education of professionals. *The Elementary School Journal, 98*(5), 511–526. doi:10.1086/461912

Shulman, L. S. (2005). Signature pedagogies in the professions. *Daedalus, 134*(3), 52–59. doi:10.1162/0011526054622015

Shulman, L. S. (2007). *It's all about time!* The Carnegie Foundation for the Advancement of Teaching. ERIC ED499494. https://files.eric.ed.gov/fulltext/ED499494.pdf

Shulman, L. S. (2015). PCK: Its genesis and exodus. In A. Berry, P. Friedrichsen, & J. Loughran (Eds.), *Re-examining pedagogical content knowledge in science education* (pp. 3–13). Routledge.

Shulman, L. S., & Shulman, J. H. (2004). How and what teachers learn: A shifting perspective. *Journal of Curriculum Studies*, *36*(2), 257–271. doi:10.1080/0022027032000148298

Shulman, L. S., & Shulman, J. H. (2017). How and what teachers learn: A shifting perspective. *Journal of Education*, *189*(1-2), 1–8. doi:10.1177/0022057409189001-202

Smit, E., Tuihof, H., Savelsbergh, E., & Beneker, T. (2022). Geography teachers' pedagogical content knowledge: A systematic review. *The Journal of Geography*, *122*(1), 20–29. doi:10.1080/00221341.2023.2173796

Tyagi, N., & Verma, S. (2022). Culturally responsive teaching: A suggestive pedagogical framework. In J. Keengwe (Ed.), *Handbook of Research on Social Justice and Equity in Education* (pp. 312–331). IGI Global. doi:10.4018/978-1-7998-9567-1.ch016

Vereijken, M. W. C., & van der Rijst, R. M. (2023). Subject matter pedagogy in university teaching: How lecturers use relations between theory and practice. *Teaching in Higher Education*, *28*(4), 880–893. doi:10.1080/13562517.2020.1863352

Chapter 6
The Impact of Learner Content and User Interface Design on E-Learning Quality:
Teaching in Times of Crises

Agyabeng Nimfah Yeboah
University of South Africa, South Africa

Leila Goosen
https://orcid.org/0000-0003-4948-2699
University of South Africa, South Africa

ABSTRACT

The purpose of the study reported on in this chapter is to investigate the impact of learner content and user interface design on improving e-learning quality and to harness the full potential of e-learning in Ghana at the basic school level. Against the background of cases on economics education and tools for educators, the main focus will be on the effective use of technologies, such as social media, movies, and TV shows, as well as, for example, music, team-based learning, think-pair-share, and other forms of active learning and computer-based learning in the classroom.

INTRODUCTION

This chapter provides a broad overview of the role of economics education in contemporary schooling, focusing on its prominence in the US curriculum. In many U.S. states, the significance of economics is underscored by its inclusion as a

DOI: 10.4018/978-1-6684-7583-6.ch006

graduation requirement or as an integral component of primary education. Yet, despite the subject's clear importance, educators often grapple with a lack of comprehensive resources to seamlessly incorporate economics into the classroom. The challenges of locating, validating, and integrating relevant materials can be daunting, especially when educators juggle multiple subjects. This chapter endeavors to simplify this task by collating essential teaching resources in this field.

Educational dynamics worldwide underwent a seismic shift due to the COVID-19 pandemic. UNESCO's 2020 report highlighted the magnitude of this impact, revealing that over 1.5 billion students across the globe were hindered from attending traditional classrooms. This disruption, affecting nearly 94% of the world's student population and hitting a staggering 99% in some lower-income countries (Goosen, 2008), prompted a swift pivot to technological solutions. The pandemic not only accentuated the value of technology in education (De Four-Babb, et al., 2022) but also accelerated the transition to virtual learning modalities (Demuyakor, 2021).

In these changing times, e-learning emerged as a robust and scalable alternative, capable of transcending geographical boundaries and serving diverse learners with relatively limited resources (Arkorful & Abaidoo, 2015). However, its adoption isn't without challenges. As highlighted by Weerathunga et al. (2021), student perceptions regarding e-learning vary widely, prompting the evolution of nuanced technology adoption theories. One of the critical pillars underpinning successful e-learning is interactivity. Gunesekera, et al. (2019) emphasized the importance of three central interactions in this domain: student-student, student-instructor, and student-content. These interactions, facilitated by Human-Computer Interaction (HCI) via user interfaces, are paramount for a smooth e-learning experience. Yet, the interconnection between student-content and the design of these interfaces, crucial for e-learning's efficacy, remains insufficiently explored.

While research on these interactions is sparse, especially in regions like Africa, the challenges and solutions might hold universal relevance. Developing countries, including Ghana, have confronted specific e-learning obstacles, from technological access to content creation (Maatuk et al., 2022). Insights from studies by Gherheş et al. (2021), Yakubu and Dasuki (2018), and Alhumaid et al. (2020) underscore the mounting reliance on e-learning and its pivotal role during crises like COVID-19.

This study, though rooted in the Ghanaian context, aims to uncover insights on the synergy between learner content and user interface design in e-learning that can be extrapolated and applied to classrooms worldwide, enhancing the global quality of virtual education.

Target Audience

This chapter, much like the overarching book it resides in, primarily caters to college students aspiring to teach economics within the K-12 spectrum. Beyond this core audience, the chapter seeks to lay down a foundation for fostering university alliances. These partnerships aim to continuously back practitioners and curriculum architects dedicated to bolstering and facilitating student achievement (Vorster & Goosen, 2017), as delineated in the 46th annual conference proceedings of the Southern African Computer Lecturers' Association (SACLA). The content of this chapter will delve into the nuances of technology integration, pertinent pedagogical strategies for classroom instruction, and diverse instructional methodologies.

Alternative Pedagogy

As part of this book, the chapter aims to provide relevant cases and examples of effective economics education issues suited for K-12 educators. The cases are written with current and future practitioners in mind, who are teaching or planning to teach economics in the K-12 classroom. The topic covered in the chapter as part of this book aims to assist current and future economic educators in *pedagogy*, methodology, practitioner examples, and practices that support a learning environment that engages and *includes all learners* and especially groups that have been under-represented in economics. Research on technology-supported teaching and learning methods for educators of learners with autism spectrum disorders and other forms of inclusive education should be considered in terms of such *inclusivity* (Goosen, 2019).

The aim of the study is to investigate the impact of learner content and user interface design on e-learning quality. The purpose of this study is to gain an in-depth understanding of the impact of learner content and user interface design on e-learning quality. The specific objectives are to:

1. Investigate the extent to which user interface design promotes student-content interaction towards e-learning quality and impacting students' performance.
2. Critically examine how learner content and user interface design can foster students' satisfaction to impact the quality of e-learning.
3. Establish the difference in performance between male and female students after using the e-learning model.
4. Compare the performance of students with access to computers at home with that of student, who do not, after using the e-learning model.
5. Compare the performance of students, who possess basic computer skills, with those, who do not, after using the e-learning model.

The study reported on in this chapter will be structured into six sections. Now that this first section had dealt with the introduction, as well as the aim and objectives of the study, the next section will provide the background to the study in terms of an overview of important literature in a conceptual review, as well as insights on the theoretical framework and foundations of SSI, SII, SCI and UID in e-learning research. The following section will detail e.g., the rationale for the study, the statement of the problem, a justification of the study, and the research questions. The latter section will also provide some insight into the research method used to find solutions through the study and recommendations. Future research directions and emerging trends will be dealt with before providing, in conclusion, a summary.

BACKGROUND

The advent of digital platforms has reshaped the educational landscape, with "The Impact of Learner Content and User Interface Design on e-Learning Quality when Teaching in Times of Crises" emerging as a pertinent topic. In this section, we assimilate a range of scholarly insights to provide a holistic understanding of this area. Our endeavor is to incorporate a variety of perspectives, whether they support, refute, or elaborate on the central theme.

Tools for Educators

In their exploration, Adu and Zondo (2023) turned their lens towards the integration of Information and Communication Technology in the teaching of economics. Set against the backdrop of social sciences and humanities, their investigation concentrated on eight Economics teachers, shedding light on the educators' perspectives. These findings are a testament to the gradual merging of technological advancements with traditional teaching practices in economics.

Sharples (2022) added another layer to this narrative by focusing on the implications of Artificial Intelligence (AI) in the education sector. Through the London School of Economics' platform, Sharples highlighted a future where AI tools, capable of crafting student essays, might necessitate a transformative shift in teaching and assessment methodologies. In fact, Geerling et al. (2023) showcased how ChatGPT can ace college-level economics programs. Much work has been performed in understanding the potential implications of teaching with AI in the economics classroom (Baidoo-anu & Owusu Ansah, 2023; Gill et al., 2024; Wolla, 2020).

Taking a more institutional perspective, Hibrida and Sumual (2022) delved deep into the performance metrics of educators at the Faculty of Economics and Business at Manado State University (UNIMA). Their analysis encompassed aspects of professional competence, motivation, and work ethics. Such studies serve as a mirror, reflecting the challenges and opportunities faced by educators in this rapidly evolving digital age. Alipio's (2020) work offers a unique vantage point, focusing on the organizational commitment of higher education economics educators. In a profession marked by high burnout rates, Alipio's structural model, emphasizing job satisfaction, becomes particularly salient.

Further collaboration between university and high school educators was championed by Hoffer and Beckstrom (2019). Their narrative underscores the mutual respect and longing for specialized knowledge between both groups, providing a compelling case for shared learning experiences. These collaborative efforts in the United States remains in strong demand as the rise of Early Colleges and career and college promise students, who are high school age, in the community college classroom. The repercussions of the COVID-19 pandemic on the world of education cannot be overstated. In this context, Kremeňová et al. (2022) documented the shifts in educators' perspectives, especially within the realm of the "operation and economics of transport."

TEACHING IN THE MODERN AGE

The convergence of cinema and education finds its voice in the work of Briguglio, Acchiardo, Mateer, and Geerling (2020). They advocate for the inclusion of behavioral economics in undergraduate curricula, suggesting that movies can serve as powerful educational tools for educators. Scott (2023) highlighted the movies are not just for undergraduate courses, but for elementary as well, showcasing lesson plans that can be paired with Disney's *Encanto*. Borup et al. (2014) offered a deep dive into the potential of video feedback in blended teaching environments. Such tools, they argued, can significantly amplify educators' social presence, thus enhancing the overall learning experience.

However, the journey of e-learning is not without its challenges. Hoogerheide et al. (2016) explored various e-learning methods, presenting a nuanced understanding of their effectiveness. While their findings are mixed, the emphasis on video modeling examples enhancing e-learning experiences, especially for male learners, is noteworthy.

Fox (2023) adeptly showcases Dunstan's (2021) 'Race, Rights, and Reform.' Through this work, educators are provided with a comprehensive narrative that highlights both the historical and diverse dimensions within the realm of economics, especially tailored for the K-12 grade spectrum. Fox's examination underscores the importance of integrating diverse perspectives, emphasizing the richness of global economic histories and their relevance for contemporary classrooms.

Alternative E-Learning

In the realm of e-learning at the university level, Ali et al. (2018) set out to understand its efficacy, amassing data from a substantial sample of 700 students via a questionnaire. Their findings, rooted in the context of Bangladesh, echoed the insights of Gamage et al. (2014), who delineated ten pivotal factors governing the effectiveness of e-learning. Notably, interactivity, collaboration, motivation, a network of opportunities, and pedagogy stood out as the topmost determinants.

Recognizing students as the central stakeholders in the e-learning ecosystem, Bahramnezhad et al. (2016) undertook a review to gauge their satisfaction levels. Their emphasis lay on tailoring e-learning programs that resonate with the unique needs of the learners, thereby enhancing the overall educational experience. As e-learning evolved, the rise of mobile learning captured

significant academic interest. Dierikx (2021) meticulously dissected the factors that would potentially steer the successful acceptance and adoption of mobile learning in higher education.

Complementing this focus on digital environments, Peters (2014) ventured into the realm of interface design, elucidating strategies to curate impactful learning experiences. Olojo et al. (2012) spotlighted the transformative potential of e-learning in the global academic landscape. Their insights underscored the prospects of adaptive learning, tailoring educational experiences to individual needs. On a more methodological note, Henson and Roberts (2006) critiqued the application of exploratory factor analysis in research. Their observations on prevalent mistakes in the domain culminated in recommendations for enriched research practices.

Shifting the lens to the immersive realm, Paes and Irizarry (2018) championed a rigorous examination of virtual reality platforms, particularly for building design reviews. Their focus converged on the interactions of human factors and the user interface. Similarly, Tilak and Bhaumik (2021) waded through the waters of graphical user interface design, underlining its security and usability aspects. Further diving into the nuances of user interface, Kořistová and Spiratos (2021) inspected virtual reality's role in shaping customer satisfaction within e-commerce settings, spotlighting the influence of varied menu styles and other UI elements.

Ritzhaupt, Kumar, and Martin (2021) provided invaluable insights for instructional designers in higher education, delving into their competencies and anticipated work dynamics. Meanwhile, in their magnum opus, 'Teaching and learning at a distance,' Simonson, Zvacek, and Smaldino (2019) laid a comprehensive foundation for understanding distance education, distilling the essence of literature to crystallize a defining perspective for their work.

GENDER AND E-LEARNING

Numerous studies had examined how gender affects how well online learning outcomes are adapted, such as Boyte-Eckis, Minadeo, Bailey and Bailey (2018). Despite several studies having "highlighted the importance of considering gender in online learning, the current literature about how male and female students would behave is still fragmented" and the effect of gender on online learning outcomes appears to be inconsistent (Wang et al., 2021, p. 190). In a paper published in the proceedings of the International Conference on Advanced Learning Technologies (ICALT), the latter authors investigated the impact of gender on online learning behavioral patterns in a comparative study based on lag sequential analysis.

More recently, Wang, et al. (2023, p. 671) agreed that although several studies made suggestions as detailed in the previous paragraph, little attention had been lavished on temporal perspectives on gender-related differences in online learning behavior. The journal article on computers in human behavior by Alghamdi et al. (2020, p. 214) reported that research had "shown that multitasking in classrooms negatively impacts students' academic performance." The latter study "investigated the indirect effects of" online and face-to-face classroom "multitasking on academic performance (i.e., Grade Point Average [GPA]) through self-efficacy for self-regulated learning (SESRL) in males and females (i.e., by gender)." Moderated mediation indicated that females performed considerably better in online learning than males because they had superior self-control.

The aim of the study reported on in the journal article on education and information technologies by Lakhal and Khechine (2021, p. 2247) was to verify whether technological factors had an influence on students' persistence in online courses in higher education. "A theoretical model encompassing seven variables was tested" to establish the moderating roles of gender, age and prior online course experience. However, other studies had found no significant difference in e-learning performance between male and female students.

DISCUSSION

This section of the chapter will present the authors' perspective on the issues, problems, etc., as these relate to the main theme of the textbook and arguments supporting the authors' position on the impact of learner content and user interface design on e-learning quality when teaching in times of crises. It will also compare with what has been, or is currently being, done as it relates to the specific topic of the chapter. Some of the theories and models used in the study reported on in this chapter are the Technology Acceptance Model (TAM), Cognitive Flexibility Theory

(CFT) and the "Unified Theory of Acceptance and Use of Technology (UTAUT)" (Weerathunga et al., 2021, p. 3). These theories share a common characteristic as to what leads to e-learning acceptance by some students. This common characteristic is the issue of interaction as a key factor for e-learning success.

There had been some exploration into the interactivity of e-learning content and interface design and how that impacts the quality of e-learning. The three interactions (SSI, SII and SCI) already mentioned in the introduction, Gunesekera, et al. (2019) argued, are the foundations for an efficient e-learning environment and that the majority of literature revealed that issues in SSI have been discussed to a satisfactory level. Regarding current issues (at the time), the study by Raynis (2018) reported "on the results of a job announcement analysis of ninety-three (93) instructional design jobs." The results were "discussed, as well as supported and contrasted with a literature review that" included reports.

The study reported on in the international journal article on instructional technology and distance learning by Arkorful and Abaidoo (2015, p. 29) investigated the role and "effectiveness of using e-learning in teaching in tertiary institutions", as well as the advantages and disadvantages of its adoption. "In institutions of higher education, the issue of utilizing modern" ICTs remains important.

Maatuk, et al. (2022, p. 35), in a journal article on computing in higher education, indicated some of the major issues, challenges and opportunities related to the COVID-19 pandemic and e-learning from the perspective of students and instructors "by extrapolating the opinions of students and faculty instructors on the use of e-learning systems in a public university during the" COVID-19 pandemic. According to the journal article on applied learning and teaching by Saxena (2019, p. 65), the "concern over gaps between industry requirements of graduate skills and attributes of the current workforce is one of the key public policy challenges". The latter author therefore suggested the Pallas advanced learning system as a research-informed virtual learning kit.

The study reported on in the international journal article on novel research in the humanities and social sciences by Odhier et al. (2019, p. 73) "reported challenges in school plant management such as" poor planning by some principals. In an investigation on the contributions of principals on school machinery and equipment management in secondary schools in Kenya, the data "collection instruments were questionnaires and" an interview schedule. The face "validity of the instruments was determined and ascertained by experts".

A study on the impact of the anxiety felt by communication engineering teachers indicated that it stemmed "from the stress caused by teaching, life and learning. It" affected "not only their teaching performance, but also their teaching" self-efficiency (Lai et al., 2020, p. 101). Therefore, an international journal of emerging technologies in learning by the latter authors reported on the perception of such teachers. The aim of the study reported on in the international journal of educational technology in higher education by Lakhal et al. (2021, p. 1) was to verify whether "the UTAUT model, enriched with anxiety and factors relating to" students' "characteristics and to the specificities of online courses", were explaining persistence in online courses in higher education through a difference-in-differences analysis.

Against the background of medical informatics, the journal article by Archambault et al. (2021, p. 1) indicated that clinical "decision support systems are information technologies that assist clinicians in making better decisions." A survey of Quebec emergency health professionals, however, showed that the adoption of these had "been limited because their content" could influence practitioners' intention to use Wiki-based knowledge tools.

The aim of a study among two French-speaking universities in Canada reported on by Lakhal et al. (2021, p. 1) in a paper presented at the open/technology in education, society, and scholarship association conference was to verify whether external factors were explaining students' "persistence in online courses in higher education. These external factors, borrowed from" a model of student progress by Kember (1995, p. 31), included open learning courses for adults, and indicated that more recent research "regarded student persistence as a multi-variate problem involving complex interactions over the period of the course."

RATIONALE FOR STUDY

E-learning is often regarded as the most suitable method for self-learning (Okediran, et al., 2021, p. 120), as it provides a wide range of materials in different formats and on all topics. "Unlike the conventional mode of education", however, carrying out the associated activities is herculean task. Therefore, the study reported on in the international journal article on multidisciplinary research and development by the latter authors "developed a system that can efficiently predict" learners' academic performance (LAP) through the adaptive neuro-fuzzy modelling of online distance learners in the era of COVID-19.

Evidence from studies during the COVID-19 pandemic era showed low student participation in some places in the United States (Catalano et al., 2021, p. 258). The international journal article on information and learning technology by the latter authors indicated that the "novel coronavirus, COVID-19, which emerged in 2019 and quickly spread to the United States, resulted in widespread closure of PreK-12 schools and universities". Transitioning to online learning during the COVID-19 pandemic was characterized by differences in access and participation among students in disadvantaged school districts.

This situation, however, was not exclusive to the United States, but was also applicable to most African countries and more specifically in Ghana. Africa was standing "at the threshold of development that requires a new approach to promote technological advancement and long-term economic growth" (Ansu-Kyeremeh & Goosen, 2022, p. 47). In a chapter as part of a book on socioeconomic inclusion during an era of online education, the latter authors were exploring the socio-economic facets of online inclusive education in Ghana, including the effects of technological advancement in academia.

The studies conducted by Catalano et al. (2021), Egielewa et al. (2022), Aboagye et al. (2021), Paschal and Mkulu (2020) and the United Nations International Children's Emergency Fund (UNICEF, 2021) reported low student participation in online learning in the COVID-19 pandemic lockdown era, even when that was the only way students could obtain access to education.

Especially the journal article on social education research by Aboagye, et al. (2021, p. 1) indicated that the challenges of students in tertiary institutions and problems "associated with the transition from conventional learning" (face-to-face) "to online learning (e-learning) in the educational system" were well-documented for the COVID-19 period. Given that e-learning was the only viable option for education during this period (Weerathunga, et al., 2021), student participation should have been higher, especially for those students, who had the necessary tools to access online content.

Problem Statement

There had been attempts to tackle teaching and learning in times of crisis by utilizing various e-learning models. Nonetheless, e-learning implementation still suffers from students' unwillingness to change from traditional classroom learning to virtual classrooms (Amanor-Mfoafo, Edonu, Akrofi, & Dowuona, 2020, p. 197). Insights from "teachers in Ghanaian basic schools" working towards undertaking e-learning during COVID-19 were obtained using an online questionnaire. Data "was collected from 108 teachers" and reported on in a European journal article on open education and e-learning studies, reflecting on "the ability of basic school teachers to teach using e-learning". Good learning design should include elements that attract students' attention and draw them to the content to be learnt (Saeed et al., 2019).

Moreover, many of the studies that had been conducted on the sustainability of e-learning appear to focus on the effectiveness of e-learning in teaching and learning. One example of the latter would be the study reported on in a journal article on English language teaching by Shifat and Khan (2022, p. 80), which "investigated the probable sustainability and effectiveness of e-learning in English language teaching (ELT) to learners in" undergraduate "English as a foreign language (EFL)" classrooms.

Additionally, the purpose of the study reported on in a Malaysian journal article on learning and instruction by Panyajamorn, Suanmali, Kohda, Chongphaisal, and Supnithi (2018, p. 1) was to examine "the effectiveness of e-learning content design" in Thai public schools "by considering two different subjects (mathematics and reading) and areas (metropolitan and rural)."

The investigation by Aali, Narenji Thani, Keramati and Garavand (2020, p. 121) reported on in a journal article on Information Technology Management (ITM) indicated that in the digital age, e-learning systems" had been employed as 'new equipment' "in the higher education system" at "different universities. Considering the importance of" the optimization of such a system, the research was "aimed at providing a model for the effectiveness of e-learning" in higher education systems.

Active Learning

All these studies seem to suggest that when all factors like technology infrastructure and access are satisfied, an e-learning model must make use of various forms of active learning to improve the quality of the online environment.

However, none of these empirical studies have directly addressed questions regarding learner content and user interface design and the impact of these on e-learning quality. This study and chapter can contribute to the value and quality aspects of the book, and is timely because as learner content and user interface design are substantially intertwined, a clear understanding of how these can improve the quality of e-learning becomes crucial. Hence the need for this study to clearly understand how learner content and the design of user interfaces impacts the quality of e-learning to fill existing literature gaps. To gauge this, the study aims to investigate the impact of learner content and user interface design on e-learning quality.

RESEARCH QUESTIONS

The study will be guided by the following primary research question: How does learner content and user interface design impact e-learning quality?

The study will further be guided by the following secondary research questions:

1. How does user interface design impact student-content interaction in e-learning to impact students' performance in an ICT subject?
2. How does learner content and user interface design foster students' satisfaction to impact the quality of e-learning in an ICT subject?
3. What is the difference in performance between male and female students after using the e-learning model?

4. What are the academic outcomes for students with computers at home, compared to those without access to computers at home, after using the e-learning model?
5. What is the performance of students, who have basic computer skills, compared to those, who do not possess basic computer skills, after using the e-learning model?

Research Ethics

Ethical issues are very important aspects in all research. Gravetter and Forzano (2015) opined that interpersonal ethics require concern for the dignity, privacy and well-being of those, who are studied in the process of data collection, analyses and reporting. These include the right to privacy, voluntary participation, no harm to participants, confidentiality and the right to withdraw from the intervention.

To gather data from eligible participants, the researcher will submit a copy of the instruments to the Cape Coast Municipal Directorate of Education to be reviewed. All ethical requirements, such as academic honesty, plagiarism, and the acknowledgement of copyright materials used, as well as computer lecturers using their institutional learning management system for Information Communication Technology (ICT) education in the cyber world (Goosen & Naidoo, 2014) as detailed in the proceedings of the 43rd conference of SACLA, as well as the institutional ethical clearance required, will be addressed. Permission will also be obtained from the eligible schools and an introductory letter and ethical clearance obtained from the Cape Coast Municipal Directorate of Education.

The respondents' consent will be sought and they will be duly informed about the voluntary nature of their participation. The respondents will be assured of their anonymity and this will also be clearly stated on the questionnaire. No respondent will be allowed to disclose his/her name or even the name of the school. Hence, the views of the respondents will be handled with the utmost care and confidentiality. Towards ensuring research integrity and the ethical management of data, a chapter in the context of e-schools and community engagement (Goosen, 2018a) was considered.

Limitations

This study will investigate the relationship between learner content and user interface design and how it impacts on the quality of an e-learning environment. This study will be delimited to only grade six students in the Cape Coast municipality "in the Central Region of Ghana" (Mintah, 2018, p. 10). The research study will be delimited to two basic schools, which will be randomly chosen from ten schools in the Cape Coast Municipal Directorate of Education. This might affect the issue of generalization. The study could be "more reliable if it was conducted in" all basic schools in Ghana. The instruments for the study will include a questionnaire and an academic performance test in computing for grade six, which will be constructed by the researcher and proofread by teachers, who are not from the selected schools. A questionnaire could have a "low response rate and the possibility of" learners' responses being biased cannot be ruled out (Mintah, 2018, p. 11). These weaknesses associated with questionnaires can "negatively influence the validity of the conclusions" that will be drawn from the study.

There will be 40 questions for use as pre-test and post-test. The study will use grade six learners, who possess a considerable number of computing skills to manipulate the intervention provided. They also exhibit traits or characteristics of junior high learners. Finally, only teachers in the selected schools will be used to administer the interventions.

Recommendations

The study by Tanye (2017) suggested that there is no national policy to direct how e-learning should be implemented, even at the university level, in Ghana. According to Tanye (2017), the "Centre for National Distance Learning and Open Schooling (CENDLOS)" (Edem Adzovie & Jibril, 2022, p. 3) was mandated to roll out e-learning solutions "through the Ministry of Education (MoE)" in Ghana to reinforce "Open and Distance Learning (ODL) at the tertiary level", as well as the pre-tertiary level, but was not successful at the junior and senior high levels in the country.

Edem Adzovie and Jibril (2022, p. 3) also reported that Ghana is a partner in various e-learning projects in Africa but had not made much progress towards the "successful introduction and implementation of e-learning solutions".

"The Universal Design for Learning (UDL) approach is increasingly drawing attention from researchers and educators as a possible solution to promote content accessibility" (Al-Azawei, Serenelli, & Lundqvist, 2016, p. 39). The journal article on the scholarship of teaching and learning by the latter authors therefore presented a content analysis of peer reviewed journals from 2012 to 2015.

The chapter on sampling techniques for quantitative research by Sarker and AL-Muaalemi (2022, p. 221), as part of a book on the principles of social research methodology, indicated that in "quantitative research, collecting data from an entire population of a study is impractical in many instances. It squanders resources like time and money which can be minimized by" making use of one of the sampling techniques, which are usually followed in the quantitative sections of a study. The "types of sampling techniques along with" the research design can contribute to non-probability sampling being selected in social science research. Ethical Information and Communication Technologies for Development (ICT4D) solutions regarding research integrity for Massive Open Online Courses (MOOCs) may be applicable (Goosen, 2018b).

The Analyze, Design, Develop, Implement, and Evaluate (ADDIE) model had been used as a fundamental approach towards creating educational and training programs by educators and instructional designers for many years. Simonson et al. (2019) made recommendations that the stages of the ADDIE model can be executed in any order and indicated that the model had become widely accepted for its effectiveness in creating successful training solutions.

FUTURE RESEARCH DIRECTIONS

The efficacy of emerging paradigms, models, and practical challenges associated with the rollout of new programs warrant further investigation in this sector. Advancements in the topic's domain beckon the scholarly community to probe deeper. To remain pertinent in classrooms, educators are advised to stay attuned to evolving trends in popular culture and technological advancements, especially by embracing innovative interfaces and applications (Raynis, 2018; Scott, 2021). A pivotal study in the Akshara multidisciplinary research journal by Malode (2022) underscores how technological advancements in Information and Communication Technologies (ICTs) have steered libraries towards a seismic transition from traditional setups to digitally advanced smart libraries. In tandem, Kaushik, Kumar, and Biswas's compilation (2019) delves into the instrumental roles library and information science professionals play, particularly in assimilating and deploying innovations and new technological trends within their operational spheres.

GENDER AND E-LEARNING

Despite a downtrend in overall higher education enrollments, online course participation continues its upward trajectory. Boyte-Eckis et al. (2018) in their exploration of business diversity, underscore the need for educators to refine their focus, emphasizing parameters such as age, gender, and ethnicity when considering preferences like midterm retest options. Building on the virtues of quality e-learning elucidated by Tanye (2017), the same study delves into a comprehensive statistical analysis of online economics students. This aims to discern insights that could bolster strategies for economics educators.

TEAM-BASED LEARNING

Mockeviciute et al. (2022) offer a rigorous systematic literature review that delves into the conditions under which feedback amplifies performance outcomes in team-based learning. This exploration, featured in a book dedicated to the nuances of managing modern organizational teams, also sheds light on prospective research avenues in the domain.

CONCLUSION

In contemporary society, e-learning has gained unprecedented prominence, a trend accentuated by the global exigencies of the COVID-19 pandemic. This underscores the imperative to elevate the caliber of e-learning offerings, catering meticulously to the multifaceted requirements of learners. Enriching e-learning's quality holds the promise of multiple dividends: heightened engagement and motivation among learners, amplified credibility for e-learning curricula, and an assurance of accessibility and effectiveness spanning diverse learner demographics. Echoing these sentiments, the deliberations at the South Africa International Conference on Educational Technologies (SAICET) posited the indispensability of educational technologies, not merely for specialized courses such as the ICT4D MOOC but as an overarching paradigm for all academic programs and institutions (Goosen, 2015).

Advancements in pedagogical methodologies, particularly within the domain of economics education, merit special attention. There has been a burgeoning interest in leveraging diverse modalities to enrich the learning experience. The integration of music and cinema into the curriculum offers a refreshing juxtaposition, marrying entertainment with rigorous academic inquiry. This innovative approach serves as a powerful conduit to contextualize complex economic theories and concepts, making them more relatable and engaging for students. Furthermore, the pivot towards team-based learning underscores the significance of collaboration and collective problem-solving, equipping students with skills that transcend academic boundaries. Simultaneously, there is a concerted push towards integrating diversity efforts, ensuring that the pedagogy is inclusive, culturally sensitive, and reflective of the pluralistic fabric of society. In sum, the landscape of economics education is undergoing a dynamic transformation, heralding a new era of inclusivity, innovation, and interactivity.

REFERENCES

Aali, M., Narenju Thani, F., Keramati, M. R., & Garavand, A. (2020). A model for effectiveness of e-learning at university. *Journal of Information Technology Management*, *12*(4), 121–140. doi:10.22059/jitm.2020.298696.2479

Aboagye, E., Yawson, J. A., & Appiah, K. N. (2021). COVID-19 and e-learning: The challenges of students in tertiary institutions. *Social Education Research*, *2*(1), 1–8. doi:10.37256er.212021422

Adu, E. O., & Zondo, S. S. (2023). Perceptions of educators on ICT integration into the teaching and learning of economics. *EUREKA: Social and Humanities*, (1), 61–71. doi:10.21303/2504-5571.2023.002530

Al-Azawei, A., Serenelli, F., & Lundqvist, K. (2016). Univeral Design for Learning (UDL): A content analysis of peer reviewed journals from 2012 to 2015. *The Journal of Scholarship of Teaching and Learning*, *16*(3), 39–56. doi:10.14434/josotl.v16i3.19295

Alghamdi, A., Karpinski, A. C., Lepp, A., & Barkley, J. (2020). Online and face-to-face classroom multitasking and academic performance: Moderated mediation with self-efficacy for self-regulated learning and gender. *Computers in Human Behavior*, *102*, 214–222. doi:10.1016/j.chb.2019.08.018

Alhumaid, K., Ali, S., Waheed, A., Zahid, E., & Habes, M. (2020). COVID-19 & E-learning: Perceptions & Attitudes of teachers towards e-learning acceptance in the developing countries. *Multicultural Education*, *6*(2), 100–115. doi:10.5281/zenodo.4060121

Ali, M., Hossain, S. K., & Ahmed, T. (2018). Effectiveness of e-learning for university students: Evidence from Bangladesh. *Asian Journal of Empirical Research*, *8*(10), 352–360. doi:10.18488/journal.1007/2018.8.10/1007.10.352.360

Alipio, M. (2020). *A Structural Model of Organizational Commitment among Higher Education Economics Educators*. Munich Personal RePEc Archive. MPRA Paper No. 99421. https://mpra.ub.uni-muenchen.de/99421/

Amanor-Mfoafo, N. K., Edonu, K. K., Akrafi, O., & Dowuona, E. N. (2020). Towards e-learning in basic schools during COVID-19: Insights from Ghanaian teachers. *European Journal of Open Education and E-Learning Studies*, *5*(2), 9–19. doi:10.46827/ejoe.v5i2.3476

Ansu-Kyeremeh, E. K., & Goosen, L. (2022). Exploring the Socioeconomic Facet of Online Inclusive Education in Ghana: The Effects of Technological Advancement in Academia. In M. Garcia (Ed.), *Socioeconomic Inclusion During an Era of Online Education* (pp. 47–66). IGI Global. doi:10.4018/978-1-6684-4364-4.ch003

Archambault, P., Turcotte, S., Smith, P. Y., Said Abasse, K., Paquet, C., Cote, A., Gomez, D., Khechine, H., Gagon, M.-P., Tremblay, M., Elazhary, N., & Legare, F. (2021, June 18). Intention to use wiki-based knowledge tools: Survey of Quebec emergency health professionals. *JMIR Medical Informatics*, *9*(6), e24649. Advance online publication. doi:10.2196/24649 PMID:34142977

Arkorful, V., & Abaidoo, N. (2015). The role of e-learning, advantages, and disadvantages of its adoption in higher education. *International Journal of Instructional Technology and Distance Learning*, *12*(1), 29–42. https://www.itdl.org/Journal/Jan_15/Jan15.pdf#page=33

Bahramnezhad, F., Asgar, P., Ghiyasvandian, S., Shiri, M., & Bahramnezhad, F. (2016). The learners' satisfaction of e-learning: A review article. *American Journal of Educational Research*, *4*(4), 347–352. http://pubs.sciepub.com/education/4/4/8/

Baidoo-anu, D., & Owusu Ansah, L. (2023). Education in the Era of Generative Artificial Intelligence (AI): Understanding the Potential Benefits of ChatGPT in Promoting Teaching and Learning. *SSRN*, *7*(1), 52–62. doi:10.2139srn.4337484

Borup, J., West, R. E., Thomas, R., & Graham, C. R. (2014). Examining the impact of video feedback on instructor social presence in blended courses. *International Review of Research in Open and Distance Learning*, *15*(3), 232–256. doi:10.19173/irrodl.v15i3.1821

Boyte-Eckis, L., Minadeo, D. F., Bailey, S. S., & Bailey, W. C. (2018). Age, gender, and race as predictors of opting for a midterm retest: A statistical analysis of online economics students. *Journal of Business Diversity*, *18*(1), 17–28.

Briguglio, M., Acchiardo, C. J., Mateer, D., & Geerling, W. (2020). Behavioral economics in film: Insights for educators. *Journal of Behavioral Economics for Policy*, *4*(1), 17–28.

Catalano, A. J., Torff, B., & Anderson, K. S. (2021). Transitioning to online learning during the COVID-19 pandemic: Differences in access and participation among students in disadvantaged school districts. *The International Journal of Information and Learning Technology*, *38*(2), 258–270. doi:10.1108/IJILT-06-2020-0111

De Four-Babb, J., Esnard, T., Bristol, L., Coye, T., Ibrahim-Joseph, L., & Perez, L. (2022). Managing the first wave. In F. Netswera, A. A. Woldegiyorgis, & T. Karabchuk (Eds.), *Higher education and the COVID-19 pandemic: Cross-national perspectives on the challenges and management of higher education in crisis times* (pp. 138–153). Brill. doi:10.1163/9789004520554_009

Demuyakor, J. (2021). COVID-19 pandemic and higher education: Leveraging on digital technologies and mobile applications for online learning in Ghana. *International Journal of Education*, *9*(3), 26–38. doi:10.34293/education.v9i3.3904

Dierikx, M. (2021, July 1). *Factors that influence the acceptance and adoption of mobile learning applications in higher education: A systematic review*. Delft University of Technology, Bachelor Seminar of Computer Science and Engineering. https://repository.tudelft.nl/islandora/object/uuid:7bea71b8-1b64-49e7-b2d9-f0741a5fe52d/datastream/OBJ/download

Dunstan, S. C. (2021). *Race, rights, and reform: Black activism in the French empire and the United States from World War I to the Cold War*. Cambridge University Press. doi:10.1017/9781108764971

Edem Adzovie, D., & Jibril, A. B. (2022). Assessment of the effects of COVID-19 pandemic on the prospects of e-learning in higher learning institutions: The mediating role of academic innovativeness and technological growth. *Cogent Education*, *9*(1), 2041222. Advance online publication. doi:10.1080/2331186X.2022.2041222

Egielewa, P., Idogho, P. O., Iyalomhe, F. O., & Cirella, G. T. (2022). COVID-19 and digitized education: Analysis of online learning in Nigerian higher education. *E-Learning and Digital Media*, *19*(1), 19–35. doi:10.1177/20427530211022808

Fox, M. E. (2023). Sarah C. Dunstan: Race, rights, and reform: Black activism in the French empire and the United States from World War I to the Cold War. *Journal of Economics, Race, and Policy*, *6*, 60–62. doi:10.100741996-022-00107-7

Gamage, D., Fernando, S., & Perera, I. (2014). Factors affecting to effective eLearning: Learners perspective. [SCIRJ]. *Scientific Research Journal*, *2*(5), 42–48.

Geerling, W., Mateer, G. D., Wooten, J., & Damodaran, N. (2023). ChatGPT has aced the test of understanding in college economics: Now what? *The American Economist*, *68*(2), 233–245. doi:10.1177/05694345231169654

Gherheş, V., Stoian, C. E., Fărcaşiu, M. A., & Stanici, M. (2021). E-learning vs. face-to-face learning: Analyzing students' preferences and behaviors. *Sustainability (Basel)*, *13*(8), 4381. Advance online publication. doi:10.3390u13084381

Gill, S. S., Xu, M., Patros, P., Wu, H., Kaur, R., Kaur, K., Fuller, S., Singh, M., Arora, P., Parlikad, A. K., Stankovski, V., Abraham, A., Shosh, S. K., Lutfiyya, H., Kanhere, S. S., Bahsoon, R., Rana, O., Dustdar, S., Sakellarious, R., ... Buyya, R. (2024). Transformative effects of ChatGPT on modern education: Emerging era of AI Chatbots. *Internet of Things and Cyber-Physical Systems*, *4*, 19–23. doi:10.1016/j.iotcps.2023.06.002

Goosen, L. (2008). A brief history of choosing first programming languages. In J. Impagliazzo (Ed.), *History of Computing and Education 3* (Vol. 269, pp. 167–170). Springer. doi:10.1007/978-0-387-09657-5_11

Goosen, L. (2015). Educational technologies for an ICT4D MOOC in the 21st century. In D. Nwaozuzu, & S. Mnisi (Ed.), *Proceedings of the South Africa International Conference on Educational Technologies* (pp. 37-48). Pretoria: African Academic Research Forum.

Goosen, L. (2018a). Ethical data management and research integrity in the context of e-schools and community engagement. In C. Sibinga (Ed.), *Ensuring Research Integrity and the Ethical Management of Data* (pp. 14–45). IGI Global. doi:10.4018/978-1-5225-2730-5.ch002

Goosen, L. (2018b). Ethical information and communication technologies for development solutions: Research integrity for massive open online courses. In C. Sibinga (Ed.), *Ensuring Research Integrity and the Ethical Management of Data* (pp. 155–173). IGI Global. doi:10.4018/978-1-5225-2730-5.ch009

Goosen, L. (2019). Research on technology-supported teaching and learning for autism. In L. Makewa, B. Ngussa, & J. Kuboja (Eds.), *Technology-Supported Teaching and Research Methods for Educators* (pp. 88–110). IGI Global. doi:10.4018/978-1-5225-5915-3.ch005

Goosen, L., & Naidoo, L. (2014). Computer lecturers using their institutional LMS for ICT education in the cyber world. In C. Burger, & K. Naudé (Ed.), *Proceedings of the 43rd Conference of the Southern African Computer Lecturers' Association (SACLA)* (pp. 99-108). Port Elizabeth: Nelson Mandela Metropolitan University.

Gravetter, F. J., & Forzano, L. B. (2015). Experimental designs: Withinsubjects design. In *Research Methods for the Behavioral Sciences* (pp. 249–278). Cengage Learning.

Gunesekera, A. I., Bao, Y., & Kibelloh, M. (2019). The role of usability on e-learning user interactions and satisfaction: A literature review. *Journal of Systems and Information Technology*, *21*(3), 368–394. doi:10.1108/JSIT-02-2019-0024

Henderson, J., & Drewes, A. (2020). *Teaching climate change in the United States*. Taylor and Francis. doi:10.4324/9780367179496

Henson, R. K., & Roberts, J. K. (2006). Use of exploratory factor analysis in published research: Common errors and some comment on improved practice. *Educational and Psychological Measurement*, *66*(3), 393–416. doi:10.1177/0013164405282485

Hibrida, A. R., & Sumual, T. E. (2022, August). Educational and teaching performance of educators at the Faculty of Economics and Business, Manado State University (UNIMA): Analysis of professional competence and motivation. *Journal of International Conference Proceedings*, *5*(2), 64–75. doi:10.32535/jicp.v5i2.1671

Hoffer, A., & Beckstrom, A. (2019). University and high school economics educators partnership: A model from La Crosse, Wisconsin. In Teaching Economics: Perspectives on Innovative Economics Education (pp. 89-96). Springer. doi:10.1007/978-3-030-20696-3_8

Hoogerheide, V., van Wermeskerken, M., Loyens, S. M., & van Gog, T. (2016). Learning from video modeling examples: Content kept equal, adults are more effective models than peers. *Learning and Instruction*, *44*, 22–30. doi:10.1016/j.learninstruc.2016.02.004

Kaushik, A., Kumar, A., & Biswas, P. (Eds.). (2019). *Handbook of research on emerging trends and technologies in library and information science*. IGI Global. doi:10.4018/978-1-5225-9825-1

Kember, D. (1995). *Open learning courses for adults: A model of student progress*. Educational Technology Publications.

Kořistová, M., & Spiratos, C. (2021). *Navigation user interface design in e-commerce and its impact on customers' satisfaction: A mixed-methods study analysing the impact of different menu styles and user interface elements*. Jönköping University.

Kremeňová, I., Fabuš, J., & Koncova, D. (2022). How the perception of educators of the Faculty of Operation and Economics of Transport and Communications regarding forms of teaching changed during the COVID-19 pandemic in 2020 and 2021. In *INTED2022 Proceedings* (pp. 5570–5574). IATED. doi:10.21125/inted.2022.1435

Lakhal, S., Heilporn, G., & Khechine, H. (2021, December). External factors explaining students' persistence in online courses in higher education: A study among two French-speaking universities in Canada. *The Open/Technology in Education, Society, and Scholarship Association Conference*, *1*(1), 1–8. doi:10.18357/otessac.2021.1.1.50

Lakhal, S., & Khechine, H. (2021). Technological factors of students' persistence in online courses in higher education: The moderating role of gender, age and prior online course experience. *Education and Information Technologies, 26*(3), 3347–3373. doi:10.100710639-020-10407-w

Lakhal, S., Khechine, H., & Mukamurera, J. (2021). Explaining persistence in online courses in higher education: A difference-in-differences analysis. *International Journal of Educational Technology in Higher Education, 18*(1), 1–32. doi:10.118641239-021-00251-4

Maatuk, A. M., ElBerkawi, E. K., AlJawarneh, S., Rashaideh, H., & Alharbi, H. (2022). The COVID-19 pandemic and e-learning: Challenges and opportunities from the perspective of students and instructors. *Journal of Computing in Higher Education, 34*(1), 21–38. doi:10.100712528-021-09274-2 PMID:33967563

Malode, V. D. (2022). *Emerging trends and technologies in library and information services in new academic environment*. Akshara Multidisciplinary Research Journal. doi:10.11648/j.ajist.20220601.12

McKibben, B., Anderson, R., & McKenzie, M. (2020). *Teaching climate change in the United States*. Taylor and Francis. Retrieved from https://api.taylorfrancis.com/content/books/mono/download?identifierName=DOI&identifierValue=10.4324/9780367179496&type=googlePDF

Mintah, P. C. (2018). *The influence of emotional intelligence on the academic performance of teacher trainees in the Central Region of Ghana* [PhD thesis]. University of Cape Coast.

Mockeviciute, A., El Baroudi, S., Gorbatov, S., & Khapova, S. N. (2022). When does feedback enhance performance in teams?: A systematic literature review and future research agenda. In *Managing team centricity in modern organizations* (pp. 115–164). Information Age Publishing.

Odhier, P. O., Ajowi, J. O., & Mwebi, B. (2019). Investigation on contributions of principals on school machinery and equipment management in secondary schools in Kenya. *International Journal of Novel Research in Humanity and Social Sciences, 6*(5), 73–88.

Okediran, O. O., Fajobi, M. O., Onawumi, A. S., Fajobi, D. T., Awoyemi, E. A., & Ojediran, J. T. (2021). Adaptive neuro-fuzzy modelling and prediction of academic performance of online distance learners in the era of COVID-19. *International Journal of Multidisciplinary Research and Development, 8*(4), 120–128.

Olojo, O. J., Adewumi, M. G., & Ajisola, K. T. (2012). E-learning and its effects on teaching and learning in a global age. *International Journal of Academic Research in Business & Social Sciences*, *2*(1), 203–210.

Paes, D., & Irizarry, J. (2018). A usability study of an immersive virtual reality platform for building design review: Considerations on human factors and user interface. *Construction Research Congress*, 419-428. 10.1061/9780784481264.041

Panyajamorn, T., Suanmali, S., Kohda, Y., Chongphaisal, P., & Supnithi, T. (2018). Effectiveness of e-learning design in Thai public schools. *Malaysian Journal of Learning and Instruction*, *15*(1), 1–34.

Paschal, M. J., & Mkulu, D. G. (2020). Online classes during COVID-19 pandemic in higher learning institutions in Africa. *Global Research in Higher Education*, *3*(3). Retrieved from www.scholink.org/ojs/index.php/grhe

Peters, D. (2014). *Interface design for learning: Design strategies for learning experiences*. Pearson Education.

Raynis, M. (2018). Analysis of instructional design job announcements (2016). *Current Issues in Emerging e-Learning*, *4*(1). Retrieved from https://scholarworks.umb.edu/ciee/vol4/iss1/9

Ritzhaupt, A. D., Kumar, S., & Martin, F. (2021). The competencies for instructional designers in higher education. In *A practitioner's guide to instructional design in higher education*. Retrieved from https://edtechbooks.org/id_highered/the_competencies_for

Saeed, M., Malallah, F., & Alasaady, M. (2019). A proposed model for designing e-learning courses. *Journal of Theoretical and Applied Information Technology*, *97*(4), 1239–1250.

Sarker, M., & Al-Muaalemi, M. A. (2022). Sampling techniques for quantitative research. In *Principles of Social Research Methodology* (pp. 221–234). Springer Nature Singapore. doi:10.1007/978-981-19-5441-2_15

Saxena, N. (2019). Pallas advanced learning systems–A research-informed virtual learning kit. *Journal of Applied Learning and Teaching*, *2*(1), 65–68. doi:10.37074/jalt.2019.2.1.8

Scott, A. B. (2021). A case study of tourism in North Carolina state parks using Google trends. *International Journal of Tourism and Hospitality Management in the Digital Age*, *5*(2), 1–14. doi:10.4018/IJTHMDA.298703

Scott, B. (2023). *Using music to enhance pedagogy in the classroom*. Presentation at the *Journal of Economics Teaching Symposium on Economics Teaching*. 10.13140/RG.2.2.34710.11847

Sharples, M. (2022). *New AI tools that can write student essays require educators to rethink teaching and assessment. Blog*. Retrieved from London School of Economics.

Shifat, N. F., & Khan, M. E. (2022). Sustainability of e-learning in the undergraduate EFL classrooms. *FOSTER: Journal of English Language Teaching*, *3*(2), 80–89. doi:10.24256/foster-jelt.v3i2.88

Simonson, M., Zvacek, S. M., & Smaldino, S. (2019). *Teaching and learning at a distance: Foundations of distance education* (7th ed.). Information Age.

Tanye, H. A. (2017). Quality eLearning in distance learning: Benefits and implications for national eLearning policy in Ghana. *International Journal of Multicultural and Multireligious Understanding*, *4*(3), 1–11. doi:10.18415/ijmmu.v4i3.73

Tilak, G., & Bhaumik, A. (2021). A review on security and usability of graphical user interface design. *Zeichen Journal*, *7*(1), 33–45. doi:10.14445/22312803/IJCTT-V67I2P104

United Nations Educational, Scientific and Cultural Organization (UNESCO). (2020). *Education: From school closure to recovery*. Retrieved November 1, 2021, from https://en.unesco.org/covid19/educationresponse

United Nations International Children's Emergency Fund (UNICEF). (2021). *Primary and secondary impacts of the COVID-19 pandemic on children in Ghana*. Accra, Ghana: UNICEF Policy and Evidence Section. Retrieved from https://orbilu.uni.lu/bitstream/10993/46437/1/UNICEF%202021.pdf

Vorster, J., & Goosen, L. (2017). A framework for university partnerships promoting continued support of e-schools. In J. Liebenberg (Ed.), *Proceedings of the 46th Annual Conference of the Southern African Computer Lecturers' Association (SACLA)* (pp. 118-126). Magaliesburg: North-West University.

Wang, H., Tlili, A., Lämsä, J., Cai, Z., Zhong, X., & Huang, R. (2023). Temporal perspective on the gender-related differences in online learning behaviour. *Behaviour & Information Technology*, *42*(6), 671–685. doi:10.1080/0144929X.2022.2039769

Wang, H., Tlili, A., Zhong, X., Cai, Z., & Huang, R. (2021, July). The impact of gender on online learning behavioral patterns: A comparative study based on lag sequential analysis. In *International Conference on Advanced Learning Technologies (ICALT)* (pp. 190-194). IEEE. 10.1109/ICALT52272.2021.00064

Weerathunga, P. R., Samarathunga, W. H., Rathnayake, H. N., Agampodi, S. B., Nurunnabi, M., & Madhunimasha, M. M. (2021). The COVID-19 pandemic and the acceptance of e-learning among university students: The role of precipitating events. *Education Sciences*, *11*(8), 436. Advance online publication. doi:10.3390/educsci11080436

Wolla, S. (2020). The economics of artificial intelligence: A primer for social studies educators. *The Councilor. The Journal of Social Studies*, *81*(2). https://thekeep.eiu.edu/the_councilor/vol81/iss2/3

Yakubu, M. N., & Dasuki, S. (2018). Assessing e-learning systems success in Nigeria: An application of the DeLone and McLean information systems success model. *Journal of Information Technology Education*, *17*, 183–203. doi:10.28945/4077

KEY TERMS AND DEFINITIONS

E-Learning: Refers to the use of digital technologies to provide access to educational content, resources, and support systems for learners and educators. It had become an increasingly popular method of education, especially in the wake of the COVID-19 pandemic, and can offer benefits such as flexibility, cost-effectiveness, and personalized learning experiences.

Interface Design: Can be defined as the process of creating the visual and functional elements of a product or system that enable users to interact with it.

Teaching: Can be defined as the intentional facilitation of learning, encompassing the design and delivery of instruction, assessment, and feedback.

Technologies: Refer to the collection of tools, methods, and systems that are designed to enhance human productivity, creativity, and communication.

User Interfaces (UIs): Refer to the graphical, textual, and auditory elements of a software application or website that enable users to interact with it. These include elements such as buttons, menus, icons, forms, and multimedia, as well as the layout and design of the interfaces. A well-designed UI should be intuitive, responsive, and visually appealing to enhance the user experience.

Chapter 7
Exploring the Role of Social Media in Enhancing K-12 Economics Education

Surjit Singha
https://orcid.org/0000-0002-5730-8677
Kristu Jayanti College (Autonomous), India

EXECUTIVE SUMMARY

The incorporation of social media into economics education is a transformative journey characterized by innovation, the resolution of obstacles, and the creation of promising opportunities. It emphasizes social media's power in engaging students, making economics concepts accessible, and promoting critical thinking. Considerations of ethics highlight the significance of digital literacy, privacy, and responsible use. In addition, social media connects students worldwide, providing cross-cultural perspectives. Emerging technologies such as virtual reality, artificial intelligence, and blockchain are poised to revolutionize economics education further. Adaptable educators and students embrace social media's potential, enriching the economics education experience. The symbiotic relationship between technology, education, and economics contains tremendous potential for preparing knowledgeable global citizens to navigate complex economic challenges.

INTRODUCTION

In the swiftly changing landscape of education, incorporating technology has assumed a central role in enhancing the educational experience of students of all ages. This transformation is most pronounced in economics education, where

DOI: 10.4018/978-1-6684-7583-6.ch007

educators constantly search for innovative methods to engage K-12 students in comprehending complex economic concepts and preparing them for the challenges of the contemporary global economy. In recent years, using social media to augment and enhance the economics education curriculum has received considerable attention as a technological innovation.

The introduction of social media platforms has revolutionized how individuals communicate, share information, and connect with the world. With billions of users worldwide, social media platforms such as Facebook, Twitter, Instagram, and TikTok have become indispensable to daily life, particularly for younger generations. Educators are increasingly utilizing social media to bridge the divide between traditional classroom instruction and the dynamic, interconnected world of economics.

This chapter examines the innovative ways educators have utilized social media to engage, enlighten, and inspire students in economics. We will investigate the various strategies, tools, and best practices educators employ to leverage social media effectively, enabling them to create enriching learning experiences that resonate with today's digitally native students. It begins by discussing the foundational concepts of economics education in the K-12 context, underscoring educators' difficulties in making economic principles relevant and understandable to young students. The paper will then examine the emergence of social media as a valuable instrument for educators, casting light on its potential to improve economics education.

Furthermore, this chapter uses real-world examples and case studies to illustrate the successful incorporation of social media into economics education. By analyzing these instances of innovation and creativity, we aim to provide educators with insights and ideas for implementing social media strategies in their classrooms. In addition, we will address concerns regarding privacy, digital literacy, and the responsible use of social media in an educational context.

It is abundantly evident that the intersection of technology and pedagogy holds tremendous potential for shaping the future of economics education. By embracing the opportunities presented by social media, educators can equip their students not only to comprehend economic principles, but also to develop into knowledgeable, critical thinkers who are prepared to navigate the complex economic landscape.

THE LANDSCAPE OF SOCIAL MEDIA IN EDUCATION

Evolution of Social Media in Education

Incorporating social media into the realm of education signifies a logical advancement in the use of technology within the educational setting. The commencement of the voyage may be traced back to the advent of the internet, which facilitated the augmentation of educators' teaching materials and the dissemination of knowledge to a broader demographic. The advancement of online technology has correspondingly led to more options for educational participation. The advent of social media platforms has provided individuals with a means to establish connections, exchange information, and engage in collaborative efforts on the internet. Educators quickly saw the pedagogical possibilities inherent in these platforms.

Sengupta and Vaish (2023) provide a significant discovery in their research, emphasizing the crucial significance of social media platforms in higher education, specifically emphasizing its amplified influence during the COVID-19 epidemic. The study highlights a significant increase in the use of social media platforms by educators, students, and educational institutions. This rise may be attributed to the rapid transition to online learning and the imposition of travel limitations. Furthermore, this study highlights the prevailing worldwide research focus on understanding the complex dynamics of social media's impact on higher education throughout the epidemic. The extensive influence of social media has had a tremendous effect on both the educational landscape and public relations and networking fields. Prominent digital sites, like WhatsApp, YouTube, Facebook (now known as Meta), LinkedIn, Instagram, and Twitter, have emerged as extensively used tools. As mentioned above, the results emphasize the significance of institutions acknowledging these dynamics to strategically use social media's potential while efficiently tackling related obstacles, increasing the overall educational experience. The progression of social media integration in the field of education may be succinctly delineated via four pivotal stages:

Web 2.0 and Online Communities: During the first years of the twenty-first century, there was a notable emergence of Web 2.0 technologies, which placed a significant focus on creating user content and fostering collaborative efforts. Online communities, forums, and wikis have become essential in facilitating the exchange of information and ideas within the academic community, including students and instructors.

The research conducted by Qassrawi and Al (2023) emphasizes the benefits of using Facebook as a Web 2.0 tool in the context of foreign language training, specifically for teaching and learning English in higher education. These factors comprise improved learner engagement, seen via higher participation levels and heightened interest among adult learners. In addition, there is a favourable correlation between the use of Facebook and improved academic performance and accomplishments among college students. Facebook serves as a supplementary platform for honing language abilities. Additionally, the platform promotes cross-cultural understanding and fosters collaborative learning, establishing meaningful relationships among students from various cultural backgrounds. Furthermore,

Facebook facilitates interactive and communicative language acquisition, providing students a significant educational encounter.

Emergence of Educational Platforms: Dedicated educational platforms like Edmodo and Moodle offered instructors safe environments to interact with students and administer coursework. These platforms enabled the incorporation of social features into the learning process in a structured manner. In their study, Stellefson et al. (2020) examined the evolving importance of social media in public health education and its potential to drive substantial advancements in health promotion. The findings of this research underscore the transformative role of social media in the field. This finding highlights the capacity of social media platforms to augment the distribution of health information, empowering users not only to access but also to create and share pertinent material.

Furthermore, it enhances the utilization of social media within the realm of promoting and disseminating health-related information, hence offering the potential for broader dissemination, heightened efficacy, and economically viable projects. However, it acknowledges specific challenges, such as effectively managing misinformation and ensuring robust user privacy protections. It recognizes that while social media has much promise, its effectiveness may differ, especially among populations with limited access to technology or insufficient digital literacy skills. The statement underscores the need for health education professionals to offer inclusive interventions that cater to all demographic groups while actively engaging with and addressing opposing perspectives that promote alternative beliefs on social media platforms. It seeks to investigate the sociocognitive and affective factors that mediate the influence of social media on health outcomes. This viewpoint fundamentally advocates for a pragmatic and efficient methodology in formulating, implementing, and evaluating social media interventions in health promotion. It entails using innovative methodologies and adopting a diverse array of multidisciplinary perspectives.

Incorporation of Social Media: As social media platforms such as Facebook, Twitter, and YouTube grew in popularity, educators began to explore methods to use them for educational purposes. The accessibility and familiarity of social media made it an attractive option for increasing student engagement. According to Meabon (2014), the primary discovery of this scholarly paper pertains to integrating mobile and electronic technologies, with a specific emphasis on social media, within the realm of public education. This integration raises essential inquiries about public education's fundamental characteristics and objectives within a democratic society. Although these technologies can augment critical educational practices and facilitate a more democratic and participatory exchange of ideas, they also present some obstacles. These entities can enable market penetration, enhance monitoring capabilities, perpetuate established educational frameworks, and restrict the perceived possibilities within education. The paper presents the results of a multiple case study that examined integrating social media into the teaching practises of five secondary school teachers. The research provides insights into teachers' changing function and identity within the framework of these technological tools.

Specialized Educational Networks: Specialized educational networks, such as Schoology and Google Classroom, have evolved in response to growing concerns about privacy and security. These systems integrated the functionality of social media with the necessary security measures for educational purposes. Staudt (2023) conducted a study. The primary discovery of this research emphasizes the use of social media by early career teachers (ECTs) to enhance their professional learning networks (PLNs) in response to the many difficulties encountered throughout the transition into the teaching profession. The issues discussed comprise external conflicts, such as the need to adjust to unfamiliar coworkers, and internal conflicts, which involve reconciling previous teaching techniques with new ones. ECTs use social media as a beneficial tool for finding assistance with educational practises, establishing connections with other educators, and overcoming resource limits. However, it is essential to highlight that academic communication technologies (ECTs) also emphasize setting limits while using social media platforms. This study emphasizes the significance of social media as a tool that facilitates early career teachers (ECTs) in successfully addressing the issues they encounter at the beginning of their careers. It also provides practical implications for ECTs, educational administrators, and leaders in the education industry. The study conducted by Trust et al. (2016) the primary discovery of this research indicates that professional learning networks (PLNs) have emerged as a vital asset for teachers in primary and secondary education (P-12), providing them with the convenience of accessing resources at any time and from any location, while also enabling them to address a wide range of interests and requirements. The findings of this study, which included examining survey responses from a sample of 732 educators, suggest that Personal Learning Networks (PLNs) have considerable promise in facilitating the comprehensive professional development of teachers. This discovery emphasizes the significance of Personal Learning Networks (PLNs) in influencing teacher learning throughout the digital era. It has implications for the forthcoming advancements in professional development within the field of education.

Benefits and Challenges of Integrating Social Media Into the Curriculum

Incorporating social media into the curriculum provides educators with various advantages; nevertheless, it also poses certain obstacles. The primary discovery of the study conducted by Alenezi et al. (2023) emphasizes the need for higher education institutions to adopt digital transformation and use information and communication technology (ICT) to remain competitive and provide education of superior quality. The speedy and successful adaptation of educational institutions is essential due to the rapid growth of technology, which necessitates a fundamental change in educational delivery techniques. Notwithstanding the possible obstacles to this transformation, digital technology in education offers many prospects for augmenting student learning outcomes and the entire educational process. Moreover, the research underscores the need for educational establishments to thoroughly evaluate their current curriculum to address the disparity between conventional educational frameworks and the swiftly progressing realm of digital education.

Fundamentally, the central discovery emphasizes the need to adopt digital education as a compulsory measure to effectively equip students for a future progressively influenced by technological advancements. In their research, Fang et al. (2014) focused on identifying and analyzing complex ethical and pedagogical issues related to the use of social media by students in the field of social work. The article's main objective was to explore and understand the implications of incorporating social media platforms into the educational practices of social work students. It presents three illustrative instances that successfully exemplify the intricacies and challenges of using social media in both personal and professional contexts. These scenarios offer a framework for evaluating the fuzzy boundary between public and private online realms, the potential of unintended receivers, and the persistent nature of distributed material on social media platforms. It ultimately presents recommendations for social work educators to effectively tackle these challenges, emphasizing the need to understand the implications of social media use in the context of social work.

Benefits

1. **Enhanced Engagement:** The interactive nature of social media encourages active participation and discussion among students, thereby improving their engagement with course materials.
2. **Real-World Connection:** Social media frequently reflects current events and trends, allowing students to apply classroom knowledge to real-world circumstances.
3. **Diverse Learning Resources:** Social media facilitates access to abundant multimedia resources, such as videos, infographics, and expert perspectives, thereby enhancing the learning experience.
4. **Collaborative Learning:** Students can collaborate on projects, share knowledge, and learn from their peers through social media platforms.

5. **Global Reach:** Social media eliminates geographical barriers, allowing students to communicate with peers and experts from around the globe, thereby fostering cultural exchange and international perspectives.

Challenges

1. **Privacy and Security:** Protecting student privacy and assuring a secure online environment is paramount but can be difficult on public platforms.
2. **Digital Literacy:** To effectively navigate the online world, students must be educated about responsible social media use, digital etiquette, and online safety.
3. **Distractions:** The same features that enhance engagement can potentially lead to a loss of concentration on educational content if used irresponsibly.
4. **Inequity:** There may be disparities in students' access to technology and social media platforms, resulting in unequal learning opportunities.
5. **Teacher Training:** Educators may need training to effectively incorporate social media into their teaching methods and navigate the rapidly changing digital landscape.

The social media landscape in education has evolved substantially, providing educators and students with numerous opportunities to enhance the learning experience. To create a safe, engaging, and equitable learning environment, the responsible integration of social media into the curriculum requires carefully considering its benefits and challenges.

LEVERAGING SOCIAL MEDIA FOR ECONOMICS EDUCATION

Engaging Students Through Micro-Blogging (Twitter) Discussions on Economic News

Twitter, a platform for microblogging, offers a unique chance for students to participate in real-time debates about economic news and events. In their chapter, Middaugh et al. (2023) have made a significant discovery, highlighting the need for a comprehensive understanding of the information environment, particularly of social media platforms like Twitter, to implement democracy education in the face of disinformation successfully. The researchers conducted an extensive examination of a large dataset consisting of 900 tweets that revolved around topics significant to teenagers on the social media platform Twitter. This investigation comprehensively examined various users, including celebrities, news organizations, and people. The various content categories included in these online debates, such as views, informative links, and calls to action, were thoroughly examined.

Moreover, their investigation revealed the complex interaction among different user categories, kinds of material, and the precise matters being examined, all impacting engagement indicators like likes, shares, and retweets. The present study not only sheds light on the complex dynamics of discourse and participation on Twitter, a widely used social media platform, but also emphasizes the significance of Twitter as a valuable venue for young people to engage with, exchange, deliberate, and articulate their viewpoints on matters about civic affairs. Significantly, it provides educators with vital insights and direction in effectively using social media platforms for civic involvement. The statement acknowledges the ever-changing character of social media platforms. It emphasizes the influence exerted by many components and individuals involved in discussions, establishing a basis for well-informed teaching approaches. This approach facilitates students' awareness of contemporary economic developments and fosters the cultivation of critical thinking and analytical skills. The primary focus of the study by Kaplan and Haenlein (2011) is on the efficacy of micro-blogs, as shown by platforms such as Twitter. The popularity of micro-blogging may be linked to its specific traits, which include the production of ambient awareness, a unique kind of push-pull communication, and the platform's ability to cater to virtual exhibitionism and voyeurism. The attributes mentioned above have not only garnered individual users' interest but have also bestowed significant value onto micro-blogs in the context of enterprises. The article highlights the potential of micro-blogging to provide advantages for firms throughout many stages of the marketing process, including marketing research, marketing communications, and customer services.

It presents a series of principles, referred to as "The Three Rs of Micro-Blogging: Relevance; Respect; Return," that provides a structure for organizations using micro-blogging platforms. Menkhoff et al. (2015), the primary discovery of this study is the introduction and examination of "pedagogical tweeting" as a social networking application that enhances competencies. Its purpose is to tackle the problem of students who do not participate or interact in classroom activities. This study elucidates the potential of Twitter's micro-blogging service as a valuable instrument for facilitating interactive discourse, addressing inquiries, and offering instructional support to educators and learners alike. The paper underscores the significance of Twitter's multi-device and multi-platform accessibility, which renders it a flexible instrument for engaging students. It facilitates collaborative knowledge formation and cultivates an environment where students actively contribute to learning. This article describes a study conducted at Singapore Management University (SMU) focusing on students' experiences enrolled in a Knowledge Management (KM) course. The research explores the students' engagement in micro-blogging activities within the context of the system. Furthermore, the study presents four hypotheses about the efficient utilization of social awareness platforms such as Twitter in the context of higher education, therefore laying the foundation for further exploration and application.

Daily News Updates: Educators can establish a Twitter account or hashtag for their class to share relevant economic news articles, infographics, and charts. These updates can be followed and responded to by students, who can then share their insights and opinions.

Live Discussions: Organizing live Twitter conversations or discussions on economic topics that are currently prevalent can be an effective way to encourage student participation and debate. Encourage the use of pertinent identifiers for discussion tracking.

Analysis and Reflection: Students can be tasked with analyzing news articles or economic policies and summarising their findings in brief tweets as part of an assignment, thereby developing their ability to communicate complex ideas concisely.

Creating Educational Content Through Short Videos (TikTok) That Simplify Complex Economic Concepts

The popular short-form video platform TikTok can be utilized to make economics more accessible and engaging for students. Nguyen and Diederich (2023) have identified a significant discovery in their study, which underscores the dualistic character of social media, with a specific focus on TikTok. This platform has been shown to enable informal learning and the building of knowledge, although mostly fulfilling social and non-knowledge-related objectives. The researchers used machine learning classifiers to analyze a large dataset of 259,508 comments on 114 TikTok videos associated with scientific and educational hashtags. The classifiers mentioned above successfully discern discrete stages in the process of knowledge building, which include the exchange of ideas, the negotiation of understanding, and the exploration of conflicting concepts.

The study's findings indicate that the predominant discourse in the TikTok setting mostly revolved around social connections rather than actively participating in knowledge development. However, films that focused on providing informative material used unique sounds and integrated analytical language were more prone to generating comments that actively engaged in the exchange and negotiation of knowledge.

The central discovery emphasizes the significance of content providers, particularly those involved in scientific communication, being aware of the current social dynamics on platforms such as TikTok. Although these platforms provide significant chances for informal learning and information exchange, the primary focus of user behaviour often centres upon social contact. Hence, it is essential for artists to meticulously contemplate how they offer and contextualize their material to foster audience participation in social knowledge production. Educators can create or curate content that simplifies complex economic concepts. According to Lampe (2023), this scholarly study's primary discovery is the effective use of TikTok's social media platform as a novel instrument for augmenting student involvement in virtual Sociology courses. This research illustrates the potential of TikTok, a venue known for its concise video format and innovative functionalities, in facilitating student involvement with sociological insights and ideas, particularly within the context of asynchronous online courses. This paper discusses a teaching activity that utilizes TikTok and shows the outcomes from an initial assessment of this teaching approach.

Additionally, it emphasizes the potential benefits of integrating TikTok into online sociology courses. This novel methodology tackles the issue of sustaining class involvement and engagement in the context of online higher education, which has gained significant relevance during the COVID-19 epidemic with the increased use of online instructional methods. In their study, Ding et al. (2023) conducted a quasi-experimental investigation to examine the impact of concise instructional videos on students' academic achievement in business statistics. The primary outcome of this study revealed a significant enhancement in students' academic performance compared to the conventional approach of virtual lectures delivered by instructors. Concise films, often lasting around two minutes or less, effectively engaged pupils' attention and piqued their curiosity.

Consequently, this led to an increased degree of student motivation, which in turn prompted them to actively engage in answering exam questions immediately after seeing the films. Furthermore, the research study found that using succinct instructional videos was particularly beneficial for students with high proficiency in mathematics, leading to enhanced performance on the statistics assessment. However, a significant association between short films and students' English proficiency levels must exist. It suggests these movies provide favourable results regardless of students' English language skills in introductory statistics courses. The study emphasizes the importance of students actively engaging with instructional films concerning their academic achievements while suggesting the potential use of brief movies to enhance student learning in higher education settings.

Explainer Videos: Create concise, engaging videos that simplify complex concepts such as supply and demand, inflation, and the gross domestic product into easily digestible segments. Utilise visual aids, graphics, and real-world examples to make content relatable.

Student-Generated Content: Encourage pupils to create educational TikTok recordings on challenging economics-related topics. It can foster parallel teaching and improve students' conceptual understanding.

Hashtag Challenges: Students are challenged to produce TikTok videos that creatively explain or implement economic concepts. Utilize class-specific hashtags to curate and distribute these videos among the class community.

Collaborative Learning Through Virtual Study Groups Using Social Media Platforms

Facebook and WhatsApp groups are examples of social media platforms that can facilitate student collaborative learning. Sabah (2023), the core finding of this study underscores the positive impact of utilizing social media, particularly Facebook groups designed for educational purposes, on various critical aspects of higher education. A comprehensive assessment identified three dimensions of use outcomes: increased perceived satisfaction, enhanced perception of academic performance, and a positive influence on the learning experience. These findings collectively demonstrate that integrating social media into higher education, as exemplified by educational Facebook groups, enhances students' overall educational satisfaction, fosters a more positive perception of their academic achievements, and positively influences their learning process. This research reinforces the growing evidence supporting the advantages of incorporating social media platforms into educational practices. It underscores the efficacy of employing the Partial Least Squares Structural Equation Modeling (PLS-SEM) approach for assessing reflective-formative constructs in a higher-order model. The primary discovery of Nungu et al. (2023) emphasizes the significant influence of online collaborative learning and the incorporation of electronic multimedia technologies on advancing STEM education in higher education settings. Students can actively contribute to co-constructing knowledge and develop crucial higher-order thinking abilities by engaging in small group interactions. This active participation in small group settings facilitates a deeper understanding of complex STEM ideas. Using multimedia tools, such as PhET simulations and YouTube videos, enhances student engagement and improves their ability to retain information, making complicated STEM topics more accessible. Despite encountering obstacles such as limited ICT resources and connection constraints, students demonstrated resilience by using readily accessible virtual labs and peer support networks. The research findings highlight the significant relationship between social and cognitive presence and student performance, emphasizing the critical role of active engagement in online collaborative learning activities. The research proposes recommendations emphasizing the need for comprehensive training programs targeting educators and students, increased internet accessibility on campuses, and the effective incorporation of multimedia resources such as Bio-interactive and Physics Education Technology (PhET) simulations to enhance STEM education. Moreover, implementing virtual labs presents itself as a practical resolution to tackle the issues related to the cost-effectiveness and availability of tangible laboratory apparatus in online STEM courses.

These online study groups can aid in the reinforcement of economic concepts.

Discussion Forums: Develop economics-specific Facebook communities and WhatsApp conversations. Students can discuss course materials, share resources, and pose inquiries outside of class.

Resource Sharing: Encourage students to share on their social media networks any relevant articles, videos, or research findings they come across. This collaborative method can enhance the educational experience.

Peer Teaching: Assign students with specific research and presentation topics for their study groups. It not only improves comprehension but also presentation and communication abilities.

Regular Check-Ins: Participate in these groups as an educator by providing guidance, answering queries, and monitoring students' progress. This virtual presence can increase motivation and engagement.

Incorporating social media platforms such as Twitter, TikTok, Facebook, and WhatsApp into economics education can make learning more interactive, engaging, and pertinent to students' lives. By adopting these innovative strategies, educators can confidently prepare students to navigate the complex economic world with confidence and a firm grasp of fundamental principles.

CASE STUDIES: APPROACHES TO SOCIAL MEDIA INTEGRATION

This section will examine three case studies illustrating innovative strategies for social media platforms to improve economics education.

Case Study 1: Using Instagram for Visualizing Economic Data and Trends

Background: A high school economics teacher recognized Instagram's potential to make economic data and trends more accessible and engaging for students. The objective was to develop a visually enticing report to comprehend economic concepts better.

Implementation

1. **Visual Infographics:** The educator initiated the creation of visually appealing infographics that summarised economic data, including unemployment rates,

inflation trends, and GDP growth. These infographics were uploaded to the economics class's Instagram account.

2. **Data Storytelling:** Each entry was accompanied by a succinct annotation that clarified the significance of the data and its practical implications. An infographic on inflation rates, for instance, was accompanied by a caption describing how it affects the purchasing power of consumers.
3. **Student Engagement:** Students were encouraged to follow the account and participate by asking questions, sharing their views, and suggesting economic topics to be visualized by the account's creators.

Outcome

- The Instagram account acquired a considerable number of student followers. Students reported a greater understanding of economic concepts and their real-world relevance.
- The visually enticing presentation made the information more accessible and memorable.

Case Study 2: YouTube Tutorials for Real-World Applications of Economic Principles

Background: A high school economics instructor created a YouTube channel to supplement his students. The channel focused on demonstrating real-world applications of economic principles, thereby making the subject matter more accessible.

Implementation

1. **Practical Examples:** The educator posted videos demonstrating the application of economic concepts such as supply and demand, opportunity cost, and elasticity to real-world situations, such as the pricing strategies of businesses and the effect of government policies.
2. **Interactive Q&A:** Each video encouraged students to submit queries or comments, nurturing discussion and enabling the instructor to elucidate misunderstandings in subsequent videos.
3. **Guest Experts:** The instructor occasionally invited business owners and economists from the local community to provide real-world insights and perspectives.

Outcome

- The YouTube channel became a valuable resource for students seeking an application of economic theories to real-world situations.
- The audience expanded beyond the classroom to include students from numerous institutions and self-learners.
- The format's interactivity promoted deeper engagement and critical thinking.

Case Study 3: Interactive Polls and Surveys on Facebook to Explore Consumer Behavior

Background: A college economics professor wished to make discussions on consumer behaviour more interactive and data-driven. Facebook was selected as the platform because of its comprehensive polling and survey capabilities.

Implementation

1. **Weekly Polls:** The instructor established a private Facebook group for the class in which weekly polls were posted. These surveys presented hypothetical consumer behaviour scenarios, such as price elasticity of demand and factors influencing consumer decisions.
2. **Discussion Threads:** After the poll results were tallied, the professor-initiated discussion threads in which students analyzed the data, explained their selections, and debated the economic theories underlying their decisions.
3. **Student-Created Surveys:** Students were tasked with designing and administering their consumer behaviour surveys using Facebook to distribute and collect responses as part of a class assignment.

Outcome

- The interactive surveys and discussions increased comprehension of consumer behaviour concepts.
- Students actively participated in the analysis of actual data and the application of economic theories.
- The platform promoted peer collaboration and interaction outside of class time.

These case studies demonstrate the adaptability of social media platforms to enhance economics education. When used creatively and strategically, social media platforms such as Instagram, YouTube, and Facebook can provide valuable resources, increase student engagement, and make economic concepts more relevant to their lives.

NAVIGATING CHALLENGES AND ENSURING ETHICAL USE

Addressing Privacy and Safety Concerns When Using Social Media With Students

1. **Clear Guidelines and Consent:** Establish explicit guidelines regarding using social media for educators and students in the classroom. Before participating in online activities, ensure that students and their parents or guardians provide informed consent.
2. **Private or Closed Groups:** Create confined or personal social media groups where only authorized users, such as students and teachers, can participate. It reduces privacy concerns by restricting access to a restricted audience.
3. **Data Protection:** When using social media platforms, educators should be aware of data protection regulations (e.g., GDPR, FERPA) and ensure compliance. Avoid revealing personal information and use secure communication methods.
4. **Online Etiquette:** Teach students suitable online etiquette, emphasizing respect, constructive communication, and accountability. Examine the effects of cyberbullying and inappropriate behaviour.

Promoting Critical Thinking Skills in Evaluating Information from Social Media Sources:

1. **Digital Literacy Education:** Integrate digital literacy into the curriculum to instruct students on critically evaluating information from social media sources. Stress the significance of fact-checking and confirming information.
2. **Source Credibility:** Encourage students to evaluate the trustworthiness of sources, including social media posts. Discuss the significance of contemplating the author's credentials, biases, and the integrity of the presented information.
3. **Media Literacy:** Include courses that teach students to distinguish between credible and unreliable sources. Instruct them on how to identify sensationalism, false information, and disinformation.
4. **Class Discussions:** Organise class discussions or assignments that require critical analysis of economic-related social media posts or articles. Encourage students to express and defend their opinions with evidence.

Balancing Screen Time with Traditional Teaching Methods:

1. **Hybrid Approach:** Adopt a hybrid strategy to balance digital and traditional instructional methods. Use social media as a supplement to instruction rather than the sole way.
2. **Structured Screen Time:** Establish explicit limits for social media use in the classroom. Ensure that screen time is focused on specific learning objectives and is followed by offline activities to reinforce concepts.
3. **Varied Activities:** Offer a variety of online and offline learning activities to accommodate various learning styles and preferences. It ensures that students have opportunities for experiential learning and interpersonal interaction.
4. **Regular Assessments:** Assess the efficacy of social media integration by regularly evaluating its influence on student engagement and learning outcomes. Adapt your approach based on the feedback and results drivers.

Incorporating social media responsibly into economics education requires addressing privacy and safety concerns, encouraging critical thinking, and maintaining a balanced approach to screen time. Educators can leverage the benefits of social media while ensuring ethical and practical use in the classroom by taking these factors into account.

FUTURE TRENDS: SOCIAL MEDIA'S ROLE IN SHAPING ECONOMIC LITERACY

Emerging Social Media Platforms and their Potential for Education

Virtual Reality (VR) and Augmented Reality (AR): Emerging technologies such as VR and AR are increasingly available via social media platforms. These immersive experiences can transport students into economic scenarios, allowing them to visualize and interact with three-dimensional complex concepts. Apps and experiences on platforms such as Facebook's Oculus and Snapchat's augmented reality (AR) lenses could provide innovative methods to teach economics. The primary discovery of this extensive analysis conducted by Al-Ansi et al. (2023) emphasizes the notable expansion in the utilization of Augmented Reality (AR) and Virtual Reality (VR) technologies within the realm of education throughout the previous twelve-year period. The advent of these technologies has resulted in a significant transformation in educational approaches, as they provide learners with immersive digital experiences, interactive learning environments, simulations, and increased levels of engagement. The considerable increase in wearable gadgets has been essential in driving this progress. Nevertheless, the research emphasizes a substantial disparity between the fast advancement of augmented reality (AR) and virtual reality (VR) technologies and their successful integration and adaptation in educational establishments. The significance of this discovery underscores the need to confront the obstacles linked to incorporating augmented reality (AR) and virtual reality (VR) in educational environments to use these technologies' capabilities for improved learning encounters correctly.

Short-Form Video Platforms: While platforms like TikTok have already garnered popularity, we can anticipate the emergence of more education-specific short-form video platforms. These platforms may provide a dedicated space for educators and students to share and consume brief, engaging economics-related educational content. The primary discovery of Zhang et al. (2023) demonstrates that the real-time dynamics of dynamic remarks substantially impact customer reactions during digital interactions. The research highlights notable findings about the impact of comments on digital material, explicitly emphasizing the significance of the timing of these remarks. Initially, a substantial surge of real-time comments adversely affects user involvement in the digital realm; however, a subsequent rise in remarks towards the conclusion yields a favourable outcome.

Moreover, the presence of a linear trend and the disparity in live comment intensity positively impact digital engagement; however, the fluctuation in intensity has a detrimental effect. The impacts of MTM (machine translation models) are intricately connected to the feelings conveyed in the real-time comments. Additionally, the research emphasizes that in-video commercials might enhance the detrimental influence of early live comments on digital engagement while reducing the negative consequences of unpredictability in live words. In general, the results mentioned above provide significant contributions to interactive marketing and give valuable recommendations for implementing influencer marketing strategies, with a particular focus on the temporal aspects of online interaction.

AI-Driven Personalization: Social media platforms will likely incorporate more advanced artificial intelligence (AI) systems for personalized learning. Personalized economics content, exams, and resources could be recommended to students based on their interests, strengths, and limitations, optimizing their learning experience. In their research, Pataranutaporn et al. (2021) investigated a significant implication of AI-generated media resulting from advancements in machine learning. This Perspective emphasizes the substantial influence that such media may exert. The emergence of technology developments has facilitated the creation of highly authentic digital representations of individuals, hence opening up avenues for fostering productive interactions across several domains. The prevailing discourse around this technology has been centred on examining its possible adverse effects. However, the objective of this Perspective is to redirect the emphasis towards its emerging advantageous applications, namely in the realms of educational assistance and enhancement of well-being. The authors provide a pipeline for developing artificial intelligence characters that are designed to be user-friendly, intending to achieve favourable outcomes. Nevertheless, the Perspective emphasizes the considerable significance of ethical concerns, underscoring the need to address ethical dilemmas and implement traceability measures to maintain trust in AI-generated media. This Perspective underscores the growing significance of generative media in the ever-evolving domain of human-AI interaction.

Blockchain for Verification: Blockchain technology could validate and credential educational accomplishments on social media platforms. It could benefit economics students who wish to demonstrate their knowledge and abilities. Alnafrah and Mouselli (2021) conducted a study. The main objective of this study is to analyze and assess the feasibility of utilizing blockchain technology as a solution for addressing the complex issues associated with managing and verifying. The proposed solution involves the establishment of a nationwide platform that utilizes hybrid blockchain technology to facilitate cooperation among various essential parties, including students, universities, government entities, policymakers, and businesses. The primary objective of this platform is to streamline the verification and accreditation procedures for academic certificates. The research highlights that this platform demonstrates both viability and the potential to serve as a complete marketplace for all actors within the higher education system. Implementing this approach can enhance the process of internationalizing education and contribute to promoting inclusive and equitable learning opportunities. This initiative aligns with the fourth Sustainable Development Goal, which guarantees quality teaching and lifelong learning for students residing in low-income countries.

The Role of Social Media in Fostering Global Economic Awareness Among Students:

1. **Cross-Cultural Experiences:** Social media allows students to communicate with peers and teachers from around the globe. Students' perspectives and knowledge of international economics can be broadened through virtual exchanges, collaborative projects, and discussions on global economic issues.
2. **Real-Time Updates on Global Economic Events:** Students can remain abreast of global economic events and trends through social media platforms. Following international news sources and experts on social media platforms such as Twitter enables students to obtain timely updates and various perspectives.
3. **Virtual Field Trips:** Social media could facilitate virtual economic field excursions to different nations or financial centres. Students could engage with local experts, investigate economic infrastructure, and acquire a global perspective on economics.

4. **Global Collaborations:** Educators can use social media to connect students with international peers for collaborative endeavours. It can lead to cross-cultural understanding and the combined solution of economic problems.
5. **Digital Diplomacy:** Social media can also serve as a platform for nurturing diplomatic relations among students interested in economics. Diplomatic simulations, international economic forums, and intellectual exchanges can occur in the digital domain, cultivating global financial awareness.

The influence of social media on economic literacy is evolving, and future trends will likely present new opportunities and challenges. As new platforms and technologies arise, educators must remain adaptable and receptive to innovative ways of integrating social media into economics education to prepare students for a constantly shifting economic landscape. To equip students with the knowledge and skills necessary for success in the interconnected world of economics, fostering global financial awareness via social media will be crucial.

DISCUSSION

One of the most remarkable aspects of social media's function in education is the ability to reconcile the distance between abstract concepts and real-world relevance. Visual content, such as infographics and brief videos, can simplify and contextualize complex economic principles. Not only do gamification elements, such as assessments and challenges, make learning more pleasurable, but they also appeal to students' competitive natures, motivating them to investigate economic concepts in greater depth. Moreover, the instantaneous feedback and interactivity of social media platforms such as Twitter and TikTok promote active learning and critical thinking, contributing to long-term retention of economic principles.

The case studies illustrated the versatility of social media in disseminating educational content. For example, YouTube channels devoted to economics provide dynamic, visual explanations of concepts comparable to having a personal tutor available. Students are afforded a risk-free environment to experiment with economic scenarios through virtual economic simulations on platforms such as Second Life, thereby enhancing the experiential nature of their education. Facilitated through social media groups and forums, collaborative learning encourages students to actively participate in discussions, share resources, and learn from their peers, nurturing a sense of community and collective understanding.

In the digital age, responsible online behaviour and digital literacy are crucial. In addition to teaching economic principles, educators must empower students with the skills necessary to navigate the vast digital landscape. Developing comprehensive digital literacy curricula that incorporate responsible social media usage, fact-checking, and critical evaluation of online sources is essential—protecting students while allowing for a collaborative and interactive learning environment and clear privacy guidelines within the educational context. Involving parents in these conversations also ensures that responsible online conduct is reinforced outside of the classroom.

The capacity of social media to connect students globally paves the way for diverse cross-cultural experiences. Collaborations between economics courses from various nations foster a global perspective and a deeper understanding of applying economic principles in diverse contexts. Virtual guest lecturers from different areas of the globe offer students distinct perspectives and broaden their horizons. This global connectivity improves economics education and prepares students for a world in which international cooperation and cultural awareness are becoming increasingly important skills.

Emerging technologies like VR, AI, and blockchain will revolutionize economics education shortly. Virtual reality can convey students to immersive economic scenarios, concretizing abstract concepts. Platforms propelled by AI offer individualized learning experiences, adjusting to each student's specific requirements and tempo. The role of blockchain in securely authenticating and sharing educational accomplishments can bring transparency and trust to credentialing, creating new avenues for recognizing students' achievements.

Integrating social media and economics education represents a revolutionary shift in how students learn and apply economic principles. The dynamic interaction between innovative teaching strategies, ethical use, global connectivity, and emerging technologies paints a bright future for economics education, in which students are not only well-equipped with economic knowledge but also equipped with essential digital literacy skills and a global perspective to thrive in the complex world of economics.

CONCLUSION

Incorporating social media into economics education is an innovative and prospective avenue for educators and students. This transformation journey has been characterized by innovative strategies, deliberate case studies, and a forward-looking approach to addressing challenges and opportunities. As we consider the function of social media in economics education, several essential insights emerge:

1. **Engagement and Accessibility:** Social media platforms have the potential to engage students in meaningful ways, making economics concepts more accessible, relatable, and applicable to their everyday lives.
2. **Innovation in Teaching:** The presented case studies demonstrate that educators can leverage the power of social media to create interactive, real-world learning experiences that cultivate critical thinking and profound comprehension.
3. **Responsibility and Ethical Use:** Managing privacy concerns, promoting digital literacy, and harmonizing screen time are essential aspects of the ethical incorporation of social media in education.
4. **Global Perspectives:** Social media provide a window to the world, allowing students to acquire global economic awareness and collaborate across borders, thereby fostering intercultural understanding.
5. **Future Trends:** Emerging platforms and technologies, such as virtual reality, artificial intelligence, and blockchain, will continue to revolutionize economics education.

Educators and students must remain adaptable and forward-thinking in this dynamic environment. Educators can continue to enrich economics education by embracing the potential of social media, thereby preparing students to flourish in the complex, interconnected world of economics. As we turn to the future, the synergy between technology, education, and economics holds great promise, as it will foster the development of informed, critical thinkers and global citizens who are prepared to face the economic challenges of the future.

REFERENCES

Al-Ansi, A. M., Jaboob, M., Garad, A., & Al-Ansi, A. (2023). Analyzing recent educational developments in augmented reality (AR) and virtual reality (VR). *Social Sciences & Humanities Open*, *8*(1), 100532. doi:10.1016/j.ssaho.2023.100532

Alenezi, M., Wardat, S., & Akour, M. (2023). The Need of Integrating Digital Education in Higher Education: Challenges and Opportunities. *Sustainability (Basel)*, *15*(6), 4782. doi:10.3390u15064782

Alnafrah, I., & Mouselli, S. (2021). Revitalizing blockchain technology potentials for smooth academic records management and verification in low-income countries. *International Journal of Educational Development*, *85*, 102460. doi:10.1016/j.ijedudev.2021.102460

Ding, N., Xu, X., & Lewis, E. (2023). Short instructional videos for the TikTok generation. *Journal of Education for Business*, *98*(4), 175–185. doi:10.1080/08832323.2022.2103489

Fang, L., Mishna, F., Zhang, V. F., Van Wert, M., & Bogo, M. (2014). Social media and social work education: Understanding and dealing with the new digital world. *Social Work in Health Care*, *53*(9), 800–814. doi:10.1080/00981389.2014.943455 PMID:25321930

Kaplan, A. M., & Haenlein, M. (2011). The early bird catches the news: Nine things you should know about micro-blogging. *Business Horizons*, *54*(2), 105–113. doi:10.1016/j.bushor.2010.09.004

Lampe, N. M. (2023). Teaching with TikTok in Online Sociology of Sex and Gender Courses. *Teaching Sociology*, *51*(4), 323–335. Advance online publication. doi:10.1177/0092055X231159091

Meabon Bartow, S. (2014). Teaching with social media: Disrupting present-day public education. *Educational Studies (Ames)*, *50*(1), 36–64. doi:10.1080/00131946.2013.866954

Menkhoff, T., Chay, Y. W., Bengtsson, M. L., Woodard, C. J., & Gan, B. (2015). Incorporating microblogging ("tweeting") in higher education: Lessons learnt in a knowledge management course. *Computers in Human Behavior*, *51*, 1295–1302. doi:10.1016/j.chb.2014.11.063

Middaugh, E., Felton, M., & Fan, H. (2023). What is in a Tweet? How Platform Features Facilitate and Constrain Civic Discourse and What It Means for Teaching Civic Media Literacy. In *Education in the Age of Misinformation: Philosophical and Pedagogical Explorations* (pp. 203–223). Springer International Publishing. doi:10.1007/978-3-031-25871-8_11

Nguyen, H., & Diederich, M. (2023). Facilitating knowledge construction in informal learning: A study of TikTok scientific, educational videos. *Computers & Education*, *205*, 104896. doi:10.1016/j.compedu.2023.104896

Nungu, L., Mukama, E., & Nsabayezu, E. (2023). Online collaborative learning and cognitive presence in mathematics and science education. Case study of University of Rwanda, College of Education. *Education and Information Technologies*, 1–20. doi:10.100710639-023-11607-w PMID:36779197

Pataranutaporn, P., Danry, V., Leong, J., Punpongsanon, P., Novy, D., Maes, P., & Sra, M. (2021). AI-generated characters for supporting personalized learning and well-being. *Nature Machine Intelligence*, *3*(12), 1013–1022. doi:10.103842256-021-00417-9

Qassrawi, R. M., & Al Karasneh, S. M. (2023). Benefits of Facebook usage (as a web 2.0 application) in Foreign Language instruction in higher education: A Meta-analysis study. *Cogent Arts & Humanities*, *10*(1), 2185447. doi:10.1080/23311983.2023.2185447

Sabah, N. M. (2023). The impact of social media-based collaborative learning environments on students' use outcomes in higher education. *International Journal of Human-Computer Interaction*, *39*(3), 667–689. doi:10.1080/10447318.2022.2046921

Sengupta, S., & Vaish, A. (2023). A study on social media and higher education during the COVID-19 pandemic. *Universal Access in the Information Society*, 1–23. doi:10.100710209-023-00988-x PMID:37361680

Staudt Willet, K. B. (2023). Early career teachers' expansion of professional learning networks with social media. *Professional Development in Education*, 1–17. doi:10.1080/19415257.2023.2178481

Stellefson, M., Paige, S. R., Chaney, B. H., & Chaney, J. D. (2020). The evolving role of social media in health promotion: Updated responsibilities for health education specialists. *International Journal of Environmental Research and Public Health*, *17*(4), 1153. doi:10.3390/ijerph17041153 PMID:32059561

Trust, T., Krutka, D. G., & Carpenter, J. P. (2016). "Together we are better": Professional learning networks for teachers. *Computers & Education*, *102*, 15–34. doi:10.1016/j.compedu.2016.06.007

Zhang, X., Zhao, Z., & Wang, K. (2023). The effects of live comments and advertisements on social media engagement: Application to short-form online video. *Journal of Research in Interactive Marketing*. Advance online publication. doi:10.1108/JRIM-02-2023-0069

Chapter 8
Social Media and Economics Education:
Addressing Challenges and Leveraging Tools for K-12 Educators

S. Baranidharan
https://orcid.org/0000-0002-7780-4045
School of Business and Management, Christ University, India

Julie Sunil
Presidency Business School, Presidency College (Autonomous), India

Sonal Devesh
Christ University, India

EXECUTIVE SUMMARY

This case study focuses on the challenges and opportunities associated with integrating social media into the K-12 economics curriculum. Ms. Smith, a high school economics teacher, faced a number of challenges when implementing social media into her teaching practices, including issues related to student engagement, cyberbullying, and privacy concerns. However, she also recognized the potential benefits of using social media in the classroom, including increased student engagement, improved collaboration and communication, and enhanced access to information and resources. To address these challenges, Ms. Smith implemented a number of remedies and measurements, including providing professional development for teachers, establishing clear guidelines for social media use, providing technical support, encouraging parent involvement, and regularly assessing the impact of social media on student learning. Through her approach, Ms. Smith was able to effectively integrate social media into her economics curriculum and enhance student learning and engagement.

DOI: 10.4018/978-1-6684-7583-6.ch008

INTRODUCTION

In recent years, the integration of technology in education has become increasingly important, with many educators recognizing the potential of social media platforms and interactive tools to enhance their teaching strategies (Al-Bahrani et al., 2015). Social media platforms, such as X (formerly Twitter) (Al-Bahrani et al., 2017; Harmon & Tomolonis, 2019; Middleditch et al., 2022), Facebook (Kirschner & Karpinski, 2010), LinkedIn (Brown & Pederson, 2020), and TikTok (Ding et al., 2023; Lai, 2021) have become a popular way for educators to share ideas, resources, and teaching strategies. Which enables students and teachers to collaborate and develop more engaging and effective educational materials. The field of economics education has been conscious that teaching impacts at earlier levels in student development influences major choices and career selection (Emerson et al., 2012). This understanding has driven economics educators to consider how to diversity teaching strategies beyond chalk-and-talk. Picault (2019) created an economics toolbox[1] to encourage the exploration of teaching that grows beyond the traditional classroom lecture. A goal of this work is to support relevant teaching methods and approaches and support lower costs for newer economics educators (Asarta, 2023; Wooten et al., 2021). This case study explores the impact of social media on economics education and the tools that educators can use to enhance student learning.

The use of social media in education has also been shown to have several benefits, including increased engagement and motivation among students, improved communication and collaboration among educators, and access to a wide range of resources and tools to enhance teaching strategies. Social media platforms also provide a space for educators to connect with other professionals in their field and share best practices, insights, and experiences (Chen, 2011).

In economics education, social media has proven particularly valuable, given the complexity of economic concepts and the challenges educators face in teaching them effectively. By leveraging social media platforms and interactive tools, educators can create more engaging and effective learning experiences for students, helping them better understand complex economic concepts and develop a strong foundational understanding of economics.

CASE

Social media has played a significant role in the education, providing educators with tools and resources to create a more engaging learning experience for students. In this case study, we will explore effective economics education topics for K-12 educators and the tools provided by social media to enhance their teaching strategies. The case study will provide a roadmap on using X (formerly Twitter) in the K-12 classroom, which aligns with previous work (Jones & Baltzersen, 2017).

A group of K-12 educators from various schools in the United States collaborated on social media to develop effective economics education topics for their students. They identified the following topics as key to the students' understanding of economics:

1. Budgeting and Saving: This topic focuses on the importance of budgeting and saving money. Educators use real-world examples to help students understand how to manage their finances.
2. Supply and Demand: This topic helps students understand how the price of goods and services is determined by supply and demand in the market.
3. Market Structures: This topic teaches students about different types of market structures, including monopolies, oligopolies, and perfect competition.
4. Globalization: This topic helps students understand the impact of globalization on the world economy, including the advantages and disadvantages of free trade.

The educators used various social media tools to enhance their teaching strategies. They used X (formerly Twitter) to share post their ideas and resources, such as articles, videos, and infographics. They also created a Facebook group where they could collaborate and discuss their teaching strategies.

To engage their students, the educators used interactive tools such as Kahoot, a game-based learning platform, and Nearpod, an interactive presentation tool. Kahoot allowed students to compete against each other in a fun and engaging way, while Nearpod provided educators with the ability to create interactive presentations, quizzes, and polls.

One real-time example of social media's impact on economics education is the use of X in the classroom. A high school economics teacher, Ms. Smith, created a class X account where she would post daily updates on current economic events and trends. She encouraged her students to follow the account and participate in online discussions related to these topics.

Through this simple use of social media, Ms. Smith was able to increase student engagement and interest in economics. Students were able to apply economic concepts to real-world situations, such as analyzing the effects of tariffs on global trade and share their opinions and insights with their peers. The use of Twitter also allowed students to practice critical thinking skills and develop their writing abilities through concise and effective communication.

In addition to social media, Ms. Smith incorporated various tools and resources to enhance student learning in economics. She used online simulations to help students understand supply and demand, and virtual stock market games to teach about market structures. She also incorporated personal finance apps to help students learn about budgeting, saving, and investing.

Overall, Ms. Smith's use of social media and effective economics education tools led to increased student engagement and interest in economics. Her students were able to apply economic concepts to real-world situations and develop important skills in critical thinking and communication.

However, there were also challenges and issues that arose in this approach. Ms. Smith had to ensure that the use of social media was appropriate and followed school guidelines. She also had to ensure that all students had access to the necessary technology to participate in online discussions and activities. Additionally, she had to carefully select and incorporate effective tools and resources that aligned with the specific learning objectives and needs of her students.

This case study highlights how K-12 educators, like Mrs. Smith, have continued to leverage social media and interactive tools to enhance their economics education strategies.

SOCIAL MEDIA IMPACT ON EDUCATION

Social media has had a significant impact on education in recent years, transforming the way educators teach and students learn. Here are some ways in which social media has impacted education:

1. Enhanced communication (Shao, 2009): Social media platforms, such as Twitter, Facebook, and LinkedIn, have provided educators with new ways to communicate and collaborate with their colleagues, share ideas, and access a wealth of resources and tools to enhance their teaching strategies.
2. Increased engagement (Erhel et al., 2022): Social media can be used to create more interactive and engaging learning experiences for students. For example, platforms like Kahoot, Quizlet, and Google Forms allow educators to create quizzes, surveys, and other interactive learning activities that help students better understand complex concepts.
3. Improved access to information (Yardi & Boyd, 2010): Social media provides access to a wealth of information and resources, which can be used to enhance teaching and learning. Educators can use social media to access the latest research, news, and trends in their field, as well as connect with other professionals and organizations.
4. Personalized learning: Social media can be used to create personalized learning experiences for students. For example, educators can use social media platforms

to tailor learning materials and resources to meet the individual needs and learning styles of each student.

5. Global connections: Social media platforms can connect educators and students from all over the world, enabling them to collaborate and learn from each other. This can help to broaden students' perspectives and expose them to different cultures and ways of thinking.

CORE PROBLEMS

The core problems in this case study include the challenges faced by Ms. Smith, a high school economics teacher, in incorporating social media and effective economics education tools into her classroom. These challenges include adhering to school guidelines for social media use, ensuring access to technology for all students, managing time effectively, personalizing instruction for each student, and accessing resources that align with the specific needs of her classroom (Amiruzzaman & Amiruzzaman, 2022; Tang & Hew, 2017). The core problem, therefore, is how to successfully integrate social media and effective economics education tools into the classroom despite these challenges, to increase student engagement and interest in economics.

CHALLENGES

While social media and interactive tools have many potential benefits for economics education, there are also several challenges and issues that educators may face when incorporating these tools into their teaching strategies. While much of the work of social media applications has been examined in mainstream western culture, there are geographic areas or student populations that could be excluded from this type of teaching method. This requires careful consideration from teachers and administrations to consider applications. Some of the challenges and issues associated with this case study include:

1. Digital divide: Not all students have equal access to technology or the internet, which may create an unequal learning environment. Educators may need to consider how to ensure that all students have access to the tools and resources they need to participate fully in social media and interactive learning activities.
2. Privacy concerns: Social media platforms often collect and share user data, which can raise privacy concerns. Educators need to be aware of these concerns and take steps to protect their students' privacy and personal information.

3. Quality control: The internet is filled with a vast amount of information, much of which is of questionable quality. Educators need to be able to evaluate the quality and accuracy of the information they find online and ensure that they are sharing accurate and trustworthy information with their students.
4. Time management: Incorporating social media and interactive tools into teaching strategies can be time-consuming. Educators need to carefully plan and manage their time to ensure that they can effectively use these tools without sacrificing other important aspects of their teaching responsibilities.
5. Technological barriers: Not all educators may be comfortable or proficient in using social media or interactive tools, which may create a technological barrier to implementation. Educators may need training or support to effectively incorporate these tools into their teaching strategies.
6. Cyberbullying and inappropriate content (Madden et al., 2013): Social media platforms can also expose students to inappropriate content or cyberbullying. Educators need to be aware of these risks and take steps to create a safe and respectful online learning environment for their students.

Problems Faced by a High School Economics Teacher, Ms. Smith

In this case study, a high school economics teacher, Ms. Smith, faced several challenges while incorporating social media and effective economics education tools in her classroom. These challenges include:

1. School Guidelines: Ms. Smith had to ensure that the use of social media was appropriate and followed school guidelines. She had to ensure that her use of Twitter and other social media platforms complied with school policies and guidelines to protect the privacy and safety of her students.
2. Access to Technology: Not all students may have access to technology outside of the classroom, such as smartphones or personal computers. Ms. Smith had to ensure that all students had access to the necessary technology to participate in online discussions and activities.
3. Time Management: Incorporating social media and effective economics education tools into the classroom can be time-consuming. Ms. Smith had to plan and manage her time effectively to ensure that the use of these tools did not disrupt the overall learning objectives of her class.
4. Personalization: Each student has their own unique learning style and pace. Ms. Smith had to ensure that the tools and resources she used aligned with the specific learning objectives and needs of her students.

5. Resources: Access to resources can be a challenge, especially for smaller or underfunded schools. Ms. Smith had to carefully select and incorporate effective tools and resources that were available and affordable for her classroom.

Problem Faced by Students

In this case study, the students faced several challenges related to the incorporation of social media and effective economics education tools in their classroom. These challenges include:

1. Technology Access: Not all students had access to technology outside of the classroom, which hindered their ability to participate in online discussions and activities.
2. Familiarity with Social Media Platforms: While most students are familiar with social media, they may not have been familiar with the specific platforms used by Ms. Smith in her class, such as Twitter. This may have caused confusion or frustration for some students.
3. Different Learning Styles: Each student has their own unique learning style and pace, and incorporating social media and effective economics education tools into the classroom may not have aligned with the learning style of every student.
4. Language Barriers: Some students may have faced language barriers when using social media and online tools, particularly if English was not their first language.
5. Cyberbullying and Safety Concerns: The use of social media in the classroom raises concerns about cyberbullying and safety, particularly if the guidelines and policies for online behavior were not properly communicated to the students.

Problems Faced by Administration and Management

In this case study, the administration and management faced several challenges related to the incorporation of social media and effective economics education tools in the classroom. These challenges include:

1. Adhering to School Guidelines: The school likely has guidelines and policies related to the use of social media in the classroom, which may have been difficult for Ms. Smith to navigate. The administration and management may have also faced challenges in enforcing these policies and ensuring that they were being followed by all teachers.

2. Providing Access to Technology: Not all students may have had access to the necessary technology outside of the classroom, which could have presented logistical and financial challenges for the administration and management in terms of providing access to technology for all students.
3. Allocating Resources: Incorporating social media and effective economics education tools into the classroom may have required additional resources, such as training for teachers or funding for software and technology. The administration and management may have faced challenges in allocating these resources effectively.
4. Curriculum Alignment: The incorporation of social media and effective economics education tools may not have aligned with the existing curriculum, which could have presented challenges for the administration and management in terms of ensuring that the learning objectives were being met.
5. Legal and Ethical Concerns: The use of social media in the classroom raises legal and ethical concerns, such as privacy and cyberbullying. The administration and management may have faced challenges in developing and enforcing policies that addressed these concerns effectively.

Problems Faced by the Parents

In this case study, the parents faced several problems related to their child's education, which were:

1. Limited Understanding of Social Media: Some parents may have limited understanding of social media and how it can be used effectively in the classroom. This lack of understanding may have caused them to be skeptical of the benefits of incorporating social media into the curriculum.
2. Concerns about Screen Time: Some parents may have been concerned about the amount of screen time their child was exposed to in the classroom, as well as the potential effects of excessive screen time on their child's health and well-being.
3. Limited Access to Technology: Some parents may not have had access to the necessary technology for their child to participate in the classroom activities, which could have created challenges for them in supporting their child's learning.
4. Concerns about Online Safety: Parents may have been concerned about the safety of their child online, especially when using social media. This concern may have led to hesitation in allowing their child to participate in the classroom activities.

CASE QUESTIONS

1. What are the benefits of using social media in economics education for K-12 students? How can it enhance their learning experience?
2. What strategies could Ms. Smith use to effectively integrate social media into her economics curriculum? How can she balance traditional teaching methods with the use of technology?
3. What measures can be taken to address the concerns of parents about the use of social media in the classroom? How can the school work to build trust and rapport with parents?
4. How can the administration and management of the school support Ms. Smith in effectively integrating social media into her curriculum? What resources and training can be provided?
5. How can the school measure the effectiveness of the use of social media in economics education? What metrics can be used to track student progress and engagement with the curriculum?

LEARNING OBJECTIVES

This case on social media in economics education and tools for educators, learners will be able to:

1. Understand the impact of social media on education, particularly in the field of economics education.
2. Identify various social media platforms and interactive tools that can be leveraged to enhance economics education.
3. Analyze the benefits and challenges of using social media in economics education.
4. Develop effective economics education topics using social media and interactive tools.
5. Evaluate the effectiveness of social media and interactive tools in economics education.
6. Apply social media and interactive tools to create more engaging and effective learning experiences for students in economics education.
7. Collaborate with other professionals in the field of economics education through social media platforms.
8. Develop a plan for incorporating social media and interactive tools into their own economics education strategies.

9. Understand the importance of staying up-to-date with emerging trends and best practices in social media and interactive tools in economics education.
10. Reflect on their own teaching practices and identify areas where social media and interactive tools can enhance their effectiveness as educators.

METHODOLOGY/APPROACHES, ANALYSIS, AND TECHNIQUES

The methodology/approaches, analysis and techniques used by Ms Smith in this case study.

Based on the case study, Ms. Smith used a variety of approaches and techniques to effectively integrate social media into her economics curriculum. Some of these include:

1. Setting clear learning objectives: Ms. Smith established clear learning objectives and guidelines for social media use in her classroom. This helped students understand how to effectively use social media as a tool for learning and collaboration.
2. Selecting appropriate platforms and tools: Ms. Smith carefully selected social media platforms and tools that were most suited to the needs of her students. This included using platforms like Twitter and LinkedIn to connect with experts in the field and to access real-world examples and case studies.
3. Modeling responsible digital citizenship: Ms. Smith modeled responsible digital citizenship by setting an example for her students in how to use social media responsibly and safely. She also provided guidance on how to manage online privacy and security.
4. Incorporating social media into group projects and assignments: Ms. Smith incorporated social media into group projects and assignments to encourage collaboration and peer learning. This helped students develop teamwork and communication skills while using social media as a learning tool.
5. Providing opportunities for reflection and feedback: Ms. Smith provided opportunities for students to reflect on their learning and share their experiences using social media in the classroom. This helped students develop critical thinking skills and provided valuable feedback to Ms. Smith on the effectiveness of her teaching approach.

Ms. Smith also used various analysis and techniques to evaluate the effectiveness of social media in her economics curriculum. She tracked metrics such as student engagement, participation, and achievement using digital tools and analytics. She also sought feedback from students and parents to make improvements to the curriculum and ensure that it was effective and meaningful for all students. Additionally, she regularly assessed the impact of social media on student learning and adjusted her approach as needed to ensure that it was effective.

Table 1. Economics education and social media tools

Effective Economics Education Topics for K-12	Social Media Tools for Educators
Understanding basic economic concepts	X (formerly Twitter), Facebook, YouTube
Personal finance and money management	Financial education apps, social media campaigns
Supply and demand	Online simulations, discussion forums
Market structures	Virtual stock market games, LinkedIn
International trade	Global online collaborations, Google Hangouts
Economic systems	Blogs, podcasts, Instagram
Government intervention in markets	X (formerly Twitter), Facebook groups, online debates
Fiscal and monetary policy	Interactive data visualization tools, webinars
Labor markets and human capital	Online career development resources, LinkedIn
Environmental economics	Green social media campaigns, environmental organizations' social media

Note: The topics listed above social media tools mentioned are just some examples that may be used to enhance economics education for K-12 students. The effectiveness of these topics and tools may depend on the quality of instruction, the specific learning objectives, and the incorporation of appropriate teaching strategies.

REMEDIES AND MEASUREMENTS

Based on the case study, Ms. Smith implemented several remedies and measurements to address the challenges and issues that arose from integrating social media into her economics curriculum. Some of these include:

1. Providing professional development for teachers: Ms. Smith advocated for professional development for teachers to help them understand how to effectively use social media in the classroom. This helped teachers develop the necessary skills and knowledge to effectively integrate social media into their teaching practices.
2. Establishing clear guidelines for social media use: Ms. Smith established clear guidelines for social media use in her classroom to ensure that students used social media in a responsible and appropriate manner. This helped to prevent

potential issues related to cyberbullying, inappropriate content, and privacy concerns.

3. Providing technical support: Ms. Smith provided technical support to students and teachers to ensure that they had the necessary resources and tools to effectively use social media in the classroom. This helped to prevent potential issues related to technological barriers and challenges.
4. Encouraging parent involvement: Ms. Smith encouraged parent involvement and communication to ensure that parents were aware of how social media was being used in the classroom and to address any concerns or issues that arose.
5. Regularly assessing the impact of social media: Ms. Smith regularly assessed the impact of social media on student learning and adjusted her approach as needed to ensure that it was effective. This helped to ensure that social media was being used in a meaningful and effective way to enhance student learning and engagement.

Overall, Ms. Smith's approach to integrating social media into her economics curriculum involved a combination of providing support, establishing guidelines and clear objectives, and regularly assessing and adjusting her approach to ensure that it was effective.

Table 2. Social media impact on tools for educators

Social Media Impact on Economics Education	Tools for Educators - Effective Economics Education Topics for K-12
Enhanced communication and collaboration	Online discussion forums, Twitter, Facebook groups
Increased engagement and interaction	Kahoot, Quizlet, Google Forms, educational games and apps
Improved access to information and resources	Blogs, websites, online journals, videos, podcasts
Personalized learning	Adaptive learning platforms, personalized learning plans
Global connections	Skype, Zoom, international online collaborations

Note: The table above social media platforms and tools that can be effective for economics education. Additionally, the effectiveness of these tools may vary depending on the specific learning objectives and needs of each individual student or class.

CASE QUESTIONS ANSWERS

1. The benefits of using social media in economics education for K-12 students include increased engagement, improved communication and collaboration, and access to a variety of resources and perspectives. It can enhance their

learning experience by allowing them to connect with peers, teachers, and experts in the field, and to access real-world examples and case studies that illustrate economic concepts. It can also provide opportunities for personalized learning and feedback, and for students to develop critical thinking and digital literacy skills.

2. To effectively integrate social media into her economics curriculum, Ms. Smith can use strategies such as setting clear learning objectives and guidelines for social media use, selecting appropriate platforms and tools based on the needs of her students, and modeling responsible digital citizenship. She can also incorporate social media into group projects and assignments and provide opportunities for students to reflect on their learning and share their experiences using social media in the classroom. It is important to balance the use of technology with traditional teaching methods to ensure that students are engaged and motivated to learn.
3. To address the concerns of parents about the use of social media in the classroom, the school can communicate the benefits of incorporating social media into the curriculum and how it can enhance their child's learning experience. They can provide information about the safety measures in place to ensure online safety, as well as guidance on managing screen time. The school can work to build trust and rapport with parents by providing regular updates and opportunities for feedback, and by involving parents in the decision-making process. Open communication and transparency are key to addressing the concerns of parents.
4. The administration and management of the school can support Ms. Smith in effectively integrating social media into her curriculum by providing resources and training, such as professional development opportunities and access to technology and software. They can also provide guidance and support for addressing concerns from parents and other stakeholders and can facilitate collaboration and sharing of best practices among teachers. It is important to ensure that teachers have the necessary support and resources to effectively incorporate social media into their curriculum.
5. The effectiveness of the use of social media in economics education can be measured using a variety of metrics, such as student engagement, participation, and achievement. Teachers can track these metrics using digital tools and analytics and can use feedback from students and parents to make improvements to the curriculum. It is important to regularly assess the impact of social media on student learning and adjust the approach as needed to ensure that it is effective and meaningful for all students.

CONCLUSION

The study addresses these concerns, the school and Ms. Smith likely worked to communicate the benefits of incorporating social media into the curriculum and how it could enhance their child's learning experience. They may have also provided information about the safety measures in place to ensure online safety, as well as guidance on managing screen time. Additionally, the school may have worked to provide access to technology for all students, regardless of their family's financial situation. Overall, the school likely worked to build trust and rapport with parents to ensure that they were comfortable with the approach to using social media in the classroom. Ms. Smith was able to successfully incorporate social media and effective economics education tools into her classroom, leading to increased student engagement and interest in economics. She was able to overcome these challenges through careful planning, communication, and flexibility to ensure that all students had access to the resources and tools necessary to succeed.

Ms. Smith worked to overcome these issues by ensuring that all students had access to the necessary technology, providing clear guidance on how to use social media platforms, personalizing instruction based on each student's learning style, and addressing any safety concerns related to social media use. By doing so, Ms. Smith was able to create a safe and engaging learning environment for all students, regardless of their individual challenges. The administration and management worked to overcome these issues by developing clear guidelines and policies related to social media use, providing access to technology for all students, allocating resources appropriately, aligning the curriculum with learning objectives, and addressing legal and ethical concerns related to social media use in the classroom. By doing so, the administration and management were able to support Ms. Smith and create a safe and engaging learning environment for all students.

The use of social media and effective economics education tools can greatly enhance student learning in economics. Educators can utilize these tools to increase student engagement, provide access to information and resources, and personalize learning experiences for their students. However, careful consideration and planning is necessary to ensure that these tools and resources are used effectively and appropriately to maximize student learning outcomes.

POSITION IN THE COURSE

This case study on the social media impact on economic education and tools for educators is suitable for a variety of courses related to education, economics, and technology. Specifically, it can be incorporated into courses on educational technology, curriculum design and implementation, economics education, and teacher professional development. It is also relevant to courses on digital literacy and internet safety. The case study can be used to facilitate discussions on the benefits and challenges of integrating social media into the classroom, as well as to explore effective approaches to address these challenges. It can also be used to examine the impact of technology on student learning and engagement, and to discuss the role of educators in effectively utilizing technology to enhance the learning experience.

TEACHING NOTES

1. Start by introducing the case study and providing some context for why it's important. You could highlight the growing use of social media in education and the potential benefits and challenges of incorporating it into the classroom.
2. Discuss the problems faced by Ms. Smith and her students. Encourage students to identify and analyze the various challenges and issues, including those related to student engagement, technology, access, and communication.
3. Review the core problem of the case study and ask students to brainstorm possible solutions. Encourage them to consider a range of potential remedies, including different teaching methodologies, the use of new technologies, and more targeted communication strategies.
4. Discuss the various approaches and techniques used by Ms. Smith to address the challenges in her classroom. Ask students to evaluate the effectiveness of these strategies and to identify any strengths and weaknesses.
5. Review the remedies and measurements taken by the administration and management team to support Ms. Smith and her students. Encourage students to evaluate the success of these efforts and to identify any areas for improvement.
6. Finally, wrap up the discussion by reviewing the key takeaways from the case study. Encourage students to reflect on what they've learned and to consider how they might apply this knowledge in their own teaching or learning experiences.
7. As an extension activity, you could ask students to research and evaluate other case studies or examples of social media use in education. Encourage them to analyze the benefits and challenges of these approaches and to identify best practices for incorporating social media into the classroom.

TEACHING OBJECTIVES

1. To understand the impact of social media on economics education and its potential benefits and challenges for K-12 educators.
2. To analyze the problems faced by teachers, students, parents, and administration when using social media in the classroom.
3. To evaluate different approaches and techniques used by educators to address these challenges, including the use of new technologies, targeted communication strategies, and innovative teaching methodologies.
4. To review the remedies and measurements taken by administration and management to support educators and students when using social media in the classroom.
5. To identify best practices for incorporating social media into economics education for K-12 students.
6. To develop critical thinking and problem-solving skills by evaluating different case studies and examples of social media use in education.
7. To encourage reflection and self-evaluation by asking students to consider how they might apply the knowledge gained from this case study in their own teaching or learning experiences.

TEACHING APPROACH AND STRATEGIES

There are several teaching approaches and strategies that can be effective for this case study. Here are a few:

1. Interactive Lecture: The instructor can present the case study and engage students in an interactive lecture, encouraging them to ask questions and share their own experiences with social media use in education. This approach can be useful for introducing key concepts and theories related to social media and economics education.
2. Group Discussion: Students can be divided into groups and asked to discuss specific questions related to the case study, such as the challenges faced by teachers, students, and parents, or the different approaches used by educators to incorporate social media into their teaching. This approach can be useful for fostering critical thinking and collaboration skills.
3. Role-Playing: Students can be asked to take on different roles, such as a high school teacher, a student, a parent, or an administrator, and act out different scenarios related to social media use in the classroom. This approach can be useful for encouraging empathy and perspective-taking skills.

4. Case-Based Learning: Students can be given other case studies related to social media use in education and asked to compare the different approaches and strategies used in each case. This approach can be useful for encouraging analysis and evaluation skills (Jones & Baltzersen, 2017).
5. Project-Based Learning: Students can be asked to design a project or activity that incorporates social media into economics education for K-12 students, using the knowledge gained from the case study and their own research. This approach can be useful for fostering creativity and problem-solving skills.

These teaching approaches and strategies can be adapted and combined depending on the specific needs and preferences of the instructor and students.

TARGETED AUDIENCE

The targeted audience for this case study on social media impact on economics education and tools for educators is primarily K-12 educators, including high school economics teachers, curriculum designers, and school administrators. However, it can also be relevant for college-level educators who are interested in exploring the use of social media in teaching economics.

This case study can also be beneficial for students pursuing education degrees, as well as students enrolled in economics courses. The case study can provide them with practical insights and strategies for incorporating social media into their future teaching practices, as well as an understanding of the challenges and opportunities associated with using social media in education.

Additionally, this case study can be useful for parents and policymakers who are interested in understanding the role of social media in education and how it can be used effectively to enhance the learning experience of students. Overall, the targeted audience for this case study is anyone who is interested in exploring the potential of social media for improving economics education and developing effective teaching strategies to engage K-12 students.

TEACHING PLAN (90 MINS)

Here is a possible teaching plan for a 90-minute session on this case study:

I. Introduction (10 mins)

- Introduce the topic of social media impact on economics education and the tools for educators that can be used to enhance the learning experience of K-12 students.
- Provide a brief overview of the case study and its key themes.

II. Case Study Discussion (45 mins)
- Break students into small groups of 3-4 people.
- Assign each group a set of discussion questions related to the case study.
- Allow 20-25 minutes for group discussion, followed by a 5-10-minute group presentation to the class on their findings and insights.
- Encourage students to share their own experiences and ideas related to the use of social media in education and economics instruction.

III. Lecture on Social Media Tools for Educators (20 mins)
- Provide a brief lecture on the different social media tools and platforms that can be used by educators to enhance economics education.
- Highlight the benefits and drawbacks of each tool and provide examples of how they have been successfully used in K-12 classrooms.

IV. Activity: Social Media Lesson Plan (10 mins)
- Ask students to create a social media-based lesson plan that incorporates at least one of the social media tools discussed in the lecture.
- Allow students to work in pairs or small groups to develop their lesson plans.
- Encourage creativity and exploration of different formats and platforms.

V. Conclusion (5 mins)
- Recap the key themes and takeaways from the case study and class discussion.
- Encourage students to continue exploring the use of social media in education and to consider how they can apply the lessons learned from this case study to their own teaching practices.

VI. Homework Assignment (Optional)
- Assign a homework assignment that asks students to research and analyze another case study related to social media in education and economics instruction.
- Ask students to write a short reflection paper on the similarities and differences between the two case studies and how they can apply the lessons learned to their own teaching practices.

Note: The timing of each section can be adjusted as needed to fit the specific needs of the class and teaching style.

NEED FOR CASE STUDY

The need for this case study arises from the increasing use of social media in education and the need to provide effective economics education to K-12 students. Social media has become an essential part of the daily lives of students, and it offers significant potential to engage students in the learning process (Al-Bahrani et al., 2017; Jones & Baltzersen, 2017). However, there are challenges associated with using social media in education, particularly in the field of economics, which requires a sound understanding of complex concepts and ideas. This case study is relevant and important for several reasons. First, it highlights the potential of social media as a tool for educators to improve economics education and engage students. Second, it provides insights into the challenges faced by educators, administrators, and parents when incorporating social media into the classroom. Third, it offers practical solutions and best practices for overcoming these challenges and maximizing the benefits of social media for education.

In addition, this case study is timely as the COVID-19 pandemic has forced many schools to switch to online and hybrid learning, making the use of social media and other digital tools even more crucial for educators. Finally, it is also relevant for policymakers and education stakeholders interested in improving economics education and leveraging technology to enhance student learning. The case study explores the impact of social media on economics education and provides educators with effective tools and strategies to engage and educate K-12 students in economics. The case study also addresses the challenges and issues associated with the use of social media in education and provides recommendations for educators, administrators, parents, and policymakers to overcome these challenges. Overall, this case study is important for educators who are looking for innovative and effective ways to teach economics to K-12 students and for policymakers who want to leverage the potential of social media to improve the quality of education in their jurisdictions.

SUGGESTED QUESTIONS FOR DISCUSSIONS

1. How can social media be used effectively in economics education for K-12 students?
2. What are some of the challenges and issues associated with the use of social media in education, and how can these be addressed?
3. How can educators ensure that the use of social media does not compromise the quality of education and learning outcomes?
4. What are the benefits and drawbacks of using social media in economics education for K-12 students?

5. How can parents and administrators support educators in the use of social media in education and ensure that students are safe and responsible online?
6. How can policymakers leverage the potential of social media to improve the quality of education and support economic literacy in their jurisdictions?
7. What are some of the effective economics education topics suited for K-12 educators, and how can social media be used to teach them?
8. What are some of the best practices for integrating social media into economics education for K-12 students?
9. How can educators assess the effectiveness of social media in economics education and adjust their teaching strategies accordingly?
10. What are the ethical and legal considerations associated with the use of social media in education, and how can educators ensure that they comply with relevant regulations and guidelines?

REFERENCES

Al-Bahrani, A., Patel, D., & Sheridan, B. (2015). Engaging students using social media: The students' perspective. *International Review of Economics Education, 19*, 36–50. Advance online publication. doi:10.1016/j.iree.2015.06.001

Al-Bahrani, A., Patel, D., & Sheridan, B. (2017). Evaluating Twitter and its impact on student learning in principles of economics courses. *The Journal of Economic Education, 48*(4), 243–253. doi:10.1080/00220485.2017.1353934

Amiruzzaman, S., & Amiruzzaman, M. (2022). Use of Twitter among college students for academics: A mixed-methods approach. *Social Sciences (Basel, Switzerland), 11*(9), 404. doi:10.3390ocsci11090404

Asarta, C. J. (2023). Student engagement and interaction in the economics classroom: Essentials for the novice economic educator. *The Journal of Economic Education*, 1–9. Advance online publication. doi:10.1080/00220485.2023.2269142

Brown, B., & Pederson, J. A. (2020). LinkedIn to classroom community: Assessing classroom community on the basis of social media usage. *Journal of Further and Higher Education, 44*(3), 341–349. doi:10.1080/0309877X.2018.1541973

Chen, G. M. (2011). Tweet this: A uses and gratifications perspective on how active Twitter use gratifies a need to connect with others. *Computers in Human Behavior, 27*(2), 755–762. doi:10.1016/j.chb.2010.10.023

Ding, N., Xu, X., & Lewis, E. (2023). Short instructional videos for the TikTok generation. *Journal of Education for Business*, *98*(4), 175–185. doi:10.1080/08832323.2022.2103489

Emerson, T. L. N., McGoldrick, K. M., & Mumford, K. J. (2012). Women and the choice to study economics. *The Journal of Economic Education*, *43*(4), 349–362. doi:10.1080/00220485.2012.714306

Erhel, S., Michinov, N., Noel, A., & Gonthier, C. (2022). Tweet to teach: Using a twitter-based instructional method to improve student motivation and academic outcomes in higher education. *The Internet and Higher Education*, *55*, 100876. doi:10.1016/j.iheduc.2022.100876

Harmon, O. R., & Tomolonis, P. A. (2019). The effects of using Facebook as a discussion forum in an online principles of economics course: Results of a randomized controlled trial. *International Review of Economics Education*, *30*, 100157. doi:10.1016/j.iree.2019.100157

Jones, M. D., & Baltzersen, M. (2017). Using twitter for economics business case discussions in large lectures. *International Review of Economics Education*, *26*, 14–18. doi:10.1016/j.iree.2017.08.001

Kirschner, P. A., & Karpinski, A. C. (2010). Facebook® and academic performance. *Computers in Human Behavior*, *26*(6), 1237–1245. doi:10.1016/j.chb.2010.03.024

Lai, H. (2021). Research on the intelligent teaching model of principles of economics course under the new media. *Journal of Contemporary Educational Research*, *5*(8), 131–135. Advance online publication. doi:10.26689/jcer.v5i8.2445

Madden, M., Lenhart, A., Cortesti, S., Gasser, U., Duggan, M., Smith, A., & Beaton, M. (2013). *Teens, social media, and privacy.* Pew Research Center. https://www.pewresearch.org/internet/2013/05/21/teens-social-media-and-privacy/

Middleditch, P., Moindrot, W., & Rudkin, S. (2022). Teaching with Twitter: An extension to the traditional learning environment. *International Review of Economics Education*, *41*, 100252. doi:10.1016/j.iree.2022.100252

Picault, J. (2019). The economics instructor's toolbox. *International Review of Economics Education*, *30*, 100154. Advance online publication. doi:10.1016/j.iree.2019.01.001

Shao, G. (2009). Understanding the appeal of user-generated media: A uses and gratification perspective. *Internet Research*, *19*(1), 7–25. doi:10.1108/10662240910927795

Tang, Y., & Hew, K. F. (2017). Using Twitter for education: Beneficial or simply a waste of time? *Computers & Education*, *106*, 97–118. doi:10.1016/j.compedu.2016.12.004

Wooten, J., Al-Bahrani, A., Holder, K., & Patel, D. (2021). The role of relevance in economics education: A survey. *The Journal of Economic Education*, *21*(1). https://libjournals.mtsu.edu/index.php/jfee/article/view/2025/1231

Yardi, S., & Boyd, D. (2010). Tweeting from the Town Square: Measuring geographic local networks. *Proceedings of the International AAAI Conference on Web and Social Media, 4*(1), 194–201. 10.1609/icwsm.v4i1.14016

ENDNOTE

1 See web reference of Picault (2019) work for course delivery methods, illustration tools, in-class activities, student projects, and confusions in the textbooks. Website: https://www.theecontoolbox.com/

Chapter 9
Moodle:
Motivational Element for Pre-Pandemic Teaching-Learning Processes

O. A. Guirette-Barbosa
https://orcid.org/0000-0003-1336-9475
Universidad Politécnica de Zacatecas, Mexico

M. A. García-Camacho
https://orcid.org/0000-0002-9645-3199
Instituto Tecnológico Superior de Fresnillo, Mexico

José G. Vargas-Hernandez
Budapest Centre for Long-term Sustainability, Hungary

J. J. Reyes-Sánchez
Instituto Tecnológico Superior de Fresnillo, Mexico

S. Castañeda-Burciaga
https://orcid.org/0000-0002-2436-308X
Universidad Politécnica de Zacatecas, Mexico

EXECUTIVE SUMMARY

This chapter consists of an investigation on the motivational factors that entail the use of the Moodle platform as an auxiliary tool within the teaching-learning process. The objective of the research was to recognize the student's perception of the use of virtual educational platforms (Moodle) as a motivational and influential factor in their learning process focused on the results it achieves. According to the results, it is possible to affirm that there is a high motivational level of the students regarding the use of the Moodle platform as well as an elevated level of motivational perception. In the same way, it was observed that there are five main components that summarize the variation between the items, motivational characteristics that were obtained and proposed as a conclusion for the effective obtaining of results when using the Moodle platform within the teaching-learning process.

DOI: 10.4018/978-1-6684-7583-6.ch009

INTRODUCTION

Current trends in education reveal the inclusion of new Information and Communication Technologies (ICT) within the teaching-learning process, thus redefining the role of teachers and students. As specified by the Organization for Economic Co-operation and Development (OECD, 2005), virtual learning refers to the use of ICT with the aim of improving and supporting learning. On the other hand, according to Barbera (2015), in the educational field the term e-learning (electronic learning) has been adopted to identify teaching mediated by communication technology, which presents alternatives for continuous training at different educational levels.

The e-learning concept, as stated by Silva (2011), contemplates technological and pedagogical aspects within the training process, where it is designed to produce learning through computer applications developed in web environments. He also points out that his main contribution from him is the change in basic assumptions, with the student being the center of the entire educational process, with an emphasis on learning rather than teaching.

In the same vein, b-learning or blended learning, is a modality that seeks to create learning environments, combining the benefits of face-to-face and virtual teaching processes, with which it is intended to integrate ICT into traditional ways of teaching. class, getting more out of the classroom (Silva, 2011). It is known as mixed or combined learning, locating those learning processes conducted through digital systems and networks, where face-to-face sessions that promote face-to-face contact are also established (Dionicio, 2014).

ICT provides correct support for the student's interaction with the tutor, in addition to promoting collaboration between peers and the joint construction of knowledge within a learning community (Silva, 2011). In this regard, Virtual Learning Environments (EVA), according to Almaráz (2014), refer to "a web platform that brings together a set of communication tools and computer resources designed to facilitate the teaching-learning process" (p. 191), as a support for face-to-face and distance teaching.

The operation of an EVA requires the integration of a platform for online learning or Learning Manager Systems (LMS), defined as a comprehensive system for the management, distribution, monitoring and control of content, as well as educational resources, within a shared collaborative environment (Silva, 2011). The best-known virtual learning platforms are Web Course Tools, FirstClass, LearningSpace, Blackboard, as well as open-source platforms (Open Source), such as Moodle, Claroline and Chamilo, among others.

In another sense, advances in training models supported by virtual instances are supported by the incorporation of ICTs, as well as pedagogical elements derived from different learning theories, such as Vigostky's socio-constructivist theories.

Within this approach, the Moodle platform (Modular Object-Oriented Dynamic Learning Environment) stands out, developed by Martin Dougiamas, which appears as a learning platform designed to provide educators, administrators and students, a system to create personalized learning environments (Moodle, 2017).

The educational ideology of the Moodle platform, according to Dávila (2011), promotes an interactive learning style, thus representing the operational and dynamic part of the teaching-learning process, manifested in what the student must "know how to know" (cognitive domain) and what they should "know how to do" (procedural mastery), thus evidencing the application of the knowledge built. Moodle's learning philosophy is framed within the so-called social constructionist pedagogy, with four main underlying concepts: constructivism, constructionism, social constructivism, as well as the concept called connected and separate.

The purpose of this study is related to the motivational factors involved in the use of the Moodle platform in the teaching-learning process. Firstly, in the introduction, the general orientation of the work is established, to later make a comprehensive review of the use of the platform motivated by factors that affect the teaching-learning results. Subsequently, the research methods are established, as well as the instrument to be used, the sample size to whom it is applied is determined. Finally, the analysis of the results is made, a discussion is made about the findings found and the conclusions are established.

BACKGROUND

Constructivism refers to the construction that the subject makes of knowledge through its interaction with the environment, contrasting previous knowledge with what results from the interaction itself, reinforcing it through application in the environment (Moodle, 2022). Where the human being gives meaning to his learning from his own conceptual structures (Dávila, 2011). From Vygotsky's constructivist theories of learning, the student constructs his own knowledge in an active way, the result of the interaction between him and the contents, which in turn causes a change in his thought Constructivism considers that the way in which knowledge is acquired can be by discovery, reception, incorporation into the cognitive structure of the student through repetition, and by the significant value it has for the subject (Garduño, 2005).

Regarding constructionism, this is based on the idea that learning is more effective when something is built that should reach others. Whereas social constructivism refers to the construction of things from one social group with a contribution to another, collaboratively creating a culture of shared constructs and meanings (Moodle, 2022). As Dávila (2011) details, the student builds knowledge by himself, with the help of a mediator and by interacting with the social group with which he shares his training process, then visualizing learning as a social process.

Another of the concepts that make up the educational philosophy of the Moodle platform is the so-called connected and separated, which emphasizes the motivations of the individual (which gives rise to the present investigation) within a discussion. Giving a separate behavior when trying to debate from an objective point of view, at the same time, a connected behavior is maintained, seeking an empathic approach to understand the interlocutor's point of view, thus achieving a constructive behavior (Moodle, 2022). It should be noted that Moodle is one of the most used platforms worldwide, since registered sites amount to 77,344, registered in 234 countries, with 100,300,607 users; where Mexico ranks fourth with 3,685 pre pandemic registrations and 9,081 post pandemic (Moodle, 2022), however, this statistic mentions the officially registered sites, not the total downloads that have been generated from the platform.

On the other hand, virtual education in Mexico and the use of digital platforms as means of learning, became evident towards the end of the 20th century, when institutional educational proposals via the Internet promoted the creation of the Red-Mex, later the National Technological Network emerged (RTN). Due to global social and economic changes, the supply and demand of new distance and online educational proposals is increasing (Martínez, 2005). The Mexican government has tried, through the México Conectado program, to promote new options for access to education through the deployment of telecommunications networks, providing broadband access in educational institutions (SCT, 2017).

The advantages of using computer technology in teaching are related to the flexibility of time and space, achieving temporary economic savings by avoiding displacements. In the same way, it is possible to update content quickly and at low cost, which allows a detailed follow-up of the student's work, in addition to tutoring and feedback from the teacher (Arriata et al. 2009). Derived from the above and considering the increase in the use of virtual platforms in the teaching-learning process, it is considered pertinent to recognize the inclusion of the b-learning modality within education from a constructivist approach, from the student's perspective as the central axis of the process.

Contemplating in this way, the motivational aspects that arise within the learning process. As stated by De la Mora (2003), motivation can be defined as "a process that causes a certain behavior, maintains the activity or modifies it" (p. 32), also details that all learning must obey a certain type of motivation. According to the author, two types of motivation in learning can be established: positive and negative. Within the first is intrinsic and extrinsic motivation, while the negative includes physical and psychological. Regarding positive motivation, this occurs when the desire to learn arises, being intrinsic when the subject himself wants to learn and extrinsic when said desire is driven by an interest or external agent, it should be noted that most of the times when this type of motivation exists motivation, what has been learned is often forgotten once the external purpose is satisfied.

Regarding the above and citing the study by Cardozo (2008), who proposes an investigation on motivation and its relationship with academic performance in university students, a high correlation was evidenced between the application of motivational, learning and performance strategies. academic. His results show how the student achieves his learning goals, in addition to the use of cognitive strategies and the use of motivational strategies as detonators of a causal relationship. On the other hand, regarding the student's perception of the use of virtual educational platforms, it should be mentioned that there are some previous studies, such as the one presented by Olmos-Miguelháñez et al. (2014), who designed and validated a scale of perceived utility on the use of the Moodle platform, evaluating content, activities, evaluative strategies, interaction and learning, such study was conducted under a face-to-face educational modality.

On the same idea is the study conducted by Estrada et al. (2013), who analyzed the perception that students have of the b-learning educational modality by incorporating the Moodle platform, evaluating aspects related to the subject, the tutor, the content, communication, and performance aspects linked to the platform. educational virtual. The results obtained showed an elevated level of student satisfaction on the implementation of the teaching-learning process under this educational modality. For their part, Cohn-Muroy et al. (2015), mention within research focused on the analysis of students' perception of the Moodle virtual educational platform, finding that it is perceived as useful and easy to use. It is then exposed, as a research objective of this work, to recognize the student's perception of the use of virtual educational platforms (Moodle) as a motivational and influencing factor in their learning process focused on the results it achieves. It should be noted that this analysis will be conducted under the student's approach (constructivism) and not on the technical utilities of the Moodle platform.

METHOD

Research Design

Due to the nature of the study, a cross-sectional, descriptive, exploratory, and non-experimental investigation is proposed.

Population

The study population was made up of university students enrolled in the four-month period January-April 2017, from the Polytechnic University of Zacatecas, Mexico.

Sample Design

The sample was determined using a probabilistic design for convenience, based on the method for studies whose main variable is qualitative and with a finite population, under the following probabilistic scheme (equation 1):

$$n = \frac{N.Z^2\left(S^2\right)}{d^2\left(N-1\right)+Z^2\left(S^2\right)} \tag{1}$$

Considering a finite population (N=1,153), with a confidence interval of 95% (Z=1.96) and a variance S of .1 (the same for the error between the population and sample mean, d), where: n=96 ≈100. The descriptive summary of the sample used can be seen in Table 1, which shows that there is much of the female population with seventy-four participants. The minimum age of the subjects was 20 years with a maximum of forty-seven. In the same way, it is observed that the predominant occupation is the study (70%), and the marital status is single as the main stratum.

Table 1. Descriptive statistics of the sample

	n=100	%
Age	20 years	24%
	21 years	30%
	22 years	24%
	More than 23 years	22%
	Total	**100%**
Gender	Femenine	74%
	Male	26%
	Total	**100%**
Ocupation besides to study	Only studies	70%
	Works	18%
	Household	6%
	Work and household	6%
	Total	**100%**
Civil status	Single	83%
	Married	13%
	Divorced	0%
	Free union	4%
	Total	**100%**

The inclusion criteria were that they were enrolled in the school year and enrollment in the Moodle virtual platform. As exclusion criteria, the refusal to participate in the study and the incomplete answer to the instrument proposed for the investigation were considered.

Instrument

An ad hoc instrument was developed, which evaluates the student's perception of the use of the Moodle platform from a motivational perspective and influence on their own learning; It should be noted that this instrument is aimed solely at recognizing the appreciation that the student has of the usefulness of the platform to facilitate learning as a motivational factor and not on the technical performance of the platform itself. The instrument was elaborated according to the social cognitive theory and dialectical constructivism, focused these from the psychology of learning. It starts from the fact that social cognitive theory highlights the idea that the subject acquires knowledge, rules, strategies, attitudes, and beliefs by observing others.

While dialectical constructivism infers that knowledge comes from the interactions of the individual with her environment (Montoro, 2015). In accordance with the above, the Motivational Perception Scale on the Use of Educational Virtual Platforms (EPMPV) is proposed, subdivided into five dimensions (see table 2), made up of twenty items. The instrument is presented on a Likert-type scale, with six response levels, ranging from not in agreement to totally agree.

Table 2. Dimensions evaluated by reagent of the EPMPV. Item Categories 1-4 Perceived self-efficacy 5-8 Expectancy-Value Theory 9-12 Motivation to achieve 13-16 Self-determination 17-20 Attribution of achievement Source: self-made.

Table 2. Dimensions evaluated by item of EPMPV

Items	Categories
1-4	Perceived self-efficacy
5-8	Expectancy-value theory
9-12	Motivation to achieve
13-16	Self-determination
17-20	Attribution of achievement

The EPMPV evaluation method was defined by the sum of the scores obtained by the student in each of the dimensions. According to the total score of the items, the ranges were established to determine the levels of motivational perception of the university students specified in Table 3, where the maximum possible score corresponds to 120 (total sum) points and the minimum to 20 (minimum sum), with a dimension between ranges of 33 points for the first two and 32 for the last one.

Table 3. EPMPV cut-off points

Range of punctuations	Perception of motivation
20-53	Low level of perception of motivation
54-87	Moderate level of perception of motivation
88-120	High level of perception of motivation

Process

The instrument was applied through a form presented in the participant's Moodle platform, which was accessed through a URL address, indicating the purpose of the research, as well as the confidential and anonymous use of their data. On the other hand, the measure of reliability with the help of Cronbach's Alpha assumes that the items (assessed on a Likert-type scale) measure the same construct. It also assumes that they are highly correlated. This method allows estimating the reliability of an instrument through a set of items, where it is expected to obtain the measurement of the same instrument, construct, or theoretical dimension.

The reliability of the scale must always be obtained with the data from each sample, guaranteeing the reliable measurement of the items in the specific research sample. To validate the instrument proposed for this work, a sample of forty elements was used as part of the piloting phase, prior to its application. An alpha of $0.89 \approx 0.9$ was obtained, which gives the instrument an acceptable reliability value. According to Nunnally (1978), within a standard exploratory analysis, a reliability value of around 0.7 is adequate. Reason it was decided to use the instrument in the application after n=100. The results obtained for Cronbach's Alpha can be reviewed in Table 4.

Table 4. Reliability statistics

Cronbach´s Alpha	Cronbach's alpha based on standardized items	N of items
.892	.901	20

Results

According to the analysis of the results, it is observed that the mean tends to show a high level of perception of motivation on the use of the Moodle virtual platform, since it is in the satisfaction interval of 88 to 120, with a standard deviation of 12.5 scale points observed (see figure 1).

Figure 1. Results

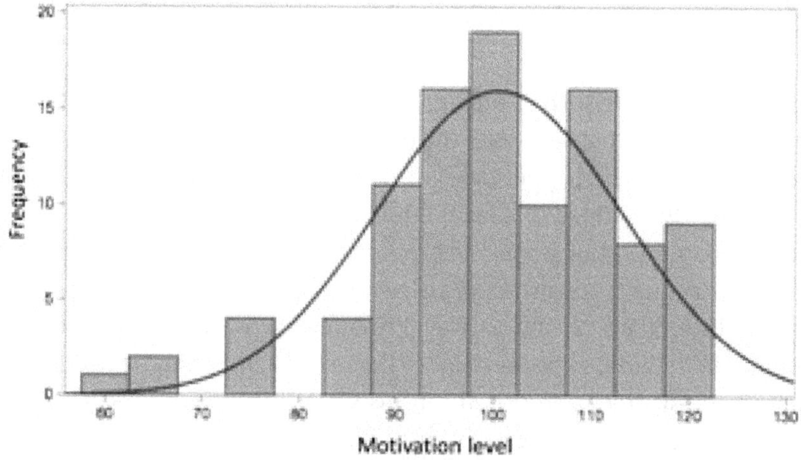

With the intention of conducting a more detailed analysis, the categories that make up the instrument were reviewed in a particular way, finding that the means in each of these are above level 4 according to the response scale. ranging from not at all agree (1) to totally agree (6), which can be observed in Figure 2 (Analysis of results by category).

Regarding the category Perceived self-efficacy, items 1, 2 and 3 reflect a high motivational level, that is, a strong conviction of the student to conduct the activities proposed in the Moodle platform, as well as their expectations, which somehow It allows you to self-regulate your behavior when you consider it necessary. However, there is no motivation on the work conducted by others as a determining factor to adapt their own behavior according to the results of others, even when they consider them positive (see figure 3).

Figure 2. Analysis of results by category

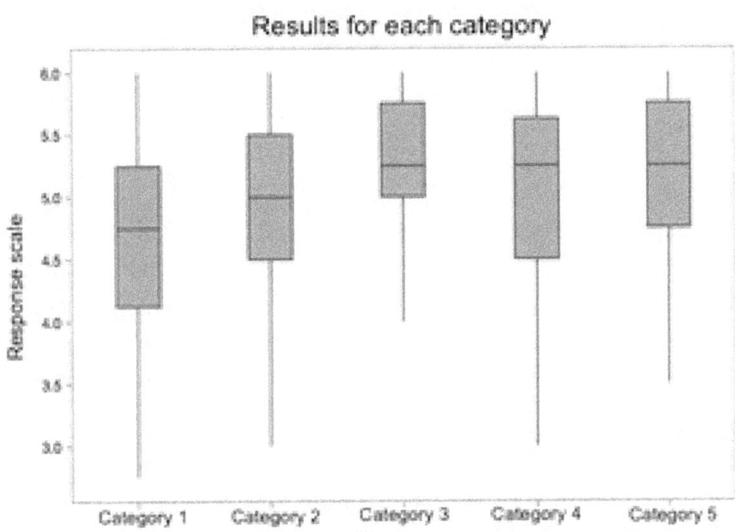

Figure 3. Perceived self-efficacy

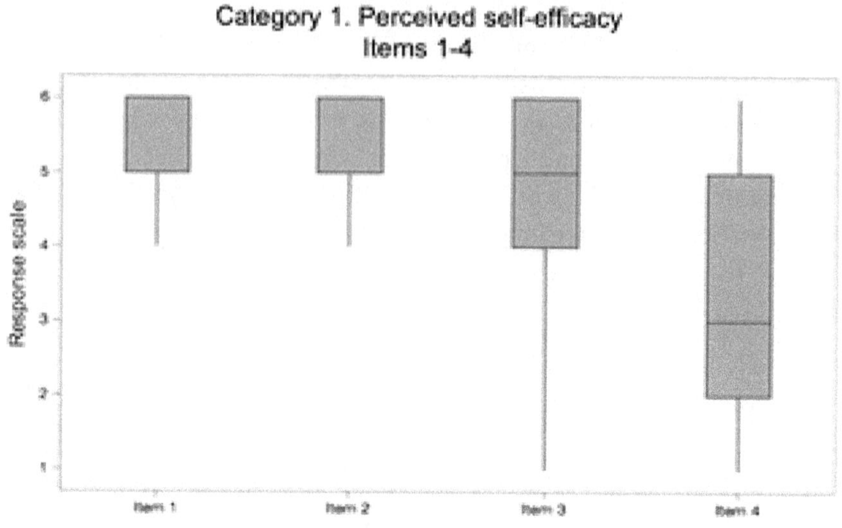

As for the expectation-value theory category, a high level of motivation can be seen in most of the items that make it up, where it can be deduced that motivation is based on the importance of overcoming the task, interest in own task, its usefulness, as well as the satisfaction and enjoyment that comes with carrying it out (see Figure 4).

Figure 4. Expectancy-value theory

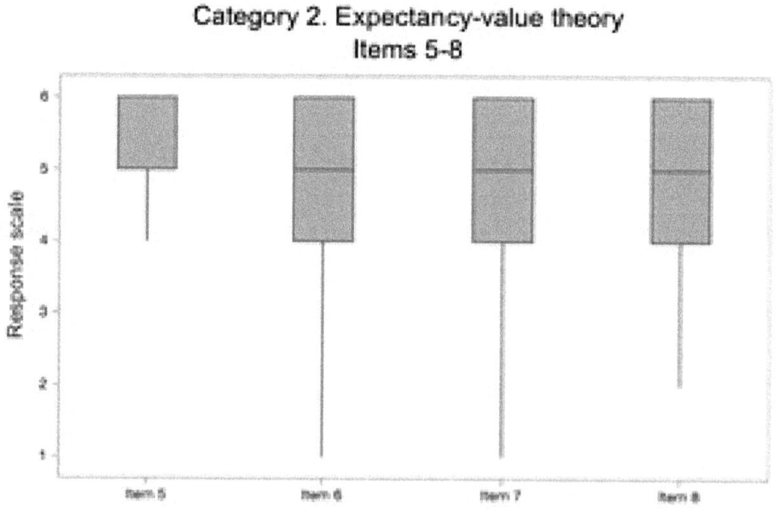

Regarding the Motivation for achievement category, there is a similar trend to the previous dimensions, observing a high motivational level, since there is a constant willingness to strive to achieve something and execute the proposed tasks, to demonstrate their competence on the topics. The above can be reviewed in Figure 5.

Figure 5. Motivation to achieve

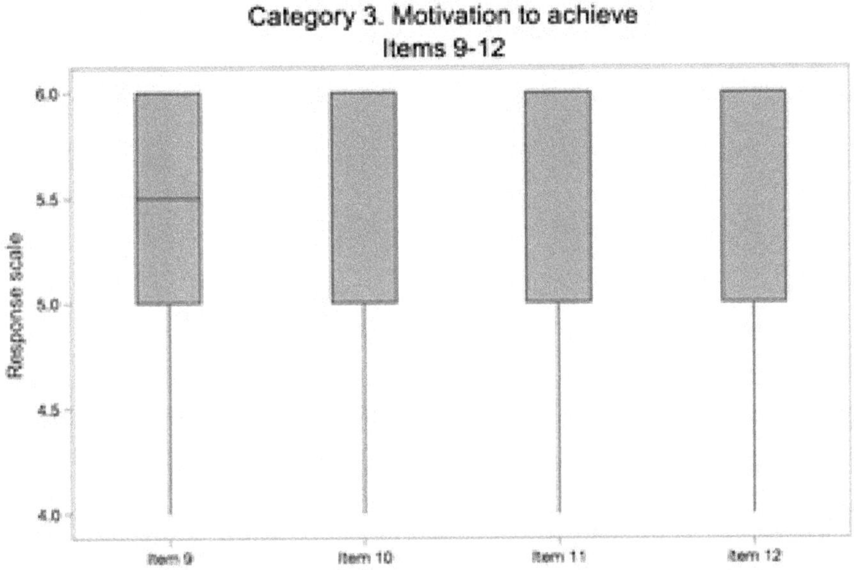

According to the analysis of the answers given in the Self-determination category, a high motivation of the students is observed in terms of autonomy, competence, and the relationship with others. Where the student tries to see himself as the cause of his actions, which in turn influences his behavior, in addition to seeking to control the results he obtains. Similarly, he tries to improve relationships with others to achieve a sense of belonging to the group (see Figure 6).

Figure 6. Self-determination

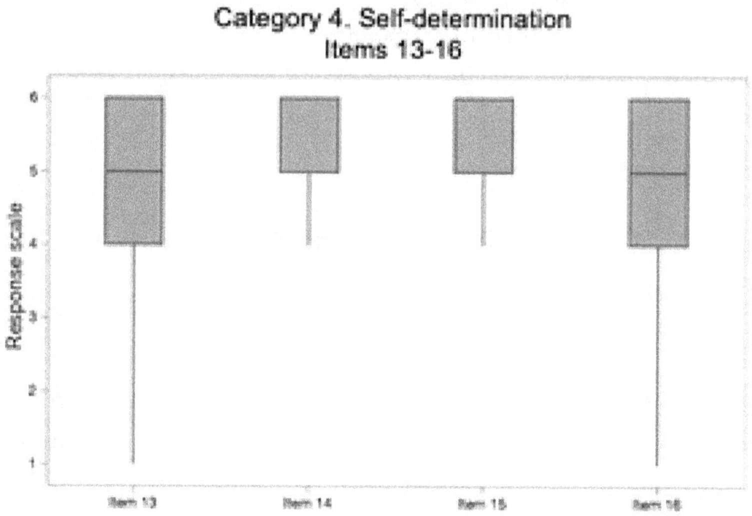

Finally, in the Achievement Attribution category, the responses were between scores 5 and 6, which denotes a high motivational level. Since the student considers the efforts made on the platform to be decisive for the results obtained, as well as his own ability to conduct the activities, even the difficulty of the task itself does not reduce his expectations of success, which can be seen in the Figure 7.

Figure 7. Attribution of achievement

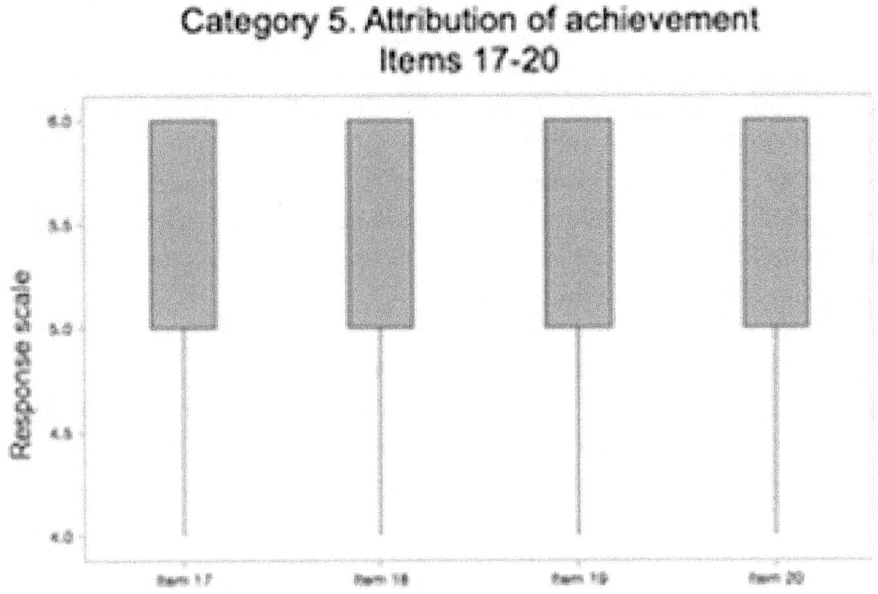

PRINCIPAL COMPONENT ANALYSIS

Principal component analysis is a statistical technique that seeks dimensionality reduction. For this work, said tool was applied, trying to explain most of the total variability of the twenty items of the **EPMPV** questionnaire, to simplify the complex and numerous relationships that could be found. The procedure was conducted using the statistical software Statgraphics.

According to Hair, et al. (1999), principal component analysis is a method that allows transforming a set of original variables into another set of variables, called the set of principal components, understood as a linear combination of the original variables, and which are characterized by being interrelated. The original variables van be taken and calculating their correlation matrix, there is usually a high degree of correlation between some of them. The foregoing leads to the assumption that the EPMPV questionnaire could be used with a set of smaller-dimensional items. Being that, if the original variables are closely related to each other, it is expected that the information can be expressed through certain main components, commonly called constructs, otherwise, the number of main components would be like that of the original variables (20 items).

According to the proposed methodology, the first step was to determine the number of components to be extracted, for which the latent root criterion was used. This technique assumes that any individual factor should justify the variance of at least one single variable, considering that each variable contributes with the value of 1 for the total eigenvalue. Therefore, only the factors that have latent roots or eigenvalues greater than one since they explain at least one variable. For their part, all those variables whose value is less than 1 were considered non-significant and were rejected for interpretation (Hair et al., 1999). As can be seen in the sedimentation graph (Figure 8), of the twenty original items of the EPMPV questionnaire, there are four main components to be extracted.

At this point, a clarification should be made, since, prior to the selection of the final set of components, the amount selected could be inconvenient. Because, if few components are used, the correct structure is not revealed and important dimensions can be omitted, which is why it was determined to select five main components, since the last component is exactly at the value of 1.

Figure 8. Sedimentation graph

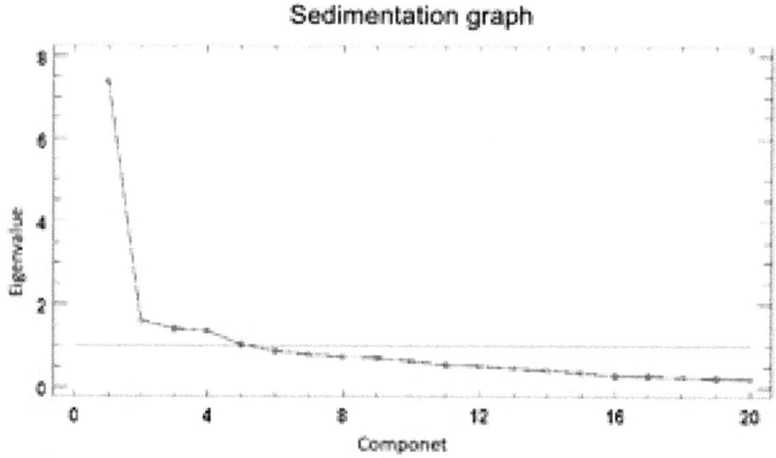

Next, the factor matrix was rotated, because, out of conviction, most researchers agree that non-rotated factorial solutions –although more direct– are not sufficient; thus, rotating the matrix removes the ambiguity that often accompanies the preliminary matrix. The ultimate objective of all rotation is to obtain some theoretically significant factors, which is why, for this work, the Varimax orthogonal rotation method was used, resulting in the matrix of Table 5.

Table 5. Varimax method rotated factor loadings

	Factor 1	Factor 2	Factor 3	Factor 4	Factor 5
Item 1	0.4208	0.2760	-0.0065	0.0643	*0.7014
Item 2	0.5390	0.3473	-0.1378	0.3151	0.3286
Item 3	0.3672	0.0709	0.2100	*0.7556	-0.0735
Item 4	-0.0268	0.1510	0.1197	*0.7815	0.1249
Item 5	0.1553	*0.7263	0.3318	-0.0813	0.3051
Item 6	0.1236	*0.8389	-0.0165	0.1647	0.1494
Item 7	0.2365	0.2890	0.2373	0.3508	0.3558
Item 8	0.1358	0.1180	*0.7500	0.3270	-0.0403
Item 9	0.1620	0.1428	*0.8531	0.0614	0.1086
Item 10	0.0831	0.2226	0.6377	0.0873	0.5574
Item 11	0.1039	0.5725	0.2719	0.0881	0.4405
Item 12	0.5735	0.5566	0.0109	0.1929	0.0898
Item 13	0.5059	0.5204	0.0312	-0.0225	0.2488
Item 14	0.6484	0.3042	0.4145	0.1289	-0.2198
Item 15	0.5804	0.5923	0.2037	0.0558	-0.1973
Item 16	0.1006	0.5922	0.2419	0.2895	0.0114
Item 17	*0.7724	0.1029	0.1233	0.0731	0.1629
Item 18	*0.7874	0.3071	0.0738	0.0218	0.1725
Item 19	*0.7253	0.0214	0.2269	-0.0389	0.4071
Item 20	0.6821	-0.0032	0.1081	0.3045	0.0691

Once the percentages of variance and communalities were determined, the last step consisted of reducing the number of variables, substituting them for a group of five substitute variables, one per factor (main component). This procedure consisted of determining the loads per factor (see Table 5) considering all those variables that presented a load value greater than 0.7 (same criteria as Cronbach's Alpha), the procedure is usually called additive scales from where Table 6 was obtained.

Table 6. Additive scales by factor (from Table 5)*

Component	Items	Category
1	item 17, items 18 e item 19	Achievement attribution
2	item 5 e item 6	Theory of expectancy-value
3	item 8 e item 9	Motivation for achievement
4	item 3 e item 4	Theory of expectancy-value
5	item 1	Perceived self-efficacy

From the above, it was obtained as a result that of the twenty original items of the **EPMPV** questionnaire, five main components were identified that summarize the variation, in this way it can be seen that:

a) **Component 1** belongs to category 5 "Attribution to achievement" contemplating items 17, 18 and 19 (17. I consider that I have sufficient capacity to develop the activities proposed in the Moodle platform; eighteen. The efforts that I make within the Moodle platform are decisive in the results obtained; and 19. The difficulty of homework does not lower my expectations of success).
b) **Component 2** belongs to category 2 "Theory of expectations-value" which includes items 5 and 6 (5. I consider it important to conduct the activities proposed in the Moodle platform; and six. I enjoy carrying out the proposed activities on the Moodle platform, such as forums, chats, wikis, glossaries, among others).
c) While **Component 3** corresponds to the category "Motivation for achievement" specifically, made up of items 8 and 9 (8. I usually do complex tasks and require a lot of effort on the Moodle platform, when I consider them useful for the future, and nine. When there are very difficult tasks on the Moodle platform, I try to do them to the best of my ability).
d) Regarding **Component 4,** it agrees with the category "Theory of expectations-value", contemplating items 3 and 4 (3. When I am not reaching my performance objectives, according to the "ratings" section within the Moodle platform, I make some extra effort to achieve them, and four. I imitate the behavior of a colleague on the Moodle platform, when it produces positive results).
e) Finally, **Component 5,** is made up only of item 1 (1. At the beginning of the course, the Moodle platform presents all the content, which allows me to recognize my performance) belonging to the category "Perceived self-efficacy".

CONCLUSION

According to the analysis of results, it was possible to observe that there are five characteristics derived from the principal component analysis that would guarantee a broad perception of the Moodle platform as a motivational factor. In this sense, the first characteristic, delimited in component five, includes the student's recognition of her own performance. In other words, the Moodle platform must specifically contain the activities to be developed, as well as the content to be reviewed.

Considering that, as García-Varcárcel (2011) points out, students resist change, since modifying their practices, beliefs or habits can cause them anxiety or insecurity, therefore, the a priori knowledge of what should be developing on the platform equates to the idea of control over your own performance.

A second characteristic, included within component four, includes the effort that the student makes to achieve their objectives, repairing the idea of correcting their performance, if this is not adequate, if the Moodle platform allows them to precisely review its degree of progress or compliance. It is necessary to mention that, in this same component, the inclusion of the level of motivation that the student gives to the behavior of one of his classmates as an agent to imitate was observed, considering it unnecessary to do it, even when he thinks that he is doing an adequate job within the platform. Therefore, the autonomy of the student and their own self-regulatory capacity within the learning process are recognized, which certainly agrees with the results of the EPMPV, in the Self-determination category, indicates that the student tends to consider himself as the origin of his actions.

Characteristic three, included in the third component, refers to the value that the student places on conducting the activities proposed in the Moodle platform, with those considered useful having greater relevance, since they can follow them regardless of the degree of difficulty. Therefore, this condition is met when the platform itself allows you to continue the tasks. This characteristic includes the concept of achievement motivation, which according to Casas, Carranza, and Ruiz (2011), comprises two dimensions: intrinsic motivation, perceived as a sign of competence and self-determination; as well as extrinsic motivation, which contemplates the subject's participation in some activity to avoid consequences and achieve success. In the previous case, the usefulness of the task would function as intrinsic motivation, and the accomplishment of this (desire for success), despite the difficulty, as extrinsic.

A fourth characteristic, derived from the analysis of principal components, included in the second component, considers the importance of adequately carrying out the tasks proposed in the Moodle platform, as well as the degree of satisfaction that this generates. Therefore, when the three previous characteristics are met, the student enjoys participating in the activities proposed on said platform.

Finally, a last characteristic is incorporated, framed within the first component, this refers to the structure of the platform from the beginning of the course, which should facilitate the self-monitoring of the student, managing to determine their academic performance in advance. In this sense, Flores and Macotela (2006) affirm that self-regulation in the motivational aspect has a direct relationship with the establishment of goals, in turn, the type of goal established is related to its execution and achievement. On the other hand, in relation to the countries with the highest implementation of LMS, the annual organization of a meeting of users of the Moodle platform, called MoodleMoots, which consists of a series of conferences focused on promoting collaboration and exchange of best practices, stands out. practices of the open source learning platform Moodle.

These meetings arise from the need to share experiences on the platform, showing what has been learned about what works and what does not work. In such a way that others become aware of those experiences and in turn can apply said knowledge to improve their own Moodle sites. MoodleMoots have been organized for more than ten years, with the participation of countries such as Mexico, Colombia, the United States, Spain, the United Kingdom, Japan, and Russia, among others (Moodlemoot, 2017). Regarding the above, according to what was stated in the 4th edition of Moodle Moot Colombia 2013, where it is stated that, of the Higher Education Institutions (HEIs) accredited in that country, 82% use the Moodle platform to support teaching (Ruíz, 2013), the foregoing considering that, of the 300 registered universities in Colombia, only 6.7% have received high-quality certification in higher education (Rincón, 2012).

For its part, Mexico has a total of 3,704 higher education institutions (SEP 2016), of which, according to the Council for Higher Education Accreditation (COPAES, 2017), 307 have at least one educational program. current accredited, corresponding to 8.29%. After an exhaustive analysis of the official web portals of these institutions, it was observed that, of these, 89.9% use the Moodle platform to support their teaching-learning process (276 IES), while 3.58% (11 IES) relies on some other virtual educational platform (Blackboard, Chamilo, etc.), and the remaining 6.52% (20 HEIs) do not specify the use of this type of teaching tools in the information contained in their official pages.

It is worth mentioning that, since the Moodle platform is a tool framed within ICT, it is constantly evolving, according to the needs of users. It is also necessary to update it to the most current versions. In the same way, it is a tool with a low level of use, since there are around 1,305 diverse types of plugins that complement its functionality, with optional download or use, of which sixty correspond to the communication area, with a total 12,387k downloads, contained in 38,583 sites (Moodle, 2022). The foregoing becomes relevant when considering that the main online activity (79%) conducted by the population in Mexico is accessing social networks, likewise, the profile of the Internet user with the highest Internet use is among the range of ages from 19 to 34 years (AMPICI, 2016), average age of students in higher education.

It is of vital importance to return to these aspects when designing and implementing courses in virtual educational platforms, making use of the complements that can improve their usefulness, considering the preferences of the population to which they are addressed, in such a way that the learning process through the interconnection of the platform to the most common social networks. In the same way, a learning environment should be noticeably clear about what is expected of students, what they do and why they do it, because, on the contrary, motivation decreases, reflecting difficulties in students to adapt activities to broader knowledge frameworks, in addition to reducing their self-regulation capacity (Dumont et al. 2010).

Based on the above and in accordance with what has been stated by the OECD, student motivation ensures the acquisition of knowledge and skills in a significant way, asserting that the teacher must provide the time, space and support necessary for the student to reflect on the learning strategies used and their influence on the knowledge acquired, hoping that the learning environments have the purpose of identifying and promoting the personal interests, as well as the intrinsic motivations of the students (Dumont, Istance & Benavides, 2010).

The foregoing becomes relevant when it is observed that, according to the results obtained, there is a high motivational level on the use of virtual platforms and that, according to said organization, the teacher who becomes aware of the motivational factors of the student, can use the information in a beneficial way for the configuration of the learning process. As Olmos-Migueláñez et al. (2014), most of the time, the use of virtual platforms, such as Moodle, far from promoting interaction with information and joint work between student and teacher, tend to be used more as mere documentary repositories, a consequence that is evident when work for the first time in such virtual environments.

In the elaboration of the present study, different limitations are recognized, among them the delimitation of the population, which is subject to a single Higher Education Institution, which makes it difficult to generalize the results. Therefore, it is suggested for future research to expand the sample, through the participation of various educational programs and institutions, as well as the homogenization of participants by gender. In the same way, it is proposed to resume the EPMPV to adapt the items according to the principal component analysis.

Within the educational philosophy of virtual platforms, the student constructs knowledge with the aid of a mediator and through interaction with the group, with motivation acting as an intermediary. Now, concerning the practical applications that can be derived from this study, it is evident that for the creation of a better online learning environment, the instructor must ensure that they describe in detail the activities that the student should carry out (how), as the student values having control over their learning (why).

Likewise, the instructor should establish, as part of the virtual learning environment, various feedback mechanisms that allow the student to recognize their progress (how), to self-regulate accordingly, since the student tends to view themselves as the origin of their actions (why). Similarly, the instructor should implement, within the virtual learning platform, activities that the student finds useful (how), as they are more motivated to engage with them, regardless of the difficulty of those tasks.

Finally, it is considered as a contribution of this research, the recommendation to focus the teaching efforts for the implementation of the Moodle platform in the care of the structure of the course prior to its start, in fact, the suggestion should be of an institutional nature, inviting the HEIs to the creation of a standard in the structures of their courses in Moodle for all their teachers. In addition, the results presented make it possible to identify the preponderant motivational factors in the student, within the use of the Moodle virtual platform. In such a way that a reference can, be established when developing and implementing b-learning, considering the characteristics of the student, as well as the technological characteristics of the platform or the contents of the subject; that is, consider the teaching-learning process from a holistic and complementary vision.

REFERENCES

Almaráz, F. (2014). La diformación para la adopción de entornos virtuales de enseñanza-aprendizaje en la universidad: un enfoque organizativo. In A. García-Valcárcel (Ed.), *Experiencias de Innovación Docente Universitaria* (pp. 191–198). Universidad de Salamanca.

Arriata, O., Galisteo, D., Pérez, M., & Martín, M. (2009). *Innovación en docencia universitaria con Moodle. Casos prácticos*. Editorial Club Universitario.

Asociación Mexicana de Internet. (2016). *12° Estudio sobre los hábitos de los usuarios de Internet en México 2016*. Recuperado de https://www.amipci.org.mx/images/Estudio_Habitosdel_Usuario_2016.pdf

Barbera, E. (2015). *Aprender e-learning*. Paidós.

Cardozo, A. (2008). Motivación, aprendizaje y rendimiento académico en estudiantes del primer año universitario. *Laurus, 14*(28) 209-237. Recuperado de https://www.redalyc.org/articulo.oa?id=76111716011

Casas, V., Carranza, G. & Ruiz, A. (2011). *Guía para la planeación didáctica en la Universidad*. México: UPN Polvo de gis.

Cohn-Muroy, D., Flores-Lafosse, N., & Villanueva, V. (2015). Percepción del uso de una plataforma virtual de aprendizaje colaborativo en una universidad peruana: Estudio de Caso. *Comunidad Latinoamericana de Objetos de Aprendizaje, 6*(1), 71-80. Recuperado de http://www.laclo.org/papers/index.php/laclo/article/view/341

Consejo para la Acreditación de la Educación Superior COPAES. (2017). *Programas acreditados*. Recuperado de http://www.copaes.org/Copaes2.0/

Dávila, A. (2011, December). Filosofía educativa de las aulas virtuales: Caso Moodle. *Compendium (Newtown, Pa.)*, 97–105. http://www.ucla.edu.ve/dac/compendium/Revista27/Compendium_27_5.pdf

De la Mora, J. (2003). Psicología del aprendizaje, Volumen 1. México: Editorial Progreso

Dionicio, A. (2014). *Intervenciones pedagógicas con b-learning (presencial-aulas virtuales)*. Editorial Dunken.

Dumont, H., Istance, D., & Benavides, F. (2010). *The Nature of Learning: Using Research to Inspire Practice*. Organization for Economic Co-operation and Development OCDE. Recuperado de https://www.oecd.org/edu/ceri/The%20Nature%20of%20Learning.Practitioner%20Guide.ESP.pdf

Estrada, R., Zaldívar, A., Mendoza, R., Nava, L., & García, O. (2013). Percepción de los estudiantes acerca de la implementación de la modalidad educativa blended learning en la Educación Superior. *Revista Electrónica de Investigación en Educación Superior, 1*(1), 1-12. Recuperado de http://sistemanodalsinaloa.gob.mx/archivoscomprobatorios/_10_articulosrevistasarbitraje/168.pdf

Flores, R., & Macotela, S. (2006). *Problemas de aprendizaje en la adolesencia: experiencias en el programa alcanzando el éxito en secundaria*. UNAM.

García-Varcárcel, A. (2011). *Integración de las TIC en la docencia universitaria*. Netbiblio.

Garduño, R. (2005). *Enseñanza virtual sobre la organización de recursos informativos digitales*. UNAM. doi:10.22201/cuib.9703231500p.2005

Hair, J., Anderson, R., Tatham, R., & Black, W. (1999). *Análisis multivariante*. Prentice Hall.

Martínez, F. (2005). *E-aprendizaje en bibliotecología: perspectivas globales*. UNAM. doi:10.22201/cuib.9703227414p.2005

Montoro, A. (2015). *Motivación y matemáticas: experiencias de flujo en estudiantes de maestro de educación primaria (Tesis de doctorado)*. Universidad Almería. Recuperado de https://www.educacion.gob.es/teseo/imprimirFicheroTesis.do;jsessionid=5ABDC9806028E030AE8456238CCD715D

Moodle. (2022). *Moodle (Página oficial)*. Recuperado de https://moodle.org/

MoodleMoot. (2017). *MoodleMoot (Página oficial)*. Recuperado de https://moodlemoot.org

Nunnally, J. (1978). *Psychometric theory* (2nd ed.). McGraw-Hill.

OCDE. (2005). E-learning in Tertiary Education Where Do We Stand? Where Do We Stand? OCDE.

Olmos-Migueláñez, S., Martínez-Abad, F., Torrecilla-Sánchez, E., & Mena-Marcos, J. (2014). Análisis psicométrico de una escala de percepción sobre la utilidad de Moodle en la universidad. *RELIEVE, 20*(2), 1. Advance online publication. doi:10.7203/relieve.20.2.4221

Otero, A. (2001). *Medio ambiente y educación: capacitación ambiental para docentes*. Ediciones Novedades Educativas.

Rincón, E. (2012). El 82% de las universidades acreditadas usan Moodle. *E-Learn Magazine*. Recuperado de http://elearningmagazine.co/2012/11/24/el-82-de-las-universidades-acreditadas-usan-moodle/?lang=es

Ruíz, N. (2013). *Moodle Moot Colombia 2013. La verdadera alternativa de la radio*. Universidad Distrital Francisco José de Caldas. Recuperado de https://laud.udistrital.edu.co/noticias/moodle-moot-colombia-2013

Secretaría de Comunicaciones y Transportes SCT. (2017). *México Conectado*. Recuperado de http://mexicoconectado.gob.mx/sobre_mexico_conectado.php?id=66

Secretaría de Educación Pública SEP. (2016). *Principales cifras del sistema educativo nacional. 2015-2016*. México: SEP. Recuperado de https://www.planeacion.sep.gob.mx/Doc/estadistica_e_indicadores/principales_cifras/principales_cifras_2015_2016_bolsillo.pdf

Silva, J. (2011). *Diseño y moderación de entornos virtuales de aprendizaje*. Editorial UOC.

Chapter 10
Influence of Data Analysis Tools in Teaching and Learning Economics

C. V. Suresh Babu
https://orcid.org/0000-0002-8474-2882
Hindustan Institute of Technology and Science, India

A. Auroshaa
https://orcid.org/0009-0001-7285-430X
Hindustan Institute of Technology and Science, India

EXECUTIVE SUMMARY

In this chapter, the authors outline a plan for implementing CBL in economics education and highlight some of the key tools and resources that can be used to enhance the learning experience. They provide access to data analysis tools for the students that can provide access to data analysis tools such as statistical software packages and online databases. This can enable them to analyze economic data more effectively and develop their data analysis skills. There is the platform to study all types of data analysis tools that may be useful to both educators and students for learning the economics. The chapter emphasizes the importance of conducting a needs assessment, developing digital resources, establishing the necessary technology infrastructure, providing faculty training, and implementing the CBL strategy across all economics courses. The chapter also highlights some of the tools and resources that can be used to support CBL in economics education, including Microsoft Excel, statistical software packages, geographic information systems, and business intelligence (BI) software.

DOI: 10.4018/978-1-6684-7583-6.ch010

INTRODUCTION

Data analysis tools have become increasingly important in teaching and learning economics in recent years. With the explosion of digital data and the proliferation of data science techniques, economists are now able to analyze and interpret complex economic phenomena with greater accuracy and depth than ever before (Suresh Babu, 2023). This has led to a growing demand for data analysis tools in economics education, as students seek to gain the skills and knowledge necessary to thrive in an increasingly data-driven world.

The use of data analysis tools in teaching and learning economics has several important benefits. First, it enables students to gain a deeper understanding of economic concepts and theories by providing them with concrete examples and real-world data to analyze. Second, it helps students develop important analytical skills, such as the ability to identify patterns, draw conclusions, and communicate findings effectively. Finally, it prepares students for a wide range of careers in economics and related fields, as data analysis skills are increasingly in demand in today's job market.

In this context, the influence of data analysis tools in teaching and learning economics cannot be overstated. From basic statistical analysis to complex econometric modeling, these tools provide students with the means to explore economic concepts and theories in greater depth, and to apply their knowledge in a real-world context. As such, they represent a powerful tool for shaping the future of economics education, and for preparing the next generation of economists to tackle the complex challenges of our time.

RELATED WORK

Define the Problem

The problem identified for the influence of data analysis tools in teaching and learning economics is the lack of practical application and hands-on experience for students. Traditional economics education often focuses on theoretical concepts and models but does not provide students with the skills and tools necessary to analyze and interpret real-world economic data. As a result, students may struggle to understand how economic concepts apply to real-world situations and may have difficulty finding employment in industries that require data analysis skills.

The lack of practical application in economics education can also lead to a lack of interest among students. Economics can be a complex and abstract subject, and without practical examples and hands-on experience, students may struggle to see the relevance and value of the subject.

The use of data analysis tools in economics education can help to address these issues by providing students with practical examples and hands-on experience with real-world economic data. By using these tools, students can see how economic concepts and theories apply to real-world situations and can develop the data analysis skills necessary for employment in a variety of industries (Kaplan et al., 2016). Additionally, the use of data analysis tools can make economics education more engaging and interesting for students, increasing their motivation and interest in the subject.

LITERATURE REVIEW

According to a study that was published in the Journal of Economic Education, using a data analysis tool in a microeconomics course helped students better comprehend economic principles and their capacity to apply those principles in practical settings (Bratt et al., 2020; Kolb & Kolb, 2005; Velegol et al., 2015). The study also discovered that using the data analysis tool helped students develop their capacity for critical thought and problem-solving (Daniel, 2015; Proitz et al., 2017; Schouten, 2017).

Another study published in the Journal of Economic Education examined the impact of a data analysis tool on students' performance in a macroeconomics course [8]. The study found that students who used the data analysis tool performed better on exams and assignments than students who did not use the tool [3].

Data analysis tools in economics education published in the Journal of Economic Surveys found that the use of these tools can help to bridge the gap between theory and practice, and can enhance students' understanding of economic concepts and their ability to analyze and interpret economic data [10].

Additionally, a study published in the Journal of Financial Education found that the use of data analysis tools in finance education can improve students' understanding of financial concepts and their ability to analyze financial data [7].

Overall, the literature suggests that the incorporation of data analysis tools in economics education can provide significant benefits for students, including improved understanding of economic concepts, enhanced data analysis skills, and improved academic performance.

SUMMARIZE

Data analysis tools have revolutionized the field of economics by enabling researchers to analyze vast amounts of data quickly and accurately. Econometric models and statistical software such as Stata, R, and Python are widely used to analyze economic data (Proitz et al., 2017). These tools have been used to study a wide range of economic phenomena, including economic growth, inequality, labor markets, international trade, and finance. Researchers use these tools to estimate the effects of various policies and interventions, to forecast economic trends, and to understand the underlying mechanisms driving economic behavior.

In recent years, there has been a growing interest in using machine learning techniques in economics, which allows for more complex and nuanced analyses. Additionally, the availability of large datasets, such as administrative data and social media data, has opened up new opportunities for research. Overall, data analysis tools have played a crucial role in advancing our understanding of the economy and informing policy decisions (Daniel, 2015).

Ensure equitable access to data analysis tools for all students. Provide resources or workshops for students who may be less familiar with technology to level the playing field. Encourage interdisciplinary collaboration between economics and data science departments. This can lead to the development of specialized courses that teach both economic theory and data analysis skills. Design assignments that require students to apply data analysis skills to real-world economic issues. This could involve analyzing trends in economic indicators, conducting market research, or evaluating policy impacts (Bratt et al., 2020)

ARGUMENTS

1. Technical challenges: Using data analysis tools can require a certain level of technical proficiency, which may be a barrier for some students. Students who are not familiar with the software or programming languages used may struggle to keep up or feel intimidated by the technical requirements (Kolb & Kolb, 2005; Velegol, 2015).
2. Overreliance on software: Relying too heavily on data analysis tools can lead to students neglecting important theoretical or conceptual aspects of economics. While software can provide useful insights and visualizations, it is important for students to also develop a deep understanding of the underlying economic concepts (Kaplan et al., 2016; Matthews, 2018; Pears et al., 2007).
3. Limitations of the data: Real-world data can be messy and incomplete, and students may not have access to high-quality data sets that are suitable for

analysis. This can limit the effectiveness of data analysis tools in teaching and learning (Kaplan et al., 2016).

4. Misinterpretation of results: Students may misinterpret or misrepresent the results of data analysis, leading to incorrect conclusions or flawed reasoning. This can be particularly problematic if students are not taught how to properly interpret and communicate the results of their analyses (Gannod, 2007).
5. Cost: Some data analysis tools can be expensive, which may be a barrier for some students or institutions. This can limit access to these tools and prevent some students from developing the skills and knowledge necessary to succeed in a data-driven world (Schouten, 2017).

The argument in the context of the influence of data analysis tools in teaching and learning economics is that the incorporation of data analysis tools can significantly enhance the effectiveness of economics education. By using data analysis tools, students can gain practical experience in analyzing and interpreting economic data, which can help to bridge the gap between theoretical concepts and real-world applications.

Furthermore, the use of data analysis tools can provide students with valuable skills that are in high demand in a variety of industries, including finance, consulting, and government. In today's data-driven economy, employers are increasingly seeking candidates with data analysis skills, and economics education that incorporates data analysis tools can help to prepare students for these career opportunities (Daniel, 2015).

In addition to providing practical experience and valuable skills, the use of data analysis tools in economics education can also make the subject more engaging and interesting for students (Proitz et al., 2017). By working with real-world data, students can see the relevance and value of economics concepts and theories, which can increase their motivation and interest in the subject. Overall, the argument is that the incorporation of data analysis tools in economics education can provide significant benefits for students, including practical experience, valuable skills, and increased engagement with the subject.

DRAFTING

Economics education has traditionally focused on theoretical concepts and models, which can make it challenging for students to understand how these concepts apply to real-world situations. Additionally, students often lack practical experience and skills in data analysis, which can limit their career opportunities in industries that require these skills. The incorporation of data analysis tools in economics education can help to bridge this gap and enhance the effectiveness of economics education.

- Data analysis tools provide students with practical experience in analyzing and interpreting economic data, which can help to reinforce theoretical concepts and improve their understanding of how economics applies to real-world situations. By working with real-world data, students can see the practical applications of economic theories and concepts, which can help to make the subject more engaging and interesting for them.
- This can be improved by the training sessions for such tools related to economics and the flow to the students will be reached.
- Using data analysis tools in economics field also provides students with valuable skills that are in high demand in a variety of industries, including finance, consulting, and government. In today's data-driven economy, employers are increasingly seeking candidates with data analysis skills, and economics education that incorporates data analysis tools can help to prepare students for these career opportunities.
- Moreover, the incorporation of data analysis tools in economics education can make the subject more engaging and interesting for students. By working with real-world data, students can see the relevance and value of economics concepts and theories, which can increase their motivation and interest in the subject. This can result in better academic performance, as well as increased engagement with the subject beyond the classroom.

In conclusion, the incorporation of data analysis tools in economics education can provide significant benefits for students, including practical experience, valuable skills, and increased engagement with the subject. As the demand for data analysis skills continues to grow across industries, it is becoming increasingly important for economics education to incorporate these tools in order to prepare students for the workforce.

FINDINGS

It can help educators to better understand and teach economic concepts by providing them with real-world data and analytical tools to illustrate economic principles. This can make economics education more engaging and relevant to students.

It can help students to develop skills in data analysis, which are increasingly important in many fields, including economics. By incorporating data analysis tools into the curriculum, students can learn how to analyze data, interpret results, and communicate findings, which are valuable skills in both academic and professional settings (Proitz et al., 2017).

Incorporating data analysis tools into economics education can help to promote evidence-based decision making. Students can learn how to evaluate the quality of data, test hypotheses, and draw conclusions based on evidence, which can help them to make informed decisions in their personal and professional lives.

Combining data analysis tools with economics education can enhance students' learning experiences, develop valuable skills, and promote evidence-based decision making, all of which are important for success in the modern economy (Daniel, 2015).

METHODOLOGY

The methodology used to develop a data analysis tool in a single platform typically involves several steps, including:

1. **Requirements gathering:** The first step is to gather and analyze the requirements for the data analysis tool. This involves identifying the types of data that will be analyzed, the specific features and functionalities that are required, and any technical or security considerations.
2. **User interface design:** Once the requirements have been identified, the next step is to design the user interface for the data analysis tool. This involves creating wireframes or mockups that show how the user interface will look and function. The design should be intuitive, user-friendly, and visually appealing.
3. **Selection of data analysis tools:** The next step is to select the appropriate data analysis tools that will be used to analyze the data. This may include statistical software packages like R or Python, or specialized data analytics tools like Tableau or Power BI.
4. **Integration of data analysis tools:** With the user interface design and data analysis tools selected, the next step is to integrate the data analysis tools into the user interface. This involves programming the application using appropriate coding languages and frameworks and integrating the data analytics tools into the application.
5. **Testing and quality assurance:** Once the data analysis tool has been developed, it needs to be thoroughly tested to ensure that it functions correctly and meets the requirements. This involves both functional testing to ensure that the application works as expected, and quality assurance testing to ensure that it is reliable and secure.
6. **Deployment and maintenance:** To deploy the data analysis tool to the intended users and to maintain it over time. This involves ongoing monitoring

and support to ensure that the application continues to function correctly and to make updates and improvements as needed.

The methodology used to develop a data analysis tool in a single platform is like the standard software development process, but with a focus on data analytics and the integration of data analysis tools into the user interface. By following a structured approach and leveraging appropriate tools and frameworks, it is possible to develop robust and effective data analysis tools that meet the needs of users in a variety of industries and contexts.

DESIGN AND DEVELOPMENT

Step 1: Defining the scope and requirements.

The first step is to define the scope of the application and the specific requirements that it needs to meet. This involves identifying the types of data that the application will analyze, the specific features and functionalities that are required, and any technical or security considerations.

Step 2: Designing the user interface.

Once the requirements have been defined, the next step is to design the user interface. This involves creating wireframes or mockups of the application that show how the user interface will look and function. The design should be intuitive, user-friendly, and visually appealing.

Step 3: Selecting the appropriate data analytics tools.

The next step is to select the appropriate data analytics tools that will be used to analyze the data. This may include statistical software packages like R or Python, or specialized data analytics tools like Tableau or Power BI.

Step 4: Developing the application.

With the requirements, user interface, and data analytics tools in place, the next step is to develop the application. This involves programming the application using appropriate coding languages and frameworks and integrating the data analytics tools into the application.

Step 5: Testing and quality assurance.

Once the application has been developed, it needs to be thoroughly tested to ensure that it functions correctly and meets the requirements. This involves both functional testing to ensure that the application works as expected, and quality assurance testing to ensure that it is reliable and secure.

Step 6: Deployment and maintenance.

The final step is to deploy the application to the intended users and to maintain it over time. This involves ongoing monitoring and support to ensure that the application continues to function correctly and to make updates and improvements as needed.

Overall, the design and development of an application for data analytics involves a complex set of steps that require expertise in both software development and data analytics. By following a structured approach and leveraging appropriate tools and frameworks, it is possible to develop robust and effective applications that meet the needs of users in a variety of industries and contexts.

Figure 1. Application pathways

TECHNICAL STACKS

1. Programming languages:

The most used programming languages for data analysis in economics are R and Python. Both languages have powerful libraries and frameworks for data manipulation, visualization, and statistical analysis.

2. Data analysis and visualization libraries:

There are a variety of data analysis and visualization libraries available for R and Python, including ggplot2, pandas, NumPy, SciPy, and Matplotlib. These libraries provide a wide range of tools for data manipulation, exploration, and visualization.

3. Databases:

For storing and managing large datasets, relational databases like MySQL, PostgreSQL, and Microsoft SQL Server are commonly used. Alternatively, NoSQL databases like MongoDB and Cassandra can be used for handling unstructured data.

4. Web frameworks:

To develop web-based data analysis tools, web frameworks like Django (Python) and Shiny (R) can be used. These frameworks provide tools for building interactive web applications and visualizations.

5. Cloud platforms:

Cloud platforms like AWS, Azure, and Google Cloud can be used for deploying and scaling data analysis tools. These platforms offer a range of services for data storage, processing, and analysis.

TOOLS AND FEATURES

For teacher reflection, researchers have utilised a variety of methods to automatically extract significant instances of interacting teacher and student conduct during instruction (Suresh Babu & Padma, 2023).

- Firstly, educators must undertake a comprehensive needs assessment. This involves delineating the pedagogical objectives related to the introduction of economics and data concepts within the context of a K-12 learning environment. Essential to this step is determining which economic principles are developmentally appropriate at various grade levels, thereby ensuring sequential and scaffolded learning experiences.
- Upon establishing these foundational objectives, attention should shift towards design. Drawing parallels to educational theories such as Constructivism, educators recognize that learning is enhanced when abstract concepts are represented visually. In this vein, data visualization becomes paramount. Effective visualization not only assists in conceptual understanding but also engenders student engagement, particularly when dealing with abstract economic data sets.
- Tool selection then emerges as the third pivotal stage. Analogous to the curatorial process in textbook adoption, educators must ascertain which software or platforms best align with their pedagogical goals. For younger students, foundational tools like Microsoft Excel may suffice. However, as students transition into the upper echelons of K-12, more advanced tools such as Tableau or rudimentary programming in Python might be considered to elevate their data analytical skills.

Following the design phase, educators would be well-advised to adopt a praxis approach—a cyclical process of action, reflection, and revision. Before the full implementation of such a curriculum, a pilot phase with a subset of students can provide invaluable insights. This feedback loop can identify potential pedagogical challenges, thereby allowing educators to make necessary refinements.

FLOWCHART

1. **Start:** The flowchart begins with the user entering the stimulator by signing in or establishing a new account.
2. **Login/Signup:** If the user is new to the stimulator, they are requested to register a new account. They can log in if they already have an account.
3. **Home Screen:** After logging in, the user is directed to the home screen, where they may access various Data Analyst tools.
4. **Dashboard:** Various data analytic tools are available in the open resource, which one is best for using your purpose can be selected for stimulating.
5. **End:** When the user logs out, the Stimulator is over.

Figure 2. Workflow chart

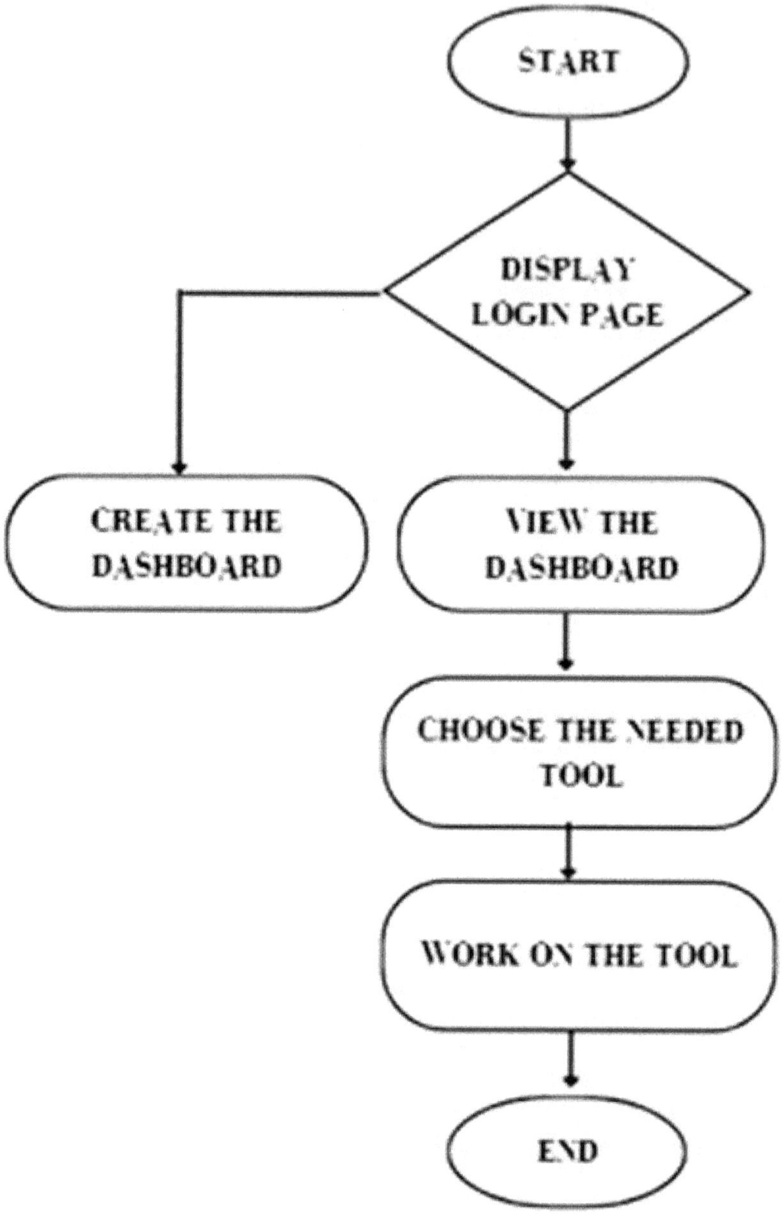

Figure 3. Class diagram

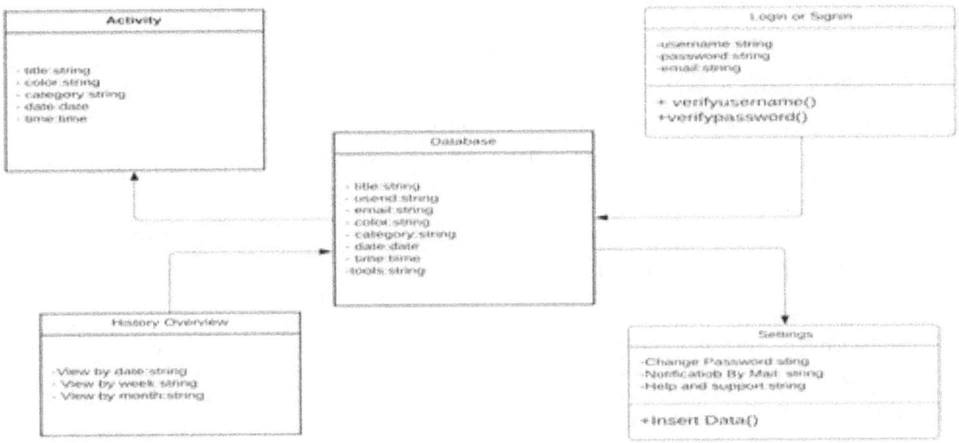

Figure 4. Use case

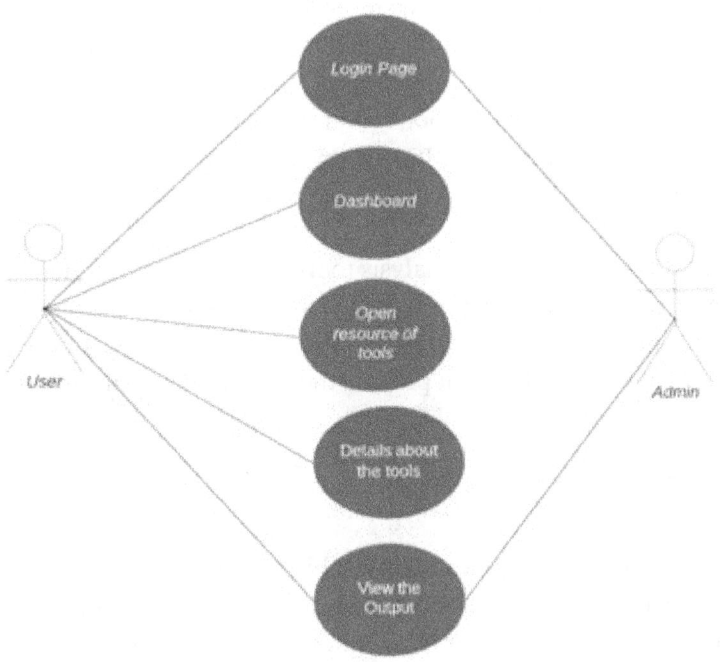

RESULTS

- Access to data analysis tools can enable students to develop their data analysis skills and become proficient in using statistical software packages to analyze economic data. This can help them to understand complex economic concepts and apply them to real-world scenarios.
- By analyzing economic data using data analysis tools, students can gain a deeper understanding of economic concepts and how they are applied in practice. This can help to reinforce their understanding of economic theory and prepare them for careers in economics.
- Providing students with access to data analysis tools can increase their engagement and motivation in learning economics. The opportunity to work with real-world economic data can be exciting and challenging, motivating students to learn more and improve their skills.
- Access to data analysis tools can help to prepare students for careers in economics by providing them with the skills and experience they need to work with economic data and apply economic concepts to real-world scenarios. This can give them a competitive advantage in the job market and increase their chances of success in their careers.
- Increased access to data analysis tools for students in economic education.
- Improved data analysis skills and a deeper understanding of economic concepts among students.
- Enhanced engagement and motivation in learning economics.
- Improved job prospects for students by developing skills in high demand in the job market.

Overall, providing access to data analysis tools is a crucial component of computer-based learning in economics. By enabling students to analyze economic data more effectively, develop their data analysis skills, and gain a deeper understanding of economic concepts, educators can prepare them for successful careers in the field.

EFFECTIVENESS

The effectiveness of data analysis tools in teaching economics can depend on a number of factors, such as the specific tool being used, the level of technical proficiency of the users, and the pedagogical approach of the instructor. However, there is evidence to suggest that the use of data analysis tools can be beneficial in several ways:

1. Enhanced understanding of economic concepts: By using data analysis tools, students can see how economic theories and concepts apply in real-world situations. This can help them develop a deeper understanding of economic concepts and theories and their practical applications.
2. Improved critical thinking skills: Data analysis tools require students to analyze and interpret data, which can help them develop critical thinking skills. This can improve their ability to make informed decisions based on data and to evaluate the validity of economic arguments and theories.
3. Increased engagement and motivation: The use of data analysis tools can make learning more engaging and interactive for students. By working with real-world data, students can see the relevance and practical applications of economic concepts, which can increase their motivation to learn.
4. Improved job readiness: Many jobs in economics and related fields require proficiency in data analysis tools. By learning these skills in the classroom, students can improve their job readiness and career prospects.

Overall, the use of data analysis tools can be effective in teaching economics, especially when combined with a pedagogical approach that emphasizes the practical applications of economic theories and concepts. By using these tools, students can overcome critical thinking skills, gain a deeper understanding of economic concepts, and improve their job readiness.

USER TESTING RESULTS

User satisfaction: User testing can help determine whether students and educators find the data analysis tools easy to use and whether they are satisfied with the results obtained. User feedback can be collected through surveys, focus groups, or individual interviews.

- Learning outcomes: User testing can also help evaluate whether students are able to apply economic concepts and theories effectively when using data analysis tools. This can be measured through assessments, tests, or other forms of evaluation.
- Technical proficiency: User testing can also help identify whether students and educators have the technical skills necessary to use data analysis tools effectively. This can be measured through observations, surveys, or other assessments.
- Accessibility and usability: User testing can also help identify any accessibility or usability issues with the data analysis tools, such as whether

they are accessible to students with disabilities or whether they are draftable with different devices and platforms.

Overall, user testing can provide valuable insights into the effectiveness of data analysis tools in teaching and learning economics. By gathering feedback from users, educators can identify areas for improvement and make adjustments to their teaching methods or the tools themselves to improve learning outcomes.

COMPARING PROGRAMS

Comparing the results of a statistical analysis conducted using a software package like R or Python to the results obtained using a spreadsheet software like Microsoft Excel can help identify any discrepancies or errors. Similarly, comparing the results of a simulation model to real-world data can help evaluate the accuracy of the assumptions and parameters used in the model. It is important to note that different data analysis tools and simulations have different strengths and limitations. For instance, statistical software packages are often more flexible and powerful than spreadsheets, but they may require more advanced programming skills to use effectively. Similarly, simulation models can provide valuable insights into complex systems, but they are only as accurate as the assumptions and data inputs used to build them.

If high school students are well trained for tools like Excel, programming languages related to data analysis, before entering the degree level they have some basic idea about the tools, also in this digital world all becomes automation. Students may be friendly to handle with tools that to related to economics. Ultimately, the choice of data analysis tool or simulation will depend on the specific research question or problem being addressed, as well as the available data and resources. Comparing results across different tools and simulations can help ensure that the analysis is robust and reliable and can help identify areas for further investigation or improvement.

FUTURE RESEARCH

Research has underscored the effectiveness of data analysis tools in enhancing the teaching and learning of economics. However, it's crucial to delve deeper into which specific tools, ranging from statistical software, data visualization techniques, to machine learning algorithms, resonate most effectively with various learner profiles and objectives. There's also emerging evidence highlighting the positive influence of these tools on student outcomes. Yet, a comprehensive understanding of how these tools distinctly affect factors like student motivation, engagement, and retention remains a gap. Furthermore, the potential of data analysis tools extends beyond academic outcomes. They can be instrumental in illuminating economic disparities, offering invaluable insights for policymakers aiming to craft equitable solutions. Particularly in sectors like education, healthcare, and financial resource accessibility, there's a pressing need to explore how these tools can help mitigate economic inequality.

Within the academic sphere, the integration of these tools into economics curricula is a trending shift. While some programs have made strides in this direction, rigorous research is warranted to discern the most effective integration strategies. Such research should address the best practices and also highlight potential challenges educators might encounter during the integration process. Lastly, the continual advent of cutting-edge technologies, including artificial intelligence, Blockchain, and the Internet of Things, necessitates a forward-looking perspective. It's imperative to investigate how these innovations might bolster data analysis in economics, especially considering their potential role in molding future economic policies.

CONCLUSION

In conclusion, providing access to data analysis tools such as statistical software packages and online databases can have a significant positive impact on students in computer-based learning for economics. By enabling students to analyze economic data more effectively, develop their data analysis skills, and gain a deeper understanding of economic concepts, educators can help prepare them for successful careers in the field. Access to data analysis tools can lead to improved learning outcomes, increased engagement, and motivation, enhanced critical thinking and problem-solving skills, and improved job prospects. These outcomes are crucial in preparing students for careers in economics and related fields and can also help them succeed in other areas where data analysis is important. Therefore, it is essential that educators provide students with access to data analysis tools as part of computer-based learning for economics. By doing so, they can help students develop the skills and knowledge they need to thrive in the modern economy and contribute to society in meaningful ways. The DATEE project can help in providing students with access to data analysis tools such as statistical software packages and online databases, enabling them to analyze economic data more effectively and develop their data analysis skills. This will improve the quality of economic education and prepare students for successful careers in the field.

USES FOR TEACHING ECONOMICS

When it comes to teaching economics, a few essential strategies come to the fore. Firstly, there is a pressing need for educators to equip students with proficiency in data analysis tools. It's imperative that students gain hands-on experience with collecting, analyzing, and interpreting data using various instruments, including statistical software packages, spreadsheets, and databases. This mastery will not only deepen their understanding of economic and financial concepts but also empower them to make data-driven decisions. Incorporating these tools directly into the curriculum is the next logical step. As suggested by Suresh Babu & Padma (2023), lessons and assignments should be meticulously crafted to compel students to apply these tools in solving authentic, real-world challenges. Such an approach can significantly sharpen their critical thinking abilities, enhancing their grasp on economic and financial tenets.

Diving into data analysis isn't solely about crunching numbers. Educators must underline the significance of data quality and accuracy. Training students to discern and rectify common data discrepancies, such as outliers, missing entries, and measurement blunders, is paramount. This ensures they don't fall into the pitfall of drawing inaccurate conclusions from flawed datasets. Additionally, the ethical dimension of data analysis in economics cannot be overlooked. Educators need to instill in students an awareness of potential biases stemming from data analysis and strategies to counteract them. Furthermore, with rising concerns about data privacy, security, and ownership, students should be well-versed in the ethical considerations surrounding these areas. Given the rapid evolution and sophistication of data analysis tools, educators face the challenge and opportunity of updating their teaching methodologies. Adapting to the shifting landscapes of economics and finance means preparing students to navigate a world where data-driven insights are superior.

IMPACTS IN ECONOMICS CLASSROOM

Enhanced learning outcomes: Data analysis tools can help students better understand complex economic concepts and theories by providing visualizations and interactive simulations that demonstrate real-world examples. This can lead to improved learning outcomes, including higher levels of engagement, greater comprehension, and improved retention of material. Improved economic analysis: Data analysis tools can help economists conduct more rigorous and precise analyses of economic data. By using statistical software, machine learning algorithms, and data visualization tools, economists can identify patterns and trends that may be difficult or impossible to detect using traditional methods. This can lead to more accurate economic forecasts and better-informed policy decisions. Increased access to economic data: Data analysis tools can make economic data more accessible to a wider audience. By using visualization tools and interactive dashboards, data can be presented in a way that is easy to understand for non-experts, including policymakers, journalists, and members of the public. Promoting data literacy: Data analysis tools can help promote data literacy by encouraging users to engage with and interpret data. This can help develop critical thinking skills and promote a deeper understanding of economic concepts and theories. Better preparation for the workforce: The use of data analysis tools in economics education can help prepare students for the modern workforce, where data analysis and visualization skills are increasingly in demand. By providing students with hands-on experience using data analysis tools, economics programs can help prepare students for careers in fields such as data analysis, market research, and business intelligence.

REFERENCES

Bratt, S., Grealis, T., Harmon, O., & Tomolonis, P. (2020). Learning Tableau: A data visualization tool. *The Journal of Economic Education*, *54*(3-4), 317–328. doi:10.1080/00220485.2020.1804503

Daniel, B. (2015). Big data and analytics in higher education: Opportunities and challenges. *British Journal of Educational Technology*, *46*(5), 904–920. doi:10.1111/bjet.12230

Gannod, G. C. (2007). Work in Progress – Using podcasting in an inverted classroom. In *IEEE Frontiers in Education Conference*. IEEE. 10.1109/FIE.2007.4418119

Kaplan, S., Leung, M., & Steinberg, R. (2016). *Teaching Economics with Dynamic Visualization and Data Analysis Tools*. https://pubmed.ncbi.nlm.nih.gov/28252210/

Kolb, A., & Kolb, D. (2005). Learning styles and learning space: Enhancing experiential learning in higher education. *Academy of Management Learning & Education*, *4*(2), 193–212. doi:10.5465/amle.2005.17268566

Matthews, M. (2018). *Using Data Analytics Tools to Teach Economics*. https://www.researchgate.net/publication/272566756_Qualitative_Data_Analysis_A_Methods_Sourcebook

Pears, A., Seidman, S., Malmi, L., Mannila, L., & Adams, E. (2007). A survey of literature on the teaching of introductory programming. In *Working group report on ITiCSE on innovation and technology in computer science education*. ACM. doi:10.1145/1345443.1345441

Proitz, T. S., Mausethagen, S., & Skedsmo, G. (2017). Investigative modes in research on data use in education. *Nordic Journal of Studies in Educational Policy*, *3*(1), 42–55. doi:10.1080/20020317.2017.1326280

Schouten, G. (2017). On meeting students where they are: Teacher judgment and the use of data in higher education. *Theory and Research in Education, 15*(3), 321-338. doi:10.1177/1477878517734452

Suresh Babu, C.V. (2023). Introduction to Data Science. Anniyappa Publications.

Suresh Babu, C. V., & Padma, R. (2023). Technology Transformation Through Skilled Teachers in Teaching Accountancy. In *Advancing STEM Education and Innovation in a Time of Distance Learning* (pp. 211–233). Global. doi:10.4018/978-1-6684-5053-6.ch011

Suresh Babu, C. V., & Rohan, B. (2023). Evaluation and Quality Assurance for Rapid E-Learning and Development of Digital Learning Resources. In M. Santally, Y. Rajabalee, & R. Rajputh (Eds.), *Implementing Rapid E-Learning Through Interactive Materials Development* (pp. 139–170). IGI Global. doi:10.4018/978-1-6684-4940-0.ch008

Velegol, S. B., Zappe, S. E., & Mahoney, E. (2015). The evolution of a flipped classroom: Evidence-based recommendations. *Advances in Engineering Education*, 4.

Chapter 11
Impact of GeoGebra on Student Learning and Inclusion of GeoGebra in the Mainstream

B. Vennila
Sri Eshwar College of Engineering, India

K. Renuga
Avinashilingam Institute for Home Science and Higher Education for Women, India

J. Ebenesar Anna Bagyam
Karpagam Academy of Higher Education, India

EXECUTIVE SUMMARY

This chapter investigates the use of ICT in education. In particular, the usage of GeoGebra as the geometrical instruction aids in the visualization of concepts, and this chapter aids in inspiring students and instructors throughout the teaching and learning process. The primary purpose of this work is to determine the effective use of GeoGebra in teaching calculus and statistical concepts among economics students whose performance is less satisfactory in math. These can be achieved by the aforementioned goals, i.e., by identifying the pupils whose performance is poor. They could be divided into two groups: research group who learns calculus and statistical concepts using GeoGebra and conventional group who learns the same concepts by traditional way of teaching. This chapter demonstrates that ICT-based learning yields superior results than conventional teaching methodology.

DOI: 10.4018/978-1-6684-7583-6.ch011

INTRODUCTION

Information and Communication Technology (ICT) holds vast potential for educators and learners to enhance educational experience. With its increasing integration worldwide, especially in developing nations, ICT is making waves in the realm of teaching and learning. A notable testament to this is the "Technology Usage and Integration" objective of India's National Education Policy (NEP) 2020, which aims to pave the way for India to become a prominent knowledge economy and a digitally empowered society. Through ICT, even rural inhabitants are now gaining access to quality education.

A common challenge among students is the perceived complexity of economic mathematical principles. While there are several software options like Stata, R, and SPSS to aid in understanding, GeoGebra, a Free Open-Source Software (FOSS), stands out for appropriate grade-level application. It uses visual representations to make economic data playful for the learning student, in how graphing can interact with one another. The software was originally developed for educational purposes as GeoGebra has its roots at the University of Salzburg in Austria, where Markus Hohenwarter created it as part of his master's thesis in 2001. The software combines geometry, algebra, spreadsheets, statistics, and calculus, making it a comprehensive tool for all educational levels and a boon for both students and teachers.

In the realm of economics, GeoGebra supports using the tool by allowing students to interact with various graphical representations. Numerous academic studies have affirmed its positive impact on students' mathematical understanding at the middle and high school grade-level (Samura et al., 2021; Yimer, 2022; Zulnaidi et al., 2020). While works have explored its content relevance to basic and higher education in mathematics, few have delved into its efficacy in illustrating the application to economics educators. This study seeks to evaluate GeoGebra's effectiveness in teaching economics-based concepts to students. It assesses students' learning progression when introduced to economic concepts through GeoGebra. The findings, while drawing comparisons with previous studies, offer unique insights given the distinct experimental conditions and subject focus. Moreover, a survey exploring the integration of GeoGebra into the curriculum has been conducted among educators, further emphasizing its growing importance in economic education.

GEOGEBRA TOOL

GeoGebra software offers six different views of mathematical objects. Three of these views are new to GeoGebra: the Graphics View, the Algebra View, and the Construction Protocol.

Figure 1. A display of the GeoGebra window with an emphasis on the algebraic view. It features a toolbar, menu bar, and various viewing options
Source: GeoGebra

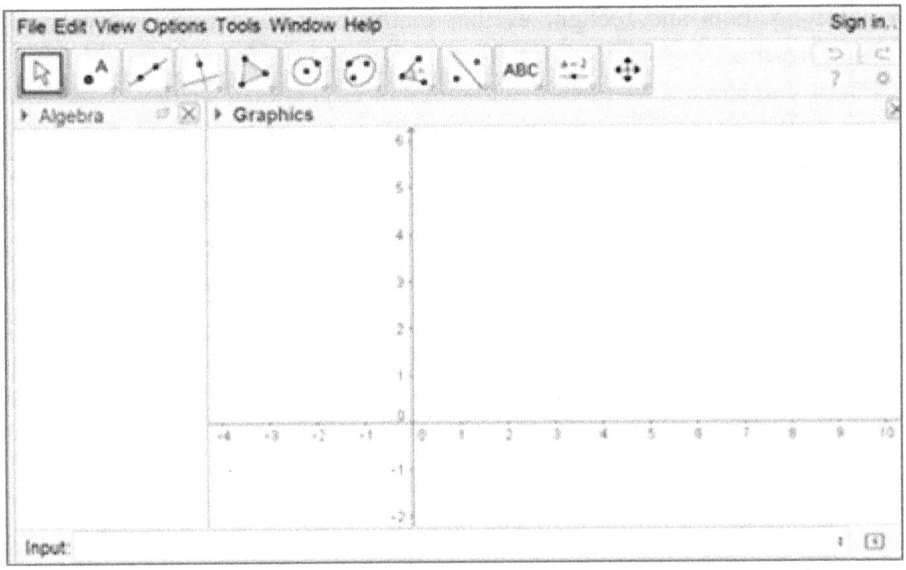

In the displayed GeoGebra interface, the toolbar is prominently situated in the upper right corner of the window. This toolbar is meticulously equipped with a comprehensive suite of geometric construction tools. These tools, which encompass functionalities to create points, lines, line segments, polygons, and angles, among others, provide educators with the capabilities to craft detailed geometric representations.

The implications of this interface for economics educators are manifold. Firstly, the tool offers a robust visual aid for teaching. By leveraging GeoGebra's functionalities, educators can simplify and elucidate intricate geometric concepts, making them more accessible and comprehensible for learners. This visual approach is particularly beneficial for delineating complex economic models and theories, which often rely on graphical representations.

Furthermore, GeoGebra's interactive nature fosters an engaging learning environment. Students are not merely passive recipients of information; they can actively interact with the geometric constructs, promoting a hands-on learning experience. Such active engagement can catalyze a profound and nuanced understanding of the underlying principles, thereby enhancing the overall efficacy of economics education.

SIGNIFICANCE

The economics educator finds that students are more likely to be uncomfortable with graphing tools and recognizes that math skills need further development for course readiness (Arnold & Straten, 2012; Ballard & Johnson, 2010). The COVID-19 pandemic saw further widening in educational achievement, which included mathematics and economics (Contini et al., 2022; Kofoed et al., 2021). Contini et al. (2022) noted a greater loss for girls and high-achieving children with low-educated parents. This work uses this mathematical tool that supports cross-disciplinary practices, which benefits a school in training students on an application that can impact beyond the economics classroom. Therefore, this paper is targeted specifically to educators who will be teaching economics in the middle or high school level, where GeoGebra is useful in the mathematics classroom. Additionally, this work could be important to curriculum specialists, school administrators, and policymakers who are interested in examining free open-source software that could benefit the classroom practitioners.

LITERATURE REVIEW

GeoGebra's capacity to foster mathematical understanding has been a focal point in educational research. The prevailing consensus in literature is viewed with a positive influence on the mathematical comprehension of middle and high school students. Samura et al. (2021) emphasized the advantages of GeoGebra in enhancing understanding of mathematical concepts, findings that are also supported by Yimer (2022) and Zulnaidi et al. (2020). A recurring theme across these studies is GeoGebra's interactivity. This software, with its ability to visually portray geometric and algebraic notions, offers students an enriched learning environment. Such immersive experiences are considered instrumental in its effectiveness.

The contributions of GeoGebra to mathematical education have been well-established. Nonetheless, the infusion of digital tools into economics education isn't exclusive to this platform. Althauser & Harter (2016) have pointed out that many mathematical lessons, even those for younger students as seen in kindergarten through 5th grade, often lack real-world relevance. They proposed economics as a potential remedy. This emphasis on real-world applications is further echoed by studies advocating for contextually relevant curricula (Farias & Balardini, 2019; Wooten & Al-Bahrani, 2021). Furthermore, Robinson & Liard-Muriente (2018) showcased how tools like "iMath" can be used in such educational settings, while Ganguli (2023) demonstrated the incorporation of mathematics in economics classrooms through approaches like the Universal Design of Learning (UDL). GeoGebra's contributions to the domain of mathematics are substantial, yet its potential in economics education is less explored. Despite its well-documented efficacy in mathematics, there's a gap in the literature regarding GeoGebra's application in economics. However, given economics' foundational reliance on graphic representations and theoretical frameworks, GeoGebra's promise as a pedagogical aid in this area is palpable.

Economics education, with its multifaceted challenges, demands tailored approaches. Arnold & Straten (2012) and Ballard & Johnson (2010) highlighted students' common difficulties with graphing utilities, advocating for an enhanced emphasis on mathematical skills to ensure a comprehensive grasp of economic principles. The upheaval caused by recent global events, especially the COVID-19 pandemic, has reshaped economics education. Contini et al. (2022) and Kofoed et al. (2021) have underscored the pandemic's exacerbation of educational divides, accentuating the urgent necessity for forward-thinking, flexible teaching strategies.

OBJECTIVE

This research aims to see how GeoGebra can be a useful tool for middle and high school economics teachers. Today, graphs and visuals are a key part of explaining tricky economic ideas. So, we believe that tools like GeoGebra can really help students get a better handle on these topics. By letting students work with and practice creating economic graphs, GeoGebra can help them understand more challenging ideas and get ready for tougher topics in the future.

We also want to compare the usual ways of teaching with methods that use GeoGebra. This will help us understand if students learn better when they use GeoGebra to understand economic graphs compared to the regular ways of teaching. Lastly, we'll ask teachers from grades 6 to 12 about their thoughts on using GeoGebra in their economics lessons. This will give us an idea of whether they think it's a good fit for the classroom and if it can make teaching economics easier and more effective.

HYPOTHESIS TESTING

The efficacy of GeoGebra, a graphical display software, in enhancing the understanding of fundamental geometrical concepts is the main subject of this research. In line with this, the study posits the following hypotheses:

Research Hypothesis (): The implementation of GeoGebra will positively impact the understanding of foundational geometrical concepts among students with lower achievement test scores.

STATISTICAL HYPOTHESIS

- **(Null Hypothesis):** The use of GeoGebra does not result in any significant difference in students' mean scores.
- **(Alternative Hypothesis):** The use of GeoGebra leads to a significant difference in the post-test mean scores of students.

RESEARCH QUESTIONS

1. To further understand the impact of GeoGebra on student achievement and educator perception, this study seeks to answer the following questions:
2. Is there a significant difference in student achievement when GeoGebra is used as a teaching tool compared to traditional methods?
3. What are educators' perceptions regarding the use of GeoGebra in teaching economics and its potential integration into the curriculum?

DELIMITATIONS

The following are the specific boundaries and scope of this research:

- **Location and Duration:** The study was exclusively conducted within two schools situated in the districts of Thiruvannamalai and Kallakurichi over a period of one month.
- **Subjects:** Two distinct groups were part of this study. The research group received instruction through GeoGebra, while the conventional group was taught using traditional methods.
- **Design and Data Collection:** This research adhered to an experimental design. Data gathering involved pre-tests, post-tests, and educator questionnaires.
- **Definitions:**
    - **Conventional Approach:** Traditional method of instruction, predominantly using a chalkboard and chalk.
    - **Research Group:** Students exposed to teaching methodologies incorporating GeoGebra.
    - **Conventional Group:** Students instructed via standard pedagogical methods.

EMPIRICAL REVIEW

Paudel (2007) conducted a study on the effectiveness of Geoboard in teaching geometry at primary level. The study's goal was to compare the academic performance of students who were taught using Geoboard to those of students who were not. For this study, the researcher chose a treatment group and a control group, with 25 students going into the treatment group and 20 students going into the control group. To analyze the data, mean, median, standard deviation, variance, and t-test were utilized. Pre- and post-testing, surveys, and interviews were all used as data collection techniques. The study discovered that the treatment group's results were superior to those of the control group based on the actual classroom.

Mukiri (2012) studied the feasibility of using GeoGebra into the teaching learning of geometry concepts in secondary school. The study's goal was to determine whether GeoGebra could be used to teach math in Kajiado, Kenya. This study's design included a mix of qualitative and quantitative methods. In this study, the performance of boys and girls before and after GeoGebra geometry instruction was compared. Two secondary schools for males, two for girls, and two for mixed students in Kajado comprised the study's sample population. During data analysis, it was discovered that there was no gender difference in students' math performance after learning in a GeoGebra setting.

Aydos (2015) investigated the impact of teaching mathematics with GeoGebra on conceptual understanding. Investigating the effects of teaching limits and continuity concepts in a GeoGebra-supported environment on students' conceptual understanding was the goal of the study. For the study, the researcher chose an experimental and control group. The data were analyzed with a t-test on gain score for the control and experimental groups as part of the research design, which also included pre- and post-tests for the examination of the data. Also, the mean, median, and standard deviation were employed by the researcher to analyze the data. The survey also discovered that students' perceptions of studying mathematics through technology have changed. The study's findings suggest that GeoGebra could be a useful teaching and learning tool.

Acharya (2015) studied the effectiveness of GeoGebra software on mathematics achievement. The report's goal was to assess the relationship between elite perceptions in learning circles using GeoGebra and student accomplishment in mathematics using GeoGebra. Two secondary schools in the Kathmandu district were chosen by the researcher as the experimental group and control group. Out of 53 pupils from two schools, 28 were in the class 9 experimental group and 25 were in the control group. For one week, the researcher employed the GeoGebra dynamic software program. Data gathering tools included a questionnaire, a pre-test, and a post-test. For the data analysis, the researcher used the mean, variance, standard deviation, and t-value. According to the study's findings, experimental group students performed better than control group students.

Lamichhane (2017) has published the thesis on effectiveness of GeoGebra on student's achievement in geometry. The study's goal was to determine whether GeoGebra software improved 10th-grade students' proficiency in parallelogram and circle geometry. To achieve the goal of the problem, the researcher employed an experimental design. The experimental group and the control group are two student groups that the researcher chooses. From the two schools, the researcher selected 75 pupils, 36 for the experimental group and 39 for the control group. Mean, variance, and standard deviation were employed by the researcher to examine and interpret the data. The data showed the experimental group outperformed the control group.

Barai (2017) had done research in GeoGebra on the topic "perception of student on the use of GeoGebra in geometry teaching ". The study's goal was to learn more about how secondary-level students perceived, participated in, and were motivated using GeoGebra in geometry instruction. 22 kids from class 9 were chosen by the researcher to participate in the experiment. For the research design, the researcher employed a mixed method. The researcher employed questionnaires, including five-point scales of the Likert type, to collect the data. For the analysis of quantitative data, mean and standard deviation were employed, and theme analysis was used for the analysis of qualitative data. After doing a data analysis, the researcher concluded that pupils in Nepal's secondary schools have a favorable opinion of GeoGebra.

Bist (2017) analyzed the use of GeoGebra in geometric construction. The objectives of this investigation were to look at how students felt about using GeoGebra for geometric building and to compare how well they did academically when using GeoGebra against a typical teaching method. Two public schools were chosen by the researcher as the experimental and control groups. The researcher was cruelly employed, the t-test and standard deviation are used to analyze the data that was gathered. The pre-test, post-test, and questionnaire were utilized to collect the data. After data analysis, the researcher discovered that students in experimental groups performed better than those in control groups.

Joshi (2017) conducted the study to determine student's achievement in trigonometry teaching through GeoGebra. The purpose of the study was to investigate how using GeoGebra to teach trigonometry affected student achievement. The quasi-experimental design was used by the researcher. 20 students were chosen for the experimental group and 22 students were chosen for the control group when the study's experimental group and control group were chosen. The researcher uses the t-test, mean, and standard deviation to analyze the data. Data analysis has shown that GeoGebra-based instruction is significantly superior to conventional methods of instruction.

The use of GeoGebra in the teaching and learning of geometry boosts student accomplishment, according to an analysis of the last four pieces of literature. It offers numerous opportunities for teaching geometry by assisting pupils in developing an intuitive sense of shape and in seeing the various forms. The usage of GeoGebra software tools facilitates a lot of content in mathematics instruction and enables students to establish the connection between symbolic and visual representation.

Martinez (2017) studied "The effects of using GeoGebra on students' achievement in secondary mathematics". The aim of the study was to evaluate the effectiveness of GeoGebra as a secondary mathematics teaching tool in terms of student accomplishment. For the study, the researcher chose two groups: an experimental group and a control group. One of them Out of 50 pupils, 22 was in the control group and 28 were in the experimental group. Pre-test and post-test designs were utilized in the quasi-experimental quantitative study. For the data analysis, the researcher used the mean and standard deviation. The researcher concluded that pupils who were taught GeoGebra performed better than other students after analyzing the data.

Belghesis and Kamalludeen (2018), was published the journal of educational technology on the topic "Teacher intention to use GeoGebra in the teaching mathematics among Malaysian teachers". The opinions of teachers regarding the use of GeoGebra in mathematics instruction were investigated. The intention gap between male and female teachers was examined. The study's goal was to examine teachers' intentions to use GeoGebra in math lessons based on their present skill levels.

Cross-sectional survey quantitative analysis was used in this study. There were 132 participants; all of them were math teachers who had taken part in a GeoGebra workshop at some point in their academic careers. The information was acquired using an online survey. Responses were collected using a five-point Likert scale with a 1–5 rating (Strongly Disagree, Disagree, Undecided, Agree, Strongly Agree). 132 survey responses in all were tallied. There were 56 men and 76 women present. To evaluate the data, the researcher used the mean and standard deviation. After that discovery, there was no discernible difference in male and female intentions to utilize GeoGebra in math instruction. Here, the two most recent reviews demonstrated the effectiveness of GeoGebra in the teaching and learning of mathematics. According to this study's findings, GeoGebra helps secondary students see how various forms relate to geometry. After analyzing the data from both experiments, it was determined that GeoGebra provided pupils with greater results than the conventional approach.

Chandramani Bohara (2019) studied the effectiveness of GeoGebra in Teaching Geometry for Students in 9th grade. The goal of this study was to determine how well GeoGebra taught geometry in 9th grade. The efficiency of the teaching of geometry using GeoGebra software was evaluated by comparing the academic performance of the students who received the instruction with and without the use of GeoGebra software. This research is quantitative and uses an experimental research approach. Two government schools were chosen by the researcher - one for the experimental groups and the other for the control group. There were 29 pupils in the control group and 27 in the experimental group. For a month, the same geometry lesson was presented to two different groups. Pre-test and post-test non-equivalent experimental design was adopted by the researcher.

The control group received traditional instruction whereas the experimental group received instruction utilizing the GeoGebra software. Both groups took a mathematics proficiency test to gather data for this study. To gauge how the experimental group felt about the GeoGebra software, a series of questions based on the five-point Likert scale were administered. With the use of SPSS software, the acquired data were examined by comparing the mean, standard deviation, and t-test.

Niroj Dahal, et al., (2022) analyzed the use of GeoGebra in teaching and learning geometric transformation in school mathematics. The purpose of the study is enabling students to visualize mathematical concepts, GeoGebra is a helpful application to enhance and improve mathematics teaching and learning. It is incredibly helpful for mathematical experiments and discoveries at all educational levels, from elementary school to university. Both Vygotsky's social learning theory and the cognitive learning theory are used as theoretical referents in this article. Twenty students from a private school in Kathmandu Valley, Nepal, in 9h grade (twelve boys and eight girls) was taught mathematics utilizing a range of examples of transformation highlighted in this study, including reflection, rotation, translation, and dilation. To assess how GeoGebra was utilized in eleven episodes, this study employed a teaching experiment, a type of qualitative research technique.

Many reviews of the literature indicate that GeoGebra is a useful tool for learning and that the experimental group performed better than the control group. It has been discovered to be an efficient teaching and learning tool for both teachers and pupils. It creates a stimulating learning atmosphere. There is a lot of study on GeoGebra's usefulness in secondary education, but little research on the concept of geometry. So, this study relates to the effect of GeoGebra in the 11th grade Calculus and Statistics for economics students.

CONCEPTUAL MODEL

Figure 2. Flow chart of the framework

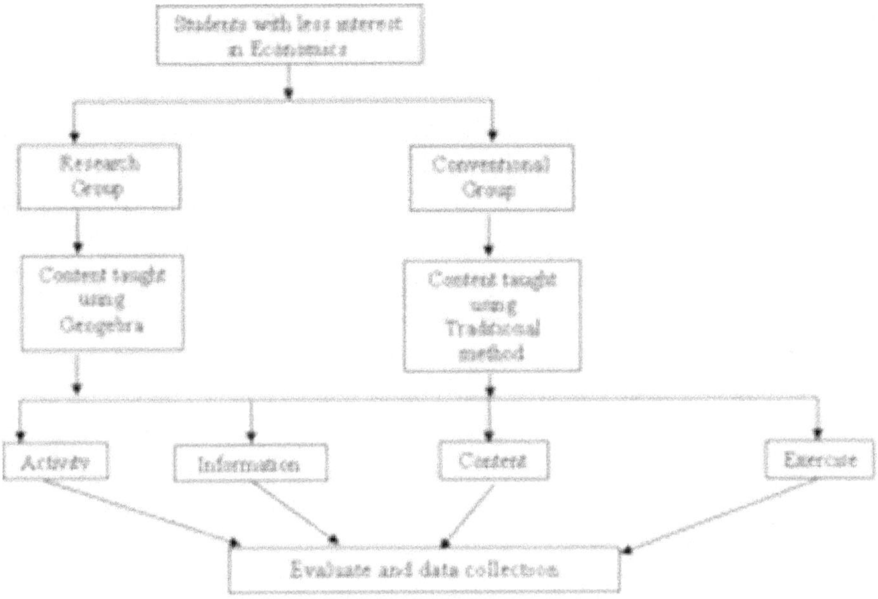

The researcher's study included both the experimental and control groups. The experimental group of pupils, who were taught using GeoGebra software, was the center of the researcher's attention. The flowchart in Figure 2 depicts the conceptual structure.

The pupils were instructed to use the usual approach in the conventional group and the software GeoGebra in the research group. The researcher looked at exercise, content, information, and activity, and she presents activities based on a particular issue. In the experimental group, the researcher was shown several visualizing shapes linked to course material. The student was inspired and given the chance to join an experimental group. Finally, the researcher examined the students' attitudes toward using GeoGebra in the experimental group by conducting assessments of the students in both groups.

For this research study, the researcher chose students from two different schools and established research groups and conventional groups. GeoGebra was used to teach research and to display the many content-related shapes. The control group received instruction using a traditional approach without the use of any ICT tools.

The researcher chose secondary-eleven mathematics as the subject matter, and both groups used the same material.

With the expert's and the subject teacher's permission, further material was included. Any content that aids researchers and subject teachers in achieving educational goals must include the information. The research group in grade eleven used GeoGebra to compile the subject-related material. The researcher focused on exercise, information, and action based on topic. Both groups participated in a teaching session with the same subject matter and different teaching strategies. The pupils in both groups then took an achievement test to assess their academic progress. After that, a teacher survey regarding the inclusion of GeoGebra in their curriculum was conducted.

METHODS

This section contains design of the study, sample of the study, tools, data collection procedure, and data analysis.

Design

Research designs are divided into three categories which are quantitative, qualitative, and mixed research. Among them this study is related to quantitative research design. The report's experimental design, a quasi-experimental one, is appropriate for this paper because it uses both a conventional group and a research group. Pupils from sixth grade who scored less on the math test are chosen for both groups. While the research group is taught using GeoGebra, the conventional group is instructed by utilizing the normal mode of instruction. Basic concepts using math for economics such measures of central tendency, correlation is taught using the GeoGebra with graphical view.

Variables

In this study the researcher used dynamic mathematical software GeoGebra as independent variable and in teaching calculus and statistics for economics at 11th grade on measures of central tendency, correlation the topic. The dependent variable was presented as the achievement of the students in that concept we've taught as well as the perception of the teachers towards inclusion of GeoGebra in curriculum. Tuition classes, teaching materials, school environment and activeness towards teaching were supposed extraneous variables.

SAMPLE POPULATION

Here, the population chosen is eleventh grade students. Due to time and budget constraints, the complete populace could not be included in this study, so researchers selected a small sample of students instead. A group of 21 pupils from a school in the Thiruvannamalai district for the research group and a group of 22 children from a school in the Kallakurichi district for the conventional group were chosen. Both groups are instructed on the same subject.

APPROACHES

In this study, two instrument questionnaires and an achievement test were used for the purpose of data collection. Also, quantitative type data collection tool was used in both groups. All data were collected based on quantitative research design based on quasi experimental design as pre-test post-test non- equivalent group design was used in this study. Pre-test and post-test were conducted in an experimental and control group. For the achievement test question, the piloting test was used to ensure the selected questions and was used split half method to find out reliability of the question. The five-point Likert scale was used to measure perception of students about GeoGebra software. SPSS 29.0 was used to analyzed and interpret the data.

Achievement Test

The identical question paper is used for both groups' accomplishment tests. Pilot testing was done on the pre-test and post-test question papers. The researcher conducted analysis on question paper with the help of subject expert. Simple questions were then adjusted for the pre-test and post-test. Within a month, the mode of instruction given to the research group is GeoGebra and for the conventional group is usual method.

VALIDITY

The reliability for the pre-test and post-test question paper is calculated from the pilot study. The reliability co-efficient r is 0.98. Validity is the most crucial instrument for analyzing the test's quality. It raises the measurement's level of quality. Teachers and topic specialists are the experts who provide the research's validity.

Questionnaire

The questionnaire was used to analyze teacher's perception towards inclusion of GeoGebra software in regular curriculum. This study contains twenty-five items of questionnaire based on five-point Likert scale. Twenty-five items of the questionnaire are categorized as GeoGebra, good software for teaching and GeoGebra enhancing student's achievement. The reliability and validity of the questionnaire was verified by supervisor before testing teacher's perception towards GeoGebra software.

Validity and Reliability: Validity is the most important tool to ensure the quality of the test. It increases the quality of measurement. In this study, validity of teacher's perception scale approved by supervisor and took ideas with expert. Cronbach's alpha test was used to determine reliability of the questionnaire. The reliability coefficient $r = 0.776$ was found for the questionnaire. The questionnaire was sent to respondents through Google form. The SPSS tool was used to analyze and interpret the data.

Control Mechanism: The control mechanism enabled the researcher to exert control over the research environment. The researcher used research design to control extraneous variables and increase the validity of the results. In this study, the researcher spent equal time with both groups and taught them independently. Both groups received the same test paper for the pre-test and post-test. In addition, the researcher double-checked the test papers for both groups. The Research and conventional groups were kept at the same distance from school.

Data Analysis

The most important aspect of the research study is the data analysis. Data collection tools and techniques serve as the foundation for data analysis procedures. The quantitative research design was used for this study. The teaching period was one month for both groups, and the same topic was taught to both groups. To assess students' achievement, a test was administered as a pre-test and a post-test to both groups. The questionnaire was designed using the five-point Likert scale, which included Strongly Agree, Agree, Undecided, Strongly Disagree, and Disagree. It was created to elicit teacher opinions on the use of GeoGebra in the classroom.

The mean, standard deviation, and t-test were used by the researcher to analyze the collected data. Percentiles were also used to assess teachers' attitudes towards the use of GeoGebra software in the classroom. SPSS 29.0 was used to analyze and interpret the data collected from both groups.

RESULTS

This section is the most important part of the research study and is about analyzing and interpreting data that has been collected. Data were collected from an achievement test (pre-test and post-test) and a questionnaire based on a five-point Likert scale in this experimental research study. This study is related to the effectiveness of GeoGebra in teaching economics at 11th grade. The objective of this research study was to compare achievement of the students between experimental and control groups and to explain teacher's perception towards GeoGebra in teaching economics at 11th grade. Two schools were selected from two different districts, Thiruvannamalai and Kallakurichi.

The data was analyzed by using SPSS 29.0. The researcher began data collection by administering pre-tests to Research and conventional groups. GeoGebra was used to teach the Research groups, while traditional methods were used to teach the conventional groups. The post-test was administered to both groups after one month of treatment, and the same test was used on both groups. The questionnaire was based on a five-point Likert scale and was administered to experimental groups to assess Teacher's perception towards GeoGebra software.

- The collected data were analyzed and interpreted under the following topics.
- Finding mean and standard deviation for pre-test
- Finding mean and standard deviation for post-test
- Comparison of achievement test scores in pre-test
- Comparison of achievement test scores in post-test
- Teacher's perception towards inclusion of GeoGebra in curriculum.
- SPSS version 29.0, a statistical program, was used to calculate.

Conventional Group

In the achievement test, there were ten items, and that test was conducted in both groups related to the topic, measures of central tendency, correlation for the 11th grade. The individual score of the students in research and conventional group in pre-test are noted. The mean and standard deviation of calculation for the conventional group of pre-test and posttest is shown in Table 1.

Table 1. Standard deviation and the average of the conventional group

Test	Mean	Standard Deviation
Pre-test	5.05	1.290
Post-test	6.00	1.195

Interpretation

It depicts the mean value of the conventional group pre-test score as 5.05, also the mean value of the conventional group post-test score and standard deviation of conventional group pre-test scores as 1.290 as well as the conventional post-test score standard deviation is, 1.195. The sample size is 22.

RESEARCH GROUP

The accomplishment test was conducted to both groups of students in 11th grade on the topic of measures of central tendency, correlation. Individual pre-test scores for students in the Research and Control groups are recorded. The pre-test and post-test mean and standard deviation of calculation for the research group is presented in table 2.

Table 2. Mean and standard deviation of research group

Test	Mean	Standard Deviation
Pre-test	5.14	1.014
Post-test	7.00	1.342

Interpretation

It shows the mean value of the research group pre-test score as 5.14, as well as the mean value of the research group post-test score as 7.00, and the standard deviation of the conventional group pre-test score as 1.014, as well as the standard deviation of the conventional post-test score as 1.342. The sample size is 21 people.

COMPARING PRE-TEST

It is the process of comparing the pre-test score of both groups. Interpret the pre-test scores of both the groups. By using the hypothesis testing, conclusion about the capabilities of students in pre-test is obtained in Table 3.

Table 3. Comparison of pre-test scores of both the groups

Group	Sample Size	Mean	Standard Deviation	t-Value	p-Value
Research group	22	5.14	1.014	0.393	0.785
Conventional group	21	5.05	1.290	-	-

Interpretation

The values obtained are calculated from the SPSS 29.0 version. From this hypothesis testing we can interpret the scores. The mean difference is 0.09, Also the t-value is 0.393 and the p-value is 0.785(>0.05). Therefore, the null hypothesis H_0 is accepted at the significance level 0.05, thus there is no significant difference between the mean of two samples. This shows that pre-test scores cannot differ by much.

COMPARING POST-TEST

It is the process of comparing the post-test scores of the research group and conventional group. Through this hypothesis testing is made, to identify the impact of GeoGebra on students. The achievement scores of research group and conventional group are differing in post- test which is shown in table 4.

Table 4. Comparison of post-test scores of both groups

Group	Sample Size	Mean	Standard Deviation	t-Value	p-Value
Research group	21	7.00	1.342	0.007	0.013
Conventional group	22	6.00	1.195	-	-

Interpretation

These values are also calculated from SPSS 29.0 version. This hypothesis recommends that, the mean difference is 1.00, Also the t-value is 0.007 and the p-value is 0.013(<0.05) which is less than significance level at 0.05 so, H_0 is rejected. Thus, there is significant difference between the mean scores. This outcome demonstrates that the accomplishment tests for the research group and conventional group were different. In other words, the outcomes of teaching mathematics using standard methods and GeoGebra are different. GeoGebra is better than the typical method.

TEACHER PERCEPTIONS

A set of questionnaires based on a five-point Likert scale were used to determine the teachers' attitudes towards the inclusion of GeoGebra in the regular curriculum. A set of questionnaires containing twenty-five items based on different dimensions was distributed to math teachers. The questionnaires were distributed to thirty teachers via Google Forms. Teachers were used to selecting the appropriate option in all items. The questionnaire set included both positive and negative statements. There are five options for students' opinions on GeoGebra software: Strongly agree, Agree, Undecided, Disagree, and Strongly disagree. The twenty-five questionnaire items were classified as whether teaching through GeoGebra is effective or unnecessary.

MEASURING EFFECTIVENESS

Teaching through GeoGebra provided effectiveness such as:

1. Enhanced student understanding and skills.
2. Improvement in student achievement test.
3. Conceptualize the content clearly.
4. Creating a more interactive learning environment.
5. Increases their participation in learning.

Table 5 depicts the effects of GeoGebra on students learning in the viewpoint of teacher.

Table 5. Questionnaire that shows GeoGebra is effective for student learning

Questions	Response for the Question				
	Strongly Agree	**Agree**	**Neutral**	**Disagree**	**Strongly Disagree**
GeoGebra in curriculum is useful for understanding of students	7	13	1	9	-
Teaching using GeoGebra will give good result in studies	8	12	4	4	1
It is appropriate tool for teaching some graphical concept	9	20	1	-	-
GeoGebra in school curriculum develop child centered learning	8	10	10	2	-
Visualized graphical concept taught using GeoGebra is remember for long term	9	12	4	5	-

Interpretation

These five questions show that agree and disagree levels. Also, most of the teachers accept that GeoGebra is effective for student learning which is shown in Figure 3. But the query is that they cannot accept the concept of inclusion of GeoGebra in curriculum.

Figure 3. Response for GeoGebra is effective for students learning

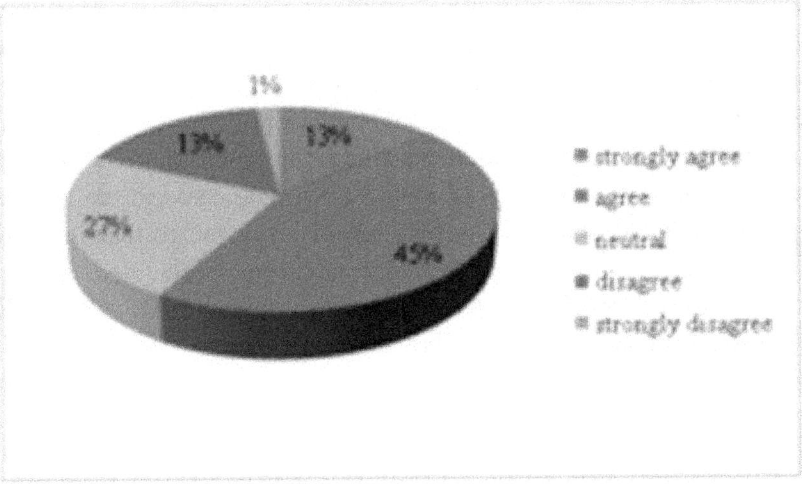

Benefits of teachers while teaching using GeoGebra

1. Easy to handle the software.
2. Less time needed to explain the concept.
3. Have confidence in teaching.
4. High response rate.

GeoGebra's effectiveness on teachers' point view is given in Table 6.

Table 6. Questions that show GeoGebra is effective for teacher's perspective

Questions	Response for the Question				
	Strongly Agree	**Agree**	**Neutral**	**Disagree**	**Strongly Disagree**
GeoGebra is good software for teaching the graphs and plotting	9	18	2	1	-
While teaching using GeoGebra I feel comfortable of students understanding	6	16	-	2	-
Inclusion of GeoGebra in curriculum is good for online education	5	18	6	1	-
More student's response for GeoGebra teaching rather than normal teaching	2	15	7	5	-
As a teacher I suggest GeoGebra is better than usual teaching	-	15	7	6	2

Interpretation

The five questions examine the impact of using GeoGebra in mathematics instruction from the teachers' perspective. Each question presents levels of agreement and disagreement. The debate here is whether GeoGebra-based teaching surpasses traditional methods. While educators acknowledge the noticeable effects of GeoGebra on student learning, they don't necessarily view it as superior to conventional teaching. They believe that while GeoGebra offers value in teaching, standard evaluation methods might not be suitable for assessing its outcomes. Therefore, a tailored evaluation approach is essential for instruction using GeoGebra. Figure 4 illustrates the interpretation of GeoGebra using a pie chart.

Figure 4. Response for the effective of GeoGebra through teacher's perspective

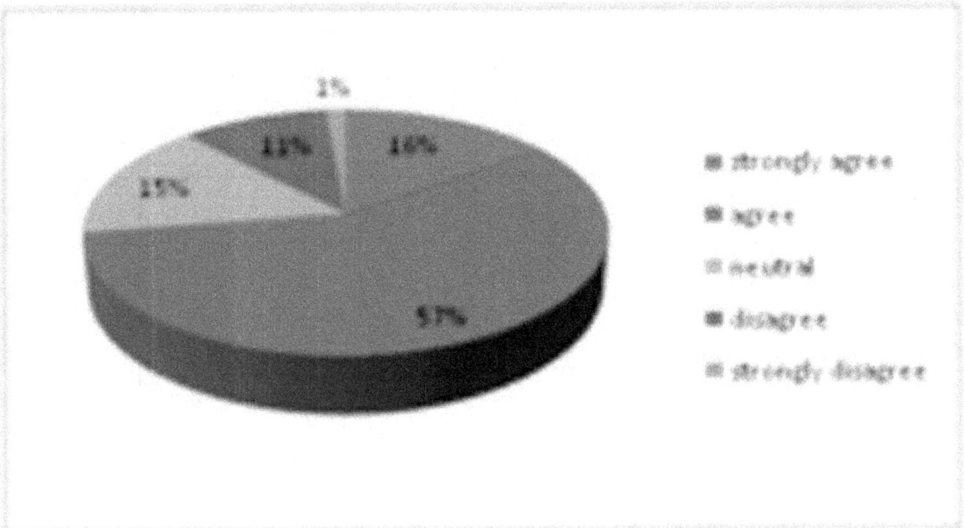

Just as every coin has two sides, so does the GeoGebra software. While we have discussed its positive aspects, it is essential to consider the challenges associated with its use. Limitations of classroom interaction could include:

- Requires significant time for lesson preparation.
- May hinder timely completion of the syllabus.
- Not suitable for every school setting.
- Unable to cover all concepts effectively.
- Lacks specific evaluation methods.
- Possibility of encountering technical issues.

These limitations provide insight into some of the challenges faced when integrating GeoGebra into the classroom. The outcomes of these challenges can often be observed in the results obtained from lessons using GeoGebra.

Feedback from teachers is compiled in Table 7. Each item received responses ranging from strongly agree to strongly disagree, with the data presented below.

Table 7. Questions that shows GeoGebra is not necessary

Questions	Response for the Question				
	Strongly Agree	Agree	Neutral	Disagree	Strongly Disagree
Teaching using GeoGebra is time consuming	2	16	8	4	-
It is difficult to cover the syllabus using GeoGebra	7	13	6	4	-
It is not appropriate for the assessment process	6	8	7	7	2
It is inappropriate for all schools to use GeoGebra in regular class session	3	15	5	6	1
GeoGebra is useful for limited number of classroom concepts	5	13	5	7	-
It is difficult to use software for school curriculum	3	12	9	6	-
As a teacher the GeoGebra approach is not suitable for evaluation	5	13	9	3	-
GeoGebra supports visual knowledge, rather than applicable knowledge	-	17	6	4	3
It is not applicable for everyday teaching usage	6	13	8	3	-
It is difficult to remember the tool name and its construction for students	3	15	7	5	-

Interpretation

This highlights the potential drawbacks of incorporating GeoGebra into the standard curriculum. While it may be challenging to integrate GeoGebra consistently in regular classes, its positive influence on student learning is evident. Therefore, GeoGebra could be employed on a practical level to enhance children's conceptual understanding.

Figure 5. Response about negative effects of GeoGebra

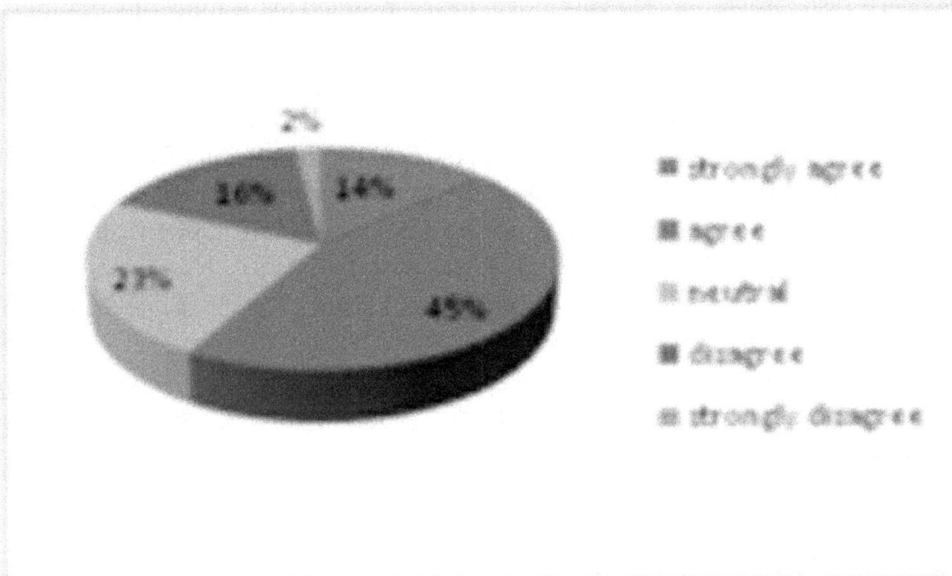

The pie chart in Figure 5 depicts the negative teacher perceptions of GeoGebra. The teachers who responded to the questionnaire accept that GeoGebra inclusion to everyday curriculum could be very difficult.

DISCUSSION

The study aimed to evaluate the efficacy of GeoGebra in teaching mathematical concepts for economics to students who exhibited reduced interest in the subject. Two schools were selected for this analysis. Both groups began with a pre-test, with the research group receiving GeoGebra-based instruction and the control group receiving traditional instruction. A post-test was subsequently administered. Comparing pre-test and post-test scores for both groups, no significant difference in achievement was observed between the groups in the pre-test, with mean scores of 5.14 for the research group and 5.04 for the control group.

However, the research group displayed heightened engagement, with student participation surpassing that of the control group. Consequently, GeoGebra-based teaching was deemed more effective than its conventional counterpart. The post-test results further supported this, revealing mean achievement scores of 7.00 for the research group and 6.00 for the control group.

A survey involving teachers across different schools provided additional insights. Teachers' responses, collected via Google forms, resulted in the following findings:

- Most teachers believed that GeoGebra positively impacts student learning.
- From a teaching standpoint, daily usage of GeoGebra can be challenging.
- Many schools lack the resources for consistent GeoGebra instruction.
- Despite its limitations, GeoGebra remains a robust educational tool.
- GeoGebra is best employed for practical demonstrations rather than routine instruction.
- GeoGebra facilitates active learning and bolsters student achievement in mathematics.

These findings underscore the benefits of GeoGebra in both student assessments and educator questionnaires.

FUTURE RESEARCH

The scope of the current study was confined to a select sample size with the primary objective to assess student performances across two distinct teaching strategies and to delve into educators' viewpoints concerning GeoGebra. Building on these initial findings, future research avenues could encompass a deeper analysis of GeoGebra's influence on tertiary education and its broader academic repercussions. There's also a rich opportunity to investigate its versatility across various sectors within economics. Capturing student feedback on GeoGebra can offer invaluable insights, especially given its prospective role in enhancing scholastic results in mathematics. Furthermore, a comprehensive evaluation of the stance of mathematics instructors towards GeoGebra would be instrumental in guiding its future integrations.

CONCLUSION

The adoption of ICT tools like GeoGebra can significantly enhance classroom learning. GeoGebra, particularly, has been recognized as beneficial from primary to tertiary education levels. The current study reaffirms that GeoGebra enhances comprehension, especially in visualizing 2D and 3D concepts. It was observed that students exposed to GeoGebra-based teaching outperformed those in traditional settings, emphasizing the software's role in graph-related instructions at school level. Therefore, while conventional teaching methods remain viable, GeoGebra offers a more enriched understanding across all student proficiencies, from below average to above average.

The survey's outcome suggests that educators value GeoGebra for its potential to elevate student achievement. However, integrating it as a standard teaching tool may present challenges. It might be more effective to deploy GeoGebra for practical, diagrammatical representation of mathematical concepts rather than daily instruction.

GeoGebra stands out as an avant-garde ICT tool for educational endeavors. By offering dynamic visual insights, it addresses and mitigates the challenges inherent in traditional teaching approaches, promoting a more technologically integrated educational setting. To maximize its benefits, it is essential to provide training for secondary educators on GeoGebra, empowering them to harness its complete range of features. Furthermore, policymakers are encouraged to champion the use of GeoGebra in classrooms to amplify student achievements. Given the compelling advantages it presents, there's a strong case for embedding GeoGebra within the secondary mathematics curriculum.

REFERENCES

Acharya, T. R. (2015). *Effectiveness of GeoGebra software on mathematics achievement*. [Unpublished Master thesis]. University Campus, Kritipur.

Althauser, K., & Harter, C. (2016). Math and economics: Implementing authentic instruction in grades K-5. *Journal of Education and Training Studies*, *4*(4), 111–122. doi:10.11114/jets.v4i4.1328

Arnold, I. J. M., & Straten, J. T. (2012). Motivation and math skills as determinants of first-year performance in economics. *The Journal of Economic Education*, *43*(1), 33–47. doi:10.1080/00220485.2012.636709

Aydos, M. (2015). *The impact of teaching mathematics with GeoGebra on the conceptual understanding of limits and continuity: the case of Turkish gifted and talented students* [Unpublished thesis] Ihsan Dogrammaci Bilkert University.

Ballard, C. L., & Johnson, M. F. (2010). Basic math skills and performance in an introductory economics class. *The Journal of Economic Education*, *35*(1), 3–23. doi:10.3200/JECE.35.1.3-23

Barai, M. (2017). *Perceptions of students on the use of GeoGebra in geometry teaching* [Unpublished Master thesis]. University Campus, Kritipur.

Belghesis, S., & Kamalludeen, R. (2018). The Intention to Use GeoGebra in the Teaching of Mathematics among Malaysian Teachers. *Malaysian Online Journal of Educational Technology*, *6*(1), 109–115.

Bist, P. R. (2017). Use of GeoGebra in Geometric Construction [Published Master Thesis]. *Imperial Journal of Interdisciplinary Research, 3.*

Chandramani Bohara. (2019). *Effectiveness of GeoGebra in Teaching Geometry* [Unpublished Master's thesis]. University Campus. Kritipur, Nepal. https//elibrary.tucl.edu.np

Contini, D., Di Tommaso, M. L., Muratori, C., Piazzalunga, D., & Schiavon, L. (2022). Who lost the most? Mathematics achievement during the COVID-19 pandemic. *The B.E. Journal of Economic Analysis & Policy*, *22*(2), 399–408. doi:10.1515/bejeap-2021-0447

Dahal, N., Pant, B. P., Shrestha, I. M., & Manandhar, N. K. (2022). Use of GeoGebra in teaching and learning geometric transformation in school mathematics. *International Journal of Interactive Mobile Technologies*, *16*(8), 65–78. doi:10.3991/ijim.v16i08.29575

Farias, C., & Balardini, F. (2018). Teaching social economics: Bringing the real world into the classroom and taking the classroom into the real world. *International Journal of Social Economics*, *46*(8), 960–976. doi:10.1108/IJSE-05-2018-0253

Ganguli, S. (2023, August 6). Building employability skills in math courses for business and economics using UDL approach. *Journal of Economics Teaching Symposium of Economics Teaching*. http://downloads.journalofeconomicsteaching.org/SET/2023/A6Ganguli.pdf

Joshi, N. R. (2017). *Students Achievement in Trigonometry Teaching Through GeoGebra* [Unpublished Master thesis]. University campus, Kritipur.

Kofoed, M. S., Gebhart, L., Gilmore, D., & Moschitto, R. (2021). *Zooming to class?: Experimental evidence on college students' online learning during COVID-19* (IZA DP No. 14356). https://docs.iza.org/dp14356.pdf

Lamichhane, D. (2017). *Effectiveness of GeoGebra on students achievement in Geometry* [Unpublished thesis]. University Campus. Kritipur.

Martinez, A. R. (2017). *The Effect of Using GeoGebra on students achievement in Secondary Mathematics* [Unpublished Master thesis]. California State University, Monterey.

Mukiri, M. I. (2012). *Feasibility of using GeoGebra in to the teaching learning of geometry concepts in secondary school* [Master thesis]. Kenya University, Kenya.

Paudel, K. (2007). *A study on the effectiveness of Geoboard in teaching geometry at primary level* [Unpublished Master thesis]. University campus, Kritipur.

Robinson, C., & Liard-Muriente, C. (2018). Math in the economics classroom: An experiment with iMath. *International Advances in Economic Research*, *24*(3), 289–290. doi:10.100711294-018-9695-7

Samura, A. O., Darhim, D., Juandi, D., Said, A. M., & Malaka, M. (2021). Improving the creative thinking ability of junior high school students through GeoGebra assisted learning community in mathematics. *International Journal of Interactive Mobile Technologies*, *15*(22), 84–98. doi:10.3991/ijim.v15i22.24797

Wooten, J., & Al-Bahrani, A. (2021). Economics in a crisis: A cautious approach to being relevant. *Journal of Economics Teaching*, *5*(4), 142–151. doi:10.58311/jeconteach/194492d686c6368d58bc577a882ddc12c9648d3b

Yimer, S. T. (2022). Effective Instruction for Calculus Learning Outcomes through Blending Co-Operative Learning and Geogebra. *Mathematics Teaching Research Journal, 14*(3), 170-189. https://commons.hostos.cuny.edu/mtrj

Zulnaidi, H., Oktavika, E., & Hidaya, R. (2020). Effect of use of GeoGebra on achievement of high school mathematics students. *Education and Information Technologies*, *25*(1), 51–72. doi:10.100710639-019-09899-y

APPENDIX

Reliability of the Questionnaire

Table 8 gives the case processing summary and Table 9 shows the reliability statistics. Table 10 produces Item Statistics and table 11 gives Total-Item Statistics in the appendix.

Table 8. Case processing summary

		N	%
Cases	Valid	30	100.0
	Excluded[a]	0	.0
	Total	30	100.0
a. Listwise deletion based on all variables in the procedure.			

Table 9. Reliability statistics

Cronbach's Alpha	N of Items
.774	21

Table 10. Item statistics

	Mean	Std. Deviation	N
GeoGebra is good software for teaching the geometrical concept	1.7333	.52083	30
GeoGebra in curriculum is useful for understanding of students	1.7333	.52083	30
Teaching using GeoGebra will give good result in studies	2.1333	.77608	30
Teaching using GeoGebra is time consuming	2.4667	.81931	30
It is appropriate tool for teaching relation between geometry and algebra	1.7333	.52083	30
GeoGebra in school curriculum develop child centred learning	2.0667	.78492	30
while teaching using GeoGebra i feel comfortable of students understanding	2.0667	.73968	30
GeoGebra tool makes all the students to participate actively in learning without individual difference	2.2667	.82768	30
Geometrical concept taught using GeoGebra is remember for long term	2.0000	.78784	30
It is difficult to cover the syllabus using GeoGebra	1.9667	.85029	30
It is not appropriate for the assessment process	2.2667	1.04826	30
inclusion of GeoGebra in curriculum is good for online education	2.2333	.77385	30
More students response for GeoGebra teaching rather than normal teaching	2.0667	.52083	30
It is inappropriate for all schools to use GeoGebra in regular class session	2.1333	.50742	30
As a student -teacher I suggest GeoGebra is better than usual teaching	2.6667	.95893	30
GeoGebra is only for particular concept not for all concept we need to taught in mathematics	2.1667	.79148	30
It is difficult to remember the tool name and its construction for students	2.4667	.89955	30
As a becoming teacher the GeoGebra teaching is not suitable for evaluation	2.3333	.88409	30
Here students visualize the but not able to apply it in notebook	2.3667	.85029	30
It is only for practical class not for theoretical examination	2.1000	.92289	30
It is not applicable for all teacher to teach technically everyday	2.2667	.90719	30

Table 11. Item-total statistics

	Scale Mean if Item Deleted	Scale Variance if Item Deleted	Corrected Item-Total Correlation	Cronbach's Alpha if Item Deleted
GeoGebra is good software for teaching the geometrical concept	43.50	47.155	.299	.768
GeoGebra in curriculum is useful for understanding of students	43.50	47.086	.309	.767
Teaching using GeoGebra will give good result in studies	43.10	42.231	.667	.743

Chapter 12
"Why Are iPhones So Expensive?": Motivation, Instruction, and Learning Strategies

Kateryna Glubochenko
V.O. Sukhomlynskyi National University of Mykolaiv, Ukraine

EXECUTIVE SUMMARY

The chapter analyzes the opportunities to use motivational and instructional design in economics education. The purpose of this chapter is to use these opportunities for teaching economics in a diverse and inclusive classroom. Based on the ideas provided, the author designs a lesson plan for teaching price-making strategies as part of economics curriculum in a diverse and inclusive environment. The author used the ARSC model, cooperative learning and inquiry-based approaches, inclusive reading strategies, backwards design, and the principles of inclusion to design learning activities for the lesson. The ARCS model is helpful in terms of capturing student interests, making the lesson content relevant for students, supporting their confidence, and satisfaction. Cooperative learning and inquiry-based learning approaches provide efficient learning activities appropriate for teaching economics in a diverse and inclusive classroom. The chapter concludes that using an inclusive approach, educators can help all students to master necessary skills in the economics domain.

DOI: 10.4018/978-1-6684-7583-6.ch012

INTRODUCTION

The purpose of this paper is to use motivation and instructional design strategies for teaching economics in a diverse and inclusive classroom. The paper also rationalizes and offers a plan of a previously adopted lesson 'Why iPhones Are So Expensive?' which aims to develop the understanding of price-making strategies in students. At the same time, papers devoted to economics education for high school students are still rather scarce. Therefore, the work contributes to the literature of economics education for teachers and education students.

Teaching economics as a separate field of knowledge assumes that students should be financially competent, understand basic economic laws and market functioning, analyze labor market trends, be aware of management and marketing issues, etc. This is a wide area of studying. Although understanding in the economics domain aims to develop all core 21st century skills, critical thinking in students can be defined as a top priority of teaching economics at high school. Thus, the learning activities designed for the lesson on price-making strategies are focused on the development of critical thinking skills. The learning strategies are built on the use of the ARCS model, the inquiry-based learning approach, formative assessment, and the inclusive approach.

Understanding ARCS Model

Motivation is an essential component of learning. The ARCS model developed by Keller (1987) analyzes attention, relevance, confidence, and satisfaction as the conditions that drive learners in their studies. The author stated that "the ARCS model of motivation was developed in response to a desire to find more effective ways of understanding the major influences on the motivation to learn, and for systematic ways of identifying and solving problems with learning motivation" (p. 2). Motivation, as some forces within an individual to do something, determines our ability to act in any field, including learning. According to Keller's ARCS model, "the attention category incorporates research on curiosity and arousal, interest, boredom, and other related areas such as sensation seeking" (Keller, 2016, p. 4). Thus, the purpose of this domain is to attract student attention mainly in the beginning of the lesson. As a motivational category of the ARCS model attention domain, perceptual arousal means that a teacher tries to find out "what can I do to capture their interest?" (Gagne et al., 1992, p. 118). So, the teacher should choose some content or activity that would make students focused on the learning process. Malone (1981) offers to use challenge, fantasy, and curiosity in order to attract student attention.

Applying the ARCS model to the lesson 'Why iPhones are so expensive?', Unit 'Understanding Economic Development', it is obvious that the purpose of the lesson is to foster students' problem-solving, critical thinking, and independent discovery learning skills, as well as their understanding of market economy functioning. Perceptual arousal as a category of the attention domain means a teacher should capture student interests. In order to do this, the teacher can begin the lesson by demonstrating to their students a very familiar product, like a donut from the school canteen, and asking them 'how much does it cost?'. Everyone will be able to answer. Then, the teacher will ask them 'why does it cost so much?'. Such a question will be an excellent example of perceptual arousal because it can surely attract student attention. Hardly any of the students tried to figure out before why quite familiar products had a certain price. Thus, they will be able to focus on the lesson contents and activities. However, this motivational category has its limitations. Interest is a very personal feeling, so teachers should know the inner world of their students very well to implement this category. At the same time, having a lesson with students for the first time makes the implementation of this category rather challenging.

Familiarity is a motivational category of the ARCS model relevance domain. Following this category, a teacher wonders, "how can I tie the instruction to the learners' experience" (Gagne et al., 1992, p. 118). Keller (2016) defined relevance as "the instructional requirements consistent with student goals, compatible with their learning styles, and connected to their past experiences seeking" (p. 4). Thus, the contents and learning activities offered for learning should be relevant for students' lives.

Applying the category of familiarity to the lesson, it is necessary to highlight that all of the students are involved in the market relations. All students buy or sell goods. So, all of them need to understand the basics of the price-making process in order to be successful in life. Moderated by the teacher, they can discuss their experience of buying and selling goods, bargaining, and setting prices. Such actions are familiar for the students. They are adolescents, so already have both buying and selling experiences. Thus, discussing possible reasons for setting the prices in context of their cases can provide the relevance to the learning process.

At the same time, implementation of this category can be also challenging for a teacher. Keller (2016) points out that "implementation problems can result from such things as poorly designed materials that lack well-written text with adequate examples and exercises" (p. 3). Thus, limitations of this category refer to the quality of contents and activities. From teachers' point of view, they may look relevant, but not reflect on students' experience, so remaining unfamiliar to the learners.

According to Keller (2016), "confidence refers to the effects of positive expectancies for success, experiences of success, and attributions of successes to one's own abilities and efforts rather than to luck or to task challenge levels that are too easy or difficult" (p. 4). Personal control is a motivational category of the ARCS model confidence domain. Guided by this category, a teacher tries to find out "how will the learners clearly know their success is based on their efforts and abilities?" (Gagne et al., 1992, p. 118). Thus, a teacher should provide the students some tools for self-assessment in order to monitor their own success in terms of learning outcomes.

Applying the category of personal control to the lesson, it is possible to organize a fair, where the students will be able to practice their newly acquired skills to set adequate prices on any products. In order to set the price and sell a product, the students will need to find out everything about their competitors, substitute goods, preferences of their consumers, and demand elasticity. Selling their products at the fair, the students will get the opportunity to test the efficiency of the prices set and become confident in their price-making mastery.

At the same time, the challenge of this category may refer to the various levels of self-confidence in students. Some students with low self-esteem may need more evidence to believe in their learning success. Robinson and Watson (2013) highlighted that "motivation cannot be guaranteed, but it can be systematically encouraged" (p. 50). Thus, although teachers foster the development of confidence in students, different students have different needs in terms of control over their own learning.

According to the ARCS model, satisfaction includes "the appropriate mix of intrinsically and extrinsically rewarding outcomes that sustain desirable learning behaviors and discourage undesirable ones" (Keller, 2016, p. 4). Natural consequences determine a motivational category of the ARCS model satisfaction domain. Following this category, teachers ask themselves "how can I provide meaningful opportunities for learners to use their newly acquired knowledge/ skill?" (Gagne et al., 1992, p. 118). As a result, a teacher should find the opportunity for students to demonstrate their knowledge. In terms of the lesson, apart from the fair discussed above, it is necessary to organize an interactive discussion to analyze the outcomes of the event. The students will have the opportunities to discuss with their peers what factors determine the prices on the fair. Discussing the results of the event can provide the natural consequences to demonstrate their newly acquired knowledge and skills. At the same time, such motivational design as part of instructional design requires a significant amount of teacher's time and efforts. So there could be a challenge of teacher's burnout.

LEARNING ACTIVITIES

Cooperative Learning

Mixing students in groups to perform cooperative group learning activities is beneficial for teaching economics in a diverse and inclusive classroom environment.

Pairing students of different learning styles or types of multiple intelligence to work together is able to highlight the strengths of all students. For instance, the curriculum assumes the development of student ability to create a marketing strategy. Learning activity assumes the tasks to make economic calculations as well as perform creative assignments. Tomlinson (2014) highlighted that "teachers in differentiated classrooms must be ready to engage students in instruction through different approaches to learning, by appealing to a range of interests, and by using varied rates of instruction along with varied degrees of complexity and differing support systems" (p. 4). Pairing the students with math intelligence and visual learning style to perform the learning activity together can be beneficial for students with different learning needs. As a result, the students with math intelligence can help the partners to make necessary calculations and determine logistics arrays (price and place). At the same time, the students inclined to creativity can inspire the partners to define a target audience, design promotion channels and develop an advertising campaign (product, promotion). Thus, they will be involved in the process of adapting the content and activities for their peers, and also learn from the strengths of each other, manifesting their best in their turn. As a result, flexible grouping strategies can be used as a method to teach students to work together and help them understand that collaboration of individuals with different interests can be beneficial for all.

Inquiry-Based Learning

The concept of supply and demand as a main price-making strategy is easy to understand via the Marshallian cross diagram. The graph demonstrates how a price is set on the intersection of the demand and supply curves. The students can choose any product at which price they would like to find out. To use the Marshallian cross diagram, the students need to do research on the factors that influence demand and supply. Working in small groups, the students will have to find out all about the competitors of a particular product, its substitute goods, preferences of their consumers, relevant legislation, and factors that determine demand elasticity.

Considering all the amount of information the students will be dealing with while making the assignment, the teacher can foster the inclusion of technology to save time and effort, and also to help the students to verify information they will find. For instance, they can use Google search to analyze the price-setting strategies of competitors or the substitute goods prices. The use of Google Forms can be helpful in terms of summarizing students' research findings, etc.

The teacher can use the practice of concept maps mostly to summarize the interactive discussions. For instance, the concept map of 'Why iPhones Are So Expensive?' discussion allows students to define the role of fashion and consumer preferences in the market economy and price-making processes. This practice is helpful in terms of activating students' existing knowledge and fostering the development of their higher-order thinking skills.

The approach of inquiry-based learning can also be implemented for studying price-making strategies in the labor market. Starting with the inquiry of professional burnout as a downside of purposefulness in the labor market, the teacher should help the students to analyze a labor supply curve and a labor demand curve to investigate the issue. Then, the students study a backward-bending supply curve of labor to make a decision of how many hours they are going to work in the future to prevent professional burnout. This economic diagram reveals a correlation between salary and substitute leisure for paid activity. So the students decide what sum would be enough for them to value their leisure time more than extra money to earn. Thus, the activity can be both independent and interactive. Cabezudo et al. (2010) pointed out that educators should help their students to develop new ways of thinking and acting by giving learners "the opportunity and competencies to reflect and share their own point of view and role within a global, interconnected society, as well as to understand and discuss complex relationships of common social, ecological, political and economic issues" (p. 10). Thus, the infusion inquiry approach can allow students to think beyond some limited paradigm.

As an example of both inquiry-based and cooperative learning approaches, a learning activity called 'Two Islands' can be used. This instruction aims to help students 'create' the production possibilities curve (PPC) by themselves because of playing a team game. PPC is a graph that demonstrates different combinations of results that can be produced in conditions of current resources and technology. The graph also illustrates the scarcity and trade-offs concepts. According to the rules, students should create two cooperative groups (two islands). Both islands can collect coconuts and catch fish. However, their work will be much more efficient in the case of the division of labor. By exploring different combinations of producing these two goods, the teams would find a win-win model of resources exchange to satisfy both teams. Interactive games have a significant beneficial potential for teaching economics (Sachdeva, 2017). Apart from exploring the economics concepts, the active learning activity also teaches the students to value communication as a power.

The learning activities of 'Why iPhones Are So Expensive?' Economics lessons require a significant level of critical thinking skills from students. At the same time, the students should have already obtained some skills to distinguish authentic and fake data and test their initial hypothesis by conducting research. So the challenge is that students will need a competent facilitator during these learning activities to help them find an answer. The research of Quigley et al. (2011), revealed four major challenges to implement an inquiry approach - measuring the quality of inquiry, using discourse to improve inquiry, pursuing the goal of teaching content through inquiry methods, and learning how to effectively manage an inquiry classroom (p. 55). The challenge of using discourse to improve inquiry seems to be the most relevant for the lesson offered.

READING STRATEGIES

As a supplemental text, the teacher can offer the students 'Power Pricing: How Managing Price Transforms the Bottom Line' by Dolan and Simon (1997). There is an academic nonfiction type of text, although it is easily written and very comprehensible. Tenth grade students are able to read more complicated types of texts in order "to develop the confidence, skills, and stamina to do the ongoing problem solving that academic text requires" (Schoenbach et al., 2012, p. 135). The text presented interesting ideas of two famous experts of price making that discussed how to change an equilibrium price to 'power' price. The authors discussed how market segmentation, promotional campaigns, competitive strategies, international pricing, and other factors can influence the price of any product.

Then, the students can discuss the role of fashion and consumer preferences in the price-making process. For instance, why iPhones are more expensive than other models of smartphones. The students can create a graphic organizer to summarize the factors of price making after reading the supplemental text. Creating infographics to summarize reading is a beneficial strategy for teaching reading because it fosters the development of students' higher-order thinking in the content area.

At the same time, it is important to allow the students to choose whether to read a hard copy of the book or its electronic variant, listen to the audio version or watch a documentary based on the book. McKnight (2014) stated that educators should "make strategic use of digital media in presentations to enhance understanding of findings, reasoning, and evidence and to add interest" (p. 163). Nonetheless, although the students will study the text individually, the reading activities for this lesson assume the use of cooperative learning or working in small groups.

INCLUSION

Differentiating economics content for diverse and inclusive students can be achieved via the implementation of Backwards Design while planning the lesson. Planning backwards, educators go through three stages: 1) identify desired results; 2) determine acceptable evidence; and 3) plan learning experiences and instruction (Tomlinson & McTighe, 2006). Differentiating content for diverse students can be applied at the second and third stages of Backwards Design (Tomlinson & McTighe, 2006, p.

15). At the same time, to define content worthy of understanding is a priority of the first stage. Thus, although diverse students have to deal with generalized content, the level of its complexity can be clarified by a teacher while planning backwards. Tomlinson and McTighe (2006) highlight that clear priorities and purposes are apparent in Backwards Design. So, it is important to know the individual features of diverse students in advance.

The research of Childre et al. (2009) revealed that Backward Design is able to improve student learning outcomes at both the elementary and high school levels. The authors demonstrated that, applying Backwards Design in classrooms with students with disabilities, a teacher should involve four key steps: 1) identify learners, 2) identify curricular priorities, 3) design assessment framework, and 4) create learning activities (p. 8). In terms of differentiating content, the authors offer to "break instructional parts of the unit into manageable elements; divide class time into mini-instruction, activity, and discussion sessions to actively immerse students in the content" (Childre et al., 2009, p. 9). Such steps give teachers the opportunities to make the lessons more meaningful by connecting the content to real life.

Halverson (2012) pointed out that Backwards Design allows students not to deal with complicated theories but helps them to develop necessary skills. For instance, some students with disabilities might have difficulties calculating the break-even point at which revenues begin to exceed costs. However, they are certainly able to determine if a particular product price was appropriate. Thus, differentiating content for diverse students is of utmost importance while teaching economics.

Planning backwards, teachers focus on cooperative learning and inquiry-based learning activities, taking into account interests and special needs of diverse students. Tomlinson and McTighe (2006) highlighted that clearly identified desired results and needed evidence allow teachers to make decisions "about what to teach and how to teach" guided by the defined priorities. Research about advantages of Backwards Design at high schools, colleges, and even universities (Carlson & Marshall, 2009; Michael & Libarkin, 2016) revealed a lot of benefits for all students in a diverse and inclusive environment. For instance, Carlson and Marshall (2009) argued for the use of Backward Design as a planning method to alter science education at the college-level. The authors offer some tips on how to plan learning experiences and instructions for adolescent students.

If prioritized learning outcomes are the development of student critical thinking and problem-solving skills in the economic domain, the teacher can plan instructional strategies that include interactive discussions, economic experiments, case studies, cooperative learning projects, and small groups activities to make activities more personalized for every diverse student. For instance, the teacher can offer such activities to practice economic skills such as calculating a household budget for students' families. It is much simpler than drawing up a budget for a company but might be more efficient for students' long-term understanding of how to keep an income and expenses balance, which is one of the identified learning goals.

Differentiating the product, Backwards Design allows teachers to plan different assessments to give students the opportunity to demonstrate that the learning goals have been achieved. Rea and Roman (2019) stated that "Backwards Design must be mindful to their audience by giving them the effectiveness of curriculum assessment" (p. 44). Therefore, assessment practices to reveal student 'acceptable evidence' should be personalized and provide constructive feedback and high expectations for diverse students (formative assessment). For instance, verbal description of an economic graph instead of making calculations can be a better choice of assessment that will allow students with auditory learning style to demonstrate their knowledge in the economics domain and be accepted as evidence of their understanding of economic laws and market principles.

Instructional strategies implemented for inclusion can be various. According to Taylor (2015), accommodations may affect content, process, product, and learning environments. Thus, the teacher can vary the level of complexity, learning activities, and ways to demonstrate what students learned, remaining in a positive and supportive learning environment. Olinghouse (2008) pointed out that "instructional accommodations are not just for students who are struggling. When accommodations are made, all students benefit" (p. 1). Table 1 presents instructional strategies that can be implemented to support an inclusive population in a classroom while teaching economics.

Table 1. Instructional principles and strategies for inclusive and diverse settings

Inclusive Students	Content	Process	Product	Learning Environment
Students with learning difficulties	Provide students with more visuals and video content to keep students engaged.	Reduce the amount of information related to one economic concept.	Allow the students for extra time while making price calculations.	Provide high expectations for student success.
Students from the pull-out program	Teachers can divide the content to better differentiate it. The student can be offered additional advanced contents to study.	Students will be offered the advanced learning activity – to make an experiment of how marketing environment changes could influence prices.	Students will be offered to participate in extracurricular research activities.	Students can be engaged as an assistant to moderate small group work.
Students with IEP	Content adaptations for IEP students must meet local and state education standards. Economic concepts will be reinforced with more concrete examples from student life to help the student better understand abstract economic ideas.	Review previously learned content prior to the learning activities.	Let the student dictate the ideas to a teaching assistant to write them down. Formulating ideas can be very helpful for the students to deepen their understanding.	Teachers can take turns while sharing instruction. This strategy can be helpful while flexible grouping.
Students that need manipulatives	Provide an overview of the content at the beginning of the lesson. This can activate the prior knowledge of all students, including the students with special learning needs.	Provide necessary health conditions to modify the activities for students.	Reduce the amount of written work and let students use adaptive devices.	One teacher works with small groups, whereas another one – with the larger group as a strategy can be used to create the environment of respectful collaboration among all students.
Students with speech difficulties	Provide students with more visuals (presentation of content) to better meet their needs.	Use scaffolding, flexible grouping, and interest centers during individual and group learning activities during the lesson.	Allow students to present their learning outcomes in writing.	Separate speaking skills from understanding while assessing the learning outcomes.
Neurodiverse students	Use lesson cycling to activate prior knowledge.	Use pre-designed graphic organizers to systematize content.	Provide a summary of important information with a list of questions to be answered.	Provide realistic but positive expectations.
ELL students	Provide study guides that feature the most important content. Introduce new economic terms (demand, supply, competition, etc.) in the beginning of the lesson. Repeat, use other words, and summarize all key points.	Make the students responsible for infographics and posters development. Summarizing the concepts by drawing them, the students can improve their language skills and learn the content simultaneously.	Let students use a spelling dictionary or electronic spelling aid. Use cooperative learning strategies to overcome student language barriers. Provide extra time. Separate content skills and language abilities.	Structure the environment for learning through flexible grouping. Provide more personalized learning opportunities. Write important ideas down on the whiteboard using colored markers for emphasis.

CONCLUSION

To sum up, the use of the ARSC model, the cooperative learning and inquiry-based approach, reading strategies, Backwards design, and inclusive principles while planning economics lessons allows a teacher to support student interests in economics topics. The ARCS model helps the teacher to capture student interests at the beginning of the lesson, make the lesson content relevant for the students, support their confidence, and satisfaction with learning activities. The strategies of cooperative learning, inquiry-based learning, and reading a supplemental text in economics are based on the idea of helping each student flourish and develop their understanding in the price-making process and market functioning. Backwards design principles for planning lessons for diverse and inclusive classrooms allow teachers to take into account different factors to meet the needs of all learners in the classroom. Such an approach can be challenging. However, knowing their students well, educators can provide them with all the opportunities to access the economics curriculum.

REFERENCES

Bloom, B. S. (1956). Taxonomy of educational objectives: The classification of educational goals. In I. Handbook (Ed.), *Cognitive domain*. Longmans, Green and Co.

Cabezudo, A., Christidis, C., da Silva, M. C., Demetriadou-Saltet, V., Halbartschlager, F., & Mihai, G. (2010). *Global education guidelines: A handbook for educators to understand and implement global education*. The North-South Centre of the Council of Europe. https://www.developmenteducation.ie/media/documents/GEguidelines-web.pdf

Carlson, D. L., & Marshall, P. A. (2009). Learning the science of research, learning the art of teaching: Planning backwards in a college genetics course. *Bioscience Education, 13*(1), 1–9. doi:10.3108/beej.13.4

Childre, A., Sands, J. R., & Pope, S. T. (2009). Backward design. *Teaching Exceptional Children, 41*(5), 6–14. doi:10.1177/004005990904100501

Dolan, R. J., & Simon, H. (1997). *Power pricing: How managing price transforms the bottom line*. Simon & Schuster.

Gagne, R. M., Briggs, L. J., & Wager, W. W. (1992). *Principles of instructional design*. https://www.hcs64.com/files/Principles%20of%20instructional%20design.pdf

Halverson, H. (2012). *Educational innovation at UW-Madison: The "Backward Design" framework* [Video]. https://www.youtube.com/watch?v=cveylXCpUmw&t=453s

Keller, J. M. (1987). Development and use of the ARCS model of Instructional Design. *Journal of Instruction Development, 10*(3), 2–10. doi:10.1007/BF02905780

Keller, J. M. (2016). Motivation, learning, and technology: Applying the ARCS-V motivation model. *Participatory Educational Research, 3*(2), 1-13. http://www.perjournal.com/archieve/issue_3_2/1-per_16-06_volume_3_issue_2_page_1_15.pdf

Malone, T. W. (1981). Toward a theory of intrinsically motivating instruction. *Cognitive Science*, *4*(4), 333–369. https://onlinelibrary.wiley.com/doi/pdf/10.1207/s15516709cog0504_2. doi:10.120715516709cog0504_2

McKnight, K. S. (2014). *Common Core literacy strategies for ELA, history/social studies, and the humanities, grades 6-12: Strategies to deepen content knowledge (grades 6-12)*. John Wiley & Sons Inc.

Michael, N. A., & Libarkin, J. C. (2016). Understanding by Design: Mentored implementation of Backward Design methodology at the university level. *Perspectives*, *42*(2), 44–52. https://files.eric.ed.gov/fulltext/EJ1126353.pdf

Olinghouse, N. (2008). *Designing lessons for diverse learners*. https://edwp.educ.msu.edu/te/wp-content/uploads/sites/49/2020/06/Designing-Lessons-for-Diverse-Learners.pdf

Quigley, C., Marshall, J. C., Deaton, C. C., Cook, M. P., & Padilla, M. (2011). Challenges to inquiry teaching and suggestions for how to meet them. *Science Educator*, *20*(1), 55–61. https://files.eric.ed.gov/fulltext/EJ940939.pdf

Rea, M. O., & Roman, J. L. (2019). Implementing backward design to improve students' academic performance in EFL classes. *Espirales Revista Multidisciplinaria de Investigación, 3*(24), 43-50. https://www.revistaespirales.com/index.php/es/article/view/422/352

Robinson, D. G., & Watson, G. S. (2013). Guidelines for the motivational design of instructional simulations. *The Journal of Applied Instructional Design*, *3*(2), 41–52. doi:10.28990/jaid2013.00127

Sachdeva, S. (2017). Making economics classrooms exciting: Role of experiential learning. *International Journal of Advanced Educational Research*, *2*(5), 83–92.

Schoenbach, R., Greenleaf, C., Murphy, L., Cziko, C., & Hurwitz, L. (2012). *Reading for understanding: How reading apprenticeship improves disciplinary learning in secondary and college classrooms*. Jossey-Bass.

Taylor, B. K. (2015). Content, process, and product: Modeling differentiated instruction. *Kappa Delta Pi Record*, *51*(1), 13–17. doi:10.1080/00228958.2015.988559

Tomlinson, C. A., & McTighe, J. (2006). *Integrating differentiated instruction and Understanding by Design: Connecting content and kids*. Association for Supervision and Curriculum Development. https://chca-oh.instructure.com/files/3649/download?download_frd=1

APPENDIX

Lesson Outline
Subject Area: Social Studies (Economics)
Grade level: 10th Grade
Topic: 'How Are Prices Set in Our Economy?' from the Unit 'Understanding Economic Development'.

Rationale of the Lesson

The purpose of the lesson is to provide all students with the opportunities to understand the patterns of market economy functioning, to become able to define optimal prices for goods and services, and to recognize the interconnectedness of multiple market factors. All students of the classroom, including diverse and inclusive learners, are future participants of the market relations. All of them will buy or sell goods, look for jobs, or start their own business. Thus, all learners need to understand the basics of the price-making process, although the depth of understanding could vary from the ability to recognize appropriate price to the ability to use economic laws and graphs to predict price fluctuations, depending on student profiles.

Lesson Objectives

By the end of this lesson, the students will be able to:

- recognize the interconnections of different economic and social factors.
- understand the basics of market economy functioning.
- determine the factors that influence product prices (competitors, substitute goods, consumer preferences, etc.).
- assess the appropriateness of product prices.

Materials Needed for the Lesson

Economics is a complicated subject related to the cognitive domain. Considering Bloom's taxonomy (1956), during the lesson, students will recall economic concepts studied previously (remember), discuss price-making strategies (understand), calculate the market price of different products (apply), find the main ideas of market functioning (analyze), define the prices for the products they want to sell (synthesis), and argue for and against monopoly in the market (evaluate). Mastering these specific learning objectives, the students will use graphic organizers, whiteboards, different visuals and graphs to illustrate the price-making process, and videos that explain the economic models of price determination in the market.

Anticipatory Set

The learning activities for the lesson include the following:

- understanding of competition – a learning activity for small groups to study the influence of competition in the market;
- the issue analysis to find out the role of substitute goods in the economy (reading the supplemental text 'Power Pricing: How Managing Price Transforms the Bottom Line' by Dolan and Simon (1997));
- an interactive discussion to define the role of fashion and consumer preferences in the market economy and price-making process ('Why iPhones Are So Expensive?');
- cooperative learning activities – the students will work with different types of content to find out the principles of demand elasticity;
- small groups activities - the students will create infographics and posters to summarize the information on price-making process;
- inquiry-based learning - as a capstone activity, the students will organize a fair to sell their handmade products for prices they have set using corresponding knowledge and skills.
- Steps to Complete the Lesson Activities:
    - a learning activity for small groups to study the influence of competition in the market;
- an issue analysis based on reading the supplemental text to find out the role of substitute goods in price-making;
- an inquiry-based interactive activity to define the role of fashion and consumer preferences in the market economy and price-making process;
- a cooperative learning activity – the students will create infographics and posters to summarize the information on price-making;
- an experiential learning activity - as a capstone activity, the students will organize a fair to sell their handmade products for prices they have set using their newly developed knowledge and skills.

CLOSING

Presentation of the research results of student teams, which have created infographics and posters to summarize the information on the price-making process. Then, the teacher will summarize the main ideas and concepts of the lesson and provide connections with previous and forthcoming topics of the unit.

ASSESSMENT

The teacher will discuss every learning activity with the students, providing detailed descriptive feedback. This topic is important for understanding social life, so the teacher will use the assessment of learning activities as a way to adjust teaching and differentiate content, process, product, and environment to make all the students master price-making. The instrument offered also allows the teacher to foster student abilities to independent discovery, problem-solving and critical thinking skills. As a formative assessment of cooperative learning activity, the teacher will use the 'Think, pair, share' method to help students think individually about the topic, discuss their ideas with a partner and then share them with the class. Students' infographics can be also used as the assessment strategy. Collaborating while designing them, the students will summarize their understanding of price-making. The Fair organized by students can be considered as a summative assessment strategy. The students will use their knowledge, skills, and understanding of price-making during this capstone learning activity. The students will be able to apply the skills they have developed, and this will be used to assess their mastery and a deep understanding of the price-making process.

Chapter 13
Wall Street Wizard:
Stock Market Simulation Game Using Flask

C. V. Suresh Babu
https://orcid.org/0000-0002-8474-2882
Hindustan Institute of Technolgy and Science, India

V. Surendar
Hindustan Institute of Technology and Science, India

EXECUTIVE SUMMARY

The stock market is a complicated and often scary arena for people inexperienced with the financial world. Stock market simulation games have been designed to solve this issue by allowing users to study and engage with the market in a fun and engaging way. This study proposes the construction of a stock market simulation web application using Flask, which will allow users to create demo accounts, learn how to purchase and sell stocks, manage their portfolios, and do real-time stock market analysis. This simulation will be intended to make stock market learning accessible and pleasurable for all users. The goal is to develop an interactive platform that educators can use to teach economics and finance to students in a fun and engaging way. This chapter will discuss how the proposed simulation would differ by including real-time analysis and a focus on portfolio management. Through the simulation, users will learn how to make educated decisions based on market research and diversify their investments to minimize risks, leading to a more financially literate society.

DOI: 10.4018/978-1-6684-7583-6.ch013

INTRODUCTION

Economics permeates every facet of society, influencing individual choices and the broader trajectories of nations. However, in K-12 classrooms, its foundational concepts can sometimes feel elusive to young students. Essential notions such as supply and demand, trade, and market mechanics, though vital, can challenge novice learners. While the integration of stock market games into economics education isn't a novel concept (Dale, 2002; White & Wagner, 2021), this chapter introduces a distinct angle: the promotion of real-time interfaces for educators. Previous studies have emphasized the benefits of gamifying economic principles and investment strategies (Al-Bahrani et al., 2018; Fabian, 2021; Lew & Saville, 2021; Rogmans, 2018). White and Wagner (2021) stood out by developing a game that encourages educators to customize interfaces. However, this work further innovates by integrating an interface with live data.

To demystify these economic ideas, educators are gravitating towards inventive classroom-specific tools. Economic simulation games have emerged as a particularly effective resource in this regard. These simulations immerse students in the world of economics, offering a hands-on platform to grapple with market strategies, gauge the repercussions of their choices, and see economic postulations in action. At the core of our endeavour is the crafting of an online economic simulation game designed specifically for K-12 students. This game, rooted in the Flask framework, grants students the autonomy to simulate economic events, steer trading choices, allocate assets, and decipher up-to-the-minute data. The ultimate aspiration? To evolve traditional economics teaching into a vibrant, participatory learning adventure.

While educational platforms like EconEdLink and Practical Money Skills already exist, our game's distinguishing feature is its incorporation of real-time data. This element introduces students to the ever-changing landscape of economics, underscoring the fluidity of decisions and their resultant outcomes. Moreover, our game champions analytical prowess, prompting students to scrutinize patterns, make educated decisions, and foster a profound grasp of economic systems.

RESEARCH PROBLEM

The issue addressed in the existing work is the requirement for efficient and interesting teaching strategies for students learning economics and finance concepts. It has been discovered that traditional teaching methods for these subjects, like lectures and textbooks, are less engaging and might not produce the best learning outcomes (Ray, 2018). The related work, therefore, seeks to investigate the use of game-based learning and supporting instructors in using cutting-edge technologies, as potential remedies to this issue. Investigating how well these strategies work to raise student engagement and academic performance in economics and finance education is the specific focus of the related work.

LITERATURE REVIEW

For some years, educational researchers have been interested in game-based learning, and there is a growing body of literature on its usefulness in improving student engagement and academic achievement in a variety of topics, including economics and finance (Choi & Noh, 2021; Rogmans, 2018; White & Wagner, 2021).

According to a comprehensive review of empirical studies on game-based learning in financial education, games can improve students' knowledge and comprehension of financial concepts, and the success of game-based learning is dependent on the game's design and execution (Gualtieri et al., 2020).

According to another study, gamification can improve student engagement and motivation in finance and economics instruction (Hsu & Lu, 2021). Furthermore, research on the influence of virtual simulation technology on economic education have indicated that it can increase students' learning transfer and capacity to apply economic ideas in real-world circumstances (Choi & Noh, 2021).

Games and simulations have been utilised to improve learning and performance in a variety of disciplines, including education, healthcare, and military training. The use of games and simulations in financial education has also received a lot of attention. There are, however, benefits and drawbacks to employing games and simulations in educational contexts.

ADVANTAGES

- Engaging and Interactive: Games and simulations are engaging and interactive, offering a fun and immersive learning experience that may encourage learners and boost their interest in the subject matter.
- Active Learning: Games and simulations promote deeper learning and information retention by allowing learners to apply concepts and skills in realistic circumstances, practise decision-making, and receive rapid feedback.
- Safe Environment: Games and simulations give a secure setting for students to experiment, explore, and make errors without fear of negative repercussions, which can encourage risk-taking and creativity.
- Real-World Application: Games and simulations may be developed to replicate real-world circumstances, allowing students to apply their knowledge and

abilities in real-world situations and improve their preparation for real-world difficulties.

DISADVANTAGES

- Limited Realism: Games and simulations may fail to adequately reflect the complexities and subtleties of real-world events, resulting in oversimplification and potentially erroneous decision-making.
- Costly and time-consuming: Developing and executing games and simulations may be time-consuming and resource-intensive, necessitating large investments in technology and skills.
- Transferability Issues: The skills and information gained in games and simulations may not simply transfer to real-world environments, necessitating further training and support.
- Technical Issues: Technical difficulties, such as software malfunctions and system failures, can derail the learning process, leading to frustration and disengagement.

GAMES AND SIMULATIONS

In recent years, game-based learning and simulation-based learning have grown in popularity in economics education. A rising number of studies have looked at the usefulness of various games and simulations in economics education. Based on similar works, shall compare and contrast several games and simulations in this area.

The Stock Market Game is a popular game-based learning tool for teaching economics. The Stock Market Game is a simulation game that allows students to invest virtual money in stocks, bonds, and mutual funds to learn about investing and personal finance. It has been demonstrated that the game improves students' financial literacy and investing understanding (Bozarth, 2020; Manzano-Leon, 2021). Some investigations, however, have found that the game does not always precisely mirror the real-world stock market (Gao & Chen, 2021).

Minecraft is another game-based learning technology that has gained popularity in economics education. Minecraft is a sandbox video game in which users may create and explore virtual environments. Minecraft has been used in economics education to teach topics such as scarcity, trade, and resource allocation. According to research, Minecraft can help pupils grasp economic concepts and improve their critical thinking abilities (Chen & Cao, 2020; Concas et al., 2020). Minecraft, on the other hand, may not be available to all pupils because it requires a computer with specified requirements and a licence to play.

Simulation-based learning, in addition to game-based learning, is commonly employed in economics education. The Virtual Economics programme, for example, includes simulations of real-world economic circumstances such as purchasing a car or establishing a business.

According to studies, the Virtual Economics programme can help pupils enhance their economic awareness and decision-making abilities (Gualtieri et al., 2020; Hsu & Lu, 2021). However, the program's ability to correctly reflect real-world economic conditions may be limited.

ARGUMENT

The researchers contend that incorporating a stock market simulation game into the classroom can enhance students' understanding of and interest in economics and finance subjects. They want to assess how well this game teaches students about the stock market and compare their findings to those of other studies on game-based learning.

The researchers tested a group of students to see how much their understanding of stock market concepts had improved both before and after playing Wallstreet Wizard. The findings revealed that the students' understanding of stock market concepts had increased in a statistically significant way. The knowledge improvement was consistent with earlier findings, the researchers found when they compared their findings to those of other game-based learning studies.

DRAFTING

The study concludes that teaching economics and finance, particularly stock market concepts, can be effectively accomplished using an economics-based tool (stock market simulation game). The educational experience offered by the game is fun and interactive, and it can help students become more knowledgeable and financially literate. The findings of this study imply that game-based learning, in particular simulation games, can be a useful addition to conventional methods of teaching economics and finance.

METHODOLOGY

The suggested stock market simulation game aims to create an interactive and informative experience for players, helping them understand the stock market and trading strategies. This game is designed to mimic real-world stock market actions, including changes in prices and events that might affect how stocks are valued.

The Python programming language and various libraries like Pandas, Matplotlib, and NumPy were used to achieve the game's goals. The game is divided into different levels, each with its own goals and challenges. The first level introduces players to the basics of the stock market and how to use the game interface. The second level involves selecting a portfolio of stocks and managing it for a specific period.

To ensure that the simulation is accurate and lifelike, historical stock price data from reliable sources such as Yahoo Finance was collected and used to simulate realistic price changes. The game also considers important news events that can influence stock values, such as when companies announce their earnings or when significant world events happen.

A pilot study was conducted with a group of children to assess the game's effectiveness. The study aimed to understand how the game impacted the students' understanding of the stock market and trading strategies. Data was collected about their performance in the game and their knowledge of the stock market before and after playing.

The proposed stock market simulation game is a valuable tool for teaching economics and financial literacy. Users can learn about the stock market in a safe and engaging manner, thanks to its interactive and realistic design. The approach used to develop the game ensures accuracy and realism, making it an excellent educational tool.

DEVELOPMENT

Realistic Gameplay Techniques: The techniques used in the suggested stock market simulation game drew inspiration from real stock markets. Players were provided with virtual money and access to actual stock market data to make investment decisions and earn profits. The game's mechanics involved simulated stock buying, selling, tracking stock market trends, and making smart investment choices.

- User-Friendly Interface: The game's user interface was designed to be easy to understand and navigate. A dashboard was created to showcase the user's portfolio, stock market insights, news updates, and other relevant information.

The interface was carefully crafted to cater to both beginners and experienced users.

- Excel for Data Management: Instead of a traditional database, the game employed Excel spreadsheets for managing crucial game data, including stock market data, user portfolios, and user details. These Excel sheets were structured to handle data effectively while offering a flexible approach to storage and retrieval.
- Real-Time Stock Market Data Integration: To provide an authentic gaming experience, real-time stock market data was integrated into the game. This data was sourced from reputable financial institutions and updated in real-time to mirror actual market fluctuations.
- Rigorous Testing and Evaluation: The game underwent comprehensive testing to ensure its reliability, eliminate bugs, and offer an engaging user experience. User feedback was also collected to pinpoint areas for improvement and gauge overall user satisfaction with the game's features and mechanics.

TECHNICAL STATEMENT

- Flask: Flask, a web framework built with Python, forms the foundation of the game's online platform. It's responsible for managing how the game interacts with users through web browsers.
- Excel for Data Handling: Instead of complicated databases, Excel sheets were used to manage game data. This allowed for smooth organization of information like stock prices, user portfolios, and other relevant details.
- Bootstrap: The game's user interface was designed using Bootstrap, a widely used toolkit for creating visually appealing and responsive web apps. Bootstrap ensured that the game works well on various devices and screen sizes.
- JavaScript: JavaScript, a versatile programming language, was employed to add interactive elements to the game. This includes real-time updates of stock prices and leaderboards.
- Pygame: The Pygame module was used to create the gaming interface itself, offering a platform to design the interactive elements of the stock market simulation.
- Yahoo Finance API: The WallStreet Wizard game taps into the Yahoo Finance API, a tool that provides real-time stock prices and financial information. By integrating this API, the game can offer players a realistic experience, enabling them to make informed investment choices.

By utilizing the Yahoo Finance API, the WallStreet Wizard game ensures that players are exposed to the latest financial trends and news, enhancing their ability to make wise investment decisions. The integration of these technologies works together to offer an immersive, educational, and engaging gaming experience.

GAME FUNCTIONS

- Step 1: The game begins with the user checking in or joining up on the Wallstreet Wizard gaming website's login/signup page.
- Step 2: After logging in, the user may set up a demo account to begin playing the game.
- Step 3: The consumer is then given a dashboard from which they may manage their stock portfolio.
- Step 4: The user may then purchase and sell stocks in the demo account using virtual money.
- Step 5: The game delivers real-time stock market information, allowing users to track the performance of their portfolio and make educated decisions.
- Step 6: The game also features portfolio management capabilities, which allow users to track their investments and make changes as required.
- Step 7: User testing and feedback collecting is an important element of the game development process since it allows developers to modify the game based on user feedback and provide a better user experience.
- Login/Signup Page: The Wallstreet Wizard game website has a login/signup page where users may log in to their current accounts or create new ones. The login/signup page is the first page that users view when they enter the game website. It features a simple form that users can fill out with their login credentials or to create a new account. The portal also has connections to the game's social media profiles as well as a support area for those who want assistance.
- Process for Creating a Demo Account: After login in or joining up, users can establish a demo account to begin playing the game. Filling out a brief form with basic information such as name and email address is required to create a demo account. After submitting the form, consumers are given a virtual money to invest in the stock market.
- Portfolio Management Tools: Various portfolio management tools are included in the game, allowing users to track their investments and make modifications as required. Users may examine their portfolio, which includes the stocks they've bought, their current valuations, and the percentage gains

or losses. Users may also add and delete stocks from their portfolios, as well as set up notifications to warn them of key market developments.

- Real-time Stock Market data: The game delivers real-time stock market data, allowing users to track the performance of their portfolio and make educated decisions. Users may examine live stock quotations, stock market news stories, and other information that might assist them make financial decisions.
- User Testing and Feedback collecting: User testing and feedback collecting are critical components of game development. Developers can utilise user testing to detect and solve possible flaws with the game's interface or functioning before it is released to the public. Feedback gathering enables developers to get user thoughts on how to improve the game's features and functions to deliver a better user experience. Surveys, user interviews, and other approaches can be used to acquire this input.

FLOWCHART

- Start: The flowchart begins with the user entering the game by signing in or establishing a new account.
- Login/Signup: If the user is new to the game, they are requested to register a new account. They can log in if they already have an account.
- Home Screen: After logging in, the user is directed to the home screen, where they may access various game features.
- Purchase/Sell Stocks: From the home screen, the user may select to purchase or sell stocks. If customers opt to purchase, they are directed to the stock selection screen, where they can pick from a list of available stocks. If they decide to sell, they are sent to their portfolio screen, where they can pick the appropriate option.
- Stock Selection Screen: The Stock Selection Screen allows the user to select from a list of available stocks and input the number of shares they wish to acquire.
- Portfolio Screen: The user may see the worth of their investments and view their portfolio.
- Real-Time Analysis: The game delivers real-time stock market analysis, displaying current market trends and how the user's investments are performing.
- End: When the user logs out, the game is over.

Figure 2. Class diagram

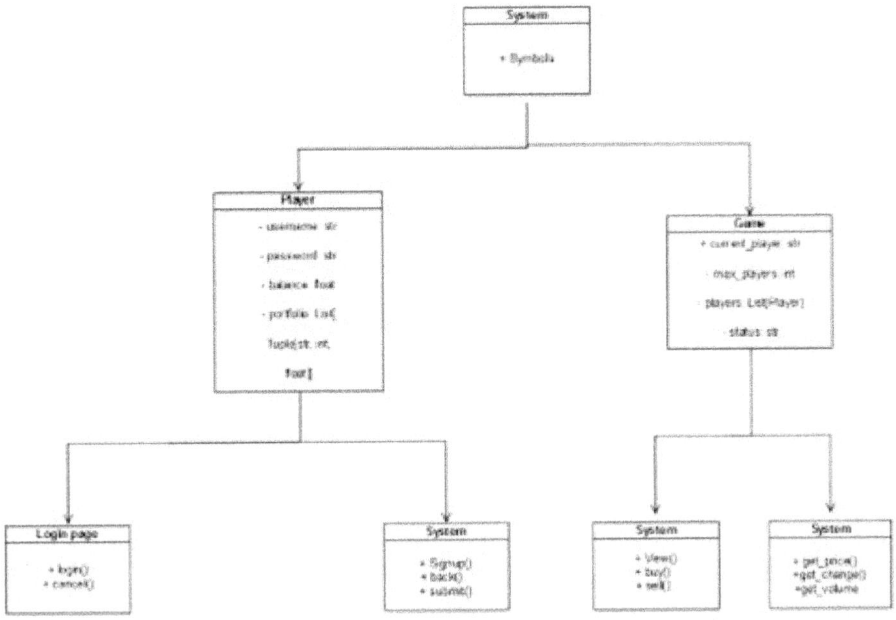

Figure 3. User case diagram

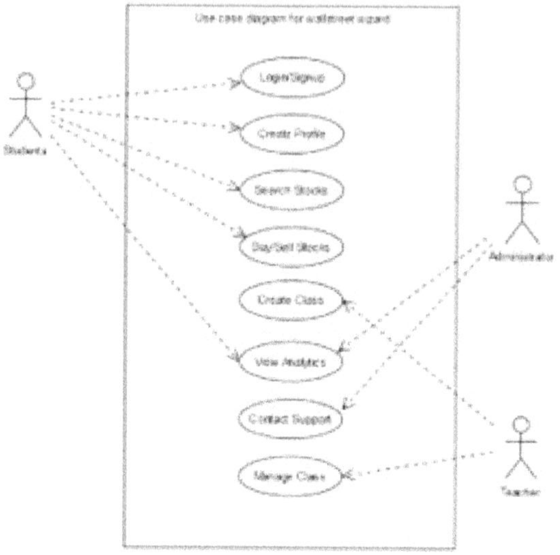

RESULTS

The researchers implemented a method that involved conducting a pre-test and a post-test to measure the increase in stock market knowledge among students who engaged with the game. Before playing the game, students took a pre-test, and immediately after playing, they took a post-test. The findings from user testing demonstrated a statistically significant improvement in students' comprehension of stock market concepts after playing the game. This underscores the game's effectiveness in teaching economics, particularly the intricacies of the stock market. The game's interactive and captivating design enabled students to apply theoretical economic principles within a practical context, contributing to their enhanced understanding.

The success of the game in teaching economics has substantial implications for both economic education and financial literacy. Games and simulations can serve as potent tools for conveying complex economic subjects, especially when conventional teaching methods fall short. By engaging with economic concepts in a dynamic and hands-on manner, students can enhance their grasp of the subject and retain their knowledge more effectively.

Nevertheless, it's important to acknowledge that the game's effectiveness could be influenced by various factors, such as student's prior exposure to economics, the design of the game, and the quality of accompanying instruction. Furthermore, it's worth noting that the study's user testing had limitations in terms of sample size, potentially affecting the broad applicability of the results. To thoroughly gauge the WallStreet Wizard game's utility in economics education, further research with larger and more diverse sample sizes is warranted. This would provide a more comprehensive understanding of the game's potential benefits in a variety of educational contexts.

Figure 4. Candle stick graph for risk and return

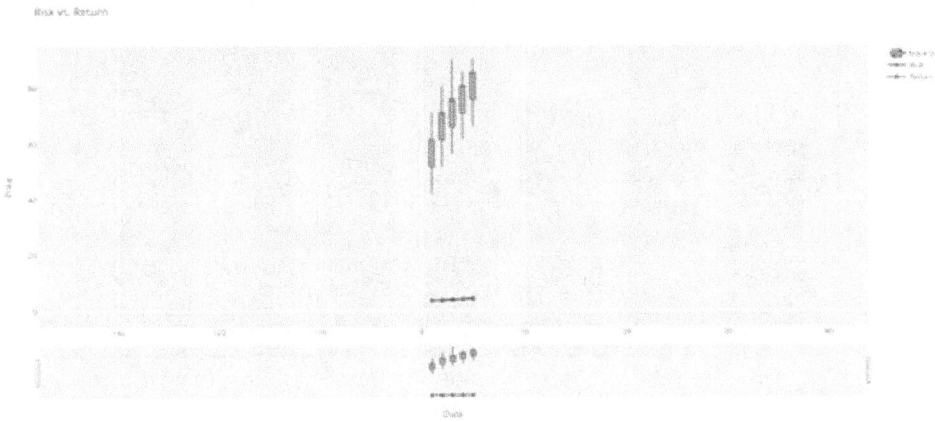

The researchers performed user testing with a sample of students to assess the efficiency of the Wallstreet Wizard game in teaching economics. The exam assessed how well students knew stock market principles before and after playing the game.

After playing the game, the students' knowledge of stock market principles improved statistically significantly, according to the user testing findings. Specifically, the students' average post-test score was considerably greater than their average pre-test score.

These findings suggest that the game has the potential to be an excellent tool for teaching pupils about economics and finance. The game can help students better comprehend how the stock market works by giving a realistic representation of it.

Figure 5. Stock price analysis graph based on every month

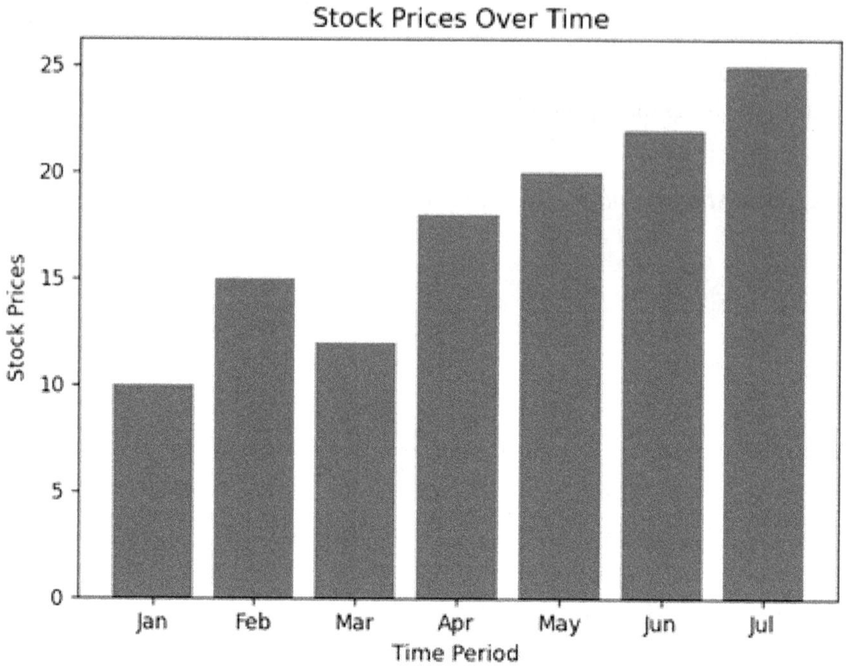

Figure 6. Portfolio performance based on the buying and selling of stocks

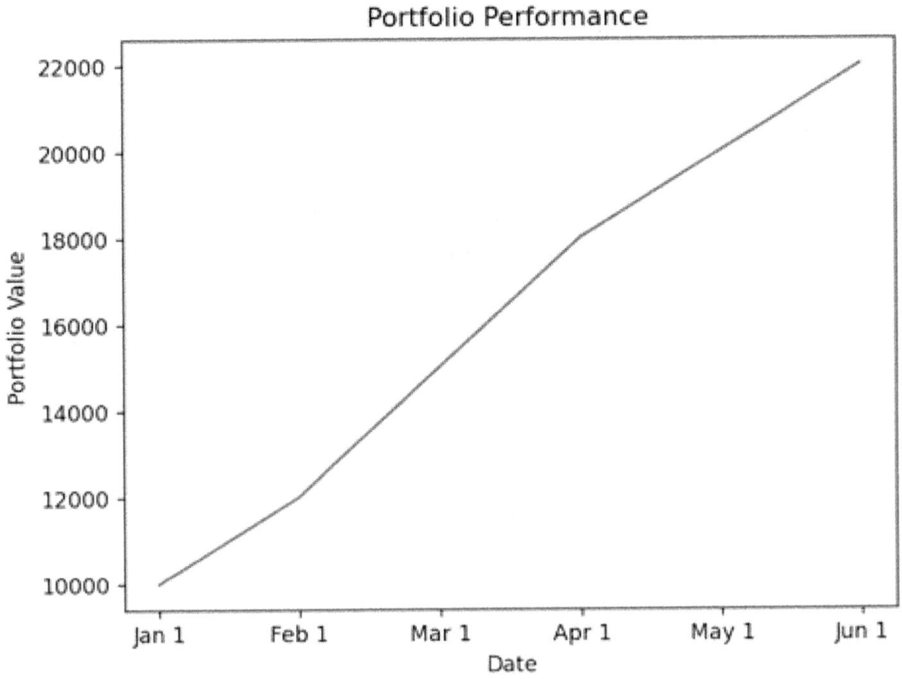

DISCUSSION

When comparing the outcomes of the WallStreet Wizard game to those of other games and simulations, it's essential to consider the unique learning goals and aims that each game and simulation seeks to fulfil. Different games and simulations may focus on distinct aspects of economics and finance education, such as microeconomics, macroeconomics, investment strategies, or financial literacy.

Various studies have highlighted the potential of games and simulations in teaching economics and financial concepts. For instance, Karp and Samuels (2001) found that students who engaged with an economics simulation game performed notably better on assessments compared to those who didn't. Likewise, Bhatt and Clemmons (2008) reported that a stock market simulation game positively impacted students' understanding of financial markets.

However, there have been instances where research yielded mixed or inconclusive results. Hwang and Lee (2012), for instance, observed that although a virtual stock trading game increased students' engagement, it didn't significantly enhance their comprehension of financial subjects.

In assessing the effectiveness of diverse games or simulations, it's crucial to examine their distinct learning objectives and design. More research is needed to uncover the most effective strategies for using games and simulations to teach economics and finance effectively.

FUTURE RESEARCH

According on the study's findings, there are various possible topics for further research relating to the Wallstreet Wizard game. Future study might involve expanding the game to include more complex stock market principles and trading methods. This would allow for a more in-depth examination of financial markets, giving pupils a better knowledge of how the stock market operates (Suresh Babu, 2022).

Another avenue for future study might be longitudinal studies to assess the long-term influence of the game on students' financial literacy and decision-making abilities. Longitudinal research would give useful insight into whether playing the game has a long-term influence on students' financial market understanding and behaviour.

Finally, future study might look at the game's potential use in other educational settings, such as online courses or as a tool for financial literacy programmes. This would enable the game to be distributed more widely and give additional possibilities for kids to learn about financial markets in an interesting and participatory manner.

CONCLUSION

To summarize, the WallStreet Wizard game has proven to be an effective tool for teaching economics and increasing financial literacy. During user testing, it was discovered that students who played the game significantly improved their understanding of stock market concepts. The user-centered design of the game produced an engaging and captivating experience.

The game's core functions, like creating accounts, managing portfolios, and real-time analysis, were developed using the Python and Flask frameworks. The integration of the Yahoo Finance API provided players with up-to-the-minute stock market data.

It's important to acknowledge that the study had limitations, such as a small group of participants and the absence of a comparison group. Future research can address these limitations and explore the game's impact on different audiences, including those with minimal economic and financial knowledge.

In essence, the WallStreet Wizard game has the potential to greatly enhance economic education and financial literacy. By offering an interactive and exciting platform to learn about the stock market, the game equips users with the skills needed to make informed financial choices. This engaging approach can simplify the teaching of economics to various age groups, making it easier for educators to promote financial understanding.

IMPLICATIONS

The planned Wallstreet Wizard game has significant ramifications for economics and finance education. The game teaches kids about stock market ideas and financial tactics in a fun and engaging way. The game gives students hands-on experience managing a virtual portfolio and making financial decisions, which can help them prepare for real-world investing.

Furthermore, the game encourages financial literacy by equipping students with the knowledge and skills necessary to make sound financial decisions. This can have a good influence on their financial well-being in the future.

The Wallstreet Wizard game has the potential to significantly improve economics teaching and promote financial literacy. The game offers a fun and dynamic learning experience that allows players to apply economic and financial ideas in a virtual setting. This can aid in the bridge between academic knowledge and practical application, which is frequently a barrier in traditional economics education.

The Wallstreet Wizard game may capture and hold the interest of users who might otherwise find economics and finance tedious and unpleasant by gamifying the learning process. This is especially true for younger students who may not have a strong interest in these areas.

By providing users with a realistic grasp of the stock market and investing methods, the Wallstreet Wizard game can assist to develop financial literacy. This can help users get the skills and information they need to make educated financial decisions and efficiently manage their own finances.

The Wallstreet Wizard game has a big potential influence on enhancing economics education and fostering financial literacy, and it deserves more investigation and improvement. The game has the potential to become a key weapon in the armoury of educators and financial organisations striving to increase financial literacy and promote economic knowledge with continuous development and extension.

REFERENCES

Al-Bahrani, A., Mahon, D., Mateer, G. D., & Murphy, P. R. (2018). PokémonGO: Applications for the economics classroom. *Journal of Economics Teaching*, *3*(2), 218–231. doi:10.58311/jeconteach/d8a48467f1a836406126d54c8e97507f474a6525

Bozarth, J. (2020). The effects of game-based learning on student engagement and academic performance in economics. *The Journal of Economic Education*, *51*(3), 217–233.

Chen, Z., & Cao, L. (2020). The application of virtual reality in financial education: An experimental study. *Journal of Financial Education*, *46*(1/2), 68–85.

Choi, D. H., & Noh, G. Y. (2021). The impact of presence on learning transfer intention in virtual reality simulation game. *SAGE Open*, *11*(3). Advance online publication. doi:10.1177/21582440211032178

Concas, G., Marulli, F., & Pani, C. (2020). Game-based learning in finance and accounting education: A systematic literature review. *Journal of Accounting Education*, *53*, 100688.

Dale, L. R. (2002). The stock market game in economics instruction. *Journal of Entrepreneurship Education*, *5*, 47–55.

Fabian, M. (2021). DevSim: A PowerPoint-based choose-your own adventure game for teaching economic development. *Journal of Economics Teaching*, *6*(2), 95–105. doi:10.58311/jeconteach/bdfda3147dc90d3efb3848d659e1c0768e0a6558

Gao, Y., & Chen, L. (2021). The effect of gamification on learning performance in financial education: A meta-analysis. *Journal of Financial Education*, *47*(1/2), 31–53.

Gualtieri, R., Dille, K., & Karlaftis, V. (2020). Game-based learning for financial education: A systematic review of empirical research. *Financial Counseling and Planning*, *31*(1), 83–97.

Hsu, C. C., & Lu, H. P. (2021). Learning effects and engagement of gamification in finance and economics education. *Journal of Interactive Learning Research*, *32*(2), 183–202.

Kasparian, C., & Namazian, A. (2020). Financial literacy and gamification: A comprehensive review of the literature. *Journal of Financial Education*, *46*(1/2), 195–220.

Lew, C., & Saville, A. (2021). Game-based learning: Teaching principles of economics and investment finance through *Monopoly. International Journal of Management Education, 19*(3), 100567. Advance online publication. doi:10.1016/j.ijme.2021.100567

Manzano-Leon, A., Camacho-Lazarraga, P., Guerrero, M. A., Guerrero-Puerta, L., Aguilar-Parra, J. M., Triguero, R., & Alias, A. (2021). Between level up and game over: A systematic literature review of gamification in education. *Sustainability (Basel), 13*(4), 2247. doi:10.3390u13042247

Ray, M. (2018). Teaching economics using 'cases' – Going beyond the 'chalk-and-talk' method. *International Review of Economics Education, 27*, 1–9. doi:10.1016/j.iree.2017.12.001

Rogmans, T. (2018). Teaching macroeconomics with the Econland Simulation Game and Learning Platform. *Journal of Economics Teaching, 2*(2), 92–103. doi:10.58311/jeconteach/892413d590665dfe858e06a93abd1697c16b00f7

Suresh Babu, C. V. (2022). *Artificial Intelligence and Expert Systems*. Anniyappa Publications.

Tan, G. W. H., Tan, K. C. D., & Teo, T. (2021). A meta-analysis of gamification in financial education. *Journal of Interactive Learning Research, 32*(2), 127–147.

White, D., & Wagner, J. (2021). Getting your students to be dynamic: Lesson and web app about market dynamics in the long-run. *Journal of Economics Teaching, 6*(2), 106–122. doi:10.58311/jeconteach/caa5a0746727f097014031 1ece607ade43c6147e

Compilation of References

Aali, M., Narenju Thani, F., Keramati, M. R., & Garavand, A. (2020). A model for effectiveness of e-learning at university. *Journal of Information Technology Management, 12*(4), 121–140. doi:10.22059/jitm.2020.298696.2479

Aboagye, E., Yawson, J. A., & Appiah, K. N. (2021). COVID-19 and e-learning: The challenges of students in tertiary institutions. *Social Education Research, 2*(1), 1–8. doi:10.37256er.212021422

Abreu, M., Veiga, F. H., Antunes, J., & Ferreira, A. (2006). Attitudes towards the school and self-interest in students from different family contexts. Activação do desenvolvimento psicológico: Actas do simpósio internacional, 194-200.

Acharya, T. R. (2015). *Effectiveness of GeoGebra software on mathematics achievement.* [Unpublished Master thesis]. University Campus, Kritipur.

Adu, E. O., & Zondo, S. S. (2023). Perceptions of educators on ICT integration into the teaching and learning of economics. *EUREKA: Social and Humanities*, (1), 61–71. doi:10.21303/2504-5571.2023.002530

Agievich, V. (2014). *Mathematical model and multi-criteria analysis of designing large-scale enterprise roadmap* [PhD thesis].

Ahmad, G. (2010). *Domain-Oriented Modeling of Indian Education System Through UML.* IUP.

Ainsworth, J. (2021). Team-Based Learning in professional writing courses for accounting graduates: Positive impacts on student engagement, accountability and satisfaction. *Accounting Education, 30*(3), 234–257. doi:10.1080/09639284.2021.1906720

Aksoy, M., & Ceylan, T. (2021). *An Action Research on Improving Classroom Communication and Interaction in Social Studies Teaching.* . doi:10.1155/2021/9943194

Al Kawas, S., & Hamdy, H. (2017). Peer-assisted learning associated with team-based learning in dental education. *Health Profession Education, 3*(1), 38–43. doi:10.1016/j.hpe.2016.08.003

Alammary, A., Sheard, J., & Carbone, A. (2014). Blended learning in higher education: Three different design approaches. *Australasian Journal of Educational Technology, 30*(4), 387–400. doi:10.14742/ajet.693

Al-Ansi, A. M., Garad, A., & Al-Ansi, A. (2021). ICT-based learning during Covid-19 outbreak: Advantages, opportunities and challenges. *Gagasan Pendidikan Indonesia*, *2*(1), 10–26. doi:10.30870/gpi.v2i1.10176

Al-Ansi, A. M., Jaboob, M., Garad, A., & Al-Ansi, A. (2023). Analyzing recent educational developments in augmented reality (AR) and virtual reality (VR). *Social Sciences & Humanities Open*, *8*(1), 100532. doi:10.1016/j.ssaho.2023.100532

Al-Azawei, A., Serenelli, F., & Lundqvist, K. (2016). Univeral Design for Learning (UDL): A content analysis of peer reviewed journals from 2012 to 2015. *The Journal of Scholarship of Teaching and Learning*, *16*(3), 39–56. doi:10.14434/josotl.v16i3.19295

Al-Bahrani, A., Mahon, D., Mateer, G. D., & Murphy, P. R. (2018). Pokémon GO: Applications for the Economics Classroom. *Journal of Economics Teaching*, *3*(2), 218–231. doi:10.58311/jeconteach/d8a48467f1a836406126d54c8e97507f474a6525

Al-Bahrani, A., Patel, D., & Sheridan, B. (2015). Engaging students using social media: The students' perspective. *International Review of Economics Education*, *19*, 36–50. Advance online publication. doi:10.1016/j.iree.2015.06.001

Al-Bahrani, A., Patel, D., & Sheridan, B. (2017). Evaluating Twitter and its impact on student learning in principles of economics courses. *The Journal of Economic Education*, *48*(4), 243–253. doi:10.1080/00220485.2017.1353934

Albiladi, W. S., & Alshareef, K. K. (2019). Blended learning in English teaching and learning: A review of the current literature. *Journal of Language Teaching and Research*, *10*(2), 232–238. doi:10.17507/jltr.1002.03

Alenezi, M., Wardat, S., & Akour, M. (2023). The Need of Integrating Digital Education in Higher Education: Challenges and Opportunities. *Sustainability (Basel)*, *15*(6), 4782. doi:10.3390u15064782

Alghamdi, A., Karpinski, A. C., Lepp, A., & Barkley, J. (2020). Online and face-to-face classroom multitasking and academic performance: Moderated mediation with self-efficacy for self-regulated learning and gender. *Computers in Human Behavior*, *102*, 214–222. doi:10.1016/j.chb.2019.08.018

Alhumaid, K., Ali, S., Waheed, A., Zahid, E., & Habes, M. (2020). COVID-19 & E-learning: Perceptions & Attitudes of teachers towards e-learning acceptance in the developing countries. *Multicultural Education*, *6*(2), 100–115. doi:10.5281/zenodo.4060121

Ali, M., Hossain, S. K., & Ahmed, T. (2018). Effectiveness of e-learning for university students: Evidence from Bangladesh. *Asian Journal of Empirical Research*, *8*(10), 352–360. doi:10.18488/journal.1007/2018.8.10/1007.10.352.360

Alipio, M. (2020). *A Structural Model of Organizational Commitment among Higher Education Economics Educators*. Munich Personal RePEc Archive. MPRA Paper No. 99421. https://mpra.ub.uni-muenchen.de/99421/

Allen, R. E., Copeland, J., Franks, A. S., Karimi, R., McCollum, M., Riese, D. J. II, & Lin, A. Y. (2013). Team-based learning in US colleges and schools of pharmacy. *American Journal of Pharmaceutical Education*, *77*(6), 115. doi:10.5688/ajpe776115 PMID:23966718

Almaráz, F. (2014). La diformación para la adopción de entornos virtuales de enseñanza-aprendizaje en la universidad: un enfoque organizativo. In A. García-Valcárcel (Ed.), *Experiencias de Innovación Docente Universitaria* (pp. 191–198). Universidad de Salamanca.

Alnafrah, I., & Mouselli, S. (2021). Revitalizing blockchain technology potentials for smooth academic records management and verification in low-income countries. *International Journal of Educational Development*, *85*, 102460. doi:10.1016/j.ijedudev.2021.102460

Althauser, K., & Harter, C. (2016). Math and economics: Implementing authentic instruction in grades K-5. *Journal of Education and Training Studies*, *4*(4), 111–122. doi:10.11114/jets.v4i4.1328

Alvarez-Bell, R. M., Wirtz, D., & Bian, H. (2017). Identifying keys to success in innovative teaching: Student engagement and instructional practices as predictors of student learning in a course using a team-based learning approach. *Teaching & Learning Inquiry*, *5*(2), 128–146. doi:10.20343/teachlearninqu.5.2.10

Amanor-Mfoafo, N. K., Edonu, K. K., Akrafi, O., & Dowuona, E. N. (2020). Towards e-learning in basic schools during COVID-19: Insights from Ghanaian teachers. *European Journal of Open Education and E-Learning Studies*, *5*(2), 9–19. doi:10.46827/ejoe.v5i2.3476

Amiruzzaman, S., & Amiruzzaman, M. (2022). Use of Twitter among college students for academics: A mixed-methods approach. *Social Sciences (Basel, Switzerland)*, *11*(9), 404. doi:10.3390ocsci11090404

Ansu-Kyeremeh, E. K., & Goosen, L. (2022). Exploring the Socioeconomic Facet of Online Inclusive Education in Ghana: The Effects of Technological Advancement in Academia. In M. Garcia (Ed.), *Socioeconomic Inclusion During an Era of Online Education* (pp. 47–66). IGI Global. doi:10.4018/978-1-6684-4364-4.ch003

Archambault, P., Turcotte, S., Smith, P. Y., Said Abasse, K., Paquet, C., Cote, A., Gomez, D., Khechine, H., Gagon, M.-P., Tremblay, M., Elazhary, N., & Legare, F. (2021, June 18). Intention to use wiki-based knowledge tools: Survey of Quebec emergency health professionals. *JMIR Medical Informatics*, *9*(6), e24649. Advance online publication. doi:10.2196/24649 PMID:34142977

Arkorful, V., & Abaidoo, N. (2015). The role of e-learning, advantages, and disadvantages of its adoption in higher education. *International Journal of Instructional Technology and Distance Learning*, *12*(1), 29–42. https://www.itdl.org/Journal/Jan_15/Jan15.pdf#page=33

Arnold, I. J. M., & Straten, J. T. (2012). Motivation and math skills as determinants of first-year performance in economics. *The Journal of Economic Education*, *43*(1), 33–47. doi:10.1080/00220485.2012.636709

Arriata, O., Galisteo, D., Pérez, M., & Martín, M. (2009). *Innovación en docencia universitaria con Moodle. Casos prácticos*. Editorial Club Universitario.

Asarta, C. J. (2023). Student engagement and interaction in the economics classroom: Essentials for the novice economic educator. *The Journal of Economic Education*, 1–9. Advance online publication. doi:10.1080/00220485.2023.2269142

Asociación Mexicana de Internet. (2016). *12º Estudio sobre los hábitos de los usuarios de Internet en México 2016.* Recuperado de https://www.amipci.org.mx/images/Estudio_Habitosdel_Usuario_2016.pdf

Atkins, M. S., Hoagwood, K. E., Kutash, K., & Seidman, E. (2010). Toward the integration of education and mental health in schools. *Administration and Policy in Mental Health, 37*(1-2), 40–47. doi:10.100710488-010-0299-7 PMID:20309623

Aydos, M. (2015). *The impact of teaching mathematics with GeoGebra on the conceptual understanding of limits and continuity: the case of Turkish gifted and talented students* [Unpublished thesis] Ihsan Dogrammaci Bilkert University.

Ayers, C. A. (2016). Developing preservice and in-service teachers' pedagogical content knowledge in economics. *Social Studies Research & Practice, 11*(1), 73–92. doi:10.1108/SSRP-01-2016-B0005

Azizan, F. Z. (2010). Blended learning in higher education institution in Malaysia. *Proceedings of regional conference on knowledge integration in ICT, 10*(1), 454-466.

Bahramnezhad, F., Asgar, P., Ghiyasvandian, S., Shiri, M., & Bahramnezhad, F. (2016). The learners' satisfaction of e-learning: A review article. *American Journal of Educational Research, 4*(4), 347–352. http://pubs.sciepub.com/education/4/4/8/

Baidoo-anu, D., & Owusu Ansah, L. (2023). Education in the Era of Generative Artificial Intelligence (AI): Understanding the Potential Benefits of ChatGPT in Promoting Teaching and Learning. *SSRN, 7*(1), 52–62. doi:10.2139srn.4337484

Bailey, J., Martin, N., Schneider, C., Vander Ark, T., Duty, L., Ellis, S., & Terman, A. (2013). Blended learning implementation guide 2.0. In J. Bailey, C. Schneider, & T. Vander Ark (Eds.), Navigating the Digital Shift (pp. 32–39). Academic Press.

Ball Hinkelmann, K. (2016). *Modelling in Enterprise Architecture. University of applied sciences northwest Switzerland.* Business School.

Ballard, C. L., & Johnson, M. F. (2010). Basic math skills and performance in an introductory economics class. *The Journal of Economic Education, 35*(1), 3–23. doi:10.3200/JECE.35.1.3-23

Bandura, A. (1977). *Social learning theory*. Prentice Hall.

Banks, F., & Barlex, D. (2021). *Teaching STEM in the Secondary School-Helping Teachers Meet the Challenge* (2nd ed.). Routledge.

Baptiste, H. P., & Leck, M. C. (2023). Lee S. Shulman: An icon of teaching. In B. A. Geier (Ed.), *The Palgrave Handbook of Educational Thinkers*. Palgrave Macmillan. doi:10.1007/978-3-030-81037-5_187-1

Barai, M. (2017). *Perceptions of students on the use of GeoGebra in geometry teaching* [Unpublished Master thesis]. University Campus, Kritipur.

Barbera, E. (2015). *Aprender e-learning*. Paidós.

Basal, A. (2015). The implementation of a flipped classroom in foreign language teaching. *Turkish Online Journal of Distance Education, 16*(4), 28–37. doi:10.17718/tojde.72185

Bean, J. C., & Melzer, D. (2021). *Engaging ideas: The professor's guide to integrating writing, critical thinking, and active learning in the classroom*. John Wiley & Sons.

Belghesis, S., & Kamalludeen, R. (2018). The Intention to Use GeoGebra in the Teaching of Mathematics among Malaysian Teachers. *Malaysian Online Journal of Educational Technology, 6*(1), 109–115.

Biewener, D. (2023, February 21). *5 Big Benefits of Blended Learning*. Simplilearn. https://www.simplilearn.com/benefits-of-blended-learning-article

Bissell, A. N., & Lemons, P. P. (2006). A new method for assessing critical thinking in the classroom. *Bioscience, 56*(1), 66–72. doi:10.1641/0006-3568(2006)056[0066:ANMFAC]2.0.CO;2

Bist, P. R. (2017). Use of GeoGebra in Geometric Construction [Published Master Thesis]. *Imperial Journal of Interdisciplinary Research, 3*.

Blackburn, R., & Rosen, B. (1993). Total quality and human resources management: lessons learned from Baldrige Award-winning companies. *Academy of Management Perspectives, 7*(3).

Block, C. (2022). 12 Reasons Your Digital Transformation Will Fail. Forbes Coaches Council. *Forbes*. https://www.forbes.com/sites/forbescoachescouncil/2022/03/16/12-reasons-your-digital-transformation-will-fail/?sh=4e5a5f751f1e

Bloom, B. S. (1956). Taxonomy of educational objectives: The classification of educational goals. In I. Handbook (Ed.), *Cognitive domain*. Longmans, Green and Co.

Boelens, R., De Wever, B., & Voet, M. (2017). Four key challenges to the design of blended learning: A systematic literature review. *Educational Research Review, 22*(1), 1–18. doi:10.1016/j.edurev.2017.06.001

Borup, J., West, R. E., Thomas, R., & Graham, C. R. (2014). Examining the impact of video feedback on instructor social presence in blended courses. *International Review of Research in Open and Distance Learning, 15*(3), 232–256. doi:10.19173/irrodl.v15i3.1821

Botturi, L., & Belfer, K. (2014). *Pedagogical patterns for online learning*. ResearchGate.

Boyte-Eckis, L., Minadeo, D. F., Bailey, S. S., & Bailey, W. C. (2018). Age, gender, and race as predictors of opting for a midterm retest: A statistical analysis of online economics students. *Journal of Business Diversity, 18*(1), 17–28.

Bozarth, J. (2020). The effects of game-based learning on student engagement and academic performance in economics. *The Journal of Economic Education, 51*(3), 217–233.

Bratt, S., Grealis, T., Harmon, O., & Tomolonis, P. (2020). Learning Tableau: A data visualization tool. *The Journal of Economic Education, 54*(3-4), 317–328. doi:10.1080/00220485.2020.1804503

Briguglio, M., Acchiardo, C. J., Mateer, D., & Geerling, W. (2020). Behavioral economics in film: Insights for educators. *Journal of Behavioral Economics for Policy, 4*(1), 17–28.

Brown, B., & Pederson, J. A. (2020). LinkedIn to classroom community: Assessing classroom community on the basis of social media usage. *Journal of Further and Higher Education, 44*(3), 341–349. doi:10.1080/0309877X.2018.1541973

Buckey, K. M. (2003). Evaluation of classroom-based, web-enhanced, and web-based distance learning nutrition courses for undergraduate nursing. *The Journal of Nursing Education, 42*(8), 367–370. doi:10.3928/0148-4834-20030801-09 PMID:12938900

Burgess, A., & Matar, E. (2020). Team-based learning (TBL): theory, planning, practice, and implementation. *Clinical Education for the Health Professions: Theory and Practice*, 1-29. doi:10.1007/978-981-13-6106-7_128-1

Burgess, A., Roberts, C., Ayton, T., & Mellis, C. (2018). Implementation of modified team-based learning within a problem based learning medical curriculum: A focus group study. *BMC Medical Education, 18*(1), 1–7. doi:10.118612909-018-1172-8 PMID:29631579

Burgess, A., Roberts, C., Lane, A. S., Haq, I., Clark, T., Kalman, E., Pappalardo, N., & Bleasel, J. (2021). Peer review in team-based learning: Influencing feedback literacy. *BMC Medical Education, 21*(1), 426. doi:10.118612909-021-02821-6 PMID:34384418

Burgess, A., van Diggele, C., Roberts, C., & Mellis, C. (2020). Team-based learning: Design, facilitation and participation. *BMC Medical Education, 20*(2), 1–7. doi:10.118612909-020-02287-y PMID:33272267

Burke, J. (2022). *Group Work in the Classroom: Types of Small Groups*. Centre for Teaching Excellence. University of Waterloo. https://uwaterloo.ca/centre-for-teaching-excellence/

Cabezudo, A., Christidis, C., da Silva, M. C., Demetriadou-Saltet, V., Halbartschlager, F., & Mihai, G. (2010). *Global education guidelines: A handbook for educators to understand and implement global education.* The North-South Centre of the Council of Europe. https://www.developmenteducation.ie/media/documents/GEguidelines-web.pdf

Cardozo, A. (2008). Motivación, aprendizaje y rendimiento académico en estudiantes del primer año universitario. *Laurus, 14*(28) 209-237. Recuperado de https://www.redalyc.org/articulo.oa?id=76111716011

Carlson, D. L., & Marshall, P. A. (2009). Learning the science of research, learning the art of teaching: Planning backwards in a college genetics course. *Bioscience Education, 13*(1), 1–9. doi:10.3108/beej.13.4

Casas, V., Carranza, G. & Ruiz, A. (2011). *Guía para la planeación didáctica en la Universidad.* México: UPN Polvo de gis.

Catalano, A. J., Torff, B., & Anderson, K. S. (2021). Transitioning to online learning during the COVID-19 pandemic: Differences in access and participation among students in disadvantaged school districts. *The International Journal of Information and Learning Technology*, *38*(2), 258–270. doi:10.1108/IJILT-06-2020-0111

Center for Teaching. (n.d.). *Team-Based Learning*. Vanderbilt University. Online available at: https://cft.vanderbilt.edu/guides-sub-pages/team-based-learning/

Cestone, C. M., Levine, R. E., & Lane, D. R. (2008). Peer assessment and evaluation in team-based learning. *New Directions for Teaching and Learning*, *2008*(116), 69–78. doi:10.1002/tl.334

Cevik, A. A., ElZubeir, M., Abu-Zidan, F. M., & Shaban, S. (2019). Team-based learning improves knowledge and retention in an emergency medicine clerkship. *International Journal of Emergency Medicine*, *12*(1), 1–8. doi:10.118612245-019-0222-2 PMID:31179926

Chad, P. (2012). The use of team-based learning as an approach to increased engagement and learning for marketing students: A case study. *Journal of Marketing Education*, *34*(2), 128–139. doi:10.1177/0273475312450388

Chandramani Bohara. (2019). *Effectiveness of GeoGebra in Teaching Geometry* [Unpublished Master's thesis]. University Campus. Kritipur, Nepal. https//elibrary.tucl.edu.np

Chan, P. E., Konrad, M., Gonzalez, V., Peters, M. T., & Ressa, V. A. (2014). The critical role of feedback in formative instructional practices. *Intervention in School and Clinic*, *50*(2), 96–104. doi:10.1177/1053451214536044

Chapman, J. (2015). *Specialization, Polymaths And The Pareto Principle In A Convergence Economy*. TechCrunch. https://techcrunch.com/2015/10/17/specialization-polymaths-and-the-pareto-principle-in-a-convergence-economy/?guccounter=1

Chen, G. M. (2011). Tweet this: A uses and gratifications perspective on how active Twitter use gratifies a need to connect with others. *Computers in Human Behavior*, *27*(2), 755–762. doi:10.1016/j.chb.2010.10.023

Chen, Z., & Cao, L. (2020). The application of virtual reality in financial education: An experimental study. *Journal of Financial Education*, *46*(1/2), 68–85.

Chhatwal, H. (2023). *Redesigning the Business Studies Curriculum of senior secondary education of Central Board of Secondary Education (CBSE), India, in the context of tuition centre in Singapore*. ResearchGate.

Childre, A., Sands, J. R., & Pope, S. T. (2009). Backward design. *Teaching Exceptional Children*, *41*(5), 6–14. doi:10.1177/004005990904100501

Choi, D. H., & Noh, G. Y. (2021). The impact of presence on learning transfer intention in virtual reality simulation game. *SAGE Open*, *11*(3). Advance online publication. doi:10.1177/21582440211032178

Christensen, C. M., Horn, M. B., & Staker, H. (2013). Is K-12 blended learning disruptive? An introduction to the theory of hybrids. Clayton Christensen Institute for Disruptive Innovation. ERIC No. ED565838.

Christensen, J., Harrison, J. L., Hollindale, J., & Wood, K. (2019). Implementing team-based learning (TBL) in accounting courses. *Accounting Education*, *28*(2), 195–219. doi:10.1080/09639284.2018.1535986

Chung, E. K., Rhee, J. A., Baik, Y. H., & A, O.-S. (2009). The effect of team-based learning in medical ethics education. *Medical Teacher*, *31*(11), 1013–1017. doi:10.3109/01421590802590553 PMID:19909042

Cleveland-Innes, M., & Wilton, D. (2018). *Guide to blended learning*. Commonwealth of Learning. https://oasis.col.org/handle/11599/3095

Cohn-Muroy, D., Flores-Lafosse, N., & Villanueva, V. (2015). Percepción del uso de una plataforma virtual de aprendizaje colaborativo en una universidad peruana: Estudio de Caso. *Comunidad Latinoamericana de Objetos de Aprendizaje, 6*(1), 71-80. Recuperado de http://www.laclo.org/papers/index.php/laclo/article/view/341

Concas, G., Marulli, F., & Pani, C. (2020). Game-based learning in finance and accounting education: A systematic literature review. *Journal of Accounting Education*, *53*, 100688.

Consejo para la Acreditación de la Educación Superior COPAES. (2017). *Programas acreditados*. Recuperado de http://www.copaes.org/Copaes2.0/

Contini, D., Di Tommaso, M. L., Muratori, C., Piazzalunga, D., & Schiavon, L. (2022). Who lost the most? Mathematics achievement during the COVID-19 pandemic. *The B.E. Journal of Economic Analysis & Policy*, *22*(2), 399–408. doi:10.1515/bejeap-2021-0447

Cress, U., Moskaliuk, J., & Jeong, H. (2016). *Mass Collaboration and Education. Computer-Supported Collaborative Learning Series* (Vol. 16). CULS.

Crittenden, V. (2005). Cross-functional education: The need for case development. February 2005. *Journal of Business Research*, *58*(7), 955–959. doi:10.1016/j.jbusres.2003.12.004

Currey, J., Eustace, P., Oldland, E., Glanville, D., & Story, I. (2015). Developing professional attributes in critical care nurses using Team-Based Learning. *Nurse Education in Practice*, *15*(3), 232–238. doi:10.1016/j.nepr.2015.01.011 PMID:25704795

Dahal, N., Pant, B. P., Shrestha, I. M., & Manandhar, N. K. (2022). Use of GeoGebra in teaching and learning geometric transformation in school mathematics. *International Journal of Interactive Mobile Technologies*, *16*(8), 65–78. doi:10.3991/ijim.v16i08.29575

Dakhi, O., Jama, J., & Irfan, D. (2020). Blended learning: A 21st century learning model at college. *International Journal of Multi Science, 1*(7), 50-65. https://multisciencejournal.com/index.php/ijm/article/view/92/72

Dale, L. R. (2002). The stock market game in economics instruction. *Journal of Entrepreneurship Education, 5*, 47–55.

Daniel, B. (2015). Big data and analytics in higher education: Opportunities and challenges. *British Journal of Educational Technology, 46*(5), 904–920. doi:10.1111/bjet.12230

Davidson, N., Major, C. H., & Michaelsen, L. K. (2014). Small-group learning in higher education—cooperative, collaborative, problem-based, and team-based learning: An introduction by the guest editors. *Journal on Excellence in College Teaching, 25*(3-4), 1–6.

Dávila, A. (2011, December). Filosofía educativa de las aulas virtuales: Caso Moodle. *Compendium (Newtown, Pa.)*, 97–105. http://www.ucla.edu.ve/dac/compendium/Revista27/Compendium_27_5.pdf

Davis McGaw, M. A. (2016). The growth of learning colleges including a case study from 2008 revisited in 2015. In E. A. Railean, G. Walker, A. Elçi, & L. Jackson (Eds.), Handbook of research on applied learning theory and design in modern education (pp. 520-544). IGI Global. doi:10.4018/978-1-4666-9634-1.ch025

Davis McGaw, M. A. (2018, November). *A global perspective on the future of education.* Keynote address presented at the National Association of State Directors of Teacher Education and Certification (NASDTEC) Conference, Minneapolis, MN.

Davis McGaw, M. A. (2019). Communities of practice: An ecosystem-based philosophy of harmony in education. In E. A. Railean (Ed.), *Handbook of Research on Ecosystem-Based Theoretical Models of Learning and Communication* (pp. 20–39). IGI Global. doi:10.4018/978-1-5225-7853-6.ch002

Davis McGaw, M. A. (2021). Designing schools as learning centers. In M. Khosrow-Pour (Ed.), *Handbook of Research on Modern Educational Technologies, Applications, and Management* (Vol. 1, pp. 359–376). IGI Global. doi:10.4018/978-1-7998-3476-2.ch022

Davis McGaw, M. A., & Evans, S. M. (2021). *Participatory pedagogy: Emerging research and opportunities.* IGI Global. doi:10.4018/978-1-5225-8964-8

De Four-Babb, J., Esnard, T., Bristol, L., Coye, T., Ibrahim-Joseph, L., & Perez, L. (2022). Managing the first wave. In F. Netswera, A. A. Woldegiyorgis, & T. Karabchuk (Eds.), *Higher education and the COVID-19 pandemic: Cross-national perspectives on the challenges and management of higher education in crisis times* (pp. 138–153). Brill. doi:10.1163/9789004520554_009

De la Mora, J. (2003). Psicología del aprendizaje, Volumen 1. México: Editorial Progreso

Dearnley, C., Rhodes, C., Roberts, P., Williams, P., & Prenton, S. (2018). Team based learning in nursing and midwifery higher education; a systematic review of the evidence for change. *Nurse Education Today, 60*, 75–83. doi:10.1016/j.nedt.2017.09.012 PMID:29045913

Della Ratta, C. B. (2015). Flipping the classroom with team-based learning in undergraduate nursing education. *Nurse Educator, 40*(2), 71–74. doi:10.1097/NNE.0000000000000112 PMID:25402712

Dello Ioio, Z. (2023). *5 reasons why digital transformation projects fail (2023)*. Enate. https://www.enate.io/blog/why-digital-transformation-projects-fail#:~:text=Technology%20is%20always%20evolving%20and,considering%20making%20their%20own%20changes

Demuyakor, J. (2021). COVID-19 pandemic and higher education: Leveraging on digital technologies and mobile applications for online learning in Ghana. *International Journal of Education, 9*(3), 26–38. doi:10.34293/education.v9i3.3904

Dierikx, M. (2021, July 1). *Factors that influence the acceptance and adoption of mobile learning applications in higher education: A systematic review*. Delft University of Technology, Bachelor Seminar of Computer Science and Engineering. https://repository.tudelft.nl/islandora/object/uuid:7bea71b8-1b64-49e7-b2d9-f0741a5fe52d/datastream/OBJ/download

Ding, N., Xu, X., & Lewis, E. (2023). Short instructional videos for the TikTok generation. *Journal of Education for Business, 98*(4), 175–185. doi:10.1080/08832323.2022.2103489

Dionicio, A. (2014). *Intervenciones pedagógicas con b-learning (presencial-aulas virtuales)*. Editorial Dunken.

Dogan, S., Çalgici, P., Arditi, D., & Gunaydin, H. (2015). *Critical success factors of partnering in the building design process. METU JFA 2015/2*. Department of Architecture, İzmir Institute of Technology.

Dolan, R. J., & Simon, H. (1997). *Power pricing: How managing price transforms the bottom line*. Simon & Schuster.

Driver, M. (2002). Exploring student perceptions of group interaction and class satisfaction in the web-enhanced classroom. *The Internet and Higher Education, 5*(1), 35–45. doi:10.1016/S1096-7516(01)00076-8

Dumont, H., Istance, D., & Benavides, F. (2010). *The Nature of Learning: Using Research to Inspire Practice*. Organization for Economic Co-operation and Development OCDE. Recuperado de https://www.oecd.org/edu/ceri/The%20Nature%20of%20Learning.Practitioner%20Guide.ESP.pdf

Dunstan, S. C. (2021). *Race, rights, and reform: Black activism in the French empire and the United States from World War I to the Cold War*. Cambridge University Press. doi:10.1017/9781108764971

Edem Adzovie, D., & Jibril, A. B. (2022). Assessment of the effects of COVID-19 pandemic on the prospects of e-learning in higher learning institutions: The mediating role of academic innovativeness and technological growth. *Cogent Education, 9*(1), 2041222. Advance online publication. doi:10.1080/2331186X.2022.2041222

Efthymiou, I. P., (2021). *Soft Skills for Children. A Guide to success for 21st century kids*. Academic Press.

Efthymiou-Egleton, I. P., Egleton, T. W. E., & Sidiropoulos, S. (2020). Artificial Intelligence (AI) in Politics: Should Political AI be Controlled? *International Journal of Innovative Science and Research Technology, 5*(2).

Efthymiou–Egleton, T. W., Sidiropoulos, S., Spanos, E., & Stougiannou, E. (2020). Big Data and Democracy. *HAPSc Policy Briefs Series*, *1*(2), 18–25. doi:10.12681/hapscpbs.26473

Efthymiou, I. P. (2020). Non-Cognitive skills and AI: A new era of learning and development. *International Case Studies Journal*, *9*(10), 42–46.

Efthymiou, I. P. (2020). Non-Cognitive Skills and AI: A New Era of Learning and Development. *International Case Studies Journal*, *9*(10), 42–46.

Egielewa, P., Idogho, P. O., Iyalomhe, F. O., & Cirella, G. T. (2022). COVID-19 and digitized education: Analysis of online learning in Nigerian higher education. *E-Learning and Digital Media*, *19*(1), 19–35. doi:10.1177/20427530211022808

Elshama, S. S. (2021). How to Apply Team-Based Learning in Medical Education? *Quantum Journal of Medical and Health Sciences*, *1*(2), 15–22.

Emerson, T. L. N., McGoldrick, K. M., & Mumford, K. J. (2012). Women and the choice to study economics. *The Journal of Economic Education*, *43*(4), 349–362. doi:10.1080/00220485.2012.714306

Erhel, S., Michinov, N., Noel, A., & Gonthier, C. (2022). Tweet to teach: Using a twitter-based instructional method to improve student motivation and academic outcomes in higher education. *The Internet and Higher Education*, *55*, 100876. doi:10.1016/j.iheduc.2022.100876

Espey, M. (2018). Enhancing critical thinking using team-based learning. *Higher Education Research & Development*, *37*(1), 15–29. doi:10.1080/07294360.2017.1344196

Estrada, R., Zaldívar, A., Mendoza, R., Nava, L., & García, O. (2013). Percepción de los estudiantes acerca de la implementación de la modalidad educativa blended learning en la Educación Superior. *Revista Electrónica de Investigación en Educación Superior, 1*(1), 1-12. Recuperado de http://sistemanodalsinaloa.gob.mx/archivoscomprobatorios/_10_articulosrevistasarbitraje/168.pdf

EURSC. (2022). *Organisation of studies*. Office of the Secretary-General of the European Schools. https://www.eursc.eu/en/European-Schools/studies/studies-organisation#:~:text=The%20European%20School%20system%20consists,seven%20years%20of%20secondary%20education

Even, R. (1993). Subject-matter knowledge and pedagogical content knowledge: Prospective secondary teachers and the function concept. *Journal for Research in Mathematics Education*, *24*(2), 94–116. doi:10.2307/749215

Fabian, M. (2021). DevSim: A PowerPoint-based choose-your own adventure game for teaching economic development. *Journal of Economics Teaching*, *6*(2), 95–105. doi:10.58311/jeconteach/bdfda3147dc90d3efb3848d659e1c0768e0a6558

Fang, L., Mishna, F., Zhang, V. F., Van Wert, M., & Bogo, M. (2014). Social media and social work education: Understanding and dealing with the new digital world. *Social Work in Health Care*, *53*(9), 800–814. doi:10.1080/00981389.2014.943455 PMID:25321930

Farias, C., & Balardini, F. (2018). Teaching social economics: Bringing the real world into the classroom and taking the classroom into the real world. *International Journal of Social Economics*, *46*(8), 960–976. doi:10.1108/IJSE-05-2018-0253

Farland, M. Z., Sicat, B. L., Franks, A. S., Pater, K. S., Medina, M. S., & Persky, A. M. (2013). Best practices for implementing team-based learning in pharmacy education. *American Journal of Pharmaceutical Education*, *77*(8), 177. doi:10.5688/ajpe778177 PMID:24159218

FastEdge. (2023). *How does educational OTT work.* FastEdge. https://www.fastedge.ai/how-does-educational-ott-work/#:~:text=Educational%20OTT%20can%20be%20thought,through%20web%2Dbased%20discussion%20boards

Fatmi, M., Hartling, L., Hillier, T., Campbell, S., Oswald, A. E., & Brown, M. (2013). The effectiveness of team-based learning on learning outcomes in health professions education: BEME Guide No. 30. *Medical Teacher*, *35*(12), e1608–e1624. doi:10.3109/0142159X.2013.849802 PMID:24245519

FeedbackFruits. (2021, August 5). *What is team-based learning*? FeedbackFruits. Retrieved from https://feedbackfruits.com/blog/what-is-team-based-learning

Felfel, H., Ayadi, O., & Masmoudi, F. (2017). Pareto Optimal Solution Selection for a Multi-Site Supply Chain Planning Problem Using the VIKOR and TOPSIS Methods. *International Journal of Service Science, Management, Engineering, and Technology*. . doi:10.4018/IJSSMET.2017070102

Ferdig, R. E., & Kennedy, K. (2014). *Handbook of research on K-12 online and blended learning*. ETC Press. http://repository.cmu.edu/etcpress/82/

Fernandez, G. C., Ruiz, E. S., Gutierrez, S. M., Gil, M. C., & Perez, F. M. (2012). Flexibility of wireless technologies in learning in robotic laboratories. In *Proceedings of the 2012 IEEE Global Engineering Education Conference (EDUCON)* (pp. 1-5). IEEE. https://doi.org/10.1109/EDUCON.2012.6201060

Fitzgerald, J. M. (2005). *A case study of a high school's development of teacher collaboration through interdisciplinary curriculum planning* (Publication No. 3173664) [Doctoral dissertation, Boston College]. ProQuest Dissertations and Theses Global.

Flores, R., & Macotela, S. (2006). *Problemas de aprendizaje en la adolesencia: experiencias en el programa alcanzando el éxito en secundaria*. UNAM.

Fox, M. E. (2023). Sarah C. Dunstan: Race, rights, and reform: Black activism in the French empire and the United States from World War I to the Cold War. *Journal of Economics, Race, and Policy*, *6*, 60–62. doi:10.100741996-022-00107-7

Fujikura, T., Takeshita, T., Homma, H., Adachi, K., Miyake, K., Kudo, M., Takizawa, T., Nagayama, H., & Hirakawa, K. (2013). Team-based learning using an audience response system: A possible new strategy for interactive medical education. *Journal of Nippon Medical School*, *80*(1), 63–69. doi:10.1272/jnms.80.63 PMID:23470808

Gagne, R. M., Briggs, L. J., & Wager, W. W. (1992). *Principles of instructional design*. https://www.hcs64.com/files/Principles%20of%20instructional%20design.pdf

Gamage, D., Fernando, S., & Perera, I. (2014). Factors affecting to effective eLearning: Learners perspective. [SCIRJ]. *Scientific Research Journal*, *2*(5), 42–48.

Gamage, K. A., Wijesuriya, D. I., Ekanayake, S. Y., Rennie, A. E., Lambert, C. G., & Gunawardhana, N. (2020). Online delivery of teaching and laboratory practices: Continuity of university programmes during COVID-19 pandemic. *Education Sciences*, *10*(10), 291. doi:10.3390/educsci10100291

Ganguli, S. (2023, August 6). Building employability skills in math courses for business and economics using UDL approach. *Journal of Economics Teaching Symposium of Economics Teaching*. http://downloads.journalofeconomicsteaching.org/SET/2023/A6Ganguli.pdf

Gannod, G. C. (2007). Work in Progress – Using podcasting in an inverted classroom. In *IEEE Frontiers in Education Conference*. IEEE. 10.1109/FIE.2007.4418119

Gao, Y., & Chen, L. (2021). The effect of gamification on learning performance in financial education: A meta-analysis. *Journal of Financial Education*, *47*(1/2), 31–53.

García-Varcárcel, A. (2011). *Integración de las TIC en la docencia universitaria*. Netbiblio.

Garduño, R. (2005). *Enseñanza virtual sobre la organización de recursos informativos digitales*. UNAM. doi:10.22201/cuib.9703231500p.2005

Geerling, W., Mateer, G. D., Wooten, J., & Damodaran, N. (2023). ChatGPT has aced the test of understanding in college economics: Now what? *The American Economist*, *68*(2), 233–245. doi:10.1177/05694345231169654

George-Walker, L. D., & Keeffe, M. (2010). Self-determined blended learning: A case study of blended learning design. *Higher Education Research & Development*, *29*(1), 1–13. doi:10.1080/07294360903277380

Gherheş, V., Stoian, C. E., Fărcaşiu, M. A., & Stanici, M. (2021). E-learning vs. face-to-face learning: Analyzing students' preferences and behaviors. *Sustainability (Basel)*, *13*(8), 4381. Advance online publication. doi:10.3390u13084381

Giachetti, R. (2012). *A Flexible Approach to Realize an Enterprise Architecture* [Paper Presentation]. New Challenges in Systems Engineering and Architecting. Conference on Systems Engineering Research (CSER), St. Louis, MO. 10.1016/j.procs.2012.01.031

Gill, S. S., Xu, M., Patros, P., Wu, H., Kaur, R., Kaur, K., Fuller, S., Singh, M., Arora, P., Parlikad, A. K., Stankovski, V., Abraham, A., Shosh, S. K., Lutfiyya, H., Kanhere, S. S., Bahsoon, R., Rana, O., Dustdar, S., Sakellarious, R., ... Buyya, R. (2024). Transformative effects of ChatGPT on modern education: Emerging era of AI Chatbots. *Internet of Things and Cyber-Physical Systems*, *4*, 19–23. doi:10.1016/j.iotcps.2023.06.002

Gleason, B. L., Peeters, M. J., Resman-Targoff, B. H., Karr, S., McBane, S., Kelley, K., Thomas, T., & Denetclaw, T. H. (2011). An active-learning strategies primer for achieving ability-based educational outcomes. *American Journal of Pharmaceutical Education*, *75*(9), 186. doi:10.5688/ajpe759186 PMID:22171114

Goffe, W. L., & Sosin, K. (2010). Teaching with technology: May you live in interesting times. *The Journal of Economic Education*, *36*(3), 278–291. doi:10.3200/JECE.36.3.278-291

Goh, S. H., Di Gangi, P. M., & Gunnells, K. (2020). Applying team-based learning in online introductory information systems courses. *Journal of Information Systems Education*, *31*(1), 1–11. https://aisel.aisnet.org/jise/vol31/iss1/1

Goosen, L. (2015). Educational technologies for an ICT4D MOOC in the 21st century. In D. Nwaozuzu, & S. Mnisi (Ed.), *Proceedings of the South Africa International Conference on Educational Technologies* (pp. 37-48). Pretoria: African Academic Research Forum.

Goosen, L. (2008). A brief history of choosing first programming languages. In J. Impagliazzo (Ed.), *History of Computing and Education 3* (Vol. 269, pp. 167–170). Springer. doi:10.1007/978-0-387-09657-5_11

Goosen, L. (2018a). Ethical data management and research integrity in the context of e-schools and community engagement. In C. Sibinga (Ed.), *Ensuring Research Integrity and the Ethical Management of Data* (pp. 14–45). IGI Global. doi:10.4018/978-1-5225-2730-5.ch002

Goosen, L. (2018b). Ethical information and communication technologies for development solutions: Research integrity for massive open online courses. In C. Sibinga (Ed.), *Ensuring Research Integrity and the Ethical Management of Data* (pp. 155–173). IGI Global. doi:10.4018/978-1-5225-2730-5.ch009

Goosen, L. (2019). Research on technology-supported teaching and learning for autism. In L. Makewa, B. Ngussa, & J. Kuboja (Eds.), *Technology-Supported Teaching and Research Methods for Educators* (pp. 88–110). IGI Global. doi:10.4018/978-1-5225-5915-3.ch005

Goosen, L., & Naidoo, L. (2014). Computer lecturers using their institutional LMS for ICT education in the cyber world. In C. Burger, & K. Naudé (Ed.), *Proceedings of the 43rd Conference of the Southern African Computer Lecturers' Association (SACLA)* (pp. 99-108). Port Elizabeth: Nelson Mandela Metropolitan University.

Gravetter, F. J., & Forzano, L. B. (2015). Experimental designs: Withinsubjects design. In *Research Methods for the Behavioral Sciences* (pp. 249–278). Cengage Learning.

Green, A., & de Bodisco, C. (2020). Using team-based learning in discussion and writing classes. *International Review of Economics Education*, *35*, 100195. doi:10.1016/j.iree.2020.100195

Grossman, P. L. (1990). *The making of a teacher: Teacher knowledge and teacher education*. Academic Press.

Grossman, P. L., & McDonald, M. (2008). Back to the future: Directions for research in teaching and teacher education. *American Educational Research Journal, 45*(1), 184–205. doi:10.3102/0002831207312906

Gualtieri, R., Dille, K., & Karlaftis, V. (2020). Game-based learning for financial education: A systematic review of empirical research. *Financial Counseling and Planning, 31*(1), 83–97.

Guerriero, S. (2014). *Teachers' pedagogical knowledge and the teaching profession: Background report and project objectives*. OECD. https://www.oecd.org/education/ceri/Background_document_to_Symposium_ITEL-FINAL.pdf

Guerriero, S. (2017). Teachers' pedagogical knowledge: What it is and how it functions. In S. Guerriero (Ed.), *Pedagogical Knowledge and the Changing Nature of the Teaching Profession*. OECD., doi:10.1787/9789264270695-6-en

Guerriero, S. (Ed.). (2017). *Teachers' pedagogical knowledge: What it is and how it functions in Pedagogical Knowledge and the Changing Nature of the Teaching Profession. Educational Research and Innovation*. OECD Publishing. doi:10.1787/9789264270695-en

Gunesekera, A. I., Bao, Y., & Kibelloh, M. (2019). The role of usability on e-learning user interactions and satisfaction: A literature review. *Journal of Systems and Information Technology, 21*(3), 368–394. doi:10.1108/JSIT-02-2019-0024

Haidet, P., Kubitz, K., & McCormack, W. T. (2014). Analysis of the Team-Based Learning Literature: TBL Comes of Age. *Journal on Excellence in College Teaching, 25*(3&4), 303–333. PMID:26568668

Haidet, P., O'Malley, K. J., & Richards, B. (2008). An initial experience with "team learning" in medical education. *Academic Medicine, 83*(10), 10–16. doi:10.1097/ACM.0b013e318183eafd PMID:11788321

Hair, J., Anderson, R., Tatham, R., & Black, W. (1999). *Análisis multivariante*. Prentice Hall.

Halverson, H. (2012). *Educational innovation at UW-Madison: The "Backward Design" framework* [Video]. https://www.youtube.com/watch?v=cveylXCpUmw&t=453s

Han, J., Park, D., Hua, M., & Childs, P. (2021). Is group work beneficial for producing creative designs in STEM design education? *International Journal of Technology and Design Education*. Advance online publication. doi:10.100710798-021-09709-y

Harmon, O. R., & Tomolonis, P. A. (2019). The effects of using Facebook as a discussion forum in an online principles of economics course: Results of a randomized controlled trial. *International Review of Economics Education, 30*, 100157. doi:10.1016/j.iree.2019.100157

Harmon, O., & Szarka, R. (2018). Using Google drawings to create homework exercises. *Journal of Economics Teaching, 2*(2), 68–78. doi:10.58311/jeconteach/cb6e720d514867854cefdc6b43a098f676b69bd6

Hayashi, K., Shibata, S., Inoue, E., Adachi, S., & Iba, T. (2022). Online Education Patterns, Part 1: Patterns for Linking Separate Worlds. *EuroPLoP'21: 26th European Conference on Pattern Languages of Programs*, 1–16. 10.1145/3489449.3490003

Heafner, T. L., VanFossen, P., & Fitchett, P. G. (2016). *A multilevel model to identify predictors of students' achievement on NAEP-Economics*. Paper presented at the annual meeting of the American Education Research Association, Washington, DC.

Helwa, H. S. (2015). Using Computer mediated Team based Learning for Developing EFL Prospective Teachers' Presentation Skills and reducing their Foreign Language Anxiety. *Arabic Studies in Education and Psychology, 58*(58), 345-388. doi:10.12816/0022419

Henderson, J., & Drewes, A. (2020). *Teaching climate change in the United States*. Taylor and Francis. doi:10.4324/9780367179496

Henson, R. K., & Roberts, J. K. (2006). Use of exploratory factor analysis in published research: Common errors and some comment on improved practice. *Educational and Psychological Measurement, 66*(3), 393–416. doi:10.1177/0013164405282485

Hettler, P. L. (2015). Student demographics and the impact of team-based learning. *International Advances in Economic Research, 21*(4), 413–422. doi:10.100711294-015-9539-7

Hibrida, A. R., & Sumual, T. E. (2022, August). Educational and teaching performance of educators at the Faculty of Economics and Business, Manado State University (UNIMA): Analysis of professional competence and motivation. *Journal of International Conference Proceedings, 5*(2), 64–75. doi:10.32535/jicp.v5i2.1671

Hiebert, J., & Morris, A. K. (2012). Teaching, rather than teachers, as a path toward improving classroom instruction. *Journal of Teacher Education, 63*(2), 92–102. doi:10.1177/0022487111428328

Hine, G. S. C. (2013). The importance of action research in teacher education programs. In *Design, develop, evaluate: The core of the learning. environment. Proceedings of the 22nd Annual Teaching Learning Forum, 7-8 February 2013*. Murdoch University. http://ctl.curtin.edu.au/professional_development/conferences/tlf/tlf2013/refereed/hine.html

Hmelo-Silver, C. E. (2004). Problem-based learning: What and how do students learn? *Educational Psychology Review, 16*(3), 235–266. doi:10.1023/B:EDPR.0000034022.16470.f3

Hoffer, A., & Beckstrom, A. (2019). University and high school economics educators partnership: A model from La Crosse, Wisconsin. In Teaching Economics: Perspectives on Innovative Economics Education (pp. 89-96). Springer. doi:10.1007/978-3-030-20696-3_8

Hoic-Bozic, N., Mornar, V., & Boticki, I. (2008). A blended learning approach to course design and implementation. *IEEE Transactions on Education, 52*(1), 19–30. doi:10.1109/TE.2007.914945

Holilah, H., Girsang, A., & Saragih, M. (2019). *Designing IT Blue Print Academic System on Higher Education with Togaf. Journal: Advances in Science*. Technology and Engineering Systems Journal. doi:10.25046/aj040232

Holton, E. F. III, Coco, M. L., Lowe, J. L., & Dutsch, J. V. (2006). Blended delivery strategies for competency-based training. *Advances in Developing Human Resources*, *8*(2), 210–228. doi:10.1177/1523422305286153

Hoogerheide, V., van Wermeskerken, M., Loyens, S. M., & van Gog, T. (2016). Learning from video modeling examples: Content kept equal, adults are more effective models than peers. *Learning and Instruction*, *44*, 22–30. doi:10.1016/j.learninstruc.2016.02.004

Horn, M. B., & Staker, H. (2011). *The rise of K-12 blended learning*. Innosight Institute. https://www.christenseninstitute.org/wp-content/uploads/2013/04/The-rise-of-K-12-blended-learning.pdf

Horn, M. B., & Staker, H. (2014). *Blended: Using disruptive innovation to improve schools*. Jossey-Bass.

Hosseini, S. M. H. (2014). Competitive team-based learning versus group investigation with reference to the language proficiency of Iranian EFL intermediate students. *International Journal of Instruction*, *7*(1), 37–47. https://dergipark.org.tr/en/pub/eiji/issue/5136/69994

Hrastinski, S. (2019). What do we mean by blended learning? *TechTrends*, *63*(5), 564–569. doi:10.100711528-019-00375-5

Hrynchak, P., & Batty, H. (2012). The Educational Theory Basis of Team-Based Learning. *Medical Teacher*, *34*(10), 796–801. doi:10.3109/0142159X.2012.687120 PMID:22646301

Hsu, C. C., & Lu, H. P. (2021). Learning effects and engagement of gamification in finance and economics education. *Journal of Interactive Learning Research*, *32*(2), 183–202.

Huang, C. K., & Lin, C. Y. (2017). Flipping business education: Transformative use of team-based learning in human resource management classrooms. *Journal of Educational Technology & Society*, *20*(1), 323–336.

Hussain, O., Dillon, Th., Chang, E., & Hussain, F. (2010). Transactional risk-based decision making system in e-business interactions. *International Journal of ComputSystSci & Eng*, *2010*(1), 15–28.

Inayati, R., Sri Handayani, S., Kustiandi, J., Haryono, A., & Wahyono, H. (2010). *The Analysis of the Difficulty in Learning Economics Subject Experienced By Students of Favored State Senior High Schools in City of Malang*. Knowledge E Publishing. https://knepublishing.com/index.php/Kne-Social/article/view/1884/4497 doi:10.18502/kss.v3i3.1884

Jääskä, E., & Aaltonen, K. (2022). Teachers' experiences of using game-based learning methods in project management higher education. *Project Leadership and Society*, *3*(1), 100041. doi:10.1016/j.plas.2022.100041

Jacobson, T. E. (2012). Team-based learning in an information literacy course. *Communications in Information Literacy*, *5*(2), 82–101. doi:10.15760/comminfolit.2012.5.2.105

Jarjoura, C., Abou Tayeh, P., & Zgheib, N. K. (2015). Using team-based learning to teach grade 7 biology: Student satisfaction and improved performance. *Journal of Biological Education, 49*(4), 401–419. doi:10.1080/00219266.2014.967277

Jeffrey, L. M., Milne, J., Suddaby, G., & Higgins, A. (2014). Blended learning: How teachers balance the blend of online and classroom components. *Journal of Information Technology Education, 13*(1), 121–140. doi:10.28945/1968

Johnson, G. B. (2013). *Student perceptions of the flipped classroom* [Master's thesis]. The University of British Columbia.

Jones, M. D., & Baltzersen, M. (2017). Using twitter for economics business case discussions in large lectures. *International Review of Economics Education, 26*, 14–18. doi:10.1016/j.iree.2017.08.001

Jonkers, H., Band, I., & Quartel, D. (2012a). *ArchiSurance Case Study*. The Open Group.

Joshi, N. R. (2017). *Students Achievement in Trigonometry Teaching Through GeoGebra* [Unpublished Master thesis]. University campus, Kritipur.

Jurdak, M. E. (2006). Contrasting perspectives and performance of high school students on problem solving in real world, situated, and school contexts. *Educational Studies in Mathematics, 63*(3), 283–301. doi:10.100710649-005-9008-y

Kang, H. Y., & Kim, H. R. (2021). Impact of blended learning on learning outcomes in the public healthcare education course: A review of flipped classroom with team-based learning. *BMC Medical Education, 21*(1), 1–8. doi:10.118612909-021-02508-y PMID:33509176

Kaplan, S., Leung, M., & Steinberg, R. (2016). *Teaching Economics with Dynamic Visualization and Data Analysis Tools*. https://pubmed.ncbi.nlm.nih.gov/28252210/

Kaplan, A. M., & Haenlein, M. (2011). The early bird catches the news: Nine things you should know about micro-blogging. *Business Horizons, 54*(2), 105–113. doi:10.1016/j.bushor.2010.09.004

Kasparian, C., & Namazian, A. (2020). Financial literacy and gamification: A comprehensive review of the literature. *Journal of Financial Education, 46*(1/2), 195–220.

Kaushik, A., Kumar, A., & Biswas, P. (Eds.). (2019). *Handbook of research on emerging trends and technologies in library and information science*. IGI Global. doi:10.4018/978-1-5225-9825-1

Keengwe, J., Onchwari, G., & Agamba, J. (2014b). Promoting effective e-learning practices through the constructivist pedagogy. *Education and Information Technologies, 19*(4), 887–898. doi:10.100710639-013-9260-1

Keengwe, J., Onchwari, G., & Oigara, J. N. (Eds.). (2014a). *Promoting Active Learning through the Flipped Classroom Model*. IGI Global. doi:10.4018/978-1-4666-4987-3

Keller, J. M. (2016). Motivation, learning, and technology: Applying the ARCS-V motivation model. *Participatory Educational Research, 3*(2), 1-13. http://www.perjournal.com/archieve/issue_3_2/1-per_16-06_volume_3_issue_2_page_1_15.pdf

Keller, J. M. (1987). Development and use of the ARCS model of Instructional Design. *Journal of Instruction Development, 10*(3), 2–10. doi:10.1007/BF02905780

Kember, D. (1995). *Open learning courses for adults: A model of student progress.* Educational Technology Publications.

Kersten, M. (2021). *Introducing SAFe® 5.* Your Operating System for Business Agility. Scaled Agile Inc.

Khatkhate, D. (2009). *Harry Johnson: Portrait of a Polymath-A Life in Economics by Donald Moggridge.* EPW. https://www.epw.in/journal/2009/51/review-article-book-reviews/harry-johnson-portrait-polymath.html

Kim, J., & Lennon, Sh. (2017). *Descriptive Content Analysis on E-Service Research. International Journal of Service Science, Management, Engineering, and Technology.* doi:10.4018/IJSSMET.2017010102

Kirschner, P. A., & Karpinski, A. C. (2010). Facebook® and academic performance. *Computers in Human Behavior, 26*(6), 1237–1245. doi:10.1016/j.chb.2010.03.024

Koehler, M. J., Mishra, P., Kereluik, K., Shin, T. S., & Graham, C. R. (2014). The technological pedagogical content knowledge framework. In J. Spector, M. Merrill, J. Elen, & M. Bishop (Eds.), *Handbook of Research on Educational Communications and Technology.* Springer. doi:10.1007/978-1-4614-3185-5_9

Kofoed, M. S., Gebhart, L., Gilmore, D., & Moschitto, R. (2021). *Zooming to class?: Experimental evidence on college students' online learning during COVID-19* (IZA DP No. 14356). https://docs.iza.org/dp14356.pdf

Kolb, A., & Kolb, D. (2005). Learning styles and learning space: Enhancing experiential learning in higher education. *Academy of Management Learning & Education, 4*(2), 193–212. doi:10.5465/amle.2005.17268566

Kolb, D. A. (1984). *Experiential learning: Experience as the source of learning and development.* Prentice-Hall.

König, J., Blömeke, S., Klein, P., Suhl, U., Busse, A., & Kaiser, G. (2014). Is teachers' general pedagogical knowledge a premise for noticing and interpreting classroom situations? A video-based assessment approach. *Teaching and Teacher Education, 38*, 76–88. doi:10.1016/j.tate.2013.11.004

König, J., Blömeke, S., Paine, L., Schmidt, W. H., & Hsieh, F. J. (2011). General pedagogical knowledge of future middle school teachers: On the complex ecology of teacher education in the United States, Germany, and Taiwan. *Journal of Teacher Education, 62*(2), 188–201. doi:10.1177/0022487110388664

König, J., Jäger-Biela, D. J., & Glutsch, N. (2020). Adapting to online teaching during COVID-19 school closure: Teacher education and teacher competence effects among early career teachers in Germany. *European Journal of Teacher Education*, *43*(4), 608–622. doi:10.1080/02619768.2020.1809650

Koppe, Ch., van Eekeleny, M., & Hoppenbrouwersz, S. (2015). Improving Student Group Work with Collaboration. Patterns: A Case Study. In *2015 IEEE/ACM 37th IEEE International Conference on Software Engineering*. IEEE. https://ieeexplore.ieee.org/document/7202977

Kořistová, M., & Spiratos, C. (2021). *Navigation user interface design in e-commerce and its impact on customers' satisfaction: A mixed-methods study analysing the impact of different menu styles and user interface elements*. Jönköping University.

Kremeňová, I., Fabuš, J., & Koncova, D. (2022). How the perception of educators of the Faculty of Operation and Economics of Transport and Communications regarding forms of teaching changed during the COVID-19 pandemic in 2020 and 2021. In *INTED2022 Proceedings* (pp. 5570–5574). IATED. doi:10.21125/inted.2022.1435

Kumar, A., Krishnamurthi, R., Bhatia, S., Kaushik, K., Ahuja, N. J., Nayyar, A., & Masud, M. (2021). Blended learning tools and practices: A comprehensive analysis. *IEEE Access : Practical Innovations, Open Solutions*, *9*, 85151–85197. doi:10.1109/ACCESS.2021.3085844

Lai, H. (2021). Research on the intelligent teaching model of principles of economics course under the new media. *Journal of Contemporary Educational Research*, *5*(8), 131–135. Advance online publication. doi:10.26689/jcer.v5i8.2445

Lakhal, S., Heilporn, G., & Khechine, H. (2021, December). External factors explaining students' persistence in online courses in higher education: A study among two French-speaking universities in Canada. *The Open/Technology in Education, Society, and Scholarship Association Conference*, *1*(1), 1–8. doi:10.18357/otessac.2021.1.1.50

Lakhal, S., & Khechine, H. (2021). Technological factors of students' persistence in online courses in higher education: The moderating role of gender, age and prior online course experience. *Education and Information Technologies*, *26*(3), 3347–3373. doi:10.100710639-020-10407-w

Lakhal, S., Khechine, H., & Mukamurera, J. (2021). Explaining persistence in online courses in higher education: A difference-in-differences analysis. *International Journal of Educational Technology in Higher Education*, *18*(1), 1–32. doi:10.118641239-021-00251-4

Lalima, & Dangwal, K. L. (2017). Blended learning: An innovative approach. *Universal Journal of Educational Research, 5*(1), 129-136. doi:10.13189/ujer.2017.050116

Lamichhane, D. (2017). *Effectiveness of GeoGebra on students achievement in Geometry* [Unpublished thesis]. University Campus. Kritipur.

Lampe, N. M. (2023). Teaching with TikTok in Online Sociology of Sex and Gender Courses. *Teaching Sociology*, *51*(4), 323–335. Advance online publication. doi:10.1177/0092055X231159091

Lapitan, L. D. Jr, Tiangco, C. E., Sumalinog, D. A. G., Sabarillo, N. S., & Diaz, J. M. (2021). An effective blended online teaching and learning strategy during the COVID-19 pandemic. *Education for Chemical Engineers*, *35*(1), 116–131. doi:10.1016/j.ece.2021.01.012

Learning, E. L. M. (n.d.). *What is Blended Learning? A Guide to Everything You Need to Know*. Retrieved from https://elmlearning.com/hub/elearning/blended-learning/

Lederman, N. G., & Gess-Newsome, J. (1992). Do subject matter knowledge, pedagogical knowledge, and pedagogical content knowledge constitute the ideal gas law of science teaching? *Journal of Science Teacher Education*, *3*(1), 16–20. https://www.jstor.org/stable/43155929. doi:10.1007/BF02614732

Lee Shing, C., Mohd. Saat, R., & Loke, S. H. (2015). The knowledge of teaching – Pedagogical Content Knowledge (PCK). *The Malaysian Online Journal of Educational Science, 3*(3). Retrieved from https://files.eric.ed.gov/fulltext/EJ1085915.pdf

Lee, Y., Capraro, R. M., & Capraro, M. M. (2018). Mathematics teachers' subject matter knowledge and pedagogical content knowledge in problem posing. *International Electronic Journal of Mathematics Education*, *13*(2), 75–90. doi:10.12973/iejme/2698 PMID:31824466

Leijen, A., Malva, L., Pedaste, M., & Mikser, R. (2022). What constitutes teachers' general pedagogical knowledge and how it can be assessed: A literature review. *Teachers and Teaching*, *28*(2), 206–225. doi:10.1080/13540602.2022.2062710

Lerner, S., Magrane, D., & Friedman, E. (2009). Teaching teamwork in medical education. *Mount Sinai Journal of Medicine: A Journal of Translational and Personalized Medicine: A Journal of Translational and Personalized Medicine, 76*(4), 318-329. doi:10.1002/msj.20129

Lew, C., & Saville, A. (2021). Game-based learning: Teaching principles of economics and investment finance through *Monopoly*. *International Journal of Management Education*, *19*(3), 100567. Advance online publication. doi:10.1016/j.ijme.2021.100567

Ley, K., & Young, D. B. (2001). Instructional principles for self-regulation. *Educational Technology Research and Development*, *49*(2), 93–103. doi:10.1007/BF02504930

Light, D., & Pierson, E. (2014). Increasing student engagement in math: The use of Khan Academy in Chilean classrooms. *International Journal of Education and Development using ICT, 10*(2), 103-119. https://www.learntechlib.org/p/147457/

Lin, W. S., & Wang, C. H. (2012). Antecedences to continued intentions of adopting e-learning system in blended learning instruction: A contingency framework based on models of information system success and task-technology fit. *Computers & Education*, *58*(1), 88–99. doi:10.1016/j.compedu.2011.07.008

Long, T., Cummins, J., & Waugh, M. (2017). Use of the flipped classroom instructional model in higher education: Instructors' perspectives. *Journal of Computing in Higher Education*, *29*(1), 179–200. doi:10.100712528-016-9119-8

Loo, J. L. (2013). Guided and team-based learning for chemical information literacy. *Journal of Academic Librarianship, 39*(3), 252–259. doi:10.1016/j.acalib.2013.01.007

Lowry, A. E. (2007). *Effects of online versus face-to-face professional development with a team-based learning community approach on teachers' application of a new instructional practice.* The Johns Hopkins University.

Maatuk, A. M., ElBerkawi, E. K., AlJawarneh, S., Rashaideh, H., & Alharbi, H. (2022). The COVID-19 pandemic and e-learning: Challenges and opportunities from the perspective of students and instructors. *Journal of Computing in Higher Education, 34*(1), 21–38. doi:10.100712528-021-09274-2 PMID:33967563

MacEntee, V., & Lewis, B. (2004). Web-enhanced course. *Issues in Informing Science & Information Technology, 1*, 951–964. doi:10.28945/790

Madden, M., Lenhart, A., Cortesti, S., Gasser, U., Duggan, M., Smith, A., & Beaton, M. (2013). *Teens, social media, and privacy.* Pew Research Center. https://www.pewresearch.org/internet/2013/05/21/teens-social-media-and-privacy/

Malode, V. D. (2022). *Emerging trends and technologies in library and information services in new academic environment.* Akshara Multidisciplinary Research Journal. doi:10.11648/j.ajist.20220601.12

Malone, T. W. (1981). Toward a theory of intrinsically motivating instruction. *Cognitive Science, 4*(4), 333–369. https://onlinelibrary.wiley.com/doi/pdf/10.1207/s15516709cog0504_2. doi:10.120715516709cog0504_2

Manzano-Leon, A., Camacho-Lazarraga, P., Guerrero, M. A., Guerrero-Puerta, L., Aguilar-Parra, J. M., Triguero, R., & Alias, A. (2021). Between level up and game over: A systematic literature review of gamification in education. *Sustainability (Basel), 13*(4), 2247. doi:10.3390u13042247

Margolis, A. R., Porter, A. L., & Pitterle, M. E. (2017). Best practices for use of blended learning. *American Journal of Pharmaceutical Education, 81*(3), 1–8. doi:10.5688/ajpe81349 PMID:28496269

Markides, C. (2011, March). Crossing the Chasm: How to Convert Relevant Research Into Managerially Useful Research. *The Journal of Applied Behavioral Science, 47*(1), 121–134. doi:10.1177/0021886310388162

Marques, M. A., Viegas, M. C., Costa-Lobo, M. C., Fidalgo, A. V., Alves, G. R., Rocha, J. S., & Gustavsson, I. (2013). How remote labs impact on course outcomes: Various practices using VISIR. *IEEE Transactions on Education, 57*(3), 151–159. doi:10.1109/TE.2013.2284156

Martinez, A. R. (2017). *The Effect of Using GeoGebra on students achievement in Secondary Mathematics* [Unpublished Master thesis]. California State University, Monterey.

Martínez, F. (2005). *E-aprendizaje en bibliotecología: perspectivas globales.* UNAM. doi:10.22201/cuib.9703227414p.2005

Matthews, M. (2018). *Using Data Analytics Tools to Teach Economics*. https://www.researchgate.net/publication/272566756_Qualitative_Data_Analysis_A_Methods_Sourcebook

McKibben, B., Anderson, R., & McKenzie, M. (2020). *Teaching climate change in the United States*. Taylor and Francis. Retrieved from https://api.taylorfrancis.com/content/books/mono/download?identifierName=DOI&identifierValue=10.4324/9780367179496&type=googlePDF

McKnight, K. S. (2014). *Common Core literacy strategies for ELA, history/social studies, and the humanities, grades 6-12: Strategies to deepen content knowledge (grades 6-12)*. John Wiley & Sons Inc.

McLaughlin, J. E., Roth, M. T., Glatt, D. M., Gharkholonarehe, N., Davidson, C. A., Griffin, L. M., Esserman, D. A., & Mumper, R. J. (2014). The Flipped Classroom: A Course Redesign to Foster Learning and Engagement in a Health Professions School. *Academic Medicine*, *89*(2), 236–243. doi:10.1097/ACM.0000000000000086 PMID:24270916

McOwen, K. S., & Farmakidis, A. L. (2020). A snapshot of medical student education in the United States and Canada: Reports from 145 schools. *Academic Medicine*, *95*(9, suppl), S1–S606.

Meabon Bartow, S. (2014). Teaching with social media: Disrupting present-day public education. *Educational Studies (Ames)*, *50*(1), 36–64. doi:10.1080/00131946.2013.866954

Megahed, N., & Hassan, A. (2022). A blended learning strategy: Reimagining the post-Covid-19 architectural education. *Archnet-IJAR: International Journal of Architectural Research*, *16*(1), 184–202. doi:10.1108/ARCH-04-2021-0081

Menkhoff, T., Chay, Y. W., Bengtsson, M. L., Woodard, C. J., & Gan, B. (2015). Incorporating microblogging ("tweeting") in higher education: Lessons learnt in a knowledge management course. *Computers in Human Behavior*, *51*, 1295–1302. doi:10.1016/j.chb.2014.11.063

Michael, N. A., & Libarkin, J. C. (2016). Understanding by Design: Mentored implementation of Backward Design methodology at the university level. *Perspectives*, *42*(2), 44–52. https://files.eric.ed.gov/fulltext/EJ1126353.pdf

Michaelsen, L. K., Knight, A. B., & Fink, L. D. (2002). *Team-based learning: A transformative use of small groups*. Greenwood Publishing Group.

Michaelsen, L. K., Knight, A. B., & Fink, L. D. (2004). *Team-Based Learning: A Transformative Use of Small Groups in College Teaching*. Stylus Publishing, LLC.

Michaelsen, L. K., & Sweet, M. (2008). The essential elements of team-based learning. *New Directions for Teaching and Learning*, *2008*(116), 7–27. doi:10.1002/tl.330

Michaelsen, L. K., & Sweet, M. (2012). Fundamental principles and practices of team-based learning. In L. K. Michaelsen, A. Knight, & L. D. Fink (Eds.), *Team-based learning for health professions education: A guide to using small groups for improving learning* (pp. 9–34). Stylus Publishing, LLC.

Michaelsen, L., & Sweet, M. (2004). *Team-based learning*. Sterling.

Middaugh, E., Felton, M., & Fan, H. (2023). What is in a Tweet? How Platform Features Facilitate and Constrain Civic Discourse and What It Means for Teaching Civic Media Literacy. In *Education in the Age of Misinformation: Philosophical and Pedagogical Explorations* (pp. 203–223). Springer International Publishing. doi:10.1007/978-3-031-25871-8_11

Middleditch, P., Moindrot, W., & Rudkin, S. (2022). Teaching with Twitter: An extension to the traditional learning environment. *International Review of Economics Education, 41*, 100252. doi:10.1016/j.iree.2022.100252

Middleton-Green, L., & Ashelford, S. (2013). Using team-based learning in teaching undergraduate pathophysiology for nurses. *Health and Social Care Education*, 2(2), 53–58. doi:10.11120/hsce.2013.00031

Mintah, P. C. (2018). *The influence of emotional intelligence on the academic performance of teacher trainees in the Central Region of Ghana* [PhD thesis]. University of Cape Coast.

Mockeviciute, A., El Baroudi, S., Gorbatov, S., & Khapova, S. N. (2022). When does feedback enhance performance in teams?: A systematic literature review and future research agenda. In *Managing team centricity in modern organizations* (pp. 115–164). Information Age Publishing.

Montoro, A. (2015). *Motivación y matemáticas: experiencias de flujo en estudiantes de maestro de educación primaria (Tesis de doctorado)*. Universidad Almería. Recuperado de https://www.educacion.gob.es/teseo/imprimirFicheroTesis.do;jsessionid=5ABDC9806028E030AE845623 8CCD715D

Moodle. (2022). *Moodle (Página oficial)*. Recuperado de https://moodle.org/

MoodleMoot. (2017). *MoodleMoot (Página oficial)*. Recuperado de https://moodlemoot.org

Morse, M. (2020). *Making a Difference Through Collaboration: A Case Study Exploring Cross-Functional Collaboration Within an Urban High School in the Northeastern United States* [PhD thesis]. The College of Professional Studies of Northeastern University.

Mosher, G. A. (2021). *Formation and development of effective student teams to facilitate team-based learning. 2013 North Midwest Section Meeting.*

Moskal, P., Dziuban, C., & Hartman, J. (2013). Blended learning: A dangerous idea? *The Internet and Higher Education, 18*, 15–23. doi:10.1016/j.iheduc.2012.12.001

Motlagh, M. K., Najarkolai, A. R., & Keshmiri, F. (2015). Team-Based learning in medical universities: Infrastructure and requirements. *Thrita, 4*(3), e29549. doi:10.5812/thrita.29549

Mukiri, M. I. (2012). *Feasibility of using GeoGebra in to the teaching learning of geometry concepts in secondary school* [Master thesis]. Kenya University, Kenya.

Müller, F. B., & Wulf, T. (2022). Blended learning environments and learning outcomes: The mediating role of flow experience. *International Journal of Management Education, 20*(3), 100694. Advance online publication. doi:10.1016/j.ijme.2022.100694

Murzi, H. G. (2014, June). Team-based learning theory applied to engineering education: A systematic review of literature. In *2014 ASEE Annual Conference & Exposition* (pp. 24-1175). 10.18260/1-2--23108

Namyssova, G., Tussupbekova, G., Helmer, J., Malone, K., Mir, A., & Jonbekova, D. (2019). Challenges and benefits of blended learning in higher education. *International Journal of Technology in Education*, *2*(1), 22–31.

Neuman, K., Kind, V., & Harms, U. (2018). Probing the amalgam: The relationship between science teachers' content, pedagogical and pedagogical content knowledge. *International Journal of Science Education*, *41*(7), 1–15. doi:10.1080/09500693.2018.1497217

Ng, D. T. K. (2022). Online lab design for aviation engineering students in higher education: A pilot study. *Interactive Learning Environments*, *30*(3), 1–18. doi:10.1080/10494820.2022.2034888

Nguyen, H., & Diederich, M. (2023). Facilitating knowledge construction in informal learning: A study of TikTok scientific, educational videos. *Computers & Education*, *205*, 104896. doi:10.1016/j.compedu.2023.104896

Nungu, L., Mukama, E., & Nsabayezu, E. (2023). Online collaborative learning and cognitive presence in mathematics and science education. Case study of University of Rwanda, College of Education. *Education and Information Technologies*, 1–20. doi:10.100710639-023-11607-w PMID:36779197

Nunnally, J. (1978). *Psychometric theory* (2nd ed.). McGraw-Hill.

OCDE. (2005). E-learning in Tertiary Education Where Do We Stand? Where Do We Stand? OCDE.

Odhier, P. O., Ajowi, J. O., & Mwebi, B. (2019). Investigation on contributions of principals on school machinery and equipment management in secondary schools in Kenya. *International Journal of Novel Research in Humanity and Social Sciences*, *6*(5), 73–88.

Odongo, C. O., & Talbert-Slagle, K. (2019). Training the next generation of Africa's doctors: Why medical schools should embrace the team-based learning pedagogy. *BMC Medical Education*, *19*(1), 1–8. doi:10.118612909-019-1845-y PMID:31699081

OECD. (2005). *Teachers Matter: Attracting, Developing, and Retaining Effective Teachers*. OECD Publishing.

Ofstad, W., & Brunner, L. J. (2013). Team-based learning in pharmacy education. *American Journal of Pharmaceutical Education*, *77*(4), 70. doi:10.5688/ajpe77470 PMID:23716738

Okediran, O. O., Fajobi, M. O., Onawumi, A. S., Fajobi, D. T., Awoyemi, E. A., & Ojediran, J. T. (2021). Adaptive neuro-fuzzy modelling and prediction of academic performance of online distance learners in the era of COVID-19. *International Journal of Multidisciplinary Research and Development*, *8*(4), 120–128.

Olapiriyakul, K., & Scher, J. M. (2006). A guide to establishing hybrid learning courses: Employing information technology to create a new learning experience, and a case study. *The Internet and Higher Education*, *9*(4), 287–301. doi:10.1016/j.iheduc.2006.08.001

Olinghouse, N. (2008). *Designing lessons for diverse learners.* https://edwp.educ.msu.edu/te/wp-content/uploads/sites/49/2020/06/Designing-Lessons-for-Diverse-Learners.pdf

Olmos-Migueláñez, S., Martínez-Abad, F., Torrecilla-Sánchez, E., & Mena-Marcos, J. (2014). Análisis psicométrico de una escala de percepción sobre la utilidad de Moodle en la universidad. *RELIEVE*, *20*(2), 1. Advance online publication. doi:10.7203/relieve.20.2.4221

Olojo, O. J., Adewumi, M. G., & Ajisola, K. T. (2012). E-learning and its effects on teaching and learning in a global age. *International Journal of Academic Research in Business & Social Sciences*, *2*(1), 203–210.

OMG. (2022). *Decision model and notation* (DMN). OMG. https://www.omg.org/dmn/

Opdecam, E., Everaert, P., Van Keer, H., & Buysschaert, F. (2014). Preferences for team learning and lecture-based learning among first-year undergraduate accounting students. *Research in Higher Education*, *55*, 400–432. doi:10.100711162-013-9315-6

Otero, A. (2001). *Medio ambiente y educación: capacitación ambiental para docentes*. Ediciones Novedades Educativas.

Paes, D., & Irizarry, J. (2018). A usability study of an immersive virtual reality platform for building design review: Considerations on human factors and user interface. *Construction Research Congress*, 419-428. 10.1061/9780784481264.041

Page, M., Schagen, S., Fallus, K., Bron, J., De Coninck, Ch., Maes, B., Sleurs, W., & Van Woensel, Ch. (2005). *Cross-curricular themes in secondary education-Report of a CIDREE collaborative project*. Consortium of Institutions for Development and Research in Education in Europe.

Palsolé, S., & Awalt, C. (2008). Team-based learning in asynchronous online settings. *New Directions for Teaching and Learning*, *2008*(116), 87–95. doi:10.1002/tl.336

Panyajamorn, T., Suanmali, S., Kohda, Y., Chongphaisal, P., & Supnithi, T. (2018). Effectiveness of e-learning design in Thai public schools. *Malaysian Journal of Learning and Instruction*, *15*(1), 1–34.

Pappas, Ch. (2022). *Cloud Based e-Learning Platforms: 10 Advantages eLearning Professionals Need To Know.* Docebo. https://www.docebo.com/learning-network/blog/cloud-based-elearning-platforms/

Parmelee, D. X. (2008). Team-based learning in health professions education. In L. K. Michaelsen, A. Knight, & L. D. Fink (Eds.), *Team-based learning for health professions education* (pp. 1–14). Stylus Publishing, LLC.

Parmelee, D. X., & Michaelsen, L. K. (2010). Twelve tips for doing effective team-based learning (TBL). *Medical Teacher*, *32*(2), 118–122. doi:10.3109/01421590903548562 PMID:20163226

Paschal, M. J., & Mkulu, D. G. (2020). Online classes during COVID-19 pandemic in higher learning institutions in Africa. *Global Research in Higher Education, 3*(3). Retrieved from www.scholink.org/ojs/index.php/grhe

Pataranutaporn, P., Danry, V., Leong, J., Punpongsanon, P., Novy, D., Maes, P., & Sra, M. (2021). AI-generated characters for supporting personalized learning and well-being. *Nature Machine Intelligence*, *3*(12), 1013–1022. doi:10.103842256-021-00417-9

Paudel, K. (2007). *A study on the effectiveness of Geoboard in teaching geometry at primary level* [Unpublished Master thesis]. University campus, Kritipur.

Pavanelli, R. (2018). The flipped classroom: A mixed methods study of academic performance and student perception in EAP writing context. *International Journal of Language and Linguistics*, *5*(2), 16–26.

Pea, R., & Lindgren, R. (2008). Video Collaboratories for Research and Education: An Analysis of Collaboration Design Patterns. IEEE Transactions on Learning Technologies, 1(4).

Pears, A., Seidman, S., Malmi, L., Mannila, L., & Adams, E. (2007). A survey of literature on the teaching of introductory programming. In *Working group report on ITiCSE on innovation and technology in computer science education*. ACM. doi:10.1145/1345443.1345441

Pereira, J. A., Pleguezuelos, E., Merí, A., Molina-Ros, A., Molina-Tomás, M. C., & Masdeu, C. (2007). Effectiveness of using blended learning strategies for teaching and learning human anatomy. *Medical Education*, *41*(2), 189–195. doi:10.1111/j.1365-2929.2006.02672.x PMID:17269953

Persky, A. M. (2012). The impact of team-based learning on a foundational pharmacokinetics course. *American Journal of Pharmaceutical Education*, *76*(2), 31. Advance online publication. doi:10.5688/ajpe76231 PMID:22438603

Persky, A. M., & Pollack, G. M. (2011). A modified team-based learning physiology course. *American Journal of Pharmaceutical Education*, *75*(10), 204. Advance online publication. doi:10.5688/ajpe7510204 PMID:22345723

Peters, D. (2014). *Interface design for learning: Design strategies for learning experiences*. Pearson Education.

Picault, J. (2019). The economics instructor's toolbox. *International Review of Economics Education*, *30*, 100154. Advance online publication. doi:10.1016/j.iree.2019.01.001

Pisonia, G., Gijlersc, H., Ha Nguyend, T., & Chene, H. (2021). Collaboration patterns in students' teams working on business cases. *CEUR Workshop Proceedings*.

Polderman, J., & Willems, J. (1998). *Introduction to Mathematical Systems Theory: A Behavioral Approach (Texts in Applied Mathematics)* (2nd ed.). Springer Verlag. doi:10.1007/978-1-4757-2953-5

Poon, J. (2013). Blended learning: An institutional approach for enhancing students' learning experiences. *Journal of Online Learning and Teaching*, *9*(2), 271–289.

Postle, G. (2003). Online Teaching and Learning in Higher Education: A Case Study. Department of Education, Science and Training. University of Southern Queensland.

Prastiwi, S., Widagdo, V., & Kamisutara, M. (2018). Enterprise architecture of education with the TOGAF framework. *The Fourth International Conference on Entrepreneurships*. https://icoen.org/icoen2018/

Proitz, T. S., Mausethagen, S., & Skedsmo, G. (2017). Investigative modes in research on data use in education. *Nordic Journal of Studies in Educational Policy*, *3*(1), 42–55. doi:10.1080/20020317.2017.1326280

ProLiteracy. (2020, February 3). *What are the challenges of implementing blended learning in adult education?* [Blog post]. Retrieved from https://www.proliteracy.org/Blogs/Article/505/What-are-the-Challenges-of-Implementing-Blended-Learning-in-Adult-Education

PushpakumaraH.JayaweeraP.ManjulanW. (2021). *Using the Open Group Architecture Framework (TOGAF) for Quality Assurance in Higher Education Teaching and Learning*. doi:10.2139/ssrn.3808691

Putri, N., & Yusof, S. M. (2009). Critical success factors for implementing quality engineering tools and techniques in malaysian's and indonesian's automotive industries: An Exploratory Study. *Journal Proceedings of the International MultiConference of Engineers and Computer Scientists.*, *2*, 18–20.

Qassrawi, R. M., & Al Karasneh, S. M. (2023). Benefits of Facebook usage (as a web 2.0 application) in Foreign Language instruction in higher education: A Meta-analysis study. *Cogent Arts & Humanities*, *10*(1), 2185447. doi:10.1080/23311983.2023.2185447

Quigley, C., Marshall, J. C., Deaton, C. C., Cook, M. P., & Padilla, M. (2011). Challenges to inquiry teaching and suggestions for how to meet them. *Science Educator*, *20*(1), 55–61. https://files.eric.ed.gov/fulltext/EJ940939.pdf

Rajalingam, P., & Rotgans, J. I. (2018). Team-based learning improves nursing students' knowledge acquisition, retention, and satisfaction: A mixed-methods study. *Journal of Nursing Education and Practice*, *8*(3), 29–39. doi:10.5430/jnep.v8n3p29

Ray, M. (2018). Teaching economics using 'cases' – Going beyond the 'chalk-and-talk' method. *International Review of Economics Education*, *27*, 1–9. doi:10.1016/j.iree.2017.12.001

Raynis, M. (2018). Analysis of instructional design job announcements (2016). *Current Issues in Emerging e-Learning, 4*(1). Retrieved from https://scholarworks.umb.edu/ciee/vol4/iss1/9

Rea, M. O., & Roman, J. L. (2019). Implementing backward design to improve students' academic performance in EFL classes. *Espirales Revista Multidisciplinaria de Investigación, 3*(24), 43-50. https://www.revistaespirales.com/index.php/es/article/view/422/352

Reguera, E. A. M., & Lopez, M. (2021). Using a digital whiteboard for student engagement in distance education. *Computers & Electrical Engineering*, *93*, 107268. doi:10.1016/j.compeleceng.2021.107268 PMID:34642507

Reid, P. (2014). Categories for barriers to adoption of instructional technologies. *Education and Information Technologies*, *19*(2), 383–407. doi:10.100710639-012-9222-z

Reimschisel, T., Herring, A. L., Huang, J., & Minor, T. J. (2017). A systematic review of the published literature on team-based learning in health professions education. *Medical Teacher*, *39*(12), 1227–1237. doi:10.1080/0142159X.2017.1340636 PMID:28664760

Remington, T. L., Hershock, C., Klein, K. C., Niemer, R. K., & Bleske, B. E. (2015). Lessons from the trenches: Implementing team-based learning across several courses. *Currents in Pharmacy Teaching & Learning*, *7*(1), 121–130. doi:10.1016/j.cptl.2014.09.008

Restall, G. C., & Clark, M. C. (2021). Team-based learning and the community of inquiry model. *New Directions for Teaching and Learning*, *2021*(165), 65–76. doi:10.1002/tl.20437

Rincón, E. (2012). El 82% de las universidades acreditadas usan Moodle. *E-Learn Magazine*. Recuperado de http://elearningmagazine.co/2012/11/24/el-82-de-las-universidades-acreditadas-usan-moodle/?lang=es

Ritzhaupt, A. D., Kumar, S., & Martin, F. (2021). The competencies for instructional designers in higher education. In *A practitioner's guide to instructional design in higher education*. Retrieved from https://edtechbooks.org/id_highered/the_competencies_for

Roberson, B., & Franchini, B. (2014). Effective task design for the TBL classroom. *Journal on Excellence in College Teaching*, *25*(3&4), 275–302. https://learntbl.ca/wp-content/uploads/2016/01/v25n34-RobersonFranchini.pdf

Robinson, C., & Liard-Muriente, C. (2018). Math in the economics classroom: An experiment with iMath. *International Advances in Economic Research*, *24*(3), 289–290. doi:10.100711294-018-9695-7

Robinson, D. G., & Watson, G. S. (2013). Guidelines for the motivational design of instructional simulations. *The Journal of Applied Instructional Design*, *3*(2), 41–52. doi:10.28990/jaid2013.00127

Rodríguez, M. C., Ramírez, L. J., & Camargo, J. M. (2019). TBL, self-assessment, and use of ICT: A methodological option to benefit the English learning process in a Colombian university. *Journal of Language Teaching and Research*, *10*(6), 1162–1172. doi:10.17507/jltr.1006.04

Roehl, A., Reddy, S. L., & Shannon, G. J. (2013). The flipped classroom: An opportunity to engage millennial students through active learning strategies. *Journal of Family and Consumer Sciences*, *105*(2), 44–49. doi:10.14307/JFCS105.2.12

Rogmans, T. (2018). Teaching macroeconomics with the Econoland simulation game and learning platform. *Journal of Economics Teaching*, *2*(2), 91–103. doi:10.58311/jeconteach/892413d590665dfe858e06a93abd1697c16b00f7

Roh, Y. S., Kim, S. S., Park, S., & Ahn, J. W. (2020). Effects of a simulation with team-based learning on knowledge, team performance, and teamwork for nursing students. *CIN: Computers, Informatics. Computers, Informatics, Nursing*, *38*(7), 367–372. doi:10.1097/CIN.0000000000000628 PMID:32349024

Rønningsbakk, L., Gudmundsdottir, G. B., & Blikstad-Balas, M. (2020). Sameness and individuality: Teacher adaptation and enactment of an innovative technology-based mathematics curriculum. *Teaching and Teacher Education, 96*, 103196. doi:10.1016/j.tate.2020.103196

Ruder, P., Maier, M. H., & Simkins, S. P. (2021). Getting started with team-based learning (TBL): An introduction. *The Journal of Economic Education, 52*(3), 220–230. doi:10.1080/00220485.2021.1925187

Ruíz, N. (2013). *Moodle Moot Colombia 2013. La verdadera alternativa de la radio*. Universidad Distrital Francisco José de Caldas. Recuperado de https://laud.udistrital.edu.co/noticias/moodle-moot-colombia-2013

Ryan, R. M., & Deci, E. L. (2000). Self-determination theory and the facilitation of intrinsic motivation, social development, and well-being. *The American Psychologist, 55*(1), 68–78. doi:10.1037/0003-066X.55.1.68 PMID:11392867

Ryan, S., Kaufman, J., Greenhouse, J., She, R., & Shi, J. (2016). The effectiveness of blended online learning courses at the community college level. *Community College Journal of Research and Practice, 40*(4), 285–298. doi:10.1080/10668926.2015.1044584

Sabah, N. M. (2020). Motivation factors and barriers to the continuous use of blended learning approach using Moodle: Students' perceptions and individual differences. *Behaviour & Information Technology, 39*(8), 875–898. doi:10.1080/0144929X.2019.1623323

Sabah, N. M. (2023). The impact of social media-based collaborative learning environments on students' use outcomes in higher education. *International Journal of Human-Computer Interaction, 39*(3), 667–689. doi:10.1080/10447318.2022.2046921

Sachdeva, S. (2017). Making economics classrooms exciting: Role of experiential learning. *International Journal of Advanced Educational Research, 2*(5), 83–92.

Saeed, M., Malallah, F., & Alasaady, M. (2019). A proposed model for designing e-learning courses. *Journal of Theoretical and Applied Information Technology, 97*(4), 1239–1250.

Sagheb-Tehrani, M. (2009). The Results of Online Teaching: A Case Study. *ISEDJ, 7*(42). http://isedj.org/7/42/

Samuels, A. J. (2018). Exploring culturally responsive pedagogy: Teachers' perspectives on fostering equitable and inclusive classrooms. *SRATE Journal, 27*(1), 22–30.

Samura, A. O., Darhim, D., Juandi, D., Said, A. M., & Malaka, M. (2021). Improving the creative thinking ability of junior high school students through GeoGebra assisted learning community in mathematics. *International Journal of Interactive Mobile Technologies, 15*(22), 84–98. doi:10.3991/ijim.v15i22.24797

Sankaralingam, K., Ferris, M., Nowatzki, T., Estan, C., Wood, D., & Vaish, N. (2013). *Optimization and Mathematical Modeling in Computer Architecture*. Morgan & Claypool Publishers.

Sarker, M., & Al-Muaalemi, M. A. (2022). Sampling techniques for quantitative research. In *Principles of Social Research Methodology* (pp. 221–234). Springer Nature Singapore. doi:10.1007/978-981-19-5441-2_15

Satterlee, B. (1996). Continuous Improvement and Quality: Implications for Higher Education. Warner Southern College.

Saxena, N. (2019). Pallas advanced learning systems–A research-informed virtual learning kit. *Journal of Applied Learning and Teaching*, *2*(1), 65–68. doi:10.37074/jalt.2019.2.1.8

Scaled Agile. (2022). *Succeeding with AI in SAFe*. Scaled Agile, Inc. https://www.scaledagileframework.com/succeeding-with-ai-in-safe/

Schempp, P. G., Manross, D., Tan, S. K. S., & Fincher, M. D. (1998). Subject expertise and teachers' knowledge. *Journal of Teaching in Physical Education*, *17*(3), 342–356. doi:10.1123/jtpe.17.3.342

Schmidt, W. H., Cogan, L., & Houang, R. (2011). The role of opportunity to learn in teacher preparation: An international context. *Journal of Teacher Education*, *62*(2), 138–153. doi:10.1177/0022487110391987

Schmidt, W. H., Houang, R. T., Coga, L., Blomeke, S., Tatto, M. T., Hsieh, F. J., Santillan, M., Bankov, K., Han, S., Cedillo, T., Schwille, J., & Paine, L. (2008). Opportunity to learn in the preparation of mathematics teachers: Its structure and how it varies across six countries. *ZDM Mathematics Education*, *40*(5), 735–747. doi:10.100711858-008-0115-y

Schoenbach, R., Greenleaf, C., Murphy, L., Cziko, C., & Hurwitz, L. (2012). *Reading for understanding: How reading apprenticeship improves disciplinary learning in secondary and college classrooms*. Jossey-Bass.

Schouten, G. (2017). On meeting students where they are: Teacher judgment and the use of data in higher education. *Theory and Research in Education, 15*(3), 321-338. doi:10.1177/1477878517734452

Scott, A. B. (2023). *Using music to enhance pedagogy in the classroom.* Paper presented at the Journal of Economics Teaching Symposium on Economics Teaching (JETSET), Newport, KY. https://doi.org/10.13140/RG.2.2.34710.11847

Scott, A. B. (2021). A case study of tourism in North Carolina state parks using Google trends. *International Journal of Tourism and Hospitality Management in the Digital Age*, *5*(2), 1–14. doi:10.4018/IJTHMDA.298703

Secretaría de Comunicaciones y Transportes SCT. (2017). *México Conectado.* Recuperado de http://mexicoconectado.gob.mx/sobre_mexico_conectado.php?id=66

Secretaría de Educaci6n Pública SEP. (2016). *Principales cifras del sistema educativo nacional. 2015-2016.* México: SEP. Recuperado de https://www.planeacion.sep.gob.mx/Doc/estadistica_e_indicadores/principales_cifras/principales_cifras_2015_2016_bolsillo.pdf

Sengupta, S., & Vaish, A. (2023). A study on social media and higher education during the COVID-19 pandemic. *Universal Access in the Information Society*, 1–23. doi:10.100710209-023-00988-x PMID:37361680

Shao, G. (2009). Understanding the appeal of user-generated media: A uses and gratification perspective. *Internet Research*, *19*(1), 7–25. doi:10.1108/10662240910927795

Sharples, M. (2022). *New AI tools that can write student essays require educators to rethink teaching and assessment. Blog*. Retrieved from London School of Economics.

Shashidhara, Y. N., & Ladd, E. (2018). Team Based Learning an Active Teaching and learning Pedagogy: A Narrative Literature Review. *Indian Journal of Public Health Research & Development*, *9*(10), 242–248. doi:10.5958/0976-5506.2018.01349.9

Shea, P., Li, C. S., & Pickett, A. (2006). A study of teaching presence and student sense of learning community in fully online and web-enhanced college courses. *The Internet and Higher Education*, *9*(3), 175–190. doi:10.1016/j.iheduc.2006.06.005

Shifat, N. F., & Khan, M. E. (2022). Sustainability of e-learning in the undergraduate EFL classrooms. *FOSTER: Journal of English Language Teaching*, *3*(2), 80–89. doi:10.24256/foster-jelt.v3i2.88

Shulman, L. S. (2007). *It's all about time!* The Carnegie Foundation for the Advancement of Teaching. ERIC ED499494. https://files.eric.ed.gov/fulltext/ED499494.pdf

Shulman, J. S. (1993). Teaching as community property: Putting an end to pedagogical solitude. *Change*, *25*(6), 6–7. doi:10.1080/00091383.1993.9938465

Shulman, L. (1987). Knowledge and teaching: Foundations of the new reform. *Harvard Educational Review*, *57*(1), 1–23. doi:10.17763/haer.57.1.j463w79r56455411

Shulman, L. S. (1986). Those who understand: Knowledge growth in teaching. *Educational Researcher*, *15*(2), 4–14. doi:10.2307/1175860

Shulman, L. S. (1998). Theory, practice, & the education of professionals. *The Elementary School Journal*, *98*(5), 511–526. doi:10.1086/461912

Shulman, L. S. (2005). Signature pedagogies in the professions. *Daedalus*, *134*(3), 52–59. doi:10.1162/0011526054622015

Shulman, L. S. (2015). PCK: Its genesis and exodus. In A. Berry, P. Friedrichsen, & J. Loughran (Eds.), *Re-examining pedagogical content knowledge in science education* (pp. 3–13). Routledge.

Shulman, L. S., & Shulman, J. H. (2004). How and what teachers learn: A shifting perspective. *Journal of Curriculum Studies*, *36*(2), 257–271. doi:10.1080/0022027032000148298

Shulman, L. S., & Shulman, J. H. (2017). How and what teachers learn: A shifting perspective. *Journal of Education*, *189*(1-2), 1–8. doi:10.1177/0022057409189001-202

Shulman, L., & Gamoran Sherin, M. (2004). Fostering communities of teachers as learners: Disciplinary perspectives. *Journal of Curriculum Studies*, *36*(2), 135–140. doi:10.1080/0022027032000135049

Silva, J. (2011). *Diseño y moderación de entornos virtuales de aprendizaje*. Editorial UOC.

Simkins, S. P., Maier, M. H., & Ruder, P. (2021). Team-based learning (TBL): Putting learning sciences research to work in the economics classroom. *The Journal of Economic Education*, *52*(3), 231–240. doi:10.1080/00220485.2021.1925188

Simonson, M., Zvacek, S. M., & Smaldino, S. (2019). *Teaching and learning at a distance: Foundations of distance education* (7th ed.). Information Age.

Smit, E., Tuihof, H., Savelsbergh, E., & Beneker, T. (2022). Geography teachers' pedagogical content knowledge: A systematic review. *The Journal of Geography*, *122*(1), 20–29. doi:10.1080/00221341.2023.2173796

Smith, A. (1987). Educational Engineering: Heuristics for Improving Learning Effectiveness and Efficiency. *Engineering Education, 77*(5), 274-79.

Sparrow, S. M., & McCabe, M. S. (2012). Team-based learning in law. *Legal Writing. J. Legal Writing Inst.*, *18*, 153.

Spencer, M. (2016). *Agile EA – the MVP – enterprise architect-Building the Business Value Chain…* https://enterprisearchitect.wordpress.com/2016/04/11/agile-ea-the-mvp/1/2

Sreehari, P. (2020). Online learning during the COVID-19 lockdown: Learners' perceptions. *Journal of Critical Reviews*, *7*(10), 300–307.

Staker, H., & Horn, M. B. (2012). *Classifying K–12 blended learning*. INNOSIGHT Institute. ERIC. https://files.eric.ed.gov/fulltext/ED535180.pdf

Staker, H., & Horn, M. B. (2013). Blended learning in the K–12 education sector. In A. G. Picciano, C. D. Dziuban, & C. R. Graham (Eds.), *Blended learning: Research perspectives* (Vol. 2, pp. 287–303). Routledge. doi:10.4324/9781315880310

Staudt Willet, K. B. (2023). Early career teachers' expansion of professional learning networks with social media. *Professional Development in Education*, 1–17. doi:10.1080/19415257.2023.2178481

Stellefson, M., Paige, S. R., Chaney, B. H., & Chaney, J. D. (2020). The evolving role of social media in health promotion: Updated responsibilities for health education specialists. *International Journal of Environmental Research and Public Health*, *17*(4), 1153. doi:10.3390/ijerph17041153 PMID:32059561

Stine, L. J. (2010). Teaching basic writing in a web-enhanced environment. *Journal of Basic Writing*, *29*(1), 33–55. doi:10.37514/JBW-J.2010.29.1.03

Suartama, I. K., Setyosari, P., Sulthoni, S., & Ulfa, S. (2019). Development of an instructional design model for mobile blended learning in higher education. *International Journal of Emerging Technologies in Learning, 14*(16), 4–22. doi:10.3991/ijet.v14i16.10633

Suresh Babu, C.V. (2023). Introduction to Data Science. Anniyappa Publications.

Suresh Babu, C. V. (2022). *Artificial Intelligence and Expert Systems.* Anniyappa Publications.

Suresh Babu, C. V., & Padma, R. (2023). Technology Transformation Through Skilled Teachers in Teaching Accountancy. In *Advancing STEM Education and Innovation in a Time of Distance Learning* (pp. 211–233). Global. doi:10.4018/978-1-6684-5053-6.ch011

Suresh Babu, C. V., & Rohan, B. (2023). Evaluation and Quality Assurance for Rapid E-Learning and Development of Digital Learning Resources. In M. Santally, Y. Rajabalee, & R. Rajputh (Eds.), *Implementing Rapid E-Learning Through Interactive Materials Development* (pp. 139–170). IGI Global. doi:10.4018/978-1-6684-4940-0.ch008

Sweet, M., & Michaelsen, L. K. (2012). *Team-Based Learning in the Social Sciences and Humanities: Group Work That Works to Generate Critical Thinking and Engagement.* Stylus Publishing, LLC.

Swoboda, A., & Feirler, L. (2016). Measuring the effect of blended learning: Evidence from a selective liberal arts college. *The American Economic Review, 106*(5), 368–372. doi:10.1257/aer.p20161055

Syynimaa, N. (2015). *Enterprise Architecture Adoption Method for Higher Education Institutions* [Doctoral Thesis]. Informatics Research Centre Henley Business School University of Reading.

Tan, G. W. H., Tan, K. C. D., & Teo, T. (2021). A meta-analysis of gamification in financial education. *Journal of Interactive Learning Research, 32*(2), 127–147.

Tang, Y., & Hew, K. F. (2017). Using Twitter for education: Beneficial or simply a waste of time? *Computers & Education, 106*, 97–118. doi:10.1016/j.compedu.2016.12.004

Tan, S. H. S., Thibault, G., Chew, A. C. Y., & Rajalingam, P. (2022). Enabling open-ended questions in team-based learning using automated marking: Impact on student achievement, learning and engagement. *Journal of Computer Assisted Learning, 38*(5), 1347–1359. doi:10.1111/jcal.12680

Tanye, H. A. (2017). Quality eLearning in distance learning: Benefits and implications for national eLearning policy in Ghana. *International Journal of Multicultural and Multireligious Understanding, 4*(3), 1–11. doi:10.18415/ijmmu.v4i3.73

Tayebinik, M., & Puteh, M. (2013). *Blended Learning or E-learning?* arXiv preprint arXiv:1306.4085. https://doi.org//arXiv.1306.4085 doi:10.48550

Taylor, B. K. (2015). Content, process, and product: Modeling differentiated instruction. *Kappa Delta Pi Record, 51*(1), 13–17. doi:10.1080/00228958.2015.988559

Team-Based Learning Collaborative. (n.d.). *What is TBL*? Online available at: https://docs.lamsfoundation.org/tbl/

The Open Group. (2011a). *Architecture Development Method.* The Open Group. https://pubs.opengroup.org/architecture/togaf9-doc/arch/chap05.html

The Open Group. (2011b). *TOGAF 9.1. The Open Group*. The Open Group.

Thompson, B. M., Schneider, V. F., Haidet, P., Levine, R. E., McMahon, K. K., Perkowski, L. C., & Richards, B. F. (2007). Team-based learning at ten medical schools: Two years later. *Medical Education, 41*(3), 250–257. doi:10.1111/j.1365-2929.2006.02684.x PMID:17316209

Thune, T. (2011). Success Factors in Higher Education–Industry Collaboration: A case study of collaboration in the engineering field. *Tertiary Education and Management, 17*(1), 31–50. doi: 10.1080/13583883.2011.552627

Tilak, G., & Bhaumik, A. (2021). A review on security and usability of graphical user interface design. *Zeichen Journal*, *7*(1), 33–45. doi:10.14445/22312803/IJCTT-V67I2P104

Tin-Chun, L. (2023). Can online discussions benefit students' learning in online courses? Evidence from teaching introduction to microeconomics. *E-Learning and Digital Media*. Advance online publication. doi:10.1177/20427530231170765

Tomesko, J., Cohen, D., & Bridenbaugh, J. (2022). Using a virtual flipped classroom model to promote critical thinking in online graduate courses in the United States: A case presentation. *Journal of Educational Evaluation for Health Professions*, *19*(1), 1–8. doi:10.3352/jeehp.2022.19.5 PMID:35219288

Tomlinson, C. A., & McTighe, J. (2006). *Integrating differentiated instruction and Understanding by Design: Connecting content and kids*. Association for Supervision and Curriculum Development. https://chca-oh.instructure.com/files/3649/download?download_frd=1

Tong, D. H., Uyen, B. P., & Ngan, L. K. (2022). The effectiveness of blended learning on students' academic achievement, self-study skills and learning attitudes: A quasi-experiment study in teaching the conventions for coordinates in the plane. *Heliyon*, *12657*(12), e12657. Advance online publication. doi:10.1016/j.heliyon.2022.e12657 PMID:36643330

Trad, A. & Kalpić, D. (2022c). Business Transformation Project's Holistic Agile Management (BTPHAM). *CBER 2022.*

Trad, A. (2021a). The transformation framework The role security in the global education system. *International Journal of Higher Education Management, 8*(1).

Trad, A. (2021b). The business transformation enterprise architecture framework for innovation: The role of artificial intelligence in the global business education (RAIGBE). The Business & Management Review, 12(1), 82-97.

Trad, A. (2022a). The Societal and Educational Transformation Projects-The Middle East's Educational Construct-The Case of the Lebanese Specific Diverse Educational System (LSDES). *The Business and Management Review, 13*(3).

Trad, A., & Kalpić, D. (2022a). Business Transformation Projects based on a Holistic Enterprise Architecture Pattern (HEAP)-The Basics. IGI.

Trad, A., & Kalpić, D. (2022b). Business Transformation Projects based on a Holistic Enterprise Architecture Pattern (HEAP)-The Implementation. IGI.

Trad, A. (2015a). *A Transformation Framework Proposal for Managers in Business Innovation and Business Transformation Projects-Intelligent aBB architecture*. Centeris.

Trad, A. (2015b). *A Transformation Framework Proposal for Managers in Business Innovation and Business Transformation Projects-An ICS's atomic architecture vision*. Centeris.

Trad, A. (2023a). *Business Transformation Project's-The Impact of Rise of Over-the-Top (OTT)*. IGI-Global.

Trad, A. (2023b). *Business Transformation Projects: The Role of Psychology-Based Resistance (RPbR). In Considerations on Education for Economic, Social, and Environmental Sustainability*. IGI Global.

Trad, A. (2023c). *The Societal and Educational Transformation Projects: The Evolution of the Lebanese Diverse Education (ELDES). In Global Perspectives on the Internationalization of Higher Education*. IGI Global.

Trad, A., & Kalpić, D. (2014a). The Selection and Training Framework for Managers in Business Innovation and Transformation Projects-An applied mathematics hyper-heuristics model. *Proceedings of the 2014 International Conference on Mathematical Methods, Mathematical Models and Simulation in Science and Engineering (MMSSE 2014).*

Trad, A., & Kalpić, D. (2014b). *The Selection, and Training Framework selection and training framework (STF) for Manager's in Business Innovation Transformation Projects–Educational Recommendations*. Journal EDEN.

Trad, A., & Kalpić, D. (2014c, June). The selection and training framework for managers in business innovation and transformation projects: The Profile and Education of a Business Transformation Manager - An enterprise architecture approach. *The Business & Management Review, 5*(1), 424–433.

Trad, A., & Kalpić, D. (2017). *An Intelligent Neural Networks Micro Artifact Patterns' Based Enterprise Architecture Model*. IGI-Global.

Trad, A., & Kalpić, D. (2020). *Using Applied Mathematical Models for Business Transformation. IGI Complete Author Book*. IGI Global. doi:10.4018/978-1-7998-1009-4

Trad, A., & Kalpić, D. (2021a). Business transformation project's architect's profile (BTPAP). *The Business & Management Review., 12*(2), 137–153. doi:10.24052/BMR/V12NU02/ART-11

Trad, A., & Kalpić, D. (2023a). *Educational Transformation Project's Remote Group Work (ETPRGW). In Shaping Online Spaces Through Online Humanities Curricula*. IGI Global.

Trust, T., Krutka, D. G., & Carpenter, J. P. (2016). "Together we are better": Professional learning networks for teachers. *Computers & Education*, *102*, 15–34. doi:10.1016/j.compedu.2016.06.007

Tucker, C. R., Wycoff, T., & Green, J. T. (2016). *Blended learning in action: A practical guide toward sustainable change*. Corwin Press.

Tuononen, T., Hyytinen, H., Kleemola, K., Hailikari, T., Männikkö, I., & Toom, A. (2022). Systematic Review of Learning Generic Skills in Higher Education—Enhancing and Impeding Factors. Frontiers in Education. *Systematic Review*. doi:10.3389/feduc.2022.885917

Tyagi, N., & Verma, S. (2022). Culturally responsive teaching: A suggestive pedagogical framework. In J. Keengwe (Ed.), *Handbook of Research on Social Justice and Equity in Education* (pp. 312–331). IGI Global. doi:10.4018/978-1-7998-9567-1.ch016

UdG. (2023). *Relationships with Secondary Schools-Polytechnic School*. UdG. https://www.udg.edu/en/eps/relacions-amb-secundaria

United Nations Educational, Scientific and Cultural Organization (UNESCO). (2020). *Education: From school closure to recovery*. Retrieved November 1, 2021, from https://en.unesco.org/covid19/educationresponse

United Nations International Children's Emergency Fund (UNICEF). (2021). *Primary and secondary impacts of the COVID-19 pandemic on children in Ghana*. Accra, Ghana: UNICEF Policy and Evidence Section. Retrieved from https://orbilu.uni.lu/bitstream/10993/46437/1/UNICEF%202021.pdf

University of Michigan. (2014). *Medical Education Day*. Program Guide Dow Auditorium and Towsley Center Lobby. Retrieved from https://medicine.umich.edu/sites/default/files/MedEdDayProgram2014.pdf

Vasan, N. S., DeFouw, D. O., & Compton, S. (2011). Team-based learning in anatomy: An efficient, effective, and economical strategy. *Anatomical Sciences Education*, *4*(6), 333–339. doi:10.1002/ase.257 PMID:21998012

Velegol, S. B., Zappe, S. E., & Mahoney, E. (2015). The evolution of a flipped classroom: Evidence-based recommendations. *Advances in Engineering Education*, 4.

Vereijken, M. W. C., & van der Rijst, R. M. (2023). Subject matter pedagogy in university teaching: How lecturers use relations between theory and practice. *Teaching in Higher Education*, *28*(4), 880–893. doi:10.1080/13562517.2020.1863352

Vlachopoulos, P., Jan, S. K., & Buckton, R. (2020). A case for team-based learning as an effective collaborative learning methodology in higher education. *College Teaching*, *69*(2), 69–77. doi:10.1080/87567555.2020.1816889

Vojtesek, J., & Hutak, J. (2019). Using multimedia in blended learning. *Software Engineering Methods in Intelligent Algorithms: Proceedings of 8th Computer Science On-line Conference 2019, 18*(1), 249-258.

Vorster, J., & Goosen, L. (2017). A framework for university partnerships promoting continued support of e-schools. In J. Liebenberg (Ed.), *Proceedings of the 46th Annual Conference of the Southern African Computer Lecturers' Association (SACLA)* (pp. 118-126). Magaliesburg: North-West University.

Wallace, M. L., Walker, J. D., Braseby, A. M., & Sweet, M. S. (2014). Now, What Happens During Class?" Using Team-Based Learning to Optimize the Role of Expertise Within the Flipped Classroom. *Journal on Excellence in College Teaching*, 25.

Walne, M. B. (2012). *Emerging blended-learning models and school profiles*. Community Foundation. Retrieved from http://www.edustart.org/volume2/issue2/Walne.pdf

Wang, H., Tlili, A., Lämsä, J., Cai, Z., Zhong, X., & Huang, R. (2023). Temporal perspective on the gender-related differences in online learning behaviour. *Behaviour & Information Technology, 42*(6), 671–685. doi:10.1080/0144929X.2022.2039769

Wang, H., Tlili, A., Zhong, X., Cai, Z., & Huang, R. (2021, July). The impact of gender on online learning behavioral patterns: A comparative study based on lag sequential analysis. In *International Conference on Advanced Learning Technologies (ICALT)* (pp. 190-194). IEEE. 10.1109/ICALT52272.2021.00064

Wang, M., Shen, R., Novak, D., & Pan, X. (2009). The impact of mobile learning on students' learning behaviours and performance: Report from a large blended classroom. *British Journal of Educational Technology, 40*(4), 673–695. doi:10.1111/j.1467-8535.2008.00846.x

Watson, J. (2008). Blended learning: The convergence of online and face-to-face education. *Promising Practices in Online Learning, 2*(1), 33-44. https://files.eric.ed.gov/fulltext/ED509636.pdf

Watson, J., Murin, A., Vashaw, L., Gemin, B., & Rapp, C. (2013). *Keeping Pace with K-12 Online & Blended Learning: An Annual Review of Policy and Practice. 10 Year Anniversary Issue*. Evergreen Education Group. https://files.eric.ed.gov/fulltext/ED566139.pdf

Weerathunga, P. R., Samarathunga, W. H., Rathnayake, H. N., Agampodi, S. B., Nurunnabi, M., & Madhunimasha, M. M. (2021). The COVID-19 pandemic and the acceptance of e-learning among university students: The role of precipitating events. *Education Sciences, 11*(8), 436. Advance online publication. doi:10.3390/educsci11080436

White, D., & Wagner, J. (2021). Getting your students to be dynamic: Lesson and web app about market dynamics in the long-run. *Journal of Economics Teaching, 6*(2), 106–122. doi:10.58311/jeconteach/caa5a0746727f0970140311ece607ade43c6147e

Whitley, H. P., Bell, E., Eng, M., Fuentes, D. G., Helms, K. L., Maki, E. D., & Vyas, D. (2015). Practical team-based learning from planning to implementation. *American Journal of Pharmaceutical Education*, *79*(10), 149. doi:10.5688/ajpe7910149 PMID:26889061

Wikipedia. (2021). Polymath. In *Wikipedia*. https://en.wikipedia.org/wiki/Polymath

Wilkinson, A. (1998). Empowerment: Theory and practice. *Personnel Review*, *27*(1), 40–56. doi:10.1108/00483489810368549

Wolla, S. (2020). The economics of artificial intelligence: A primer for social studies educators. *The Councilor. The Journal of Social Studies*, *81*(2). https://thekeep.eiu.edu/the_councilor/vol81/iss2/3

Wong, P., Jumat, M. R., Lee, I. C. J., Foo, K. X., Goh, S. P. L., Ganapathy, S., Lai, S. H., & Hwang, N. C. (2020). Redesigning team-based learning facilitation for an online platform to deliver preclinical curriculum: A response to the COVID-19 pandemic. *MedEdPublish*, *9*(135), 135. doi:10.15694/mep.2020.000135.1

Wooten, J., & Al-Bahrani, A. (2021). Economics in a crisis: A cautious approach to being relevant. *Journal of Economics Teaching*, *5*(4), 142–151. doi:10.58311/jeconteach/194492d686c6368d58bc577a882ddc12c9648d3b

Wooten, J., Al-Bahrani, A., Holder, K., & Patel, D. (2021). The role of relevance in economics education: A survey. *The Journal of Economic Education*, *21*(1). https://libjournals.mtsu.edu/index.php/jfee/article/view/2025/1231

Yakubu, M. N., & Dasuki, S. (2018). Assessing e-learning systems success in Nigeria: An application of the DeLone and McLean information systems success model. *Journal of Information Technology Education*, *17*, 183–203. doi:10.28945/4077

Yardi, S., & Boyd, D. (2010). Tweeting from the Town Square: Measuring geographic local networks. *Proceedings of the International AAAI Conference on Web and Social Media, 4*(1), 194–201. 10.1609/icwsm.v4i1.14016

Yimer, S. T. (2022). Effective Instruction for Calculus Learning Outcomes through Blending Co-Operative Learning and Geogebra. *Mathematics Teaching Research Journal, 14*(3), 170-189. https://commons.hostos.cuny.edu/mtrj

Yukelson, D. (1997). Principles of effective team building interventions in sport: A direct services approach at Penn State University. *Journal of Applied Sport Psychology*, *9*(1), 73–96. doi:10.1080/10413209708415385

Zachman, J. (2015). *Defining Enterprise Architecture: Economics and the Role of I.T. Business Rules Community*. https://www.brcommunity.com/articles.php?id=b841

Zandia, F., & Tavana, M. (2011). *A fuzzy group multi-criteria enterprise architecture framework selection model.* Elsevier.

Zhang, J., Wu, W., & Li, H. (2018). Enhancing building information modeling competency among civil engineering and management students with team-based learning. *Journal of Professional Issues in Engineering Education and Practice*, *144*(2), 05018001. doi:10.1061/(ASCE)EI.1943-5541.0000356

Zhang, X., Zhao, Z., & Wang, K. (2023). The effects of live comments and advertisements on social media engagement: Application to short-form online video. *Journal of Research in Interactive Marketing*. Advance online publication. doi:10.1108/JRIM-02-2023-0069

Zimmerman, E. (2019). *Microsoft Teams VS Google Classrooms: Tools for Blended Learning. EdTech Magazine*. Retrieved from https://edtechmagazine.com/k12/article/2019/02/google-classroom-and-microsoft-teams-education-find-blended-learning-tool-works-best-perfcon

Zingone, M. M., Franks, A. S., Guirguis, A. B., George, C. M., Howard-Thompson, A., & Heidel, R. E. (2010). Comparing team-based and mixed active-learning methods in an ambulatory care elective course. *American Journal of Pharmaceutical Education*, *74*(9), 160. Advance online publication. doi:10.5688/aj7409160 PMID:21301594

Zulnaidi, H., Oktavika, E., & Hidaya, R. (2020). Effect of use of GeoGebra on achievement of high school mathematics students. *Education and Information Technologies*, *25*(1), 51–72. doi:10.100710639-019-09899-y

About the Contributors

Brad Scott serves as Faculty – Economics within the Business Department under the College of Technical Programs at Rowan-Cabarrus Community College in Salisbury, North Carolina. He is also an adjunct instructor and doctoral student (D.B.A. – Economics) with the Godbold College of Business at Gardner-Webb University. Mr. Scott started writing and presenting work in K-12 economics education after beginning his teaching career with Mallard Creek STEM Academy (Charlotte, NC), a K-8 Charter School. He holds a M.S. in Applied Economics from Southern New Hampshire University and B.A. from Lenoir-Rhyne University. Brad Scott is an active member of the American Economic Association and the National Association of Economics Educators.

Melanie E. Fox is a Clinical Assistant Professor and Director of the Purdue Center for Economic Education. She joined Purdue University's Daniels School of Business in August 2023. Prior to joining the faculty at Purdue, she was the Director of Undergraduate Studies in the Department of Economics at Virginia Tech. Her career of more than 20 years in economic education has included co-creating the Economic Scholars Program at the Federal Reserve Bank of Dallas and developing the economics content on Khan Academy. Dr. Fox holds a B.A, M.A., and Ph.D. from the University of Houston.

* * *

Vennila B. is working as an Assistant Professor in the Department of Mathematics, Sri Eshwar College of Engineering, Coimbatore. She has teaching as well as research experiences for about 10 years. She has completed her Ph.D. in Mathematics from Bharathiar University, Coimbatore in the year 2019 in the field of Queueing theory. Her research interests include queueing theory, fuzzy queue, neutrosophic logic and optimization techniques. She has published more than 15 papers in reputed national and international journals. She has presented 3 research papers at various international conferences. She is a life member of ISTE and ISEAS.

C. V. Suresh Babu is a pioneer in Content Development. A true entrepreneur, He floated Anniyappa Publications, a company which is very active in bringing out books related to Computer Science and Management. Dr. C. V. Suresh Babu has also ventured into SB Institute, a centre for knowledge transfer. He holds Ph.D in Engineering Education from National Institute of Technical Teachers Training & Research, Chennai along with seven Master degrees in various disciplines such as Engineering, Computer Applications, Management, Commerce, Economics, Psychology, Law and Education. He also has the UGC-NET/SET qualifications in the disciplines of Computer Science, Management, Commerce and Education to his credit. Personal blog: https://sites.google.com/view/cvsureshbabu/.e2f99afb-1a1c-43c5-978b-f2cacc9d88ea

Martha Ann Davis McGaw, of the Davis-McGaw Family Foundation, has a M. Ed. with a focus on diversity, identity and bias. CCTL cognate; a B. A. in psych. Currently on the advisory boards of IWS, Inc, a breast cancer support for underserved communities and Peach State Opera. Ms. Davis McGaw has 8 years experience as a PCADV certified Domestic Violence and Sexual Assault Counselor; three years as an Olweus' certified Bullying Prevention Counselor; 12 years in retail management. Davis McGaw's current focus centers on equity in education, placing learners, from K through doctoral level, at the center of every educational policy, initiative and institution. Her work is informed through her experiences as a public educator promoting informal education initiatives while a direct services counselor; as Director of Teen Services and Interim Unit Director of a Boys and Girls Club; a parent of seven children educated in eight different nations. The Davis McGaw Family Foundation was established as a commitment to the development of an equitable, affordable, diverse educational system in the U. S. A. with the goal of promoting economic stability for all.

Iris-Panagiota Efthymiou is a Lecturer at the University of Greenwich and the University of East London, UK. Executive, institutional director, author, and keynote speaker with over 20 years of experience in entrepreneurship, international affairs, and executive leadership roles. Possesses a solid foundation in research, management, consultancy, and strategic development. Iris has worked as a college director and created her Public Affairs consultancy. She worked with politicians, Diplomats, entrepreneurs, academics, and journalists, and spoke at the UN Headquarters in Geneva. She is a Board Member of HAPSc, and a Scientific Associate of the Lab-HEM, of the University of Piraeus. She published over 15 books, 40 articles, and Book chapters in peer-reviewed journals, and she is the Chief Editor of the Journal of Politics and Ethics in New Technologies and AI. Iris has a Ph.D. in Behavioural

Economics, a Master's in Health Economics and Management, and Bachelor's in Economics. https://irisefthymiou.com/.cdc8022d-bae2-4cd8-8c42-68f1e3a52c63

Kateryna Glubochenko, , is Department of Economics, Management, and Finance, PhD, M.Ed., associate professor at V.O. Sukhomlynskyi National University of Mykolaiv, Ukraine. The area of expertise includes Teaching Management and Marketing, Management and Marketing Curriculum Design, Distance Learning, the Development of Student Creativity. She has published over 30 research papers and textbooks.

Leila Goosen is a full professor in the Department of Science and Technology Education of the University of South Africa. Prof. Goosen was an Associate Professor in the School of Computing, and the module leader and head designer of the fully online signature module for the College for Science, Engineering and Technology, rolled out to over 92,000 registered students since the first semester of 2013. She also supervises ten Masters and Doctoral students, and has successfully completed supervision of 43 students at postgraduate level. Previously, she was a Deputy Director at the South African national Department of Education. In this capacity, she was required to develop ICT strategies for implementation. She also promoted, coordinated, managed, monitored and evaluated ICT policies and strategies, and drove the research agenda in this area. Before that, she had been a lecturer of Information Technology (IT) in the Department for Science, Mathematics and Technology Education in the Faculty of Education of the University of Pretoria. Her research interests have included cooperative work in IT, effective teaching and learning of programming and teacher professional development.

Ebenesar Anna Bagyam J. is working as an Assistant Professor in Department of Mathematics, Karpagam Academy of Higher Education, Coimbatore. She has teaching as well as research experiences for about 15 years. She has completed her Ph.D. in Mathematics from Avinashilingam Institute for Home Science and Higher Education for Women, Coimbatore in the year 2016 in the field of queueing theory. Her research interests include queueing theory, fuzzy queue, optimization technique, and machine learning. She has published more than 25 papers in reputed national and international journals. She has presented 6 research papers at various international conferences. She is a life member of IMS and ISCA. At present, she is guiding research scholars in the field of queueing theory, machine learning, and optimization techniques.

Nitish Kumar Minz is an exceptional Bachelor of Commerce student specializing in Business Administration and Management at K.R. Mangalam University.

With an unwavering commitment to excellence and a remarkable work ethic, Mr. Minz has consistently demonstrated his dedication to academic and professional pursuits. His academic achievements extend beyond the classroom, as he has made significant contributions to several research papers and book chapters that are currently in the final stages of publication. His insightful contributions and research expertise have earned him recognition within his field of study. Mr. Minz holds a prestigious position as the Secretary of Extension and Outreach Activity in the Student Council of K.R. Mangalam University. In this role, he has showcased exceptional leadership skills, effectively managing various projects and strategic initiatives. Through his internship at KEIC (KRMU Entrepreneurship & Incubation Center), he has honed his project management and strategic planning abilities, gaining valuable hands-on experience in the field. Furthermore, Mr. Minz has been selected as NEP SAARTHI- Student Ambassador for Academic Reforms in Transforming Higher Education at K.R. Mangalam University. This esteemed role demonstrates his passion for educational reforms and his commitment to improving the quality of higher education. As a Student Ambassador, Mr. Minz actively engages with fellow students, faculty, and staff, promoting a culture of academic excellence and facilitating positive changes within the university. Recognizing his outstanding accomplishments and exceptional contributions, Mr. Minz has recently been honored with the prestigious Chancellor's Excellence Award. This esteemed award serves as a testament to his dedication, hard work, and exemplary performance throughout his academic journey. Mr. Nitish Kumar Minz's academic prowess, research contributions, leadership roles, and recognition through awards highlight his exceptional abilities and potential for future success. He continues to inspire and make a significant impact within the academic community, demonstrating his commitment to excellence in all his endeavors.

Anshul Saluja has a PhD in Educational Policy from the National Institute of Educational Planning and Administration (NIEPA), New Delhi and has also attained M.Phil. from NIEPA, New Delhi. She holds UGC-NET (JRF) in Education. She has been a recipient of the University Grants Commission-Junior Research Fellowship, University Grants Commission-Senior Research Fellowship and MHRD-NIEPA Senior Research Fellowship during her M.Phil. and PhD. Her area of specialization is School Participation of Children at the Elementary Level of Education. She did her Master's in Psychology with a specialisation in Counselling Psychology. Her other academic possessions are Master in Education (M.Ed.), Bachelor of Education (B.Ed.) and Bachelor of Science (H) Botany. Besides, she has also cleared CTET (Central Teacher Eligibility Test) and HTET (Haryana Teacher Eligibility Test). She is working as an Assistant Professor in the School of Education, K. R. Mangalam University. She teaches the subjects like Child Development, Childhood and Growing Up, Cognition and Learning, Basic Concepts and Thoughts in Education, Contemporary India and Education, Biology etc. She has been guiding students in writing research papers and some of my students have presented their papers at national seminars and conferences. She has been the speaker and moderator of various webinars organized by K. R. Mangalam University. She has organized FDPs and seminars at the school level as co-ordinator. Besides, being an assistant professor at the School of Education, she has been assigned an additional charge of Assistant Dean, Student Welfare, K.R. Mangalam University. Being on this post, she has been the convener of the Induction-cum-Orientation Programme for Freshmen (2021-22), Induction Programme for Freshmen (2022-23) and inter-university events. She is also heading NAAC Criteria 5 at the university level and is a member of various important committees (like the university discipline committee, and grievance redressal cell). She has published papers in UGC care-listed journals and Scopus journals. She has attended several seminars/conferences and has presented many papers on issues related to education in various national and international seminars/conferences and has also attended several workshops. She is the Editorial Board Member of the International Journal of Education, Culture, and Society ().

Symeon Sidiropoulos is Adjunct Lecturer at the Department of Economics of the University of Piraeus. He holds a BA in International and European, Economic and Political Studies from the University of Macedonia, a Master's Degree in the Environment and Health Management from the Medical School of Athens and a PhD in Global Health Policies and International Organisations from the University of Piraeus. He is President of the Hellenic Association of Political Scientists and member of the Academic Board of the Laboratory of Health Economics and Management of the University of Piraeus.

Surjit Singha is a dedicated researcher interested in UN Sustainable Development Goals, Organizational Climate, Workforce Diversity, Organizational Culture, HRM, Marketing, Finance, IB, Global Business, Business, AI, Women Studies, and Cultural Studies. Currently serving as a faculty member in the Department of Commerce at Kristu Jayanti College (Autonomous), Dr. Surjit holds prestigious positions as Editor, reviewer, and author for renowned Global Publications and Journals. With over 13 years of extensive experience in Administration, Teaching, and Research, both in Industry and Higher Education Institutions (HEIs), Dr. Surjit is committed to imparting knowledge and guiding students in their research pursuits. As a research mentor, Dr. Surjit is vital in nurturing young minds and fostering academic growth. Leading a team of approximately 35 faculty members, Dr. Surjit also heads website management, promotion, and social media publicity efforts. Dedicated to continuous learning, Dr. Surjit boasts certifications as a Life

Skill Trainer by RGNYID, a Microsoft Innovative Educator by Microsoft, and a Yoga Volunteer certified by The Yoga Certification Board, Ministry of AYUSH, Gov. of India. A trailblazer in academia, Dr. Surjit has guided and mentored 21 student projects in the academic year 2022-23, resulting in all 21 students publishing papers under Dr. Surjit's astute guidance. As NSS Faculty Mentor, Dr. Surjit has successfully mentored 65 students in the academic year 2022-23, ensuring all students achieve credits and qualifications. Dr. Surjit Singha has made substantial contributions to research with an impressive track record of over 65 publications as articles, including chapters in books, edited books, and various textbooks. Dr. Surjit continues to excel in academia after being granted 2 US Copyrights and receiving two fully funded minor research projects (Completed and Published) from Kristu Jayanti College (Autonomous). With a firm commitment to excellence in education and research, Dr. Surjit Singha elevates the institution's status and fosters an environment of knowledge dissemination and growth. ORCID iD: https://orcid.org/0000-0002-5730-8677.8c936200-c771-4e0d-9333-eb6f58324ce8

Julie Sunil is Associate Professor at Presidency Business School. She has over fifteen years experience in teaching masters in management courses. Her area of expertise includes Marketing and General Management Practices. She has contributed several research papers and case studies in national and international journals of repute.

Index

M

O

P

Q

R

S

T

U

W

Recommended Reference Books

IGI Global's reference books are available in three unique pricing formats:
Print Only, E-Book Only, or Print + E-Book.

Order direct through IGI Global's Online Bookstore at **www.igi-global.com** or through your preferred provider.

ISBN: 9781799887096
EISBN: 9781799887119
© 2022; 413 pp.
List Price: US$ **250**

ISBN: 9781799874157
EISBN: 9781799874164
© 2022; 334 pp.
List Price: US$ **240**

ISBN: 9781668440230
EISBN: 9781668440254
© 2022; 320 pp.
List Price: US$ **215**

ISBN: 9781799889502
EISBN: 9781799889526
© 2022; 263 pp.
List Price: US$ **240**

ISBN: 9781799885283
EISBN: 9781799885306
© 2022; 587 pp.
List Price: US$ **360**

ISBN: 9781668455906
EISBN: 9781668455913
© 2022; 2,235 pp.
List Price: US$ **1,865**

Do you want to stay current on the latest research trends, product announcements, news, and special offers?
Join IGI Global's mailing list to receive customized recommendations, exclusive discounts, and more.
Sign up at: **www.igi-global.com/newsletters.**

Publisher of Timely, Peer-Reviewed Inclusive Research Since 1988

IGI Global
PUBLISHER of TIMELY KNOWLEDGE

www.igi-global.com Sign up at www.igi-global.com/newsletters facebook.com/igiglobal twitter.com/igiglobal

www.ingramcontent.com/pod-product-compliance
Lightning Source LLC
LaVergne TN
LVHW081348300926
849161LV00008B/2095
* 9 7 8 1 6 6 8 4 7 5 8 3 6 *